MONEY & MORALS

IN AMERICA

MONEY & MORALS

IN AMERICA

A History

PATRICIA O'TOOLE

CLARKSON POTTER/PUBLISHERS
NEW YORK

Published by Clarkson N. Potter/Publishers, 201 East 50th Street, New York, New York 10022. Member of the Crown Publishing Group.

Random House, Inc. New York, Toronto, London, Sydney, Auckland
www.randomhouse.com

CLARKSON N. POTTER, POTTER, and colophon are trademarks of Clarkson N. Potter, Inc.

Printed in the United States of America.

Design by Maggie Hinders

Library of Congress Cataloging-in-Publication Data

O'Toole, Patricia.
Money and morals in America: a history / Patricia O'Toole.
Includes bibliographical references and index.
1. Wealth—Moral and ethical aspects—United States—History.
2. Wealth—Religious aspects.   3. Money—Biblical teaching.
I. Title.
HB835.O85   1998   97-50263
241'.68—dc21

ISBN 0-517-58693-2

10 9 8 7 6 5 4 3 2 1

First Edition

To Kathryn, Paul, Rob, Melissa, Sean, Maeve, Emily, James, Kate, Joe, and Ellen—who inherit this world

CONTENTS

FROM TIME IMMEMORIAL men have lived by the principle that "self-preservation is the first law of life." But this is a false assumption. I would say that other-preservation is the first law of life. It is the first law of life precisely because we cannot preserve self without being concerned about preserving other selves. The universe is so structured that things go awry if men are not diligent in their cultivation of the other-regarding dimension. "I" cannot reach fulfillment without "thou."

—MARTIN LUTHER KING JR.,
Where Do We Go from Here?

PREFACE

OF WEALTH AND COMMONWEALTH

I DIDN'T KNOW it at the time, but the work for this book began
on August 17, 1989, on Lafayette Square in Washington, D.C. I
had come down from my home in Connecticut to interview the
new head of the Small Business Administration for my monthly *Lear's*
magazine column on business and society. I was not thrilled by the
assignment. I had agreed to it because the column I wanted to do,
about who would sue whom for what in connection with the *Exxon
Valdez* oil spill in Alaska a few months earlier, could not be written
until the plaintiffs were ready to file their grievances in court.

Frances Lear was generous with writers, so I was at the Hay Adams
Hotel, elegantly quartered in an eighth-floor room with French doors
opening onto a little balcony and the city's best view of the White
House. It was three-thirty in the afternoon, and I had risen at four in
the morning to fly to Richmond on another errand. I drew a bath and
resolved to lounge around in one of the hotel's famously thick
bathrobes until I was lounged out. Five minutes into this decadence,
conscience had me dialing the Small Business Administration to con-
firm the plans for the next morning. The assistant who took my call
informed me that the interview had been canceled and could not be
rescheduled. A crisis, he said.

After a fitful night, I got up early and went out for a walk in
Lafayette Park, the greensward of Lafayette Square. I had visited many
times while working on my last book, a biography of Henry Adams

and his friends. I saw the neighborhood through their eyes, circa 1890, so my vision always needed correcting to take in the modern buildings, tour buses, and sprinkling of protesters along the Pennsylvania Avenue edge of the square, the edge nearest the White House. But it soon became clear that despite all I knew about Lafayette Park, including the size of its squirrel population, I had missed something: the human population at seven in the morning. There in the shrubbery were people under blankets and people in sleeping bags. Awkward as it felt to be in their bedroom, I made myself walk all the paths of the park and the sidewalk around it in hopes of finding only two or three sleepers, in which case I could entertain the possibility that they were fresh-air eccentrics. The number was on the order of two or three dozen.

Back on my balcony, waiting for breakfast to arrive, I couldn't see the sleepers anymore. The park foliage was too dense. The eight stories between me and the dispossessed might as well have been eight planets.

It was still too early to call *Lear's* with the bad news about the Small Business Administration, so I sat down with breakfast and learned from *The Washington Post* that the state of Alaska, the major plaintiff in the oil spill litigation, had filed its suit. I was saved. Lucky, lucky me. Remembering that investigators from the National Transportation Safety Board had amassed reams of paper on the accident, I decided to spend the day plowing through their documents in preparation for my interviews with the Alaskans.

I packed, dressed, and filled a Hay Adams laundry bag with the remains of breakfast—a feast or two of brioches, croissants, muffins, jams, apples, bananas, grapes, and oranges. As soon as I checked out, I crossed the street, walked into the park, and handed the bag to two men on a bench. I will always remember the deadness of their eyes. These men did not look as if they had lost all joy; they looked as if they had had it bombed out of them. They tore into the bread.

As I went about my business that day, I could not stop seeing the faces of these men (whose sons? whose brothers?). Nor could I stop thinking about the seven A.M. body count in Lafayette Park. Or wondering what emergency in the Small Business Administration, or anywhere else in the United States government, could be more dire than the one on display in the front yard of the White House.

Being a writer, I wanted to set down what I had seen and arrive at some understanding of it. In spare moments I began making notes for what I thought would be a book about the 1980s, about how greed had strangled the American dream. Although I devised a fine narrative structure, I never did manage to find the right voice. Everything I wanted to say came out at the top of my lungs (verbs like "strangled," unprintable nouns). With talk shows offering the public so many diatribes for free, I could not imagine why anyone would be moved to stop by a bookstore and pay good money for mine. And much as I wanted to blame the strangling on Wall Street debt pushers and supply-side Reaganites in Adam Smith neckties, I suspected that in the American epic of having and having not, junk bonds and supply-side economics were bit players.

A few months before my morning in the park, President George Bush had used his inaugural address to call for a kinder, gentler America, and there had been much pious talk about the need to recover our sense of community. I wondered: Had such a sense ever flourished in America outside the paintings of Norman Rockwell? As far back as the 1830s, a visiting French count, Alexis de Tocqueville, had thought that democracy in America was driving a wedge between individual and community. To his eye, the typical American was "habitually engaged in the contemplation of a very puny object: namely, himself." Americans believed that "they owe nothing to any man, they expect nothing from any man; they acquire the habit of always considering themselves as standing alone, and they are apt to imagine that their whole destiny is in their own hands." Indifferent to ancestors, descendants, and contemporaries, Tocqueville said, the American was thrown back upon himself, a state that would imprison him "entirely within the solitude of his own heart."

Tocqueville did not foresee that the American sense of separateness would come to have radically different consequences for rich and poor.

By the end of the twentieth century, solitude for the rich meant safety, privacy, and nearly unlimited freedom to indulge one's individuality. For the poor, solitude was worse than prison. It was a desert—vast, unsheltering, unanswering.

Curious about whether Americans had always felt their separateness more than their togetherness, I went back to colonial history and read my way to the present. The surprise was not the outsized "me first" aspect of the story but the passionate, never-ending debate about the relationship between private gain and public good. From the beginning, it seems, America has represented both El Dorado and the city upon a hill. Columbus came as a prospector for the Spanish crown, the Puritans to create a better society, and the dissonance between these ambitions has always been a central fact of American life. Henry Demarest Lloyd, a contemporary and critic of the robber barons, saw the conflict as an all-out war, pitting "wealth against commonwealth." I have come to think of it as a tension between money and morals, between selfish desires and shared obligations.

"Moral," of course, is a provocative word, particularly in our time, when clashes between one moral code and another are frequent, public, and heated. Which is the greater moral good: a high minimum wage, which would assure hundreds of thousands of workers a decent standard of living, or a low one, which benefits millions of consumers by reducing prices? Should a Third World country struggling to build its industrial base be required to spend billions outfitting its factories with state-of-the-art pollution control devices, or would those billions be better spent on the alleviation of poverty? Should a welfare recipient have to work?

As I researched and wrote this book, I read about morals in the works of philosophers, ethicists, theologians, psychologists, sociologists, political scientists, and political economists. The definitions that mean most to me center on the idea that a moral act takes into account a fundamental condition of existence: to be human is to live in a community. By this reckoning, I am not required to sacrifice my life for others or even to put their interests ahead of mine, but my actions must proceed from an understanding that I belong to a world beyond my puny self.

In the phrase "moral act," "act" is as critical as "moral." Toward the end of 1990, as the court was determining the prison sentence for Michael Milken, the celebrated financier and felon of the 1980s, he sent a letter to the judge. Among other things, he said he could not understand the viciousness of his critics. "I have been faced with the challenge that not only am I portrayed as a fraud, but everything my life stood for is called a fraud, and all the principles I have spoken about my whole life are hollow." They were hollow. With principles, what counts is not speaking about them, even for a whole life, but living them. Act is all.

In the realm of money, the overriding moral issue is one of fairness—of who gets and who doesn't and what happens as a result. Most discussions of economic fairness are quickly derailed by the observation that fairness, being subjective and situational, is a poor set of scales for weighing economic decisions. Ask an employee to name the fair wage for her job and she is likely to give a higher figure than her employer would. Unable to resolve the difference on purely moral grounds—concluding somehow that $9 an hour is "right" and $8 or $10 is "wrong"—we have instead followed the advice Adam Smith gave more than two centuries ago in *The Wealth of Nations:* Let the market decide. Champions of this view tend to ignore Smith's appreciation of the mischief that can arise when one party to a transaction controls significantly more resources than the other. The market may be a level playing field, but the game can hardly be called fair when disparities of power and wealth inflate some players to the size of Chicago Bears linebackers while most bulk tiny as Cub Scouts.

Adam Smith was a professor of moral philosophy at the University of Glasgow, and contemporary moralists with an interest in economics have observed that discussions of fairness are more productive when they focus on unfairness. In 1985, at a conference on the morality of the market, held in Vancouver, British Columbia, one participant pointed out that Aquinas had written twice as much about injustice as about justice. Another noted Aristotle's counsel to seek the essence of justice by contemplating situations that arouse our feelings of injustice. (One need not read Aristotle or Aquinas to understand injustice. I would guess that nearly every child of six has an exquisite sense of it as a result of living at the mercy of powerful, often arbitrary adults.) There is also something to be gained by debating questions of economic justice in terms of more fair/less fair rather than fair/unfair. In the end we may disagree about the level of the income tax rate or the size of a chief executive's paycheck, but our difference will be one of degree, not substance.

There would be less tension between money and morals if marketplace capitalism were as good at spreading wealth as it is at creating it. American private wealth is more heavily concentrated now than at any other time since we started keeping track of such things. By 1995, the richest 1 percent of the citizenry owned 40 percent of the pie, double the size of its slice in 1976. Most American families are not as well off as they were in 1973 despite the fact that many of them are now supported by two incomes. Their lower standard of living would matter little if it merely cut into pleasures such as travel and eating out, but affluence has become increasingly necessary for access to safe neighborhoods, good education, and adequate health care.

The deterioration is bound to affect morals as well as money. In the 1840s, watching the market claim its place at the center of American life, Ralph Waldo Emerson remarked that "the subject of economy mixes with morals" because poverty "demoralizes." When a person is "driven to the wall," Emerson wrote, "the chances of integrity are frightfully diminished." In short, goodness requires spare change. Those sleeping in parks and breakfasting on the leftovers of the fortunate cannot be expected to act with much concern for the well-being of others.

"But what am I supposed to do?" the rich man asks. Indeed. Most of the rich have acquired their fortunes through their own enterprise, inheritance, or other legitimate means. Many give generously to charity.

Having followed the rules, those who live in the upper economic stratum generally fail to see why anyone would hold them accountable for the deteriorating standard of living of 60 percent of their fellow Americans. "Where is the cause and effect?" asks a friend who belongs to the 1 percent, writes large checks to charity, and lives a morally exemplary life.

"Just because we can't see it yet doesn't mean it doesn't exist," I answer.

She raises an eyebrow.

"The laws of gravity operated long before Isaac Newton discovered them," I say. Wishing I had an unassailable explanation, I vow to continue searching for the still-unwritten law of the mechanics of money, the mathematical expression that will verify what we already know: Money flows toward money. Unless the flow is redirected, the concentration will continue, as will the decline in the general standard of living.

By positing a tension between money and morals, I do not mean that money is necessarily evil and morals are necessarily good. The American chronicle plainly shows that not every opportunist is a greedy knave (Andrew Carnegie's enthusiasm for giving away his fortune makes my point), nor is every idealist a friend of society (any number of cult leaders and militia commandants come to mind). In the course of working on this book, I have been struck again and again by the extent to which individual Americans, past and present, carry within them the tension between money and morals. As a people, we want to get rich *and* do good, be J. P. Morgan *and* Mother Teresa.

In some corner of the heart, each of us knows this, just as we know that human beings are destined to go through life with seemingly incompatible desires for intimacy and autonomy. But the continuing idealization of the self-made man, the fantasy that success will come to all who yank their bootstraps, and the rest of the relentlessly individualistic rhetoric of American culture makes it hard for the better angels of our nature to take wing. We have come to believe that we are what classical economics says we are: creatures driven by self-interest, obsessed with maximizing personal gains. And when that is the drift of

the conversation, one is dismissed as a chump or a naïf for speaking of
the pleasures of extending a kindness with no expectation of a reward
or for musing aloud that a nation as affluent as ours ought to be able
to provide each of its inhabitants with a place to sleep.

If the opulence of the few and the deprivation of the many were the
whole story, a book on the subject would be too dreary to read, much
less write. What intrigued me as I explored the relationship of
Americans and their money were the brilliance, zeal, and sheer variety
of the efforts to harmonize wealth and commonwealth over the last
350 years. I wanted to write about these endeavors in the hope of
reconnecting readers to a large, and largely forgotten, part of their past.
Americans are forever striking out for virgin territory—geographic,
social, economic, and intellectual. Entranced by the possibilities of
starting over, we continually lose sight of what came before us. Like an
amnesiac, a nation unaware of the meanings of its experience is hampered in conquering its weaknesses and building on its strengths. We
invent even when it might be more profitable to imitate. The socially
responsible corporation existed long before the founding of Ben &
Jerry's, for example. And we persist in believing that we have yet to
devise the ideal American day care system even though we had it during World War II. We also claim not to know how to cope with the
economic ramifications of racism despite the fact that sound analyses
of the problems and imaginative solutions have existed for decades.
The history of money and morals in America is a trove of ideas, examples, and warnings of value to anyone concerned about deepening our
sense of commonwealth. (Curiously, we take for granted that a strong
sense of the common good is a hallmark of high civilization, but having no shared definition of the common good, we can pledge no
allegiance to it.)

Because the tension between money and morals has been an
American constant, there is no grand historical arc worth tracing—no
rise of this or decline of that. Spared the confines of such arcs, I
decided to structure the book as a series of biographical narratives, a
decision that proved fortuitous on two counts: stories of individuals,
acting on their own or in small groups, give flesh and blood to an

abstraction, and few stories reveal character as fully as stories of money—of how one gets it and what one does with it.

Another author could have assembled a different cast for such a book, but in assembling mine, I was guided by personal predilection, narrative possibility, and Henry James. James observed that it was a complex fate to be an American, and I wanted to show the fated in all their complexity—grasping, generous, boneheaded, desperate, cruel, profligate, tender, shoving, resisting, ingenious, flashy, stingy, fretful, quixotic, exploited, enraged, ignored, willful, scheming, determined, intolerant, inspired. Borrowing a scaffold from the title of a Wallace Stevens poem, "Thirteen Ways of Looking at a Blackbird," I settled on thirteen chapters, each offering its own perspective on money and morals:

The daring of John Winthrop, who imagined that he and his fellow Puritans could found a society upon Christ's most extravagant demand, "Love one another."

The perils of selflessness, discovered in Colonel James Oglethorpe's colonization of Georgia, where noble aspirations doomed the venture by leaving insufficient room for the pursuit of self-interest.

Benjamin Franklin's felicitous blend of profit making and public service, a combination that made him a model for generations of accomplished private citizens who have applied their talents and influence to the public good.

The clash of high ideals and hard times in the textile mills of Lowell, Massachusetts, where mill owners thought they had created an industrial utopia while workers considered themselves enslaved.

Emerson and Thoreau, who first protested their materialistic age by dropping out and later used their literary powers to crusade against the Northern commercial class for its complicity in Southern slavery.

The self-destructive inertia of the slaveholding cotton planters of Georgia.

The strange case of Andrew Carnegie, who saw no contradiction between the ruthless business practices that produced his fortune and the magnanimity of his philanthropy.

Henry Ford's Five-Dollar Day, which doubled his employees' pay but forced them to open their homes to company investigators who threatened pay cuts if they disapproved of a workers' private life.

The back-to-the-land romance of the Agrarian poets of Tennessee, who feared the ascendancy of big business and Wall Street during the 1920s and loathed the intangibility of modern life.

The record-breaking productivity and enlightened management at Henry J. Kaiser's West Coast shipyards during World War II.

The courtship of the corporate establishment by civil rights leader Whitney Young, who did his utmost to show white America that great economic issues are almost always great moral issues.

William C. Norris, supercomputer pioneer and social inventor, who saw that corporations could profit by solving major social problems.

The shareholder activism of Timothy H. Smith and the Interfaith Center on Corporate Responsibility, a coalition of religious investors who use their standing as stockholders to press corporations for socially progressive policies on equal opportunity, environmental protection, and other matters.

To write the book, I worked from letters, diaries, journals, speeches, sermons, pamphlets, court records, corporate documents, presidential papers, transcripts of congressional hearings, oral histories, my own interviews, even sheet music. The research took me to scholarly and corporate archives, historical societies, and libraries from Cambridge to Berkeley and Minneapolis to Savannah. Toward the end, I also ventured into cyberspace, coming home with insights from scholars in other countries on the effects of the growing American presence in the global marketplace. Without the Internet, I probably would not have thought to look at Asian journalists' accounts of events in Burma or to seek Third World points of view on Third World debt, much of which is owed to American banks.

The fact that the materials for each chapter varied widely in scope and kind opened opportunities for a variety of narrative approaches, and I took them. When I found voices particularly engaging, for example, I set up the story in ways that let the subjects talk. I have modernized spelling and punctuation, trusting that any loss in piquancy will be offset by gains in digestibility. Where I have written "Negro" instead of "African American" or "Indian" rather than "Native American," I have done so to blend my prose style with conventions of other eras.

My chronicle of the contest between money and morals ends in 1997, but the contest itself goes on, raising questions about the nature of the common good, the relation of self and society, who gets ahead and who is left behind, and how we conceive of our connection to the dead-eyed men in the park.

1

MORE THAN ALL THE WEALTH IN THE WORLD

THE PURITANS ABOARD the *Arbella* sensed the bounty of Massachusetts before they reached it. On the seventy-first of their seventy-six days at sea, they stopped to fish and easily caught dozens of large cod. With the next sunrise came an offshore wind bearing a smell of earth, a smell that reminded their leader, John Winthrop, of gardens. Four days later, at four o'clock on the morning of June 22, 1630, they fired two cannons to announce their arrival, jubilation apparently overriding consideration for the slumbering inhabitants of the village of Salem. Winthrop and his party steered into Plum Cove, dropped anchor, and went ashore. Wild strawberries abounded. The newcomers helped themselves.

Behind them were tempests (meteorological and human), seasickness, stillbirths, fears of pirates, orgies of swabbing, crime (swearing, fisticuffs, disobedience), and punishment (manacles, leg irons, weights around the neck). All that distinguished this transatlantic voyage from others of its day were a few sheets of paper on which Winthrop asked his companions to join him in a covenant based on the most inspired of Christ's imperatives: Love one another.

Winthrop's entreaty, "A Model of Christian Charity," declared that society was a body of separate parts, love the only thing capable of holding the parts together, and togetherness the only means of survival. God had made some individuals rich, some poor, some powerful, and some weak in order to display His range and create opportunities to work His spirit upon the wicked—preventing the mighty from devouring the weak and the poor from rising up against the rich, for instance. Above all, God had made a limitless variety of individuals to assure that "every man might have need of other[s]," thus knitting humankind together "in the bond of brotherly affection," Winthrop wrote. Once held by that bond, individuals would cease to feel their separateness and would strive together for the glory of God and "the common good of the creature Man."

To Winthrop, love was everything. The soul coveted it "more than all the wealth in the world," he said. "Nothing yields more pleasure and content to the soul than when it finds that which it may love fervently, for to love and live beloved is the soul's paradise, both here and in heaven." Of all graces, love—"free, active, strong, courageous, permanent"—was the most godly. Of all sins, self-love was the most deadly. Adam had fallen because he put his own desires first, and Christ had given His life to demonstrate the importance He attached to loving others more than oneself. In their new world, Winthrop said, "there are two rules whereby we are to walk toward one another: justice and mercy." Those who had must aid those who had not, and public good must come before private interest.

But if they embraced "this present world" and their "carnal intentions," he warned, "the Lord will surely break out in wrath against us, be revenged of such a perjured people, and make us know the price of the breach of such a covenant." To avoid this "shipwreck," as Winthrop called it (choosing a metaphor sure to impress a traveler in midocean), the people of Massachusetts must "rejoice together, mourn together, labor together, always having before our eyes our Commission and community."

If they succeeded in loving one another, Winthrop promised, God would bless them in all ways. The governor closed by asking them to remember that New England would be "as a city upon a hill," watched by Old England and by God. If they turned their hearts away from heaven, they would perish, and their failure would "open the mouths of enemies to speak evil of the ways of God." John Winthrop could imagine such a fate, but he would not permit it.

AT forty-two, Winthrop was starting over, hoping to build a new world to replace an old one fallen apart. Born in comfortable circumstances, he studied at Trinity College, Cambridge, and began practicing law after training at Gray's Inn. Widowed twice in his twenties, he married Margaret Tyndal when he was thirty. But by the end of the 1620s, he had lost his place in the Court of Wards, and an agricultural depression had slashed the income from the Suffolk country estate left to him by his father. He despaired of giving his own sons a foothold in the world and could not think of his future or of England's without dread.

In portraits, John Winthrop is a dark-bearded man with penetrating eyes, a long nose, and a broad forehead. On the voyage to Massachusetts, he began keeping a journal, and if his eyes mirrored his soul as well as his journal did, they must have registered emotions stretching from majesty to merriment to kindness to fury. He was methodical, persuasive, seemingly devoid of self-aggrandizement, and compassionate except when he felt his authority under attack.

As a Puritan, Winthrop belonged to a small sect that had come into being in the decades of spiritual ferment following Henry VIII's establishment of the Church of England in 1536, after splitting with Rome. In their earliest days, Puritans concentrated their purifying on religious practices, hoping to persuade the Church of England that its elaborate rituals and decor were impediments to the individual's communion with God. Puritans also insisted upon the ultimate authority of the Bible. Both positions distressed the Anglican clergy by implying that despite its place at the center of English political life, it might be spiritually superfluous.

Puritanism proved no easier on Puritans than on prelates. An individual was called to the faith by God. Once summoned, a Puritan faced ceaseless demands to labor (earthly callings being the visible manifestations of spiritual ones), to spend hours at prayer, to forswear fancy dress and the theater, and to make each thought, word, and deed an emblem of the glory of God. Puritans viewed themselves as a chosen people, an opinion undoubtedly reinforced by the fact of their small numbers and the sheer hopelessness of their aspirations. Few were called, fewer chosen, the price of membership so high it could never be paid in full.

Exhilarating as these stringencies were to God's elect, most seventeenth-century Englishmen looked at Puritans and saw spoilsports made peevish by an excess of piety. An early Puritan chronicler noted that the Church of England ignored the pleas for reform and burrowed deeper into depravity by permitting "lewd and profane persons to celebrate a Sabbath like the heathen to Venus, Bacchus, and Ceres; in so much that the multitude of irreligious, lascivious, and popish-affected persons spread the whole land like grasshoppers."

By the time John Winthrop had come of age, the whole land was in fact spread with ills—political chaos, economic upheaval, disease, and crime. The Puritans, recognizing the chastening hand of God, were unsurprised. But as they contemplated the future, they found themselves in a predicament familiar to anyone who has been a member of a much-loved group when it lost its way: What is the right thing to do? Stay put and work for change? Or leave with one's ideals intact and try to practice them elsewhere?

England's rampant destitution vexed Winthrop with questions he could not answer. "Why meet we so many wandering ghosts in shape of men, so many spectacles of misery in all our streets, our houses full of victuals, and our entries of hunger-starved Christians? Our shops full of rich wares, and under our stalls lie our own flesh in nakedness." Wherever he looked in the late 1620s, he saw violence and sin. "Cruelty and blood is in our streets, the land aboundeth with murders, slaughters, incests, adulteries, whoredom, drunkenness, oppression, and pride where well-doing is not maintained, or the godly cherished, but idolatry, popery and whatsoever is evil is countenanced; even the least of these is enough, and enough to make haste out of Babylon." Fearing even greater afflictions, he prayed that God would provide the Puritans with "a shelter and a hiding place."

The most likely refuge was Massachusetts, where England already had a few outposts. And the most likely vehicle of escape was the Massachusetts Bay Company, which was managed and largely owned by Puritans. Based in London, the company had been chartered by the crown in 1629 for the purpose of founding a colony to take Christianity to the natives, trade with them, start fisheries and agricultural enterprises, and in general seize every chance to add to the king's power and purse. It occurred to the Puritans of the Massachusetts Bay Company that if they moved the seat of the company's operations from London to Massachusetts, they would have almost unlimited freedom to start a godly kingdom and run it as they saw fit.

Appealing as that sounded to some Puritans, including John Winthrop, others wondered whether God wanted such a kingdom. Removing the godly at a time of crisis would be a great wrong to church and country, the skeptics argued. Nor did they approve of Winthrop's desire to persuade the ablest Puritans to join him. They also challenged the right of Englishmen to help themselves to land long possessed by "other sons of Adam" and predicted that the natives' resentment would make them troublesome neighbors. Nature and experience argued further against the plan: Massachusetts lacked natural barriers to invasion, and no English settlement in North America could yet be counted a success.

Winthrop, determined to prove that the case for Massachusetts was stronger than the case against, formulated counterarguments and solicited other opinions. A good Christian could serve God anywhere, he said. He justified taking the best people on the ground that a mighty work required mighty workers. Native claims to the land meant little to most seventeenth-century Europeans. In taking possession of the Americas, they operated on their legal principle of *vacuum domicilium,* an ingenious dignification of a patently rapacious idea: If land was empty, it was available, and no payment was necessary unless natives claimed ownership. The earth was "the Lord's garden, and He hath given it to the sons of men to be tilled and improved," Winthrop said. The natives' lack of tilling only strengthened the Puritan sense of entitlement.

God Himself seemed to have special designs for Massachusetts. Only a dozen years before the landing of the *Arbella,* He had cleared the way for settlers by wiping out more than a third of the natives in a plague. ("Miraculous," said the Puritans.) Winthrop hoped to win the natives' goodwill but expected to prevail whether he got it or not. An English settler already in Massachusetts had assured him that forty men with muskets could hold their own against five hundred warriors with bows and arrows. More important, Winthrop considered it "a good work" to take the gospel to the natives. Whether the natives would take to the gospel he did not know, but he thought the Puritans should not pass up an opportunity to "raise a bulwark" against Jesuit missionaries in the New World. Untroubled by the absence of cliffs and other natural fortifications, Winthrop noted that Holland had managed to thrive despite similar vulnerabilities.

Winthrop found the failures of previous English settlements instructive but not discouraging. In his judgment, the organizers had erred because they had aimed "chiefly at profit," put themselves at the mercy of greedy merchants who cut off supplies in hard times, enlisted "rude and misgoverned persons" as settlers, and entrusted their government to the irresolute and the inexperienced. Winthrop intended to avoid these mistakes and believed that if Massachusetts prospered, it would be a haven for other Puritans. Calamity was imminent, he felt sure, "and who knoweth but that God hath prepared this place for a refuge for many whom He meaneth to save in the general destruction."

At summer's end in 1629, having received the king's approval to shift the company's seat to Massachusetts, the shareholders elected Winthrop as governor. In spite of his relatively small financial stake in the Massachusetts Bay Company, he defeated three other candidates for the post. The reasons for his victory are not entirely clear, but the case he had made for moving to New England was powerfully reasoned. Winthrop's seriousness, his determination to succeed, and his obvious devotion to a cause larger than himself undoubtedly appealed to investors who understood the riskiness of the venture. "Oh, that He would give me a heart now to answer His goodness to me, and the expectation of His people," he wrote Margaret.

For the next nine months, the governor and his aides busied themselves hiring sixteen ships and recruiting a thousand pious settlers—women, children, and men who were carpenters, masons, smiths, potters, coopers, fishermen, and farmers. Provisions were gathered, and in the spring of 1630, the hold of the *Arbella* began to fill with 10,000 gallons of beer, 3,500 gallons of water, much bread and cheese, and hundreds of barrels containing the ingredients of thousands of meals that must have been stupefyingly dull: salted cod and beef, peas, oatmeal, and flour. For flavor there was butter, salt, mustard seed, vinegar, and suet. Winthrop left no sign that he doubted the rightness of his decision to leave, but as the departure approached, he was not without regret. Merely reading a letter from Margaret, who would not join him in Massachusetts for more than a year, had "dissolved my head into tears," he said.

WHATEVER joy the first fleet of Massachusetts Puritans felt at their deliverance from the terrors of the sea was soon tempered by other discoveries. During the previous winter, more than a quarter of the three hundred English settlers who preceded the Puritans to Massachusetts had succumbed to disease, cold, or the vagaries of the food supply. The survivors—weak, hungry, badly housed—inspired little confidence. Dozens of the Puritans who came with Winthrop decided not to stay, preferring the certain perils of another transatlantic passage to the unknown terrors of the wilderness.

Toward the end of June, after a few days in Salem, Governor Winthrop and his aides headed south through the woods in search of a town site, ultimately selecting a spot near Beacon Hill. They named the settlement Boston, after an English stronghold of Puritanism. The first test of Winthrop's faith soon followed, and he noted the event with one terse sentence in his journal: "My son H:W: was drowned at Salem." Henry Winthrop, one of the governor's eight children, had gone with a group of ship's officers to look at a native encampment.

On the way, they spied a canoe across a river and decided to borrow it to save themselves a long, hot walk to the next ford in the stream. Henry, twenty-two and vigorous, had volunteered to swim over for it.

The little that John Winthrop said of the drowning when he wrote his family showed his reluctance to question God's will. There was a lesson to be drawn from such events, he told another of his sons: "the Lord teach you and the rest by it to remember your Creator in the days of your youth, and to improve your time to His service, while it lasts." Despite God's "stroke upon my son Henry," he wrote home to Margaret, the rest of the family was safe, and God upheld "our hearts that we faint not in all our troubles."

Troubles were legion. Cows and goats were dying, calves were being eaten by wolves. The governor felt obliged to order his first execution. Christmas Eve wrapped New England in a bitter cold that did not abate till spring. Fowl and game were plentiful, but the density of the forests made it hard for a hunter to get a clear shot. Shivering in tents and drafty huts, the settlers had little to eat but clams, mussels, and whatever acorns they could chisel from the frozen ground. By New Year's Day, two hundred of them had died. Many more were ill.

There was no doubt that this was the voice of God, but it was difficult to make out what He was saying. Had the Puritans been abandoned? Or did God mean to test them, as He had tested His other chosen people? Unwilling to believe that the Puritans had been forsaken, Winthrop concluded that they had incurred the Lord's displeasure. Precisely how, he declined to say, though he wrote Margaret that "Satan bends his forces against us, and stirs up his instruments to all kinds of mischief, so that I think here are some persons who never showed so much wickedness in England as they have done here." In hopes of regaining divine favor, he ordered a day of atonement.

But the greatest shock on this alien shore was a pleasant one. Trees came down, houses went up (and stayed up, once the governor banned wooden chimneys), crops flourished, livestock multiplied, and in 1631 Winthrop commissioned the construction of a small sailing ship, *The Blessing of the Bay,* to start a trade along the coast. By 1632, Richard

Saltonstall, one of the Massachusetts Bay Company's largest shareholders, saw profits wherever he looked—from masts, clapboards, fishing, tar, pitch, hemp, and flax. What the settlers did not need themselves they expected to sell elsewhere. Saltonstall urged an English acquaintance to "encourage good men to come over, for here is land and means of livelihood sufficient for men that bring bodies able and minds fitted to brave the first brunts."

Braving the first brunts, onerous as they were, proved a minor challenge compared to the struggle of loving one another. With the demand for houses far exceeding the supply of sawyers, carpenters, and masons, a bidding war broke out within weeks of the *Arbella's* landing. Craftsmen in the building trades routinely gouged their customers, and customers of ample means paid so well that the less affluent were priced out of the market. As the havoc and rancor spread, the Court of Assistants—Massachusetts Bay Company directors who served as a combination of cabinet and legislature for the colony's first few years—imposed wage controls in the summer of 1630. Maximum pay for building craftsmen was set at two shillings a day. Breaking the law would cost customer and craftsman ten shillings apiece. When some customers bent the rules by offering free meals to their hired hands, the court mandated a 25 percent pay cut for workmen fed on the job.

Governor Winthrop and his assistants also instituted a series of price controls as prices of food, clothing, and other necessities shot heavenward. Massachusetts merchants were ordered to charge only a third more than their goods would fetch in England. Wage and price controls came and went, returned and were repealed again, with the court alternately responding to public outcries and despairing of enforcement. Winthrop noted in his journal that when wages were too tightly controlled, workmen tended to leave the labor market, contenting themselves with subsistence farming while they built up their own properties. Eventually the court called upon town governments to monitor wages. Winthrop also ordered each town to appoint an agent to buy all the goods from every incoming ship in exchange for the right to resell them at profits within the guidelines set by the court.

But enterprising sailors would not be stopped from smuggling goods ashore to make their own trades.

Cheating inspired a flurry of regulations designed to compensate for the shortage of love that sellers felt for buyers. To address the deceits of tanners, the court ordered the appointment of tanning experts to regulate quality. Complaints about barrels that leaked because of wormholes led to official standards and inspections. Every baker was required to give his loaves a distinctive brand in order to facilitate the discovery and punishment of those who gave short weight. A merchant guilty of overcharging was obliged to return double the excess and to pay a fine levied at the discretion of the court.

Theft and fraud brought vivid punishments intended to convince the populace to steer a narrow course. Stealing a loaf of bread, a sheet, or a pair of shoes called for a whipping. There were fines for unauthorized borrowing of horses and for peddling quack medicines. An ambitious servant who engaged in a bit of freelance trading without his master's permission was fined and flogged.

In dealing with the scoundrels, Governor Winthrop drew on the full range of his feelings, sometimes playing the despot, sometimes the pragmatist, and sometimes the indulgent parent. One winter, on learning that a man had been filching wood from a neighbor, Winthrop promised to rehabilitate the malefactor. The thief, asked to account for himself, explained that he had taken the wood because he and his family had none. Winthrop made his own woodpile available to the man and laughingly reported his success in "reforming" a criminal. "[I]n the infancy of plantations," Winthrop wrote, "justice should be administered with more lenity than in a settled state" because people were more apt to transgress out of ignorance and desperation than real evil. But his lenity coexisted with a conviction that only a strong hand would keep his fallible, self-loving charges on a righteous path.

While the Puritans thought of themselves as a community of saints, it required more saintliness than most humans could muster for a merchant to put customers' welfare ahead of his own, especially when shortages dealt him an advantage. The merchant who happened to have a stock of bridles or window glass at a moment when his competitors had none was inclined to make the most of his luck until the arrival of new goods restored a measure of competition.

The most celebrated case of mercantile grasping came before the court in 1639, when Robert Keayne of Boston was accused of allowing himself unconscionable profits. He was said to have marked up such goods as nails, thread, and gold buttons by more than 100 percent on some occasions. Members of the court had no doubts about Keayne's guilt but disagreed about the gravity of his offense. Some wanted to fine him £200, others £100. Winthrop initially took a hard line, viewing the practices as inexcusable because Keayne was a wealthy man, professed to be a true Christian, and had ignored earlier warnings against overcharging. Worst of all in Winthrop's judgment, Keayne seemed blind to the necessity for impeccable behavior by members of "a church and commonwealth now in their infancy, and under the curious observation of all churches and civil states in the world."

Those in favor of the smaller fine argued that it was in the nature of trade to exploit whatever advantages a market presented, that Keayne was not the only sharpster among Boston's merchants, and that because the Bible required no more than double restitution, a fine of £200 seemed unduly punitive.

Keayne was ordered to appear in church to "acknowledge and bewail his covetous heart." Overcome by tears as he struggled to explain himself, he pleaded ignorance of his wholesale prices in some instances and argued that he had believed—mistakenly, he had come to understand—that when a merchant lost money on one item, there was no sin in making it up on another. After debating whether Keayne should be excommunicated, the congregation concluded that an admonition would suffice. As Winthrop reported the proceedings, it was decided that Keayne had been misled by "false principles" but had shown himself "otherwise liberal in his hospitality, and in church communion."

Keayne felt the sting of his public humiliation for the rest of his life. Thirteen years after the trial, in disgrace again because of drunkenness, he began writing a will that filled 158 pages in the colony's probate records. Thirty pages railed against the cruelty of the judgment, and another thirty attempted to prove his innocence with details from his account books. Keayne consoled himself with thoughts of the day "when I and they, the judges and the judged, shall stand naked before one throne, where there will be no respect of persons, when all sentences and the causes of them will be called over again before a greater judge and a higher tribunal than man's can be."

IN Keayne's ordeal it is possible to see that the Puritanism of New England, for all its insistence on stability, was instability itself. The Puritans in the wilderness were like a row of iron filings suspended between two equally powerful magnets—held in place by a tension so perfect that it snapped at the least disturbance and scattered the filings in all directions. Puritanism demanded hours of worship and daily Bible reading, yet the business of conquering the wilderness needed constant toil. A good Puritan was expected to be economically self-sufficient, but he was also supposed to subordinate personal interests to the needs of community. The cardinal virtue, self-denial, pitted a human against most of the longings recognizable as human. It was wrong to make a monastic withdrawal from society, equally wrong to embrace the world. A Puritan lived trembling on the edge of a blade, ever in danger of a bloody plunge to perdition.

The calling, the divine summons to Puritanism as well as to one's earthly vocation, was a knot of contradictions. On the one hand, it gave Puritan patriarchs a compelling justification of the status quo: the mighty were mighty and the weak weak because God had made them so. To aspire to another station was to flout His will. On the other hand, the calling demanded a sweaty devotion to work, and assiduity amid the vast opportunities of Massachusetts regularly produced wealth and a change of station.

Few subjects agitated the Puritan mind more than wealth. It was both a sign of God's blessing and a powerful temptation to the sin of pride (how satisfying to be among the elect of the elect!) and to the sins of the flesh. Orthodoxy required a Puritan to dress plainly, but judging by the court's steady issuance of sumptuary laws, the appetite for fancy clothing was insatiable. The Puritan leadership was especially distressed by the sartorial ostentation of the lower classes, who were supposed to content themselves with "raiment suitable to the order in which God's providence has placed them." The court banned short sleeves, disclosing as they did "the nakedness of the arm." Also forbidden were wide sleeves, billowing breeches, clusters of ribbon, luxurious cuffs, and double ruffs, presumably because all of them required excessive quantities of fabric. Lace was outlawed for provoking "the nourishing of pride and exhausting of men's estates."

Even here the Puritans were ambivalent. While they would not have wastrels and peacocks in their own province, they saw nothing amiss in profiting from the immoderation of others, so they allowed lace makers to continue in their callings as long as they promised to sell their handiwork only to "such persons as shall and will transport [it] out of this jurisdiction." The court also ended the drinking of toasts, declaring that they served no purpose, often led to drunken brawling, and wasted wine and beer. Such sentiments did not prevent the Puritans of Massachusetts from entering—and prospering in—the rum trade.

Avarice was a highway to hell, but riches were not. "Riches are consistent with godliness," the Reverend Samuel Willard declared, "and the more a man hath, the more advantage he hath to do good with it." Here was divine encouragement to wax fat and an invitation to imagine it a noble aim because the richer a man became, the more wealth he would allow to trickle down to less fortunate Christians.*

*The connection between Puritan attitudes toward wealth and the rise of capitalism has been the subject of a long debate that began in 1905 with the publication of *The Protestant Ethic and the Spirit of Capitalism* by Max Weber. Weber argued that the Puritans' dedication to their calling plus their simple way of life led naturally to the accumulation of wealth, which was then put to work as capital—money used to produce more money. Weber saw New England's budding capitalists as rational, entrepreneurial, and individualistic. His critics have countered that the spirit of capitalism predated Protestantism by centuries, that hard work had been a Christian virtue since the days of St. Paul, that the calling implicitly forbade acquisitiveness because it required contentment with one's place in the social order, that individualism was frowned upon in a world requiring near total submission to authority, that laissez-faire capitalists would not have regulated prices and wages, and

Poverty saved an individual from indulging worldly appetites but was no proof of sainthood. The able-bodied poor of seventeenth-century Massachusetts were suspected of being willfully deaf to their callings. A scarcity of labor that persisted for decades made employment easier to find and more remunerative in Massachusetts than in England, so idleness was nearly as intolerable as sodomy. Nevertheless, Governor Winthrop insisted that all the poor be cared for, and towns and churches regularly cooperated in distributing food and alms. As local taxes rose and the ranks of the poor increased, grumblers drew increasingly sharp distinctions between the worthy poor and the idle poor. Beggar and vagabond were forced to move on, often with whips at their backs. Many villages forbade strangers to visit for more than a fortnight, and hosts had to pledge that their guests would not become an expense to the town.

Puritans opened their purses to relieve the starkest miseries of the poor but felt no duty to help their fellow beings rise in the world. As employers and policy makers, they were unshakable in the conviction that generosity was economically and morally unsound. Winthrop, holding an attitude that persisted into the twentieth century, believed laborers should not earn much more than they needed for subsistence because high wages led to high prices and encouraged workers to slack off.

In the early 1630s, when Winthrop and the Court of Assistants first regulated the wages of carpenters and others in the building trades, they acted partly for the well-being of the community and partly to discourage bad habits. Able to earn enough in four days to support themselves for a week, the craftsmen began lazing about. They also spent freely on tobacco and "strong waters," which Winthrop considered "a great waste to the commonwealth" since the

---

that if Puritan devotion to thrift had been as strong as Weber thought it was, the Massachusetts court would not have felt obliged to pass laws designed to restrain spending on clothes, nor would the colony's early industrial development have been hindered by a shortage of capital. (See R. H. Tawney, *Religion and the Rise of Capitalism* [1926]; H. M. Robertson, *Aspects of the Rise of Economic Individualism* [1933]; and Gabriel Kolko, "Max Weber on America: Theory and Evidence," *History and Theory* 1:3 [1961].)

proceeds tended to flow out of Massachusetts to sellers in Virginia and other colonies.

WERE it not a sin, pride would have been the most appropriate feeling for the Puritans to have as their first decade in Massachusetts came to an end. Through grit and perseverance, they had transformed twelve thousand acres of rocky, forested wilderness into farmland yielding more than enough wheat, corn, and rye to feed the twenty thousand inhabitants of Boston and the surrounding towns. The common good had been vigorously promoted by Governor Winthrop and his assistants, who spurred the construction of dams, mills, and other public works with a variety of economic incentives. To speed the development of commercial fishing, they granted fishermen exemptions from military service and certain taxes. The town bull, available to serve all cattle, was as much a feature of life as were common pastures and common woodlots. Local officials were empowered to draft laborers for public construction projects. To assure that crops did not rot in the field for want of hands at harvesttime, constables had authority to compel the aid of merchants and others not regularly employed in farming. The inhabitants of Massachusetts may not have loved one another, but the governor excelled at devising ways of making them act as if they did.

Next to Winthrop, the man most responsible for the successes of the 1630s may have been the archbishop of Canterbury, whose persecution of English Puritans drove wave upon wave of them to the shores of Massachusetts. Upward of fifteen thousand immigrants arrived with their life savings, and their needs for food and housing apace, expanded demand for goods and services. Land values climbed steadily, and by 1640, prosperity was, if not universal, refreshingly widespread.

Then milk and honey ceased to flow. Impeached as a traitor, the archbishop went to the Tower of London in 1640, an event that "caused all men to stay in England in expectation of a new world," Winthrop said in his journal. The drying up of immigration deprived the colony's farmers, merchants, and artisans of new customers and cut off the supply of cloth, furniture, and other English goods brought to Boston aboard ships carrying new settlers. Corn and grain lost virtually all of their value, and cattle prices plunged 75 percent. Farmers could not pay merchants, who routinely extended credit between harvests. Merchants in turn could not settle their debts with suppliers in England. By autumn, the Court of Assistants was so alarmed by the amount of property being confiscated for nonpayment of debt that it ordered all such proceedings reviewed by panels of "3 understanding and indifferent men."

Pointing to the collapse of crop and livestock prices, the court urged servants, laborers, and workmen to lower their wages proportionately and "be content to partake now in the present scarcity, as well as they have had their advantage by the plenty of former times." This time the court stopped short of imposing wage controls but warned that it would be considered "great opposition in any that shall transgress the intention of this order, and will have them proceeded with accordingly." The court also decreed that corn, fish, and other commodities be accepted in settlement of debt. To reduce imports, committees were appointed to investigate the prospects of home manufacturing of linen and wool.

The governor escaped none of the hardships of the depression. By his calculation, the cost of running a proper governor's household came to £500 a year, £300 of which he funded with his own money, largely from the sale of his estate in England. Absorbed in public affairs, he left his private fortunes in the care of his bailiff, James Luxford, who proved most untrustworthy. Luxford often borrowed money from Winthrop's friends, who naturally assumed that the bailiff was acting at the governor's request. Winthrop knew nothing of the loans until hard times forced the friends to seek repayment. It also appears that Luxford sometimes overcharged when he sold Winthrop's produce and livestock, and he sometimes overpaid when he hired his own friends for odd jobs. For forgery, lying, and other offenses, Luxford was bound to the public whipping post, where his ears were cut off. And then, the court records dryly note, Luxford was given "liberty to depart out of our jurisdiction."

To repay the £2,600 he owed to creditors, Winthrop was forced to revoke his will. For the future, he put his trust in the benevolence of the Lord, "who hath promised not to fail or forsake me but will be an husband to my wife and a father to our children, as He hath hitherto been in all our struggles." His brother-in-law made him a present of a calf, which arrived with a comforting reminder from the story of Job, who had been "raised to a full estate in this way by his friends." Another friend observed that after Job had been brought low by the Lord, the Lord had "blessed his latter days more than his former." The people of Massachusetts collected £500 for Winthrop, and Winthrop managed to accumulate the rest of what he owed, but he had to sell his house in Boston and most of his farm. Recalling the depression some years later, he brimmed with melancholy: "Indeed it was a very sad thing to see how little of a public spirit appeared in the country, but self-love too much."

For all his own public spirit, Winthrop had a keen appreciation of the sovereignty of self-love in the human character. Neither promises of paradise nor threats of damnation could obliterate self-love, so the most Winthrop could do was try to contain it by yoking private gain to public good wherever possible. Suspicious of monopolies and other economic arrangements that favored the few, Winthrop and the Court of Assistants nevertheless granted broad privileges to entrepreneurs in the belief that their successes would benefit the colony as a whole. Hugh Peter, a clergyman and civic-minded entrepreneur who had spurred the development of commercial fishing by organizing a central store to sell fishing equipment at reasonable prices, was enlisted to raise capital for shipbuilding so that Massachusetts could expand its trade. With obvious satisfaction, Winthrop noted in his journal that the task was difficult "for want of money, &c. but our shipwrights were content to take such pay as the country could make."

A saltworks, an ironworks, and mines were encouraged with concessions lasting anywhere from ten years to eternity. The most ambitious of the early industrial enterprises was an ironworks started by John Winthrop Jr. In 1641, bearing promises of tax exemptions, land grants, mineral rights, and other privileges, he sailed to London in search of investors. Sympathetic English Puritans chartered the Company of Undertakers for the Iron Works of New England, appointed the younger Winthrop as manager, and sent him home in 1643 with £1,000 and a platoon of miners and foundry men. Within five years, output of guns, pots, and other cast-iron wares reached a ton a day.

But the more the works produced, the more money it lost. Transportation of manufacturing equipment from England was prohibitively expensive, the workers bumptious. "[N]otwithstanding all our care," the Londoners explained, "we have been necessitated to send some for whose civilities we cannot undertake, who yet we hope by the good example, and discipline of your country, with your good assistance may in time be cured of their distempers." Their distempers proved incurable, their expertise spotty. As losses swelled, acrimony led to lawsuits, countersuits, and the bankruptcy of the ironworks.

Hampered by shortages of capital and skill, manufacturing grew slowly in Massachusetts despite the government's generous incentives. Prosperity, when it returned, could be traced almost entirely to trade. Once the colony had ships of its own, it found export markets for salted fish, grain, cattle, leather, clapboards, barrels, and masts.

CATCHING the first scent of Massachusetts four days before anchoring at Salem, Winthrop had thought immediately of gardens—of land that was cultivated, not wild. This was no accident. He and his companions believed that the Lord had commanded them to improve the earth, replacing the chaos of wilderness with the order of the English countryside. They took as their text Genesis 1:28–29: "Be fruitful and multiply, and replenish the earth, and subdue it: and have dominion over the fish of the sea, and over the fowl of the air and over every living thing that moveth upon the earth."

In the beginning, fearful of wolves and unpredictable natives, the Puritans huddled inside the city upon a hill and submitted to the control of the governor and his Court of Assistants. As survival became easier, more than a few settlers began to yearn for freedom, which they imagined they would have if they lived out of sight in the next cove or on the far bank of some bridgeless river.

Torn between the belief that a godly society demanded closeness and the conviction that a godly people should tame the wilderness, the Puritans embraced both. Social controls gradually tightened, with authorities dictating who could settle where, who could sell land to whom, who could board ships and when, and who would be allowed to visit. Jesuits were denied admittance except in emergencies—a shipwreck, say—and made to depart on the next available conveyance. At the same time, new towns sprang up regularly, and speculation on wilderness real estate was feverish.

As the Puritans read Genesis, God wanted them to exercise dominion over the natives as well as the wilderness. They hoped their conquest of the Massachusetts Pequots would be a gentle one. "Offend not the poor natives, but as you partake in their land, so make them partakers of your precious faith," a Puritan cleric advised his fellow Christians. "Who knoweth whether God have reared this whole plantation for such an end."

In the matter of loving one another, Pequots were models of Christian charity, said a settler who befriended them—"so loving that they make use of those things that they enjoy (the wife only excepted) as common goods, and are therein so compassionate that rather than one should starve through want, they would starve all." It was the rest of Christianity that bedeviled the natives. Good Christians were expected to cover their bodies, and with clothing came the burden of laundry. They were also expected to trade leisure for work, trust in a god they could not see, and seek no sexual pleasure outside monogamous marriage. Converts were few.

In earthly affairs, relations between Puritans and natives were conducted on Puritan terms. The court regulated commerce between white man and red, forbade natives to be paid in gold or silver, and restricted the natives' access to firearms. It also sought to protect the natives on numerous occasions—ordering the whipping of a young settler convicted of making indecent proposals to a squaw, demanding recompense when settlers' hogs ravaged native cornfields, and making wine available out of a belief that it would be unjust to "deprive the Indians of any lawful comfort which God allows to all men."

The peace between Puritans and Pequots ended in 1637 with a war begun by the Puritans in retaliation for the slaying of two English traders. After a few skirmishes, several hundred Pequots, women and children included, took refuge in their fort on the Mystic River. The English set it ablaze and shot all who tried to escape. Between five hundred and seven hundred Pequots perished. The survivors never again threatened Puritan authority.

The gaping disparity between the ideal of loving one another and the slaughter of the Pequots could not be denied, but it could be explained. By "one another," the Puritan did not mean strangers or infidels, he meant his fellow Puritans. The Pequots also had the misfortune to roil the Puritans at a moment when Governor Winthrop faced two other challenges to his authority. The idea of separating church and state was anathema in the Bible commonwealth, and in 1636, when a radical young preacher named Roger Williams refused to stop telling his congregation in Salem that civil authority should end at the meetinghouse door, he was exiled to England. Although Winthrop agreed that Williams must be silenced, he liked him enough to break ranks with the Court of Assistants and give him advance notice of the banishment. On Winthrop's advice, Williams fled to the wilds of Rhode Island.

The other dissenter in need of squelching was Anne Hutchinson, whose home had become a sort of spiritual salon, a gathering place for those who wanted to talk about what they heard from the pulpit. Hutchinson led the discussion, and the discussion led to heresy. Orthodox Puritanism held that salvation was a gift from God, but an individual had to prepare for it by living a life filled with good works. Hutchinson wanted to replace this "covenant of works" with a "covenant of grace," which rested on the appealing idea that an individual would be notified of salvation by a revelation from God. Grace rendered good works unnecessary. Hutchinson's credo, propagated by a brother-in-law who was a Boston preacher, grew so popular that it became the sole issue in the election of 1637. Winthrop and the old guard managed to beat back the heretics' candidate for governor, but not without chicanery: they moved the polling place from Boston, where Hutchinson's thinking was most widespread, to Cambridge. Hutchinson was tried, convicted of "traducing the ministers," and exiled.

Perhaps the greatest threat to Winthrop's power came from Puritanism itself. There was an irreconcilable contradiction between the Puritan creed, which demanded absolute faith, and the intense rationality the Puritans brought to their relationships with God and with one another. In business, family, and government, Puritans saw relationships largely in terms of contracts—binding agreements in which nothing is taken on faith. A contract, arrived at by negotiations that culminate in mutual consent, proceeds from two assumptions: that the parties involved are capable of making rational choices and that they have a right to exercise the choices they make. As Governor Winthrop discovered, such ideas were inherently democratic. Chafing against the near dictatorship of the governor and the Court of Assistants, the inhabitants of Massachusetts wanted to know why, having freely entered into the covenant outlined in "A Model of Christian Charity," they had almost no say in determining how it would be carried out. The Puritan fathers replied that the settlers had agreed to God's terms, which were not negotiable. The argument did not hold. By asking his fellow Puritans to join him in a covenant, Winthrop had—intentionally or not—invited them into a relationship based on consent. Ever after they had balked at submitting.

EARLY in the spring of 1649, Governor John Winthrop, then in his sixty-first year, died of a cold. To his family he left £103 worth of household furnishings of the most rudimentary sort, many tools, a few firearms, and some clothing (much of it characterized as "ould" in an inventory of his worldly possessions). With its balls of twine, pewter candlesticks, chains, fish hooks, and spectacles, the inventory was the testament of a man who lived what he preached.

Winthrop's spiritual legacy is rich and tangled. On the voyage to New England, he had entreated his companions to love one another and for two decades had done his utmost to make them live the ideal. The poor were suspect but supported. For the greedy there were fines, price controls, and public opprobrium of the sort heaped upon Robert Keayne. The common good was well tended, with incentives to build public works and stimulate manufacturing, trade, and employment.

But love had its limits. None was wasted on natives or strangers. Religious dissenters and persons with democratic hankerings were accused of loving self more than society. The Puritan regarded himself as a man of his word, yet he also wanted every verbal agreement confirmed in writing, and his document of choice, the contract, was rooted in mistrust rather than brotherly love. A prosperous and devout Puritan might insist that he was merely the steward of his worldly possessions, with the true ownership reserved to God. All the same, he took the precaution of writing wills and deeds, which lodged ownership in quarters well this side of heaven. Diligence and thrift, once regarded as signs of putting the life of the spirit before the life of the flesh, came to be valued as strategies for accumulating wealth. The city upon a hill had been conceived as a haven from the evils of the world, but for many, the haven came to feel less sheltering than controlling. Part of the attraction of the wilderness beyond Boston was its release from watchful authorities and from the constant pressure to prove one's neighborly love. Opportunity, prosperity, democracy—all were potent forces in the life of Puritan Massachusetts, and all tended to fuel individual ambitions at the expense of Winthrop's collective ideal.

The failure of this experiment in love speaks more to the nature of ideals than to the shortcomings of John Winthrop. Between the real and the ideal there is always a gap, and as if in obedience to some law of physics, the gap becomes electrically charged—crackling, unstable, destined to change. But as easy as it was to say that the dream of a city upon a hill had been too grand, the alternative, a city ruled by self-interest, seemed small and base. Winthrop could not make the citizens on his hill love one another, but the thoughtful among them regretted that. Impossible to attain, his ideal also proved impossible to ignore. Puritanism would fade, but the tension between wealth and commonwealth would not.

2

Not for Self, but for Others

E NGLAND IN THE year 1729 was two countries—one as poor and brutalizing as the England that had unmoored John Winthrop, the other thriving. The wharves of London, Bristol, and Liverpool were thick with ships, farmland sprouted factories, and the cities accreting around these enterprises seemed veritable engines of wealth. On a tour of Britain in the 1720s, Daniel Defoe, the author of *Robinson Crusoe,* noticed that towns with even a few prosperous families attracted craftsmen, providers of services, and purveyors of a steadily expanding array of goods. Incomes seemed to be rising faster than prices, creating ever more customers for china and other wares previously beyond the means of all but the rich. The turning of the commercial wheels generated more employment, which stimulated more consumption, and so gloriously on. The phenomenon had been pointed out to Defoe by Bernard de Mandeville, a physician and poet who delighted Londoners with *The Fable of the Bees, or Private Vices, Public Benefits.* Abstemiousness helped no one, Mandeville said, while luxury "Employ'd a million of the Poor, And odious pride a million more."

The new wealth did not trickle all the way down. Relief rolls grew, and thousands were forced into workhouses, which had been invented a few decades earlier to make the poor toil for their alms. Each year in London, four thousand men went to prison for failure to pay their debts. Privately owned and run for profit, the prisons were foul, crammed, violent, and pestiferous. The inmate who survived hunger or assault stood a good chance of succumbing to infection.

Nevertheless, the new prosperity was sufficiently commonplace to chill sympathies for the poor. As far as Defoe could tell, rising wages had inspired the lower orders to work less and idle more. Others took an even darker view, insisting that the trouble with the poor was that they were not poor enough. "The only way to make the poor industrious is to lay them under the necessity of labouring all the time they can spare from rest and sleep," one magistrate proclaimed. Starvation wages would not only instill the habit of diligence, they would improve the balance of trade by making English goods affordable in foreign markets.

Here and there, gentlemen with softer hearts applied themselves to charitable endeavors and voiced their discomfort about the widening chasm between rich and poor. Viscount Percival, member of the House of Commons and intimate of King George II and Queen Caroline, worried that great wealth led to great luxury, "and luxury extravagance, and extravagance want, and want knavery." Percival told the queen that he would not have England poorer, "yet it were better if riches were more equally divided."

And in 1729, Colonel James Edward Oglethorpe, an impassioned young aristocrat with a seat in the House of Commons, captured the public imagination by leading a parliamentary inquiry into the state of the nation's jails. Haunted by the death of a friend, a scholar who had contracted smallpox in a debtors' prison, Oglethorpe inspired Parliament to pass a bevy of reforms and secure the release of ten thousand imprisoned debtors.

Oglethorpe's act was a shining deed in a dark world, but as one observer soon noted, freedom gave the penniless little beyond "the wretched advantage of starving at large." When a respected writer on trade suggested breaking the cycle of debt and imprisonment by sending the poor abroad to form new English colonies, Oglethorpe was intrigued. Here in one simple idea lay the seeds of many good things: for the indigent, a start on a life better than any they were likely to know in England; for the crown, reduced expenditures on poor relief;

for manufacturers, cheaper sources of hemp, silk, cotton, tobacco, and other raw materials; and for the empire, more "trade, navigation, and wealth."

Australia had not yet appeared on the imperial horizon, so the most promising site known to Oglethorpe and his associates was the unclaimed wilderness between the English colony of South Carolina and the Spanish territory of Florida. Sir Robert Montgomery, a Scot who had explored the region with the ambition of winning a colonial charter for himself, had pronounced it "the most amiable country of the universe."

It lies in the same latitude with Palestine herself, that promis'd Canaan, which was pointed out by God's own choice, to bless the labors of a favourite people; it abounds with rivers, woods, and meadows. Its gentle hills are full of mines, lead, copper, iron, and even some of silver; 'tis beautiful with odoriferous plants, green all the year. Pine, cedar, cypress, oak, elm, ash, or walnut, with innumerable other sorts, both fruit or timber trees grow everywhere so pleasantly that tho' they meet at top, and shade the traveller, they are, at the same time, so distant in their bodies, and so free from underwood, or bushes, that the deer, and other game, which feed in droves along these forests, may be often seen near half a mile between them.

The air is healthy, and the soil in general fruitful, and of infinite variety; vines, naturally flourishing upon the hills, bear grapes in most luxuriant plenty. . . . The orange and the lemon thrive in the same common orchard with the apple, and the pear-tree. Plums, peaches, apricots, and nectarines bear from stones in three years' growing. The planters raise large orchards of these fruits to feed their hogs with; wheat ears have been measur'd there seven inches long, and they have barley, beans, pease, rice, and all our grains, roots, herbs, and flowers not to speak of numbers of their own, which we can find no names for; beef, mutton, pork, tame poultry, wild fowl, sea and river fish, are all there plentiful.

Oglethorpe joined Percival, several of their fellow members of Parliament, a handful of clergymen, and other public-spirited gentlemen in building a case for colonizing this Eden. The king would extend his military and political might in North America, Oglethorpe and his associates predicted. Britain would reduce its annual imports by £300,000 through the establishment of a silk industry in the new territory, which was said to be rich in mulberry trees, the leaves of which are used to feed silkworms. The indigent would be "carried gratis to a land of liberty and plenty," Oglethorpe wrote. There they would "immediately find themselves in possession of a competent estate, in a happier clime than they knew before, and they are unfortunate, indeed, if here they cannot forget their sorrows."

The planners named their paradise Georgia, after the king, and in 1732, it pleased His Majesty to grant them a charter. To assure that the benefits of the colony accrued to the colonists, Oglethorpe and his fellow altruists departed from the common practice of organizing the venture as a joint-stock company. Georgia was to be a trust, funded not by investors but by donations, lotteries, and parliamentary appropriations. Like a newborn child, the colony was given twenty-one years to mature, with the charter reverting to the crown in 1753. Until then, management reposed in the Trustees for Establishing the Colony of Georgia in America, who forbade themselves to own so much as a mulberry tree lest their private interests clash with the public good. *Non sibi, sed aliis,* read the motto on their seal. "Not for self, but for others." They numbered twenty-one: Oglethorpe, Percival, ten other members of Parliament, five clergymen, a philanthropist, a clerk, a country squire, and a government official. Percival (soon to become the first earl of Egmont) would preside over the Trustees in London, and Oglethorpe would lead the settlers to the new land.

By the Trustees' arithmetic, a gift of £20 was enough to carry a man to Georgia, outfit him with clothing and tools, and feed him from a common store for the year they thought it would take him to become self-sufficient. In an early fund-raising pamphlet, Benjamin Martyn, secretary to the Trust, invited "the man of benevolence" to imagine "those who are now a prey to all the calamities of want . . . masters of little possessions, which they can leave to their children; and then let him think if they are not happier than those supported by charity in idleness." In Mandeville's world of fops, Martyn said, "Common is the

complaint we hear that public spirit is lost among us, and that no one
pursues any dictates but those of his interest. I hope this is not true, I
do not think it is; but if there is any foundation for it, it is time to
awaken people to a love of their country, to see her welfare, and to promote it." To put public interest ahead of private gain was "the perfection of virtue."

In screening prospective settlers, the Trustees turned away the "ras-
cally" and those deemed able to "get their bread at home." The candidates who rated a mention in Egmont's diary fit the Trustees' image of
themselves as rescuers of the deserving poor. There was, fresh from
debtors' prison, a Mr. Reyley—merchant, bookkeeper, husband, and
father of two small children. "He appeared a great object of charity,
and we ordered him to bring certificates of his honesty and good
behavior from the two last persons he was bookkeeper to," Egmont
wrote. One Mr. West, a "broken" blacksmith lately jailed for his debts,
was accepted after convincing the Trustees he was "an honest, sensible
man." Two contingents of persecuted Protestants, from the Austrian
city of Salzburg and the Piedmont region in Italy, gained asylum in
Georgia, partly because some of them knew the arts of making silk and
wine, partly for humanitarian reasons.

But tolerance had its boundaries. Some in Parliament, fearing that
Salzburgers might overrun the colony, urged that there be no more
than one of them for every four Britons. Papists were barred on the
assumption that "they would only be spies upon our colony to inform
the French or Spaniards." And when English Jews collected money to
underwrite a band of Jewish settlers, the Trustees ordered the funds
returned because of a rumor that other benefactors would balk at aiding a cause not wholly Christian.

In addition to settlers sent "on the charity," with a year's subsidy, the
Trust considered applicants willing to go at their own expense and servants who agreed to indentures of either four or five years. The chief
enticement for all was a grant of land, typically five hundred acres for
the private adventurers, fifty for charity colonists, and twenty to
twenty-five for the indentured.

Fearful that their once prodigal sons might slide back into debt, the Trustees attached a long list of restrictions to the land grants. Property could not be used as collateral for loans. Nor could it be sold, a rule meant to discourage the speculative itch that Egmont disparaged as "the stock-jobbing temper." To make Georgia a society of small farmers and to keep the settlers close to one another in case of attack by the Spanish or the natives, no one would be permitted to own more than five hundred acres. Land could not be inherited by women for fear that it would lie fallow if there were no hands to work it, that there would be no males to defend it, and that if one landed heir married another, a family would amass overly large holdings.

The same paternalism led the Trustees to ban rum and other hard liquor. They would soon prohibit slavery as well, though not from humanitarian compunction. They believed it would deprive poor whites of work, threaten security by introducing a people whom the Spanish might easily persuade to revolt, and promote the very laziness that the Trustees hoped to cure by giving the lower classes the demanding gift of wilderness.

On paper, Georgia was a miniature of Sir Isaac Newton's clockwork universe, a beautiful little cosmos with every part fitted precisely to every other part, the whole a thing to excite the hopes of the poor, the kind, the creators of empire.

By the autumn of 1732, the Trustees had accepted ninety adults and twenty-three children for Oglethorpe's first voyage to Georgia. The emigrants assembled at Gravesend, a port near the mouth of the Thames, and installed themselves aboard the *Anne*, a sturdy frigate of two hundred tons. Seven Trustees attended the embarkation, and on learning of an infant passenger not yet christened, they put up two guineas "to make the company merry" on the day of the ceremony.

The settlers composed a petition expressing thanks, pledging obedience, and requesting a list of benefactors so that their names might be inscribed on a pyramid to be erected in their honor in Georgia. At eight o'clock on the morning of November 17, after a four-gun salute and a last-minute change of pilots (the first having been found "in liquor"), the *Anne* weighed and came to sail.

The christening of Georgius Marinus Warren occurred a few days later, with Oglethorpe as godfather and the company made merry by many quarts of eggnog and "a handsome supper." The meals issuing from the galley of the *Anne* had considerably more charm than those aboard Winthrop's *Arbella*. There were potatoes, onions, carrots, generous rations of butter, soups, mutton, pork, beef, fowl, fish, tea, wine, beer, and on Christmas, mutton, beef broth, pudding, and pints of eggnog for all.

But if the cuisine had improved since Winthrop's day, the elements had not. From one dawn to the next, the wind might blow the *Anne* 172 miles or 12. Christmas brought gales that snapped a topmast and sprang a sail. "Squally" days greatly outnumbered fair ones, and a passenger could do little in a storm but pray for its end. Between storms, beds were aired, and Oglethorpe drilled the men with firearms and bayonets. Sleeping quarters were scrubbed with vinegar once a week. The ocean's fauna and flora—tropical birds, flying fish, vast blankets of seaweed—were noted with interest.

The colonel carried broth to the sick, caught a dolphin and gave his portion to the "big-bellied" women aboard the ship, and turned small occasions into special feasts. When scuffles broke out, he brokered the peace and restored the company's cheer with a round of drinks. In more stubborn cases, he was not above delivering "a good kick on the arse."

On January 13, 1733, near Charleston, South Carolina, Oglethorpe spied land—a line of trees "just above the horizon, no disagreeable sight to those who for seven weeks have seen nothing but sea and sky." With satisfaction, he reported that only two passengers, both of them babies ailing from the start of the voyage, had died, and that many of the emigrants, "half starved through want before they left London," had returned to health "with food and care."

Told that the colonists might balk at following him to the wilderness once they had sampled the comforts of Charleston, Oglethorpe left his passengers aboard the *Anne* while he visited the governor of South Carolina and gathered intelligence for the last leg of the journey. When he returned, the *Anne* headed down the coast, to the mouth of the Savannah River, then sailed inland for another ten miles, dropping anchor at the base of a forty-foot bluff. There, on February 1, James Oglethorpe deposited the first Georgians and put them to work settling the place they called Savannah, after the river.

A staircase, the work of a construction party advanced by the governor of South Carolina, awaited them, and Oglethorpe's tent was up within the hour. Surveying the "Landskip" from his perch atop the bluff, he found it "very agreeable, the stream being wide, and bordered with high woods on both sides." He had reason to believe the place would prove healthful, too, since the South Carolinians had told him that a small Indian nation, the Yamacraws, had chosen to situate their village on the bluff.

A delegation of Yamacraws came to welcome the strangers on their first day, and as implausible as it sounds in view of the sorrowful history of North America's natives and its immigrants, the reports sent to England in 1733 say that the Yamacraw chief, Tomochichi, told Oglethorpe that his people had four desires: status as subjects of His Majesty, gifts of land among the settlers, permission to send their children to the white man's school, and instruction in Christianity. By all accounts a practical man, Tomochichi may have hoped that by aligning his tribe of one hundred with the English, he could protect it from the neighboring Creeks, who had banished the Yamacraws after a falling-out.

By the end of the second day, all tents were pitched, and by the end of the third, all provisions had been hauled up the bluff. On the fourth day, the Sabbath, the Reverend Dr. Herbert performed a service of thanksgiving, and on the tenth, Oglethorpe could spare a moment to write the Trustees that except for the babies who had died at sea, all his charges were alive.

After six weeks on the frontier, one colonist wrote to his family in England that Oglethorpe was "both great and good" and predicted that in spite of runaway hogs, ants that "bite desperately," and a few "Grumbletonians" in their ranks, "there is no room to doubt but that we shall be a flourishing people." With hoes supplied by the Trust, they had only to plant their crops and wait for nature to deliver the seven-inch ears of wheat and the rest of the luxuriant plenty promised by Sir Robert Montgomery.

THE first flaws in the Georgia plan appeared in the summer, when Oglethorpe reported that his wards had grown "very mutinous and impatient of labor and discipline." New settlers had begun to arrive, and few comported themselves as the Trustees would have wished. A day after debarking from the *Georgia Pink,* Mary Preston, pregnant and newly widowed, was arrested for picking the pocket of a man lost in a fog of rum. The perpetrator pleaded that she too was a victim of intoxication and had committed the theft unawares. For his rum drinking, the man was sent to the stocks. Mrs. Preston's trial was postponed until after her lying-in.

There is no compelling evidence that the ban on rum kept anyone from drinking it. It was easily purchased from the South Carolinians, who lived on the other side of the Savannah River and obligingly delivered by night or came grinning by day with casks marked "cider." "Many of the newcomers, in spite of all I can do, drink very hard," Oglethorpe told the Trustees. "I fear a mortality will soon happen amongst them." Long a foe of hard liquor, Oglethorpe believed it spoiled mother's milk, and he worried about the hazards of mixing strong drink with Georgia heat.

More ominously, the Georgians clamored for slaves, having watched them working for South Carolinians doing business in Savannah. The thought of being able to order others to labor in the broiling sun exercised understandable thrall, and the colonists readily accepted the notion that such an arrangement was foreordained since the African, unlike the Englishman, was at home in the heat.

Colonel Oglethorpe ordered the slaves returned to South Carolina, staved every rum barrel he could find, and tried to sweeten tempers with an extra allowance of wine. He refused to consider the demands for rum and slaves because they conflicted with the Trust's master plan for Georgia and because his power in the colony was total. Unlike Governor John Winthrop of Massachusetts, who had shared his authority with the Court of Assistants, Oglethorpe governed alone. He was judge and jury, a one-man parliament, commander-in-chief, and omnipotent executive answerable to no one but the Trustees in far-off London.

But as autocrats go, Oglethorpe is notable for his selflessness and incorruptibility. The surviving accounts of Georgia's first year show a tireless thirty-six-year-old leader determined to bring a dream to life. He ordered the building of a communal cowpen and established a public garden as a nursery for vegetables, fruits, mulberry trees, and grapevines. Before summer, he had formed an alliance with the outlying Creeks, whose support was critical in protecting Georgia from the Spanish to the south and the French to the west. More important, the Creeks ceded to England all the lands they did not use—thousands of square miles—keeping only three coastal islands and requesting a campground for their visits to Savannah.

Progress was indisputable, Oglethorpe wrote the Trustees at the end of 1733. "Providence itself seems visible in all things to prosper your designs calculated for the protection of the persecuted, the relief of the poor and the benefit of mankind." The Spaniards had not attacked, the natives were friendly, and the South Carolinians had been generous with expertise, labor, and money. Savannah's population stood at 259, fifty houses had gone up, and a lighthouse was under construction on Tybee Island, near the mouth of the Savannah River. The administrative house was in order, with civil government and criminal courts working smoothly and the militia kept in fighting trim by regular drills.

But in keeping with an unwritten law of colony founding, everything would cost more and take longer than expected. The bill for a new house, originally estimated at £20, ran to twice that. Public buildings stood framed but unsheathed for months while Savannah waited for funds from London. The Tybee Light went unfinished for so long that Oglethorpe threatened to hang the chief of the construction crew, and crew members were judged so unreliable that they were denied the pleasure of buying from the trading boats on the river. They would squander their pay, it was said, and "make themselves sick by drinking drams and eating trash."

Confident in Oglethorpe's honor and judgment, the Trustees had sent him to Georgia without defining his responsibilities or his authority. Officially he was free to govern as he saw fit, but the idea of unlimited power inevitably discomfited Englishmen proud of their parliamentary traditions. Both the Georgians and the Trustees regularly accused Oglethorpe of overstepping. His first arrogations were financial—requests for reimbursements, submitted without records of how the money had been spent. The omission put the Trust in an awkward position, Egmont said. Without the supporting invoices, the Trust could be easily cheated and was vulnerable to charges of mishandling donations and parliamentary appropriations. But if reimbursements were delayed, the Trust risked injuring the colony's standing with creditors. The problem was addressed but not resolved. Savannah's accounting remained lax, Oglethorpe rarely caught up on his paperwork, and bills often went unpaid for more than a year. Oglethorpe frequently advanced his own money as a stopgap, but the expedient was not appreciated in London, where the Trust seemed continually surprised by the size of his bills and where Parliament often balked at requests for more money for Georgia.

The colonists accumulated grievances of their own. In the beginning, disputes festered overlong because Oglethorpe was slow to appoint magistrates. Once installed, the magistrates commanded little respect because they were seen as Oglethorpe's agents rather than as impartial administrators of justice. Believing that their peers would be more lenient than the magistrates who handled most cases, colonists soon began pressing for more jury trials. Oglethorpe advised the Trust against the practice, predicting that miscreants would get off too lightly. If he worried that easy justice would breed lawlessness and disrespect, he was too late. This Prohibition era, like its twentieth-century descendant, made scofflaws of most of the populace.

Frustrated by the ambiguities of their relationship with Oglethorpe, the Trustees in 1737 created the post of secretary of Georgia and filled it with William Stephens, a former member of Parliament. Egmont, who considered Stephens "a man of cool temper and excellent sense, and great industry and punctualness," was elated to think that the Trust at last would have "constant information of the state of the colony, concerning which hitherto we had been kept too much in the dark."

STEPHENS provided much light, but it was slow to penetrate. With the best of intentions, the Trustees had attached tight restrictions to land ownership, unaware that they were lengthening the odds against Georgia's success. Prohibited from borrowing against their land, settlers seldom could afford to improve it. They were also denied the usual means of securing the credit most farmers needed to survive from one harvest to the next. Barred from selling their land, the colonists were indeed safe from the temptation to speculate, but they were also trapped—unable to trade one patch of land for another or the whole for a chance at a life in some pursuit other than agriculture.

When a landholder died without male heirs, his property reverted to the Trust. Egmont prided himself on granting exceptions, but the idea that a man without sons or brothers might toil for a lifetime only to have his property go back to the Trust discouraged many such landowners from exerting themselves. Trying to convey the pervasiveness of the settlers' frustration with the land policy, one settler wrote the Trustees, "However weak these arguments are, I do assure your honors that the greatest number of people here are guided by them."

But the greatest person among them was not. Oglethorpe, mindful that most Georgians had landed in Georgia through their financial ineptitude, believed that if they were allowed do as they pleased with their land, they would lose it. To make his point, he noted that almost everyone in Savannah in 1739 was in hock to a pair of rum peddlers who would welcome the end of the restrictions so they could "take the lands for the debts, monopolize the country and settle it with Negroes."

As early as 1733, South Carolinians sniffing a real estate boom in Georgia had promised Oglethorpe "considerable presents" if he would convince the Trust to grant them huge tracts of land and permission to own slaves. He refused. "If we allow slaves," he wrote the Trustees, "we are against the very principle by which we associated together, which was to relieve the distressed." Slavery would "occasion the misery of thousands in Africa . . . who now live free there," and large planters would ruin the small farmers who were supposed to be the mainstay of Georgia society. Oglethorpe also cautioned the Trustees against allowing female inheritance or making any other changes in the terms of land tenure. There were "infinite difficulties" in enforcing the present laws, he said, and new laws would compound the confusion.

One of the difficulties was the land itself. Savannah freeholders were given fifty acres—one-eighth of an acre for a house in town, four and seven-eighths acres a short distance away, the rest farther out. "No regard was had to the quality of the ground," one settler complained. Some of these arbitrarily allocated lands turned out to be pine barrens, some swamps. The grants were also sliced into "long pointed triangles, which considerably increased the extent of the enclosure, and rendered [a] great part of each lot entirely useless." The colony's surveyor, Noble Jones, was a busy and distractable fellow whose slapdash work set off innumerable disputes. Many settlers were understandably reluctant to work their land until boundaries and titles were cleared up.

The folly of thoughts that seemed so wise in London could be summed up in one unhappy fact: By 1738, the Georgians had cultivated only one thousand of the fifty-nine thousand acres granted by the Trust. This poor showing plus prodding from local officials who disagreed with Oglethorpe convinced the Trustees that the land tenure rules were too strict, and in 1740, they gave colonists permission to acquire as much as two thousand acres through marriage or bequests.

THE greatest gulf between London and Savannah, wider than the Atlantic itself, was the gulf between the Trustees' motives for founding Georgia and the settlers' reasons for going there. Acting not for themselves, but for others, the Trustees expected those others to be equally high-minded—appreciative, diligent, obedient, willing to put the common good first and believe that individual prosperity would follow. Of the 3,200 persons who settled in Georgia during the years of the Trust, 1,100 English emigrants and 1,000 European Protestants were sent "on the charity." Nearly 700 more came as private adventurers, another 400 as indentured servants. Unlike the Puritans of Massachusetts, they were not a community bound by a shared belief. Accident had thrown them together, and they had little incentive to care about one another or a larger good.

With their own fortunes at risk, the private adventurers had reason to work hard and did. So did the Europeans, who seemed genuinely thankful to have been given refuge from religious persecution. But the English charity colonists displayed little of the gratitude and industry envisioned by the Trustees. Indolence, insubordination, and inebriation were chronic among charity colonists and indentured servants alike. The servants regularly defected to other colonies before serving out their time. By 1740, at least one Trust official was able to see that persons "who had been useless in England were inclined to be useless also in Georgia."

However unseemly, the obduracy of the settlers was understandable. Hardships crowded them on every front. The communal store, established to protect them from the shortages chronic in a wilderness, was sometimes empty, and sometimes the storekeeper refused to distribute the goods promised by the Trust. Provisions went bad, and merchants from other colonies exploited the Georgians' inexperience by price gouging.

The plow, long used in England, was mysteriously absent from Georgia. "I despair of ever doing any great matters by pecking with a hoe," a settler complained to the Trustees in 1738. "[I]t might be of very great service to the colony if your honors would please to assist them with a few English plows for I am sure that one man and a boy with but a couple of oxen or horses shall do more than ten men with their hoes . . . and I think [that] would be better also than that inhumane and abominable using of Negroes." Poor in plows, the Georgians were unexpectedly rich in spelling texts, one thousand of which had been donated by a Mr. Leak, bookseller of Bath. With scant time for study, however, most colonists continued to spell by ear, describing the clearing of land as "tegious" if done alone and ruinously "extravigant" if carried out by the few day laborers available for hire.

Settlers were also dangerously ignorant of their new world. The plans called for a society of small farmers, but only 15 of the 149 men who arrived in 1733 had any agricultural experience. Seeds were often planted too close together, or too late, and flimsy fences collapsed before cattle and hogs eager to dine on some crops and trample the rest. Once on the loose, cows often declined to come home. They preferred swamps, the deeper the better, and if not soon retrieved, were nabbed by thieves or slaughtered on the spot. To deter rustlers, Oglethorpe ordered that cattle be branded. Slaughterers were hard to catch, and juries rarely convicted them.

The ban on rum did not elevate the moral tone of Georgia and inadvertently penalized the economy. Money that might have stayed in Georgia flowed to South Carolina, and the prosperity that might have come from exporting Georgia timber to the West Indies never materialized since the West Indies had nothing to trade but rum. During Georgia's first two decades, imports outpaced exports by six to one, draining the colony of cash and impairing credit, since merchants knew that few Georgians could honor their bills.

FIRED by ambitions of building a huge silk industry, Oglethorpe had engaged a small group of Italian silk makers even before sailing to Georgia. They arrived in a cantankerous mood that never lifted. What followed was a long comic opera and an expensive lesson in the perils of harnessing a dream to persons who do not share it.

Paul Amatis, chief of the silk makers, registered his dismay with the

Trust's leisurely approach to reimbursements by going on strike. That crisis passed, but Amatis soon died, and the care of the silk enterprise passed to one of his companions, a Mrs. Camuse. Known for an "exceeding fine hand" at winding silk, she also had an exceeding fine appreciation of her indispensability. As William Stephens put it, Mrs. Camuse, "knowing too well the English of sine qua non, finds it in her power to set what value on her self she pleases." Her demands—for money, livestock, and land—were exquisitely timed, forcing Stephens to accede for fear of losing the entire year's production if she stayed her fine hand at some crucial moment.

In the fall of 1738, Oglethorpe informed the Trustees that all was finally well with Mrs. Camuse. She and her family were beginning to enjoy Savannah, their latest reels of silk thread were excellent, and the public garden was filled with mulberry trees.

But Oglethorpe overestimated the constancy of Mrs. Camuse. During one mulberry leaf shortage, she tried to make a killing by going to Stephens's house and offering to sell leaves to the Trust at the rate of three pence for each of her own one thousand trees. A "monstrous sum," Stephens thought, since he knew that many of the trees were saplings. Afraid of turning her down, he temporized, sending her home without an answer. Then he summoned reinforcements, rode to her plantation, and there, bolstered by his fellows, drove a better bargain for the Trust. On another occasion, Stephens noted that she had dropped by his house, "modestly demanding two steers to be delivered her for her family."

More serious was her refusal to take apprentices. After much probing, Stephens learned that she feared for her job and her life. In the Italian Piedmont, where she had been raised, teaching a foreigner how to make silk was a crime punishable by death. "'Tis no longer strange that she insists on pretty high terms," Stephens wrote to London. Tossing between his hope that the silk business could succeed and his worry that the whole enterprise rested on "too precarious a bottom: Mrs. Camuse's temper," Stephens urged the Trustees to maintain their subsidy while he persevered in his efforts to win her cooperation.

After holding out for a full decade, Mrs. Camuse agreed to train two young girls from Ebenezer, a nearby settlement of Austrian refugees. When the girls returned to Ebenezer, the village pastor, John Bolzius, reported that Mrs. Camuse had given them busywork and insisted that she could not reveal the whole of her art until the third year of the apprenticeship. The girls thought they had seen enough to be able to wind silk on their own if a carpenter could make the tools, but once again Piedmont stymied Ebenezer. "I am told that Mrs. Camuse keeps [the tools] as a secret and don't let anybody have a pattern thereof," Bolzius wrote the Trustees. To end her monopoly, he asked that equipment and instruction manuals be sent from England. The Trust obliged, and in 1746, the people of Ebenezer began making silk. Seeing that theirs was not as fine as Mrs. Camuse's, they sought her advice. She stayed true to character—"unwilling to tell us the least article," Bolzius said.

Mrs. Camuse was not the only impediment. Mulberry leaves, vulnerable to spring frosts and haphazard horticulture, were often scarce. Silkworms easily fell victim to undernourishment, vermin, overcrowding, mold, cold, and heat. There was also, Stephens said, an "unaccountable backwardness . . . in our dames and damsels to attend the worms during their time of feeding." The reluctance, ascribed to meager pay and a feminine aversion to worms, punctured a cherished fantasy: since most of the work was light enough to be performed by women, the Trustees had imagined that women would take it up. They did not. Nor did men, who could earn twice as much at any other kind of labor.

Stephens met one year's shortages of leaves and worms with cocoons purchased from South Carolina. Georgia's annual output of silk thread jumped from fourteen pounds to forty, but the high price of the South Carolina cocoons meant that "the sale of a pound of spun silk in London would in no wise answer the expense of raising it." Annoyed that monies intended to promote the growth of Georgia had gone elsewhere, the Trust ordered the colonists to raise their own silkworms and announced that it would pay no more than two shillings for a pound of cocoons. Seeing little profit in the arrangement, most Georgians chose to raise no silkworms at all, and production plummeted to seven and one-half pounds of spun silk.

As one disappointing year followed another, Stephens's appraisals of the silk prospects began to cycle with the seasons. His hopes budded in spring, blossomed in summer as he hunted down new sources of mulberry leaves, and shriveled the moment he saw that his ministrations had come, once more, to nothing. "I profess solemnly that nothing in the whole course of my service has sat so close on my thoughts as how to get that manufacture promoted," he sighed at the end of August 1744. Silk, he told the Trustees a year later, "never comes into my thoughts without giving me great pain."

Mrs. Camuse died in 1750. Silk flourished briefly under the tutelage of others and with financial incentives from Parliament, but as England's displeasure with its American colonies grew, the subsidies dwindled and the silk business evanesced. The broken threads occasioned no mourning. As early as 1740, the earl of Egmont had noted that "exceeding good cotton grows in Georgia," and by 1790, when the last reels of raw silk passed through the Savannah customs house, cotton had become the stuff of Georgia's dreams.

OGLETHORPE'S choice of Savannah as the place to settle put a hundred miles of peace of mind between the first Georgians and the Spaniards in Florida, but ultimately Georgia's noble experiment was threatened less by distant enemies than by fellow Englishmen in South Carolina. As every Savannahian could see, nothing could be finer than to be in Carolina. There a man could drink what he chose, buy as much land as he could afford, and do with it as he pleased. He could also own slaves, sparing himself the hardest physical labors and saving enormous sums in wages and provisions. Depending on who did the ciphering, white servants were either four or six times more expensive than slaves.

The push for slaves had begun with Samuel Eveleigh, a Charleston merchant who extended credit to Oglethorpe and the Trustees in the

hope of winning large grants of land and a monopoly on the trade
with the native tribes of Georgia. In a letter to London in April 1733,
scarcely two months after Oglethorpe's landing, Eveleigh advised the
Trustees that the absence of slaves in Georgia would prove "a great
prejudice if not a means to overset your noble design" simply because
of the heat. In another letter, he asserted that without the labor of
slaves, Georgia would produce no surplus commodities, "and without
that, no trade can be carried on there to satisfaction. It can't be supposed that the Trustees know the circumstances of this country so well
as those who have lived several years in it."

Others took up the cause. Patrick Tailfer, a physician who described
himself as one of "the better sort of people in Savannah," tried to sway
the Trustees with medical and economic arguments. The heat was not
only alien to Englishmen, it was unhealthy for them, causing "distempers which render them useless for almost one half of the year," Tailfer
said. Dietarily, white men required "meat, bread and other victuals,"
while Negroes lived "in good plight and health upon salt [meat?],
Indian corn and potatoes, which they raise themselves with no expense
to the master but the seed." Tailfer also noted that indentured servitude, unlike slavery, was temporary. When indentures expired, an
employer faced two unpalatable choices: a long, costly voyage to
Britain to recruit new servants or taking a chance on those "harden'd
abandoned wretches" shipped to Georgia by the Trust. The wretches
often ran away, blending easily among other whites, "whereas Negroes
would always be known and taken into custody unless they could produce a certificate from their master."

Tailfer proposed that slaves be used in only the most strenuous
labors, reserving lighter unskilled jobs and the crafts for whites.
Elaborating Eveleigh's point about slaves and trade, Tailfer said, "It
seems impossible to raise any quantity of produce with white servants
only, and even if it should be done, we could not dispose of it [through
exports] because our neighbors in Carolina would always undersell us,
having their work so very much cheaper than ours."

William Stephens warned the Trustees that Tailfer was an idler and a dandy who "has lived and dressed in a superior manner to any of this place; and has vanity enough to set up for a dictator." Oglethorpe shared Stephens's low regard for Tailfer but argued against slavery on grounds of security. In South Carolina, slaves outnumbered whites, and Oglethorpe believed it was only a matter of time before the slaves sought revenge.

Tailfer persevered, and in 1739, he and and his brother-in-law, Robert Williams, collected more than one hundred signatures on a petition asking the Trustees to end the landholding restrictions and the ban on slaves. Defeated by these policies, the petition said, Georgians were leaving for other colonies.

Stephens urged the Trustees to ignore "these finders of everyone's faults but their own. . . . Such a multiplicity of riff raff I look on as I would on sheep's excrements." Oglethorpe forwarded a cooler judgment, speculating that many of the signers had felt pressed to add their names because they owed money to Tailfer and Williams. Change the land tenure rules and allow slavery, Oglethorpe warned, and "the province is ruined." Debtors would clean their slates by giving their deeds to Tailfer and Williams, who would stitch small farms into large plantations, and large plantations could prosper only with slave labor.

In 1739, the Trustees made one concession, allowing property owners without sons to bequeath land to any relative except a Catholic one. The ban on slavery would stand. The Trustees would not, they said, be party to the introduction of a "baneful commodity" sure to "destroy all industry among the white inhabitants" and create a world in which slaves would become the terror of their masters.

Oglethorpe praised the decision and reported that it had "in a great measure quelled the troublesome spirit." Tailfer and his ilk were planning to leave Georgia, and those who had elected to stay had new reason to appreciate the wisdom of the Trust's antislavery law. In September, a slave insurrection in South Carolina ended the lives of forty Negroes and twenty whites.

But at the very moment when Oglethorpe and Stephens were rejoicing in the thought that the slavery issue had been settled, two

Georgians in London were pressing the Trust to reconsider. One of the petitioners was Tailfer's brother-in-law, a surprise to no one. The other was Stephens's son Thomas. Thomas, who clerked for his father, had had a few clashes with Oglethorpe and the colony's storekeeper, and William Stephens had sent Thomas off to London in the hope that a holiday would leave him "easy in his thoughts."

In October 1739, a few days after telling the Trustees that Savannah was thriving, Thomas met privately with Egmont and confided his opinion that the colony was becoming "a desert" because of the high cost of labor. He also accused Oglethorpe of high-handedness. When Egmont noted the discrepancy between Thomas's opinions and his father's reports, Thomas said his father was afraid to write the truth because of Oglethorpe's vindictiveness. Thomas claimed to possess several depositions that would destroy Oglethorpe, but when Egmont asked to see them, Thomas balked.

Next the younger Stephens set out to convince Parliament that money appropriated for Georgia was money wasted because the colony would never succeed without slaves. Egmont was outraged, and when news of Thomas's doings reached William Stephens in Savannah, he found his eyes "brim full of tears."

The London battle over Georgia stretched on and on. On one side, the Trustees lobbied for increased public funds to offset a steady decline in private benefactions. On the other, Thomas Stephens insisted that public funds were not needed; private investors would put up the necessary capital if they were permitted to own slaves and large, unencumbered properties. From South Carolina, Tailfer and others tried to goad the Trustees into owning up to their failure. No shame would attach to them for admitting that "from unforeseen emergencies their hypothesis did misgive . . . but all the world would exclaim against that person or society who through mistaken notions of honor . . . would persist in pushing an experiment contrary to all probability, to the ruin of the adventurers."

In 1742, trying once more to hold back the tide, the Trust ended the ban on rum. In June, after savaging the honor of Oglethorpe and the

Trustees, Thomas Stephens was summoned to appear on his knees in the House of Commons, where he was rebuked by the Speaker. For a moment, it appeared that the antislavery camp would prevail. But in July, Parliament refused to vote funds for Georgia. Egmont protested by resigning from the governing council of the Trust and calling upon other council members to do likewise. They declined and immediately ordered William Stephens to canvass the Georgians on "the use and introduction of Negroes."

Stephens's report reached London early in 1743. He himself disliked the institution of slavery, he said, but had concluded that if the law were changed, he would become a slaveholder because of the prohibitive cost of white servants. Stephens suggested a cautious introduction. For security's sake, he thought the rules should require the presence of at least one white male for every four slaves. To assure that Negroes would not take jobs from whites, he urged that slaves be confined to the country, where they would clear and till the land. He also advised against the common practice of allowing a master to hire out his slaves, an arrangement that only resulted in giving the master the means "wherewith to live idle, and voluptuously."

The last bar to slavery fell in 1743, when Oglethorpe returned permanently to England, citing a need to tend to his financial affairs and a desire to resume his career in Parliament. William Stephens, the colony's president, was left in charge. Without Egmont to carry the standard in London and Oglethorpe as watchdog in Georgia, only one question about slavery remained: When? In the public houses of Savannah, would-be slaveholders regularly hoisted their tankards and proposed toasts to "the one thing needful." Betting that the one thing would soon be secured, adventurers began investing in Georgia, just as Thomas Stephens had predicted. Between 1743 and 1749, the annual influx of private capital swelled from £510 to £16,320.

The Trust neither lifted the ban on slavery nor enforced it, and by 1748, it was widely known that slaves were hard at work in Georgia, most of them at discreet distances from Savannah. A year later, the Trust, with advice from William Stephens, drew up rules for slaveholding in Georgia. The code imposed fines and other punishments for "endangering the limb of a Negro" and for interracial sexual congress. It forbade intermarriage and prohibited apprenticing a slave in any trade except the making of barrels, presumably because they would be needed for Georgia's exports. The code also prescribed the one-to-four ratio of whites to slaves suggested by Stephens and required that every purchase and sale of Negroes be entered in the official records. Slaves were not to work on the Sabbath, when their masters could either "permit or oblige them to attend some time on that day for instruction in the Christian religion."

The new rules took effect in 1750, after the Trustees persuaded His Majesty's Privy Council that slavery would prove "a benefit to the said colony and a convenience and encouragement to the inhabitants thereof." Thus convenienced and encouraged, Georgia immediately began to prosper. Few noticed or cared when the Trustees, citing their "total inability" to raise funds for the colony, surrendered their charter in 1752.

THE story of Georgia's founding is often presented as a triumph of greed over altruism, the demise inevitable and hastened by the kindly but misguided gentlemen of the Trust. They were, it is said, hopelessly naive in their belief that the Georgians would not covet the life of their slaveholding neighbors in South Carolina. But in the matter of slavery, it seems truer to say that the Trustees were not nearly idealistic enough. Their case against slavery was military and economic, not moral. While individual members of the Trust occasionally voiced revulsion at the idea of one human being owning another, it did not occur to them to use their influence to work for the abolition of slavery throughout the British Empire.

As planners and managers of Georgia's economy, the Trustees miscalculated everything. With no personal financial stakes in the venture, they eliminated conflicts of interest, but they also insulated themselves from all risk. They stood to lose nothing if Georgia failed. It is futile yet irresistible to wonder how the pinch of pecuniary loss might have altered the Trustees' decisions on land tenure, rum, and on scores of other practical matters.

The ocean between Britain and Georgia compounded the administrative challenges. Except for Oglethorpe, none of the Trustees ever set foot in their colony, so their information was secondhand and, in many instances, self-interested. It was also stale. A letter written in Savannah in one month might not find a London-bound ship until the next, and the ship might call at several ports en route. When the Londoners drafted their reply, the swiftest passage would not carry it back in Savannah in fewer than seven weeks. To people trying to scratch a living from dirt they could not even be sure they owned, the long silences and the Trustees' reluctance to alter policy must have been profoundly discouraging.

The Trust's choice of Colonel Oglethorpe as leader was sound. His philanthropic interests were deep. He was honorable, vigorous, young, and resolute. His soldiering had equipped him for the dangers of the frontier. But the Trustees erred in allowing him the powers of a czar. Passionately committed to the Trust's dream of Georgia, he viewed compromise and change as doors to defeat. As an aristocrat and a military officer accustomed to privilege and command, he preferred government by edict rather than by ballot or negotiation and rarely reversed his decisions. Unable to bargain with Oglethorpe or appeal to representatives whose power served as a check on his, the Georgians justifiably felt deprived of rights enjoyed by British subjects elsewhere. Oglethorpe floated righteously above their protests, as serene and infuriating as any patriarch who believes he understands the needs of his people better than they do.

The fatal blunder was the Trustees' misreading of human nature. In their enthusiasm for their own goodness, they imagined that the settlers too would be lit by noble fires, ready to sacrifice all for a grand cause. But selflessness does not thrive on destitution. Struggling to sustain themselves, forbidden to mortgage or sell their property, unable to compete with slave labor, the first Georgians understandably developed an outsized craving for the things of this world.

When private gain and public good collide, individual wealth often triumphs at the expense of commonwealth. Georgia was different, a strange case that stands as a warning to social reformers at every point on the ideological spectrum. The Trustees' design failed because its insistence on selflessness crushed all possibility of individual prosperity. "Not for self, but for others" was a fine sentiment for earls, but it was a rare pauper who could cherish the thought.

3

VIRTUOSO

GEORGIA ESCAPED THE grave, but had there been need of an epitaph, none would have served better than this: "The most exquisite folly is made of wisdom spun too fine." The thought came from a Philadelphian acquainted with Georgia's troubles, a man who called himself Poor Richard and published an almanac filled with practical advice for farmers and moral guidance for all. "Do good to thy friend to keep him, to thy enemy to gain him," he counseled. He declared that "God helps them that help themselves" and that "Whate'er's begun in anger ends in shame." He preached thrift—"Beware of little expenses, a small leak will sink a great ship"—and inveighed against greed: "O *Avarice!* How blind are thy votaries! How often by grasping at too much do they lose all, and themselves with it!" He saw virtue and happiness as mother and daughter and warned of the hazards of associating with the wicked: "He that lies down with dogs shall rise up with fleas."

Poor Richard's creator, a printer named Benjamin Franklin, had published his first almanac on December 19, 1732, a day when the first Georgians were somewhere on the Atlantic, tarring the sides of the ship carrying them toward the American coast. Near the end of his long life, Franklin said Georgia's travails owed much to the poor character of the settlers, but the young Franklin had more in common with the Georgians than the old Franklin chose to report. In 1723, at the age of seventeen, he had skipped out on an indenture to his brother, a printer in Boston. A few weeks later, arriving at Philadelphia's Market Street wharf, he was as hard-pressed as any of the first Georgians, although he refused to show it. In return for his help in rowing the boat that had brought him down the Delaware, the owners offered to waive his fare. Franklin insisted on giving them a shilling, "a man being sometimes more generous when he has but a little money than when he has plenty, perhaps through fear of being thought to have but little," he wrote in his autobiography. His first stop was a bakery, where he asked for three cents' worth of bread and was presented with three "great puffy rolls." Satisfied by one, he bestowed the other two on a woman and child waiting on the wharf.

Even without fishes, the loaves signaled that this was no ordinary young man. At the age of ten he had gone to work for his father, a maker of candles and soap; at twelve he was bound over to his brother's print shop; at sixteen he embraced vegetarianism. The money he saved on food he spent on books, and the time he gained by not dining with his carnivorous brother at a nearby boardinghouse he invested in reading. His mind clear because of his modest meal, he conquered arithmetic, which he had twice failed in school. He also mastered the geometry of navigation and introduced himself to grammar, rhetoric, and logic.

When Philadelphia looked at the newcomer, it saw nothing of his accomplishments, nothing of his promise, nothing in fact but the obvious—gray eyes, sandy hair, and a stocky five-foot-nine-inch frame. The decade between Franklin's elating arrival and the success of *Poor Richard* was a gauntlet of broken business promises, debt, litigation, his father's rejection of a request for help, and the marriage of his beloved to another suitor. A business rival who learned of his plans to start a newspaper rushed in ahead of him. More often than he approved of, he surrendered to "that hard-to-be-governed passion of youth," one consequence of which was the birth of a son, William, to a woman Franklin declined to name. Even the excitement of founding Philadelphia's first public library was diminished by the realization that the great puffy roll of his pride was still not fully digested. Few cared to contribute until he stopped presenting the idea as his, crediting it instead to friends who had asked him to seek the aid of "lovers of reading."

Perhaps sobered by his reverses, Franklin undertook two ambitious projects to remodel his morals. Borrowing an idea from Cotton Mather, the Puritan divine, Franklin organized twelve of his friends into a men's club. They puckishly called themselves "the Junto," literally meaning "joined" in Spanish and used to signify a cabal or secret society. Meeting on Friday nights for the purpose of mutual improvement, they took turns posing questions for group discussion. By Franklin's design, debates were to proceed "in the sincere spirit of enquiry after truth, without fondness for dispute, or desire of victory." If Franklin's surviving questions are typical, the Junto's talks ranged from science ("Whence comes the dew that stands on the outside of a tankard that has cold water in it in the summer time?") to economics ("Does the importation of servants increase or advance the wealth of our country?") to human nature ("Wherein consists the happiness of a rational creature?"). Franklin said his friends in the Junto taught him the art of conversation and helped him find customers for his struggling new printing firm.

Franklin's second personal reformation project aimed at nothing less than moral perfection. "I wished to live without committing any fault at any time," he remembered in his autobiography. He soon realized the enormity of the challenge but refused to admit its impossibility. When he decided that the mere desire to be virtuous was not enough, he systematically set about uprooting bad habits and planting good ones in their place. Moral perfection, he decided, would follow from the mastery of twelve virtues: temperance, silence, order, resolution, frugality, industry, sincerity, justice, moderation, cleanliness, tranquillity, and chastity. After someone told him that he was "generally thought proud," he added humility to the catalog. To measure his progress toward perfection, he drew up charts listing the virtues down one axis and the days of week across the other. For many years he examined his conduct daily and noted each transgression with a black spot in the appropriate category.

Franklin professed surprise at the quantity of his faults and occasionally had the good sense to wonder whether "such extreme nicety as I exacted of myself might be a kind of foppery in morals, which if it were known would make me ridiculous." Foppery there was, and it has been ridiculed. In the novel *Israel Potter,* published in 1855, Herman Melville caricatured Franklin as an old man so full of prescriptions and injunctions that he destroyed young Israel's pleasures. Mark Twain complained that Franklin's maxims "were full of animosity toward boys. Nowadays a boy cannot follow out a single natural instinct without tumbling over some of those everlasting aphorisms and hearing from Franklin on the spot. If he buys two cents' worth of peanuts, his father says, 'Remember what Franklin has said, my son,— "A groat a day's a penny a year;"' and the comfort is all gone out of those peanuts. If he wants to spin his top when he is done work, his father quotes, 'Procrastination is the thief of time.'"

In the twentieth century, Franklin has been derided as "the founder of all the Kiwanians" and a jailer of the human spirit. Believing that the man needed liberation, not perfection, D. H. Lawrence scorned Franklin's quest for self-control. "The soul of a man is a dark vast forest, with wild life in it. Think of Benjamin fencing it off!" Lawrence supposed that Franklin had done his thinking in good faith, but "what we think we do is not very important. We never really know what we are doing. Either we are materialistic instruments, like Benjamin, or we move in the gesture of creation, from our deepest self, usually unconscious."

The unconscious was a modern invention, as unimaginable to Benjamin Franklin as the Internet. Whatever the value of Lawrence's dissection, there remains something poignant about a young man devising and practicing a system of moral calisthenics in hopes of making himself a better person. Lawrence and Franklin journeyed in opposite directions, Lawrence the artist pressing ever inward to probe the mysteries of his own soul, Franklin the social creature driving toward community, away from the promptings and temptations of self.

EARLY in his twenties, Franklin renewed his acquaintance with Deborah Read, his first love, whose brief marriage to John Rogers had ended in disaster. Soon after the wedding, Deborah had been told that John already had a wife. Now she and Benjamin Franklin wanted to marry, but finding the first Mrs. Rogers to prove John's bigamy was difficult. It was also rumored that John had died. If true, that removed one obstacle but threw up another: his debts—known to be considerable—would devolve to his successor in marriage. On September 1, 1730, love conquered all. Benjamin and Deborah entered into a common-law marriage and took the infant William into their home.

Benjamin began to prosper. He bought the *Pennsylvania Gazette* from his rival and made it the most widely read newspaper in America. The colony of Pennsylvania appointed him as its official printer, assuring his firm a steady flow of work. And he became a venture capitalist of sorts with a scheme for making money by helping others. In exchange for a share of the profits, he started one of his journeymen in a printing business in Charleston, South Carolina. Perhaps because of his own early hardships and the sting of his father's rejection, Franklin assisted several young men in establishing businesses. The profits from these partnerships added appreciably to his wealth.

His greatest publishing success, also begun during the early years of his marriage, was *Poor Richard's Almanack,* which took his brand of moral betterment to the public. Almanacs, paperbound books small enough to slip into a pocket, were calendars that showed the phases of the moon, laid out timetables for the tides, and made wild guesses at the weather. Almanacs were also catch-alls for riddles, jokes, verses, proverbs, recipes, agricultural tips, and facts of the believe-it-or-not variety.

Franklin knew the genre well, having printed almanacs for others, and the name *Poor Richard* undoubtedly derived from *Poor Robin,* an almanac published by his brother James in Rhode Island. Since his first literary endeavors, written under the name of Silence Dogood, Franklin had often used pseudonyms, and for his almanac he created the personae of the impoverished Richard Saunders and his long-suffering wife, Bridget. Poor Richard's almanacs typically began with short essays. Some offered practical advice—on health, nutrition, the arts of wine making and ice fishing. Others explored scientific subjects such as the life of the mosquito and the wonders of the microscope. Now and again Poor Richard thanked readers for their "gracious and kind encouragement," a gesture that enabled him to sound winsomely self-effacing even as he trumpeted the almanac's success.

Poor Richard prided himself on his weather forecasts, but maxims were his real distinction. He thought of his pithy sayings as "scraps from the table of wisdom" and over twenty-five years shared more than nine hundred of them. Some he wrote himself; many were pirated. All were uttered in his unmistakable voice.

> Opportunity is the great bawd.
> Early to bed and early to rise, makes a man healthy, wealthy and wise.
> Well done is better than well said.
> He that would have a short Lent, let him borrow money to be repaid at Easter.
> Keep your eyes wide open before marriage, half shut afterwards.
> He that falls in love with himself will have no rivals.
> Lying rides upon debt's back.
> What you would seem to be, be really.
> No gains without pains.
> Vice knows she's ugly, so puts on her mask.
> Haste makes waste.

Poor Richard's Almanack sold well—nearly ten thousand copies a year—a fact suggesting that however priggish Franklin seemed to later intellectuals, eighteenth-century Americans were more pleased than put off. In his autobiography, one of the classics of American literature, Franklin said he had seen his almanac "as a proper vehicle for convey-ing instruction among the common people, who bought scarce any other books." He had stressed industry and frugality "as the means of procuring wealth and thereby securing virtue, it being more difficult for a man in want to act always honestly, as (to use here one of those proverbs) *it is hard for an empty sack to stand upright.*"

As decocted in scores of how-to-succeed manuals written since Poor Richard's day, Franklin's aphorisms seem to be the credo of that quintessential American, the self-made man. But the popularity of

Franklin's advice on getting and spending has obscured his deeper concern with virtue, by which he meant service to others. According to Poor Richard, the noblest question in the world was "What good may I do in it?" The pursuit of wealth was laudable—to a point. Self-sufficiency brought independence, but "Avarice and happiness never saw each other." Debt was to be avoided because it left one at the mercy of creditors, but lending was a form of goodness and a source of pleasure. Somewhere between the hells of debt and greed lay a heaven where "A wise man will desire no more than what he may get justly, use soberly, distribute cheerfully, and leave contentedly."

EARLY to bed, early to rise made Benjamin Franklin wealthy enough to retire in 1748, when he was forty-two. He retained a half-interest in his printing firm, continued to write *Poor Richard* for another decade, and invested in more printing businesses being started by young men. The combined proceeds gave him a handsome living. He intended to spend the rest of his life on "philosophical studies and amusements." By philosophical he meant scientific, and although he had not yet flown his famous kite, he had distinguished himself as the inventor of the Franklin stove and the founder of America's first scientific community.

Franklin's wood stove, designed about 1740, did away with most of the cold drafts admitted by conventional fireplaces and gave off twice the heat with one-fourth the wood. When the governor of Pennsylvania offered him a ten-year patent on the stove, Franklin heeded Poor Richard's counsel to put public good ahead of personal gain: "I declin'd it from a principle which has ever weigh'd with me on such occasions, viz., That as we enjoy great advantages from the inventions of others, we should be glad of an opportunity to serve others by any invention of ours, and this we should do freely and generously." For the same reason he later gave away the lightning rod, explaining how to make one in the 1753 edition of *Poor Richard's Almanack*.

In 1743, Franklin had organized the first learned council in the New World, the American Philosophical Society. Explaining the need for such a body, he noted that every colony had a few individuals with the time and means "to cultivate the finer arts and improve the common stock of knowledge," but the sheer size of America kept them from getting to know one another. As a result, useful information went uncommunicated. Franklin proposed to connect these "virtuosi" by mail. With the society as a clearinghouse, members would exchange information on "all philosophical experiments that let light into the nature of things, tend to increase the power of man over matter, and multiply the conveniences or pleasures of life."

The purview of the society would be broad: new plants and their uses, techniques for improving cider and wine, medical discoveries, improvements in animal husbandry and mining and manufacturing, advances in chemistry and mathematics, labor-saving devices, better transportation, more maps and surveys. Members would send their news and questions to the society's headquarters in Philadelphia, where their letters would be discussed by fellow scientists. Copies would be forwarded to members with similar interests. The society would also fund scientific studies and once a year publish "such experiments, discoveries, improvements, &c. as may be thought of public advantage."

The virtues preached by Poor Richard and monitored by Franklin in his book of charts emphasized the individual's relation to society, but the code applied mainly to private life: society to Franklin meant family, friends, business associates, scientific colleagues. Soon after he retired, however, he began serving as an alderman of Philadelphia and a member of the Pennsylvania Legislature, and as his civic participation expanded, so did his concept of virtue. Convinced by his involvement in government that public-spirited action was essential to the well-being of cities, colonies, and nations, he lost no opportunity to promote the idea that virtue ought to be practiced in public as well as in private.

His 1749 "Proposals Relating to the Education of Youth in Pennsylvania," for example, was both a fund-raising appeal for Philadelphia's first college (forerunner of the University of Pennsylvania) and a sermon on the virtue of civic activism. Franklin spoke not on his own authority but with reference to John Milton, John Locke, and other sages, noting that wise men had always seen education as "the surest foundation of the happiness both of private families and of commonwealths." The ideal curriculum for the new college would include a fair hand, drawing (a "universal language"), "leaping" and other physical exercise, mathematics, English, languages pertinent to the students' intended professions, natural history, horticulture, the history of commerce, mechanics, geography, "ancient customs," history, and morals. The overarching goal of higher education, in Franklin's view, was to produce graduates who understood that true merit consisted of "an inclination join'd with an ability to serve mankind, one's country, friends and family." Franklin's brief for education was simple and compelling: Nourish the youth and the adult will nourish society.

Franklin also used his growing influence to support the founding of Philadelphia's first hospital. Writing in his old newspaper, the *Pennsylvania Gazette,* he described the success of Europe's hospitals, which cured many who otherwise would have died, made doctors more skillful by exposing them to a broad range of cases, provided instruction for medical students, offered superior hygiene and nutrition, and were highly economical because a hospital nurse could serve ten patients while a private nurse tended one. "In short," Franklin concluded, "a beggar in a well regulated hospital stands an equal chance with a prince in his palace for a comfortable subsistence and an expeditious effectual cure of his diseases."

Franklin's plea brought in more private donations, but not enough, so he took his cause to a public forum, the Pennsylvania Legislature. Rural legislators resisted. They argued that since the hospital would be in Philadelphia, Philadelphians should pay for it. They also doubted the city's desire for an institution that would attract the poor. Franklin seized the moment to propose what may have been the first challenge grant in the history of philanthropy: If he and his allies could raise £2,000 in private contributions, would the colony match it? Believing that he would not succeed, his opponents readily agreed. Franklin took their promise to prospective donors, explaining that each pound they gave would raise two pounds for the hospital. "The subscriptions accordingly soon exceeded the requisite sum, and we claim'd and receiv'd the public gift," he recalled decades later, still thrilled by the memory of his shrewdness.

Franklin successfully championed plans to pave and clean Philadelphia's streets and to light the city at night. The lighting had been suggested by someone else, but Franklin the activist brought the idea to fruition, and Franklin the scientist improved the streetlamp. The first lamps, imported from London, lacked bottom vents and trapped smoke inside the globes. After a few hours, the soot blocked the light. Come morning, the globes needed cleaning, during which many were broken. At Franklin's suggestion, the globes were replaced with four-paned glass boxes so that a mishap would be likely to shatter only a single pane. A long funnel set in the box and "crevices admitting air below" drew the smoke up and out of the lamp, enabling it to glow brightly through the night.

Franklin's public interests broadened again in 1754, when he drafted the Albany Plan of Union, which aimed to bring seven northern colonies into a defensive alliance against the French in Canada. The plan called for a federation governed by a council of representatives from each of the member colonies. The council, under the leadership of a president-general, would have the power to levy taxes, appoint civil officials, and manage Indian and military affairs. To build support for his plan, Franklin drew the first American political cartoon, an image of a snake chopped into several pieces. "Join, or die," read the caption. Franklin's plan was approved unanimously by the delegates to Albany but found no friends in provincial capitals, where colonial governors and legislatures saw it as a usurpation of their powers.

The defeat of the Albany Plan was offset by Franklin's triumphs as postmaster of the American colonies. In 1753, Franklin and the postmaster of Williamsburg, Virginia, were jointly appointed to the office of deputy postmaster and "Manager of His Majesty's Provinces and Dominions on the Continent of North America." His Majesty's

American postal operations were a shambles, and the new appointees were promised the handsome salary of £300 apiece if they could show a profit of at least that much. Left on his own when the other deputy fell ill, Franklin formulated policy, systematized accounting, standardized and printed postal forms, and set up faster routes. Mail began moving three times a week instead of one. Profits followed. As Carl Van Doren pointed out in his magisterial biography, Franklin's post office achieved what his Albany Plan had not: it unified the colonies.

IN the summer of 1757, when he was fifty-one, Franklin left Philadelphia to serve as Pennsylvania's agent in London. Anticipating an indefinite stay, he left the business of publishing *Poor Richard* to others and on the voyage to England composed his last preface, a compendium of the previous twenty-five years' worth of advice on worldly success. His essay, soon dubbed "The Way to Wealth," became a perennial best-seller, which is unfortunate because the fame of Franklin's practical advice has reinforced the mistaken impression that he cared more for private gain than public good.

In many respects, Franklin's five-year stay in London seemed to be one long meeting of the world's grandest Junto. Already admired by the British for his electrical experiments, he was quickly ushered into clubs and coffeehouses frequented by many of London's most accomplished citizens—scientists, explorers, philanthropists, and a pair of litterateurs named Johnson and Boswell.

By the end of 1764, when Franklin began a second English sojourn, much had changed. England had wrested Canada from the French, but the conflict had more than doubled the national debt. To trim it, Parliament hit upon the idea of raising American taxes, a proposition that seemed eminently reasonable in London. The average Englishman contributed fifty times more than the average American to the imperial exchequer, and Americans benefited more than the English from the considerable sums spent to fend off the French and the Indians along the sprawling western frontier.

But as Poor Richard had observed, "The horse thinks one thing, he that saddles him another." The first of the new taxes, passed in 1764, increased duties on sugar, coffee, textiles, indigo, and wine from sources outside the British empire. It also lengthened the list of American goods exportable only to destinations within the empire, where they did not always command the highest price. Americans began complaining of taxation without representation. The following year their protests came near rebellion with the passage of the Stamp Act, which imposed a tax on legal papers, licenses, diplomas, newspapers, and documents of every other description—including almanacs. Nine colonies retaliated by organizing a boycott of English goods.

English merchants quickly felt the injury and demanded that the act be repealed. When the House of Commons agreed to consider the matter early in 1766, Franklin was summoned to appear. Questioned at length over several days, he explained that the tax offended Americans because they had no representatives in Parliament and because they were taxed more heavily than the British supposed. Pennsylvania, for example, laid out £500,000 for the late war on its western frontier and had received only £60,000 in reimbursements from Parliament. The tax was also impractical. It would be difficult to collect because hard currency was in short supply in the colonies, a situation Franklin blamed on England's refusal to let the Americans issue paper money. Franklin also thought it unjust to expect rural colonists to make expensive journeys to the city to purchase stamps for their documents in order that "the crown might get sixpence."

He also made plain his belief that whatever the crown gained in revenue was being lost in loyalty. Before the Stamp Act, Franklin said, Americans had "submitted willingly to the government of the crown, and paid, in all their courts, obedience to acts of Parliament." Governing the colonies had required no force—merely "a little pen, ink, and paper. They were led by a thread. They had not only a respect but an affection for Great Britain; for its laws, its customs and manners, and even a fondness for its fashions, that greatly increased the commerce."

A friend of repeal asked the last two questions, and Poor Richard answered.

Q. *What used to be the pride of the Americans?*
A. To indulge in the fashions and manufactures of Great Britain.
Q. *What is now their pride?*
A. To wear their old clothes over again till they can make new ones.

Frugality, once the way to private wealth, had been elevated to public virtue. No one was more surprised than Franklin, who had doubted that Americans would have either the will or the means to persevere in austerity.

The Stamp Act was repealed in March 1766, but over the next decade, as Americans inched toward their divorce from Britain, Poor Richard's creator poured considerable energy into persuading English newspaper readers that America did not need Britain. Calling himself "Homespun," he reported that the colonists had discarded the tradition of wearing mourning clothes, "yet nobody sighs for Norwich crapes or any other of the expensive, flimsy, rotten black stuff and cloths you used to send us." Determined to grow their own wool, Americans had also given up eating lamb, with the result that "the sweet little creatures are all alive to this day, with the prettiest fleeces on their backs imaginable." Drafting the Albany Plan of Union, running the post office, and serving as London agent for four colonies had deepened Franklin's sense of himself as something more than a Pennsylvanian and a British subject. He was an American, connected to other Americans from Boston to Savannah by interests that transcended old bonds to colony and empire.

Franklin also accused the British of avarice, the deadliest sin in Poor Richard's catechism. To Britons who might not know, Franklin explained that Americans were forced to send raw materials to England for manufacture and purchase the finished product "loaded with the charges of a double transportation." The English, "not content with the high prices at which they sell us their goods . . . have now begun to enhance those prices by new duties. . . . Thus they get all our money from us by trade, and every profit we can anywhere make by our fishery, our produce, and our commerce, centers finally with them!" He signed himself "F.B.," a disguise so thin it bordered on insult.

Avarice was not only reprehensible, it was self-destructive, Franklin argued. Given that the colonies enriched Britain by £2 million a year, would it not be more intelligent to carry on as before, steadily increasing the returns, than introduce "these new-fashioned vigorous measures to kill the goose which lays the golden eggs?"

As the rift widened, Franklin's anger pushed him to satire more savage than anything in the pages of Jonathan Swift. Since the Americans would not be subdued, Franklin wrote, General Gage, Britain's commander in chief in North America, should be sent instructions "that all the males there be c—st—d." Gage's army should proceed through all the towns, taking with it "a company of sowgelders. . . . On their arrival at any town or village, let orders be given that on the blowing of the horn all the males be assembled in the market place. If the corps are men of skill and ability in their profession, they will make great dispatch, and retard but very little the progress of the army." The general should be given authority to see that John Hancock, Sam Adams, and other ringleaders were "shaved quite close."

The benefits would be manifold, Franklin predicted. "In the course of fifty years it is probable we shall not have one rebellious subject in North America. This will be laying the axe to the root of the tree. In the meantime a considerable expense may be saved to the managers of the opera, and our nobility and gentry be entertained at a cheaper rate by the fine voices of our own c—st—i, and the specie remain in the kingdom, which now, to an enormous amount, is carried every year to Italy. It might likewise be of service to our Levant trade, as we could supply the Grand Signor's seraglio and the harems of the grandees of the Turkish dominions with cargoes of eunuchs."

Hoping to avert a war, Franklin continued meeting with British officials until a few weeks before the first exchanges of gunfire at Lexington and Concord in April 1775. And when he left England, it was because of news from home. His wife, who had stayed in Philadelphia because she disliked travel, had died of a stroke.

ON the fourth of July 1776, Thomas Jefferson was thirty-three, John Adams forty, George Washington forty-four. Benjamin Franklin was seventy and the most radical of the rebels. When his loyalist son William, governor of New Jersey, was arrested and imprisoned, Franklin attempted (in vain) to convert him to the rebels' cause but did not use his influence with American authorities to work for William's release. Franklin called for independence well before most of his colleagues in the Second Continental Congress, and he urged that the Declaration of Independence permit the government to limit the size of property holdings. Having seen the riches of England's landed aristocracy and the misery of nearly everyone else, he believed that some restraint on wealth was necessary to assure the greatest happiness of the greatest number.

Before the year was out, Franklin went abroad again, to Paris, as one of three commissioners charged with building French support for the American Revolution. He returned in 1785 and two years later took part in the last great episode in America's founding, the Constitutional Convention in Philadelphia. Moving toward this moment and for many years afterward, the founders were as preoccupied with virtue as Poor Richard had been, but where he had answers, they had only questions. Would Americans rise to the demands of a republic and nurture the common good, or would they prove as corruptible and greedy as the citizens of republics past? Was it wiser to govern by appealing to the virtues of the people or by restraining their vices? Prosperity was healthy, but where was the line between enough and too much?

"Will you tell me how to prevent riches from becoming the effects of temperance and industry?" John Adams inquired of Thomas Jefferson. "Will you tell me how to prevent riches from producing luxury? Will you tell me how to prevent luxury from producing effeminacy, intoxication, extravagance, vice and folly?" Elsewhere Adams noted that while the world claimed to admire intellect and virtue, it also encouraged "ambition and avarice by taking the most decided part in their favor." To build a government "upon a supposition that nations and great bodies of men, left to themselves, will practice a course of self-denial is either to babble like a new-born infant or to deceive like an unprincipled imposter."

For Franklin, the contest between self and other, between the pleasures of wealth and the duties of commonwealth, had been slight. Poor Richard had called worldly opportunity "the great bawd," but Franklin himself had found the bawd's seductions easy to resist—a consequence not so much of his virtues as his tastes. He happened to prefer science and public service to the pursuit of power and wealth. He understood that he was an exception but believed that through reason and good example, persons of influence had the power to inspire the multitudes to think and act in spheres larger than self-interest. In his fund-raising letter for the University of Pennsylvania, he had pointed out that such an institution would not only add to the prosperity of Philadelphia, it would burnish character. From fine character came public spirit and from public spirit came excellent societies. Who but dolts and scoundrels would oppose such an end?

Like Franklin and Adams, Jefferson saw the dangers of "self-love," a quality he considered "the sole antagonist of virtue." But where Adams fretted and Franklin prodded, Jefferson calmly trusted. "It has been said that we feed the hungry, clothe the naked, bind up the wounds of the man beaten by thieves, pour oil and wine into them, set him on our own beast and bring him to the inn because we receive ourselves plea-sure from these acts," he wrote to a friend. He agreed but felt that this explanation failed to answer the ultimate question: "These good acts give us pleasure, but how happens it that they give us pleasure? Because nature hath implanted in our breasts a love of others, a sense of duty to them, a moral instinct, in short, which prompts us irresistibly to feel and to succor their distresses. . . . The Creator would indeed have been a bungling artist had he intended man for a social animal without planting in him social dispositions." The fact that some humans lacked these dispositions did not prove the deficiency "a general characteris-tic of the species."

For James Madison, the essential characteristic of the species was rivalry, an observation that led to the idea of equipping the machinery of government with levers and brakes to keep rival forces in balance. "Ambition must be made to counteract ambition," he wrote in the *Federalist*. "It may be a reflection on human nature that such devices should be necessary to control the abuses of government. But what is government itself but the greatest of all reflections on human nature? If men were angels, no government would be necessary." Such ruminations on human fallibility had been part of American meditation on virtue since Thomas Paine popularized them in *Common Sense,* a pamphlet published early in 1776. "Government, like dress, is the badge of lost innocence. . . . For were the impulses of conscience clear, uniform, and irresistibly obeyed, man would need no other lawgiver."

Many philosophers of the eighteenth century put more stock in reason than in conscience, but John Adams took the side of those who understood that reason too had its limits. "We see every day that our imaginations are so strong and our reason so weak, the charms of wealth and power are so enchanting, and the belief of future punishments so faint, that men find ways to persuade themselves, to believe any absurdity, to submit to any prostitution rather than forgo their wishes and desires. Their reason becomes at last an eloquent advocate on the side of their passions, and [they] bring themselves to believe that black is white, that vice is virtue, that folly is wisdom and eternity a moment."

Because passions were woven into "the texture and essence of the soul," government would be unwise to ignore them, Adams thought. Instead they should be "arranged on the side of virtue." He believed that ambition and other "selfish affections" could be steered toward virtue because as strong as the passions were, human beings had also been endowed with "the desire of reputation in order to make us good members of society." The virtuous—those who put their country ahead of themselves when the need arose—were esteemed, while the selfish were held in low regard. For Adams as for Franklin, such virtue was the essence of government. A nation, like Christianity itself, could "stand on no other basis," Adams wrote, but "standing on this it is founded on a rock. Standing on any other ground it will be washed away by the rains or blown down by the winds."

When the Constitutional Convention opened on May 25, 1787, Franklin was too ill to attend. Still weak when he appeared a few days later, he allowed another delegate to read his first proposal, an argument against salaries for officials of the new government. Men were dominated by two great passions, Franklin had written. "These are ambition and avarice; the love of power and the love of money. Separately, each of those has great force in prompting men to action, but when united in view of the same object, they have in many minds the most violent effects. Place before the eyes of such men a post of honor that shall at the same time be a place of profit, and they will move heaven and earth to obtain it." No one rose to disagree, but the convention declined to act on his suggestion.

A few days later, as delegates debated whether to leave the selection of judges to the executive or the legislative branch, Franklin amused the convention by explaining that the Scots had neatly solved the problem by giving the choice to lawyers, who "always selected the ablest of the profession in order to get rid of him, and share his practice."

That suggestion was also declined, but on June 11 Franklin triumphed with an idea that ended a deadlock threatening to sink the convention and the hope for a national government. Delegates from thickly settled states had been insisting that the federal legislature be based on proportional representation, with one member for every forty thousand inhabitants. Delegates from small states demanded a system of equal representation, an arrangement that would give tiny Delaware as much power as a populous state like Pennsylvania. The Great Compromise, as Franklin's proposal came to be known, created a Congress of two chambers, a House of Representatives based upon proportional representation and a Senate to which every state would send two members.

In his last speech to the convention, Franklin urged delegates to set aside their objections to particulars of the newly drafted Constitution and consent to the whole. Perfection was impossible, and he doubted that any future assembly could produce a finer document. He intended to add his name to it, he said, "because I expect no better, and because I am not sure that it is not the best."

On September 17, thirty-nine of the fifty-five delegates signed. As Franklin watched, he noticed that George Washington's chair was adorned with a picture of the sun, and Franklin remarked on the difficulty of painting sunrises that could be distinguished from sunsets. During the debates of the convention, he said, his hopes for the new nation had alternately soared and plunged, and he had often looked at the sun on Washington's chair "without being able to tell whether it was rising or setting, but now at length I have the happiness to know that it is a rising and not a setting sun."

The pleasure the elder statesman took in the American sunrise was reminiscent of the exuberance of the runaway boy arriving in Philadelphia sixty-four years before. Once again the world shone with possibility. The Constitution had created a republic, and a republic, Franklin thought, was the finest form of government—"if you can keep it." Poor Richard and Benjamin Franklin had taught the citizenry everything it needed to know. Ideals were pointless unless they were lived. Virtue was as virtue did.

4

THE BEAUTIES OF FACTORY LIFE

FRANKLIN TILTED HIS sermons toward the encouragement of virtue rather than the excoriation of vice, and the flaws most exasperating in his moral cosmos were not personal but collective: the shortsightedness of Pennsylvania legislators who opposed his public works projects, the power lust of colonial governors who rejected his Albany Plan of Union, the avarice of the British empire. His long years abroad had also persuaded him of the evils of manufacturing, an activity still rare in his native land. "Manufactures are founded in poverty," he wrote from England in 1760, nearly a decade before James Watt hitched the Industrial Revolution to his steam engine. It seemed to Franklin that manufacturers prospered by preying on Britain's landless multitudes. When he learned of the high death rate in Manchester, he blamed it on manufacturing, which condemned workers to destitution, forced them to labor and live in unwholesomely close quarters, and tempted them to self-destruction by gin. Franklin supposed that as long as a man could afford to buy land of his own, he would prefer the independent life of the farmer to the subservience of toiling for others, and as long as there was "land enough in America for our people, there can never be manufactures to any amount of value."

Such sentiments were near universal among the Americans of Franklin's day, when all but a twelfth of the population lived on farms and the yeoman was the hope of the young republic. In the judgment of Thomas Jefferson, manufacturers were "panders of vice" and merchants nearly as bad. "The wealth acquired by speculation and plunder is fugacious in its nature and fills society with the spirit of gambling. The moderate and sure income of husbandry begets permanent improvement, quiet life, and orderly conduct both public and private." Financially independent, the yeomanry was thought to be above corruption, and champions of the agrarian life imagined that the relatively equal distribution of wealth in a nation of small farmers would mute the ructions between rich and poor.

The chorus in favor of manufacturing was small but had as its lead tenor Alexander Hamilton, the nation's first secretary of the treasury. After two years of studying the state of American industry (puny), Hamilton informed the House of Representatives in 1791 that agriculture, hallowed though it was, would not make the United States a great nation. With nothing but crops to sell, America was in a weak bargaining position, and the cost of shipping goods across the vastness of the Atlantic considerably upped the price of exports and imports. It stood to Hamilton's reason that a country able to keep itself in essentials was safer than one dependent on foreigners.

Hamilton also saw that agricultural economies could suffer mightily in the busts that inevitably followed booms in commodity prices, and he observed that the productivity of farmers would always be crimped by nightfall, the changing of the seasons, and human stamina. But machines toiled day and night without wages or complaint. Anticipating that Americans would oppose industry because it would take labor away from farms, where strong backs were in short supply, Hamilton noted that England's cotton manufacturing was carried on almost entirely by women and children. The secretary urged Congress to nurture industry with patents, tax incentives, quality standards, more roads and canals, speedier methods of moving money from place to place, lower duties on imports of raw materials, higher tariffs on finished goods made abroad, and a ban on the export of manufacturing technology.

Congress yawned.

Here and there, entrepreneurs who shared Hamilton's hopes opened waterpowered mills to spin cotton into yarn, but as often as not, they failed. They lacked technical expertise, and their workers disliked factory life. An Englishman touring American spinning mills in the 1790s discovered that their employees yearned to leave "as soon as they have saved up a few pounds, in order to become landholders up the country, and arrive at independence." Franklin had been right.

The grand industrial dream of Alexander Hamilton did not materialize until two decades later, when manufacturing enamored a young Boston merchant and real estate speculator named Francis Cabot Lowell. The product of two New England dynasties, Francis was born in 1775, a few days before Paul Revere saddled up for his midnight ride. At fourteen Francis was sent to Harvard, where he excelled in mathematics and tomfoolery. Caught building a bonfire in Harvard Yard, he was asked to leave but allowed to complete his studies under the eye of a parson in a village up the country. "I presume few if any of his class equal him in mathematics and astronomical attainments," the parson wrote to Francis's father, Judge John Lowell. "He is very accurate in calculating and projecting eclipses." Francis finished his coursework in time to graduate with his class in 1793.

To the disappointment of Judge Lowell, Francis passed up the traditional family pursuits—law, politics, and religion—for the trading firm of his uncle William Cabot. Cabot sent him to sea as a supercargo, whose job it was to oversee the acquisition and disposition of the goods in the hold. Within a decade, Francis had done well enough to buy a score of properties on Boston's waterfront and, according to his brother, renovate their father's "dilapidated fortunes."

Francis Cabot Lowell spoke plainly, usually in dollars and cents. He knew what he was willing to pay and took care to limit his risk. Writing to one of his Southern purchasing agents, he specified that his commodities "be shipped to Boston or New York by coasters whose masters are known to be careful and judicious, and in sums not exceeding $2,500 in any one bottom." Seeking a cooper to make casks for rum, he promised good wages—$400 a year—for the right candidate:

"a young man unmarried that loves work better than women," ready to "do any thing that he is wanted for," and willing to be hired "on trial before we engage him for a year."

Lowell's health was rarely as hale as his finances, and in 1810 he settled in Edinburgh with his wife and their four children for an extended holiday. Curious about textile manufacturing (at which the Cabots had failed expensively when he was a boy), he began visiting factories in Scotland and England. He soon decided to learn all he could in hopes of starting his own manufacturing enterprise when he returned to Massachusetts.

Britons with industrial know-how were sworn to secrecy and forbidden to emigrate, leaving Lowell with the challenge of mastering enough particulars to be able to copy the newest marvel of textile technology, the power loom. With the new loom and yarn-spinning machinery already available in the United States, Lowell dreamed of being the first to put both spinning and weaving under one roof. Bales of cotton would arrive at the back door of his factory, and bolts of cloth would come out the front. He also hoped to create an American version of New Lanark, a model factory village near Edinburgh, which recruited its operatives from the countryside, paid them more than the going rate, and housed them comfortably in a progressive community.

Back in Boston in 1812, Francis took the notes and drawings from his industrial espionage to the best mechanic he knew and engaged him to build a power loom. At the Boston Stock Exchange, where he went in search of capital for his new venture, the Cabots turned him down. The scoffing of one of his cousins scared away others. Nathan Appleton, the grandee of Boston's mercantile community, had promised Lowell $10,000 for the new company but now thought it prudent to trim his gamble by half. Undiscouraged, Lowell found a site on the Charles River, in Waltham, with sufficient waterpower for the mill he had in mind. He incorporated his Boston Manufacturing Company early in 1813 and by autumn had raised the $400,000 he figured he needed to build a mill, a machine shop, and boardinghouses for the young women he planned to hire. From the outset, the enterprise was a behemoth, backed by ten times more capital than the typical spinning mill in Rhode Island.

The buildings of the new factory were ready before the power loom worked properly, and when the company tried to market its first textiles through the only Boston retailer who carried fabrics, there were no buyers. Once past these shoals, however, the Boston Manufacturing Company sailed smoothly and at high speed. Lowell cloth, as it came to be known, was sturdy sheeting, a yard and an inch wide. It was inexpensive and, for the price, of excellent quality. Sales, handled by Appleton's trading house, shot from $3,000 in 1814 to $345,000 in 1822. Within a few years of its founding, the company began rewarding shareholders with annual dividends averaging 20 percent.

Decades later, reminiscing about the company's beginnings, Nathan Appleton noted that Francis Cabot Lowell had chosen to staff the mills by recruiting women in their late teens and early twenties with the idea that they would come from the farms of New England, stay for a year or two, and then return to the countryside. The arrangement left male hands on the farm, where they were needed, and Lowell hoped the short tenure would prevent the miseries he had seen among Britain's factory population. To Appleton, the idea of hiring farmers' daughters had seemed eminently sound. "Here was in New England a fund of labor, well educated and virtuous. It was not perceived how a profitable employment has any tendency to deteriorate the character." Appleton recalled that it was Lowell who decided that the employees would live in boardinghouses run by "respectable women, with every provision for religious worship. Under these circumstances, the daughters of respectable farmers were readily induced to come into these mills." So readily that the Boston Manufacturing Company began keeping a waiting list for job applicants.

FRANCIS Cabot Lowell died in 1817, at forty-two, but lived long enough to lobby successfully for a tariff protecting his textiles from cheaper imports and to see the ink in the company's ledgers darken from red to black. The Waltham factory soon outgrew the power supplied by the indolent Charles, and company officials began scouting for other sites. Thirty miles northwest of Boston, at the confluence of the Merrimack and Concord Rivers, they found a spot that would be to American manufacturing what the Tigris and Euphrates had been to Eden. With rapids dropping more than thirty feet in a mile, the Merrimack abounded in waterpower. There were canals, too: the Pawtucket, which bypassed the rapids, could serve as an added source of power, and the Middlesex would make it easy to float cotton bales up from Boston and finished goods back down.

Early in 1822, Jackson, Appleton, and their associate, Kirk Boott, incorporated the Merrimack Manufacturing Company, capitalized at $600,000. They purchased the Pawtucket Canal and quietly bought up the farms along the tumbling Merrimack. The new town would be called Lowell, in memory of their friend, and they dared to imagine a day when it would boast a thousand inhabitants. None of them foresaw that by 1835 they and a chosen few others would own a $6,650,000 agglomeration of eight textile corporations with twenty-two mills and 6,500 employees. The town would have 17,000 citizens, a number that soon doubled, and by 1850 Lowell, City of Spindles, was a virtual metropolis—the second-largest city in Massachusetts.

Modest ambitions notwithstanding, Lowell's founders left no aspect of their undertaking to chance, and as they set the course of life in Lowell, they proceeded with morals as well as money in mind. Nearly all of them belonged to an elite of some forty families who ruled the business, politics, and society of Boston. From the seventeenth century to the twentieth, wherever the annals of the city fall open, the page is likely to feature a Lowell, Cabot, Winthrop, Higginson, Lee, Jackson, Quincy, Adams, Saltonstall, Endicott, Channing, Warren, Minot, Otis, Eliot, Phillips, Brooks, Perkins, Dana, Prescott, Parkman, Sturgis, Bigelow, Lodge, Sargent, Bowditch, Loring, Peabody, Holmes, Forbes, Derby, Lyman, Perkins, Russell, Coolidge, Amory, Sears, Storrow, Appleton, or Lawrence. Cabots married Lowells, Lowells married Jacksons, Jacksons married Cabots, and so on until nearly everyone on Beacon Hill was at least a cousin of everyone else.

The families of Beacon Hill were a great tribe, joined by birth, marriage, and financial dealings even more intertwined than the helixes of their DNA. Their code of honor has been traced to their Puritan beginnings, but whatever Puritanism remained had been highly secularized by the time Francis Cabot Lowell pirated the power loom. Where the first American Winthrops and Endicotts sought a balance between the concerns of this world and those of the next, their nineteenth-century descendants considered it sufficient to balance moneymaking with good citizenship, philanthropy, and cultural pursuits. The next world had ceased to weigh. Avarice, once a deadly sin, had paled to mere folly. "Mercantile honor is as delicate and fragile as that of a woman," Nathan Appleton explained. "It will not bear the slightest stain. The man in trade who has been found to equivocate or falter in his course becomes a marked man. He is avoided." The tribe's adherence to its code probably owed less to the long reach of Puritanism than to the close embrace of family. The man who knows he will be held accountable to the brothers, uncles, and cousins who have entrusted him with their money has ample incentive to do the right thing regardless of his character.

Beyond investing in one another's enterprises, the tribe founded financial institutions to assure its members a ready supply of business capital and to manage its personal fortunes. Their power and wealth allowed them to mobilize enormous sums for their textile mills, the mills multiplied their wealth, and their wealth increased their power. No money machine is perpetual, but the gears of this one meshed so smoothly that it showed few signs of wear until the 1920s.

THE town of Lowell and the Merrimack Manufacturing Company began taking shape in 1823 under the direction of Kirk Boott, one of the Waltham venture's first shareholders. An engineer trained at Sandhurst, Britain's military academy, Boott started with the givens. Mill buildings had to be narrow and large windowed to capture as much daylight as possible. The length of a mill was a factor of the available waterpower: most forceful nearest the waterwheel, the power dimmed as it flowed through the shafts driving the gears of the looms and other machines. In Lowell, the waterpower thrown off by the Merrimack faded into insignificance beyond 350 feet or so. The operatives' tasks were narrowly defined and arranged to smooth the flow of work from one stage to the next. Whatever could be automated was, and wherever Lowell's mechanics saw an opportunity to increase the operating speed of existing machinery, they took it. Five and six stories high, the Lowell mills long ranked among the largest buildings of New England. With their red-brick facades, white window frames, and an occasional fillip in the form of a belfry or cupola, they were sternly handsome. The grounds, landscaped with precision, suggested the taming of nature rather than nature itself, an impression soon reinforced with the addition of fences.

In 1810, after an unimpressive year at Harvard, Boott had been sent abroad by his father. He served briefly as a junior officer in the British army, an experience that seems to have left him with an appetite for command. While a fellow officer recalled Lieutenant Boott as "a gallant soldier and a great favorite in the corps" as well as a fine shot at billiards, the construction crews and early factory workers of Lowell remembered him as haughty, imperious, and quick to impose discipline by riding crop. Lowell's first church, St. Anne's, was named for Boott's wife and served members of his faith, Episcopalianism. Whether millworkers belonged to the congregation or not, they were forced to attend services at St. Anne's and to support the church through monthly payroll deductions. Unlike most of Beacon Hill, which prided itself on sharing the republican ideals of the Yankee farmer, Boott believed in reminding the lower classes of their place and keeping them in it. Though such speculation is fruitless, it is natural to wonder how relations between capital and labor might have fared had modern American factory life not begun under the heel of Kirk Boott.

Boott dominated with the complicity of the factory itself, which controlled the worker by controlling the nature and pace of work. The farmers of New England were legendary for their diligence, but they enjoyed the freedom to decide when to stop for lunch, cool off in the river, or leave one task for another. Their daughters at Lowell would have no such latitude. They were awakened by bells, summoned to the factory and sent home by bells, and required to work six days a week, at first for eleven and then more than twelve hours a day. The neighborliness and general sense of social equality they had known at home would not figure in their relationships with employers. They saw little of the mill owners, who stayed in Boston. Management of each factory was entrusted to a resident agent, who in turn put an overseer in each workroom. The consequent social order—a handful of managers atop a mass of workers—was feudal, not democratic. Lowell, the city on the hill of American industrialization, ran on absolutism and noblesse oblige.

For a time, though, autocracy mattered less than the sirens calling from the banks of the Merrimack. Word of the experience of working in Waltham had spread, and young women were eager to come to Lowell when the first mill opened in 1823. They wanted money to send home to poor families, help brothers through college, accumulate dowries, and taste the joys of financial independence. In an era when most hired hands were paid in kind or credit, Lowell's workers received hard cash. Lowell also paid year-round, a decided advantage over the seasonal compensation associated with farming. While the standard Lowell wage of $3.25 a week was not extravagant, the first operatives considered themselves decently paid. After paying for room and board, they had $2.00, which was more than most of them could have earned anywhere else.

Lowell also offered escape. Before the mills in Waltham and Lowell, most young unmarried women remained at home with their parents. A plucky girl with bookish leanings might go off to teach school, and young women from poor families sometimes found work as domestics, but few other socially acceptable doors opened to them. Factory girls, as they proudly called themselves, could enjoy the companionship of a wide circle of friends their own age. Boardinghouse governance was strict but free of the emotional underbrush ensnaring parents and grown children.

To a degree (although not of the baccalaureate kind available to their brothers), Lowell even offered intellectual stimulation—lending libraries, night school courses, and, in time, the *Lowell Offering,* a literary magazine written and edited by the girls themselves. Fifty cents bought a season pass to twenty-five lectures at the local lyceum, where Ralph Waldo Emerson, John Quincy Adams, and other eminences enjoyed rapt attention. Lowell's lyceum "was always crowded, and four-fifths of the audience were factory-girls," Professor A. P. Peabody of Harvard recalled. "When the lecturer entered, almost every girl had a book in her hand, and was intent upon it. When he rose, the book was laid aside, and paper and pencil taken instead; and there were very few who did not carry home full notes of what they had heard. I have never seen anywhere so assiduous note-taking. No, not even in a college class."

Perhaps because the mills were novelties in America and the Lowell mills so clearly superior to their English counterparts, the first wave of factory girls seldom complained about their long hours, their ten o'clock curfew, the bells that rang them out of bed at four in the morning, or the alien, incessant demands of their mechanical work partners. Newcomers stymied by galloping machinery tended to blame themselves. In the *Lowell Offering,* Sarah Bagley, who came to the mills from New Hampshire, claimed that the din of the factories made them ideal for contemplation. "There all the powers of the mind are made active by our animating exercise; and having but one kind of labor to perform, we need not give all our thoughts to that, but leave them measurably free for reflection on other matters." Another factory girl talked herself out of minding the overpowering noise when it occurred to her that "people learn to sleep with the thunder of Niagara in their ears, and the cotton mill is no worse." A colder-eyed Lowell worker came nearer the truth when she said that the weaving rooms sounded "as if ten thousand wind mills were set in motion by a hurricane."*

---

*The noise and bone-deep vibration still can be experienced in the weaving room of the Boott Cotton Mills, one of several buildings open to the public at the Lowell National Historic Site.

Lowell prospered for a decade, weathering three recessions and starting seven more textile corporations: the Hamilton, Appleton, Lowell,
Middlesex, Tremont, Lawrence, and Boott. Between 1826 and 1836,
shareholders received annual dividends averaging 11.4 percent—nearly
twice the rate the entrepreneurs paid on their industrial bank loans in
Massachusetts. Their financial triumphs and the apparent success of the
factory girl system made Lowell an almost obligatory stop for foreign
visitors.

Charles Dickens found the girls well dressed and abloom with
health. "The rooms in which they worked were as well ordered as
themselves," he wrote in *American Notes*. Plants thrived on mill win-
dowsills, and it seemed to him that the factories provided as much
"fresh air, cleanliness, and comfort as the nature of the occupation
would possibly admit." Knowing that English readers would disapprove
of the social striving implicit in the lyceum lectures, Dickens nudged
his countrymen to rethink their assumptions. "Are we quite sure that
we in England have not formed our ideas of the 'station' of working
people from accustoming ourselves to the contemplation of that class
as they are, and not as they might be?" he asked. "I know no station in
which . . . any one of these pursuits is not most humanising and laudable. . . . I know no station which has a right to monopolise the means
of mutual instruction, improvement, and rational entertainment; or
which has ever continued to be a station very long after seeking to do
so."

Anthony Trollope saw Lowell as a "philanthropical manufacturing
college," where the girls were looked after more like students "at a
great seminary than as hands by whose industry profit is to be made
out of capital." Lowell, Trollope thought, was "the realization of a
commercial Utopia. . . . I should not call the place elegant [but] it
struck me at once that some great effort at excellence was being
made."

Contemplating their creation, Lowell's founders were no less
delighted than Trollope and Dickens. Demand for their cloth might
rise and fall, but with generations of experience in speculation, they

happily sold textile shares when the market boomed and bought during busts. William Appleton, Nathan's cousin and an original investor in several Lowell corporations, reckoned that such well-timed comings and goings had added $2 million to his fortunes. For Patrick Tracy Jackson, the beauty of factory life was manufacturing itself. The industrialist, he wrote, could take "raw material and by the skillful treatment of it add to its value, by which the capitalist and the operative were profited; and the public were gainers if he could produce a useful article."

It was an unassailable theorem as long as no one lumbered it with questions about who had the power to determine prices, wages, and the parceling out of profits. Only Nathan Appleton seems to have understood his debt to happenstance. "It was wholly accident that I went into [cotton manufacturing]," he readily admitted, "and the truth is that my mind has always been devoted to many other things than money-making. That has never been a passion with me, or ever a subject of much concern. Accident and not effort has made me a rich man."

ACCIDENT and not effort ended the decade-long honeymoon between the men who owned the mills and the women who worked in them. In 1834, after a three-year slide in dividends, the mill owners believed they faced another difficult year. The cost of raw cotton had doubled since 1830, and demand for textiles had slowed, forcing manufacturers to lower prices in the hope of sparing themselves an ugliness of factory life: warehouses stacked high with unsold goods.

Eager to minimize the damages, the directors of the Lowell companies proposed cutting the factory girls' wages by 25 percent. More than 1,500 of the 6,500 employees on the payrolls were men, who earned on average two and one-half times more than the women, but cutting the men's pay does not appear to have figured in the discussions. Nor, apparently, did the directors consider idling the factories. As Jackson had observed on another occasion, "Capital once invested in buildings and machinery cannot be withdrawn. The business must be pursued,

or the ruin is immediate and irretrievable." To a capitalist, unproductive capital was as reprehensible as the town layabout. The directors
ordered their mill agents, who managed the factories, to "act in concert . . . and endeavor to do what is right between the parties." When
the agents replied that 25 percent was draconian and suggested 12.5
percent, the directors pushed for more. The agents met them halfway,
warning that deeper cuts would prove "unfavorable to the procure-
ment of good help in future."

The good help of the present felt betrayed and set about organizing
a strike. One of their leaders was fired. Her co-workers walked off the
job, marched from mill to mill, and factory girls paraded eight hundred
strong through the streets, where they committed the unladylike act of
public speaking and pledged not to return to work for less than full pay.

The hubbub lasted a week. A few girls were fired, and a few quit,
but most, having little choice, returned to work at the new lower wage.
The class boundary staked out by Kirk Boott was now starkly visible,
with capital and management on one side of the line and labor on the
other. The factory girls had come to understand, without benefit of
Karl Marx, that they were not partners in a great social experiment
designed for mutual gain; they were cogs in a machine run for the
profit of others. Mill agents dismissed the disturbances as the work of
a handful of "Amazons" but were stunned that so many women had
joined the rebellion. Mill owners declined to record their feelings
about the revolt, but in their later writings, which emphasized the
magnanimity of Lowell's founders and the equality of American labor
and capital, it is easy to sense the impatience they must have felt with
girls who did not appreciate how well off they were compared with
their sisters in Manchester.

The factory girls struck again in 1836 when the corporations tried
to raise the price of room and board after the boardinghouses reported
that payments no longer covered expenses. Business was good, so the
corporations might have made up the difference, but they chose not to.
The girls staged numerous short walkouts over several months, ultimately winning the participation of nearly 2,000 of the 6,800 work-

ers in the mills. It appears that the girls triumphed, although it is not clear whether the corporations increased their contributions or simply turned the problem back to the boardinghouses.

Whatever elation followed must have burst in the financial panic of 1837, which set off the longest, deepest depression Americans had known. For the next five years, the factory girls of Lowell, like laborers throughout the country, were more concerned about keeping their jobs than improving their lot.

Had Dickens and Trollope applied their customary perspicuity to the Lowell presented to them in the 1840s and 1850s, they would have discovered a multitude of discontents inside the neatly coiffed heads of the factory girls. Boardinghouses were crowded, and the workday had bulked from eleven to nearly twelve and a half hours. Machinery was retooled to run faster, requiring the operatives to step up their pace. Employers also made the girls "stretch out" to tend more machines. "Frequently a firm would actually slow down machinery and simultaneously increase the number of machines assigned to each worker," Thomas Dublin explains in *Women at Work,* a history of Lowell's beginnings. "Then, after an initial breaking-in period, the speed of the machinery would be increased steadily." As the machines whirred faster, the owners lowered wages "to ensure that earnings did not increase at the same rate as output. Only in this way could the firm cut unit labor costs and in the face of declining cloth prices maintain profit margins."

Shareholders got their dividends, consumers got affordable fabrics, and managers fared very well. Overseers received bonuses for exceeding production goals, an achievement made possible only by extracting more work from the operatives. As a sardonic joke of the time had it, an operative was a person who worked in a factory and earned three times as much as she was paid. Nathan Appleton considered it "the best economy" to fill the office of mill agent "with men of the highest character and talent" and "pay such salaries as will command the entire services of such men," but the beauty of his logic escaped those on the factory floor. In 1842, after employers blamed another wage cut on the seemingly interminable depression, a factory girl wondered, "Why do they not cut down the fat salaries of their Agents, who roll about this city in their carriages, living at ease in fine houses, with servants of both sexes to do their bidding?"

> But this is never done. The poor *laborers* must bear all the *burthens.* If there are any losses to be sustained, or any diminution of profits likely to affect the *dividends,* the difference must always be made up by the hard working female operatives, who are occasionally very *pathetically* told that the factories are only kept running at all from motives of *pure charity towards them.* Let us see a little more equality—a little more sincerity in this matter, and then perhaps we may have a little more charity.

Shareholders did feel the squeeze in 1842, when dividends plunged to a record low of 3.5 percent. But they rebounded to 7 percent in 1843, soared to 15 percent in 1844, and topped 17 percent in 1845. None of this good fortune was shared with the factory girls, whose weekly wages were 12.5 percent lower in 1845 than in 1844. By 1850, wages at the Hamilton Company were 9 percent lower than in 1836, a trend that probably prevailed in Lowell since the corporations typically acted together so that none would have an advantage over another.

The slaves who planted, tended, picked, ginned, baled, and loaded the cotton bound for the Lowell mills troubled few consciences in the textile industry, and as working conditions deteriorated in the mills, many factory girls came to believe that they too were enslaved. Laborers could either "work as the capitalist dictates, or . . . starve!" one operative protested. "And if they do work, the capitalists derive *nine elevenths* of the products of their labor. How much better, then, we ask, is the condition of some of our *white* northern laborers, than some of the *black* southern slaves?"

Sarah Bagley, who had once praised the mills and the benevolence of their managers in the *Lowell Offering,* could no longer contain her anger with those who said it was false to equate factory girls with slaves because the girls had the freedom to leave. "Let us look a little at this

remarkable form of freedom," she wrote in the *Voice of Industry,* one of
the era's most influential labor publications.

A slave too goes voluntarily to his task, but his will is in some manner
quickened by the whip of the overseer. The whip which brings us to
Lowell is NECESSITY. We must have money; a father's debts are to be
paid, an aged mother to be supported, a brother's ambition to be aided,
and so the factories are supplied. Is this to act from free will? When a
man is starving he is compelled to pay his neighbor, who happens to
have bread, the most exorbitant price for it, and the neighbor may
appease his conscience, if conscience he chance to have, by the reflection that it is altogether a voluntary bargain. Is any one such a fool to
suppose that out of six thousand factory girls of Lowell, sixty would be
there if they could help it?

The *Voice of Industry* condemned Negro slavery but held that the
wage slavery of the North was equally wrong. Other workers feared
that American laborers would soon be no better off than the oppressed
masses of Europe. Out of patience after reading of yet another book
by "[t]hose who write so effusively about the 'Beauties of Factory
Life'" in Lowell, an operative who signed herself "Juliana" noted that
it was easier to "smooth over and plaster up a deep festering rotten system . . . than it is to probe to the very bottom of this death-spreading
monster."

The difference between having and having not stirred new resentments and, in the mind of one Lowell factory girl, "serious reflection
on the injustice of society." In an encounter with mill owners' daughters, she learned that they "had an abundance of leisure, could attend
school when and where they pleased, were fashionably dressed, were
not obliged to work any except when they pleased." Try as she might,
she said she could "never see the justice of one set of girls working all
the time in order that another set should live in ease and idleness."

In the eyes of the factory girls, the mill owners were hypocrites,
boasting to the world of the high moral tone they had created in
Lowell but simultaneously relegating the girls to a lower class. Mill

managers were equally culpable, blithely declaring labor the equal of capital but rarely bothering to tip their hats to factory girls, much less receive them in their parlors. The suggestion that factory girls were not as good as the next person was an affront to the egalitarianism they had learned in the quilting bees, barn raisings, and town meetings of their New England villages.

"The rich are growing richer and the poor, poorer, and Mammon is usurping sovereignty in all places," the *Voice of Industry* lamented. Now and then laborers staged a short strike or a rally, but protest was risky. Troublemakers were fired, their names added to blacklists shared with textile factories throughout New England. Fearing for their jobs, workers hid behind pen names and vented their grievances in the *Voice of Industry* and other workers' papers that flourished in New England in the 1840s.

On the rare occasions when a mainstream newspaper or magazine portrayed the hardships in Lowell, champions of the status quo rushed their rebuttals into print. In *Lowell, as It Was, and as It Is,* the Reverend Henry A. Miles, a local clergyman, argued that although the hours were long, the work was light. He doubted the girls' accounts of the exhaustion caused by the seventy-two-hour workweek and blamed what illnesses there were on the girls themselves. Some came to Lowell without the requisite strength for the job, according to Miles, while others lived in the grip of "that devotion to fashion which is characteristic of the sex" and failed to dress properly in bad weather. "Moreover, there is something in the monotony of a mill-life which seems to beget a morbid hankering for little artificial stimulants of the appetite, and the tone of the stomach is frequently deranged by a foolish and expensive patronage of the confectioner."

The *Lowell Offering,* underwritten by the corporations, demurely campaigned for longer mealtimes, but Harriet Farley, the *Offering*'s editor, was as skeptical as the Reverend Miles of the girls' complaints of overwork. Her evidence: the high caliber of the poems and essays they contributed to the *Offering,* writing that had won plaudits from Dickens himself. "The din and clatter of the Mill had not confused the brains of the workers, and no cotton fuzz had obscured the brightness of their ideas," Farley said. Reminding the girls that they owed their employers an honest day's work, she suggested that they nourish their strength by limiting their nights out. No doubt influenced by Nathan Appleton's pronouncements on the subject, Farley held that capital and labor were bound by common interests and would prosper by working together. Ill positioned to confront the Lowell corporations, she preferred to believe that labor stood to gain more by cooperation than conflict.

Long hours aside, mill owners were not indifferent to the health and safety of their employees. Where possible, moving mechanical parts were encased. When the agent of the Lawrence Manufacturing Company discovered that a chemical used in fitting up the mills irritated the stomachs of his workmen, he quickly sought a substitute. A worker with a mild case of smallpox was sent home as a precaution against an epidemic, and inoculations were offered to the rest of the company's employees.

But there is no doubt that the mills were hard on the lungs. Cotton lint filled the air, humidity was deliberately high to keep threads from breaking, and there were fumes from sizing, dyes, and the hundreds of whale-oil lamps needed to counter the darkness of winter. The benefits of masks were understood, but they were seldom worn because the girls did not consider them fashionable.

The true state of the girls' health remains unknown. Elisha Bartlett, M.D., Lowell's first mayor, reported that when he asked 2,610 factory girls to tell him whether their health had improved, stayed the same, or deteriorated during their time in Lowell, 6 percent reported gains, 59 percent said they noticed no difference, and 34 percent claimed they felt less well. Bartlett saw nothing worrisome in the results and does not appear to have inquired into the nature or seriousness of the maladies of the 34 percent.

At the end of 1844, the discontent swirling through the air with the fumes and cotton dust coalesced into the first union of American working women, the Lowell Female Labor Reform Association.

Evidently anticipating a long struggle, the twelve charter members, all
factory girls, chose as their motto "Try again." From their slender ranks
they elected ten officers, with Sarah Bagley as president and chief organizer. Miss Bagley, thirty-nine, quickly resigned from her job at the
Hamilton Company's mills, where she had worked for eight years, to
devote herself to labor's campaign for a ten-hour workday.

The seeds of the ten-hour movement had been germinating since
1840, when President Martin Van Buren signed an executive order setting ten hours as the legal workday for federal employees and contractors. Lowell operatives sent their first ten-hour petition to the
Massachusetts Legislature in 1842, and when there was no response
from the gold-domed statehouse on Beacon Hill, they tried again in
1843 and 1844. The legislature remained silent. In 1845, the Lowell
Female Labor Reform Association tried once more.

> We the undersigned peaceable, industrious and hardworking men and
> women of Lowell, in view of our condition—the evils already come
> upon us, by toiling from 13 to 14 hours per day, confined in unhealthy
> apartments, exposed to the poisonous contagion of air, vegetable, ani-
> mal and mineral properties, debarred from proper Physical Exercise,
> Mental discipline, and Mastication cruelly limited, and thereby hasten-
> ing us on through pain, disease, and privation, down to a premature
> grave, pray the legislature to institute a ten-hour working day in all of
> the factories of the state.

The new petition was signed by Sarah Bagley, two male colleagues
in labor reform, and two thousand factory workers, most of them
women, from Lowell, Fall River, and Andover.

William Schouler, chairman of the Committee on Manufactures of
the Massachusetts House of Representatives, agreed to hold hearings
on the ten-hour day if representatives of the Lowell Female Reform
Association would come to Boston to testify. If Schouler hoped that
feminine decorum or the ardors of the journey would keep them away,
he was mistaken. Sarah Bagley and others appeared on the appointed
day, February 13.

Schouler was up to the challenge. Owner of the *Lowell Courier,* he knew the city well and was a steadfast friend of the corporations. He made a show of investigating working conditions by taking his committee on a tour of two of Lowell's largest mills, where the visitors found nothing untoward. "Grass plots have been laid out, trees have been planted and fine varieties of flowers in their season are cultivated within the factory grounds," Schouler wrote in the official report. "In short, everything in and about the mills and boarding-houses appeared to have for its end, health and comfort."

Summarizing the testimony of several witnesses, Schouler missed few opportunities to cast doubt on their credibility. Of Olive Clark, who had worked at the Lawrence Corporation for five years, he noted straightforwardly that she considered the air impure "on account of the small particles of cotton which fly about" and that she believed "the long hours had an effect on her health." But when quizzed by the committee, she had admitted that her health "never was good," that her employers treated her kindly, that the work was "not laborious," and that she had "never spoken with the agent or overseer about working only ten hours." Schouler seemed to imply that before the hearings, Miss Clark had not been moved to complain, a suggestion that ignored the threats of dismissal and blacklisting faced by workers who did express grievances.

Based on the hearing and the trip to Lowell, the committee unanimously concluded that legislation creating a ten-hour workday was unnecessary, unwise, and unjust. Why, Schouler wondered, should the state hold corporations to such a rule but leave individuals and partnerships unregulated? He also cited the dearth of persuasive evidence that long hours alone damaged "the public morals, the physical condition, or the social well-being of society" or that the factory system was "more injurious to health than other kinds of indoor labor."

Furthermore, said Schouler, a ten-hour law in Massachusetts would "close the gate of every mill in the State" because manufacturers elsewhere would be free to keep longer hours. By trimming the workweek from seventy-two hours to sixty, a ten-hour day inevitably would affect wages, and wages, Schouler maintained, were "a matter which experience has taught us can be much better regulated by the parties themselves than by the Legislature. Labor in Massachusetts is a very different commodity from what it is in foreign countries. Here labor is on an equality with capital, and indeed controls it, and so it ever will be while free education and free constitutions exist. . . . Labor is intelligent enough to make its own bargains, and look out for its own interests without any interference from us."

Schouler conceded that it would be better if hours were shorter, mealtimes longer, and the air cleaner, but, he added, "we say the remedy is not with us. We look for it in the progressive improvement in art and science, in a higher appreciation of man's destiny, in a less love for money, and a more ardent love for social happiness and intellectual superiority." Labor had made possible the "magnificent results" of the factory system in Massachusetts, "and labor will continue to improve upon it."

Furious, Sarah Bagley described Schouler's account of the testimony as "so changed in its connection or removed from its original position that it was made to say what we never said, or thought of saying. . . . The Chairman of the Committee manifested a great desire to bring out everything that would look bright and beautiful upon the side of manufactories. Now to this I do not object—but I do object to his wish to conceal the deformities of which we had a right to complain." She and others accused him of "withholding from the legislature all the most important facts in the defence made by our delegates."

Miss Bagley vowed that she and her allies would be back and caustically proposed that they ask the legislature "to extend to the operatives the same protection they have given to animals, and our condition will be greatly improved." Denouncing Schouler as "a corporation machine, or tool," the Female Labor Reform Association vowed to persuade their male allies, who voted, to cast their ballots for his opponent.

To the astonishment of all, Schouler lost. But the legislature was no more responsive without him, and a year later he regained his seat.

Sarah Bagley, America's first woman labor leader, moved on, becoming the nation's first woman telegrapher. The corporations, thanks largely to a long flood of Irish immigrants willing to work on any terms, fended off the ten-hour day for several more decades.

THE clash of capital and labor at Lowell was a clash of points of view. From Beacon Hill, which measured its benevolence against the hell of Manchester, the beauties of factory life were beyond dispute. But to weary, stupefied factory girls, Lowell was nearer purgatory than paradise. The beauties of factory life, it seemed, were in the eye of the beholder.

The capitalists saw themselves not as utopians but as pragmatists with high moral standards. Rather than try to perfect society or humankind, they meant to refine their corporations and use a share of the profits to promote their version of the public good. To the old Puritan notion that a rich man was only the steward of his wealth, the Lowell entrepreneurs added the fetching new idea that the management of a corporation was merely the steward of its shareholders' wealth. Thus positioned, corporate directors in a tussle with labor could contend that they were unable to raise wages or shorten the workday because the money in question belonged to all who owned the company's stock. The argument sounds selfless, but only until one remembers that the directors of the Lowell corporations were also the largest shareholders.

Believing that they had more than fulfilled their obligations to their workers, the Boston capitalists considered their profits just, considered the profits theirs, and would have considered it impudent had anyone suggested that their generous contributions to charity might more properly belong to labor.

The animosity of labor leaders who spoke of "drivelling cotton lords" must have stung the humane, public-spirited gentlemen who owned the mills, but one of the most perceptive European visitors, a young aristocrat named Alexis de Tocqueville, had warned of such conflict. Without setting eyes on the factory girls or even paying much heed to manufacturing elsewhere in the United States during his 1831–32 travels, he nevertheless had divined that industry could injure democracy by separating owner and worker. The worker was the dependent of an employer he knew only in the factory. They contracted to exchange labor for wages but felt no obligation to one another. "The aristocracy created by business rarely settles in the midst of the manufacturing population which it directs; the object is not to govern that population, but to use it," Tocqueville wrote in *Democracy in America*. "I am of the opinion, on the whole, that the manufacturing aristocracy which is growing up under our eyes is one of the harshest that ever existed in the world; but at the same time it is one of the most confined and least dangerous. Nevertheless, the friends of democracy should keep their eyes anxiously fixed in this direction."

If America's first manufacturers were the least dangerous of aristocrats, it was largely through their own inadvertent doing. By emphasizing the high-mindedness of their social designs in Lowell, they encouraged the rest of the world, their employees included, to judge them by ideals and to press for what might be rather than content themselves with what was.

5

IN THE DIRECTION OF DREAMS

O N THE FOURTH of July in 1845, Sarah Bagley and two
thousand friends of labor from Lowell and other New
England mill towns threw themselves a grand picnic in
Woburn, Massachusetts. A brass band greeted their trains and serenaded
their procession to a grove said to have been "tastefully arranged" for
the occasion. Whether the festoons ran to red, white, and blue or taste-
fulness of another ilk went unreported as the *Voice of Industry*'s correspondent galloped into an account of the day's main attraction, Miss
Bagley's address. Her tone was "refined and delicate," the *Voice* said, and
the crowd was so still that the rustling of leaves could be heard "softly
playing in the wind between the intervals of speech."

However genteel her manner, Sarah Bagley was in a pugnacious
mood. She spoke of censorship by the *Lowell Offering,* which had
refused to print her articles on workers' rights, the tyranny of factory
labor, and the corporations' new drive to lengthen the workday. Ten
years in the mills had made Sarah Bagley an expert on working conditions, and in her judgment, the *Offering* was giving "a false representation to the truth," allowing the corporations to put "a gloss on their
inhumanity." When she announced that the factory girls of Lowell
intended to fight the longer hours, the grove rang with "loud and
unanimous huzzas."

Miss Bagley took her seat amid the cheers, and Albert Brisbane, a
distinguished visitor from New York, rose to speak. Brisbane had

grown famous by introducing Americans to the ideas of Charles
Fourier, a French utopian who had divined the secret of world bliss: If
humankind regrouped into small farming communities, cooperation
would supplant competition, and poverty would vanish. Each "phalanx," as Fourier called his little paradises, was to be populated by some
1,700 members who pooled their capital, shared profits and living
quarters, and divided the toil in accord with their talents and inclina-
tions. Many hands making light work, phalanx life would abound in
time for leisure, art, and intellect.

Brisbane's proselytizing, carried on in newspapers and a book
brashly entitled *The Social Destiny of Man,* inspired Americans to found
some three dozen Fourierist communities in the early 1840s. But on
this day in Woburn, the reporter for the *Voice* did not find a word of
Brisbane's worth quoting. Labor's lack of interest may have reflected its
lack of capital. Or perhaps the rapid corruption of Lowell's early ideals
had soured the very notion of a planned community. Or perhaps this
audience rightly sensed that the social destiny of the masses would be
worked out in factories, not in phalanxes.

A DOZEN miles to the west of the great picnic, near Concord,
another skeptic of communal living was passing his first full day in a
utopia of one. Henry David Thoreau, settling into his new cabin at
Walden Pond, was not quite twenty-eight but already had set his mind
against experimental communities. "I had rather keep bachelor's hall in
hell than go to board in heaven," he told his journal in 1841 after
declining an invitation to join the celebrated phalanx down the road,
Brook Farm. He thought the arrangement would spoil his virtue
because a boarder had no true home.

Instead, Thoreau had gone to the woods, explaining that he "wished
to live deliberately, to front only the essential facts of life, and see if I
could not learn what it had to teach, and not, when I came to die, discover that I had not lived." He wanted to "live deep and suck out all
the marrow of life" and "cut a broad swath and shave close, to drive life
into a corner, and reduce it to its lowest terms, and, if it proved to be

mean, why then to get the whole and genuine meanness of it, and publish its meanness to the world; or if it were sublime, to know it by experience, and be able to give a true account of it."

The path to Walden had been stony. As a boy in Concord, Thoreau was nicknamed "Judge" for his solemnity, which included a decidedly unboylike aversion to parades. At Harvard, he preferred the solitary pursuits of reading and walking to the company of fellow students. Without apology he declared, "I love to be alone. I never found the companion that was so companionable as solitude." Thoreau looked like the outsider he felt himself to be. He peered at Concord through eyes that were otherworldly—crystalline, with only a tinge of gray. (Or was it blue? Acquaintances disagreed.) Five feet seven and lean, he was indifferently barbered, skittish, awkward in the parlor. To avoid small talk, he often marched into a house, delivered his message, and marched out.

"H is military"—ill at ease "except in opposition," said Ralph Waldo Emerson, Concord's other famous man of letters. When an acquaintance admitted that she loved Thoreau but did not like him, Emerson understood. He himself found it easier to imagine clapping an arm around an elm than around Thoreau. Thoreau too would have understood. He found resistance "delicious" and once confessed an affinity for war because "it so apes the gait and bearing of the soul."

Born in 1817, Thoreau graduated from Harvard in 1837, a year memorable for a financial panic that dropped the country into one of its deepest depressions. Emerson sketched the troubles in his journal: "Cold April; hard times; men breaking who ought not to break; banks bullied into the bolstering of desperate speculators; all the newspapers a chorus of owls." Emerson heard "loud cracks in the social edifice" and was jangled by a rumor that sixty thousand laborers soon would be out of work. A "formidable mob," he thought—powerful enough "to break open banks and rob the rich and brave the domestic government." In this bleak season, Thoreau was lucky to find a job as a schoolteacher in Concord but lasted only a few weeks. Unwilling to continue following orders to flog students, he resigned.

A year later, he and his brother John took over another school, Concord Academy, delighting their charges with natural history lessons in the woods, field trips to newspapers, mathematics classes taught with the aid of surveyor's instruments, and freedom from the threat of corporal punishment. The school closed in 1841, when John fell ill. On New Year's Day of 1842, he nicked a finger while stropping a razor, developed tetanus, and soon died, a tragedy echoed in Henry's thoughts about shaving close and understanding life before it was taken away.

Unsure where to turn, Thoreau accepted an invitation to join Emerson and his family in their big white clapboard house on Lexington Road. He agreed to serve as handyman and gardener in exchange for room and board, and it was understood that his household duties would be light, leaving many hours for rambling the countryside, reading his way through the books in Emerson's study, and writing.

How the two men met is unclear, but an introduction would have been almost inevitable in their sociable village of two thousand. From the beginning of their friendship, Emerson admired Thoreau's devotion to simplicity. "Everything that boy says makes merry with society though nothing could be graver than his meaning," Emerson told his journal after passing a winter afternoon with his young friend. Fourteen years older than Thoreau and many degrees cooler in temperament, Emerson saw the absurdity of pitting the simple life against a "doubledealing quacking" age. The humor escaped Thoreau, who considered it a point of honor to be a misfit in their "nervous, bustling, trivial" time.

Both Emerson and Thoreau would wrestle with the double dealers and bustlers, delivering the first great American critique of the most powerful new force of their day, the marketplace. As both men saw, the rise of large-scale manufacturing and the vast sales territories being opened by new railroads, canals, and riverboats meant that business no longer operated on the fringes of the nation's life. The market touched everything. Money—how it was pursued and how it was used—served as "a delicate meter of civil, social, and moral changes," Emerson wrote in an essay on wealth. Their objection to its ascendancy was not rooted in the old Puritan conviction that the love of money bred a selfishness that separated the individual from God and community. Emerson and Thoreau feared that a preoccupation with wealth separated a man from his innermost self by requiring him to sacrifice his individuality on the altar of public opinion. "Public and private avarice make the air we breathe thick and fat," Emerson wrote toward the end of the 1830s. "There is no work for any but the decorous and complaisant."

EMERSON'S early years, like Thoreau's, were filled with hesitations and false starts. Son of a Unitarian minister, he had disappointed his parents first by his inability to read until he was three and then by a middling performance at Harvard. Fourteen when he entered, in 1817, he skimped on homework to leave more time for his own reading and for writing in his journal. During his four years in Cambridge, the boy Ralph Emerson sprouted into a five-foot-eleven man who wished to be known as Waldo. Gangly and narrow in the shoulders, he had a head of thick chestnut hair, a nobly Roman nose, bright blue eyes, and a round, deep, beckoning cello of a voice.

After a few years of teaching school, Emerson returned to Harvard to study divinity, was ordained, and served briefly as pastor of one of Boston's largest Unitarian congregations. He left the clergy in 1832 because of a spiritual crisis undoubtedly magnified by the death of his wife, Ellen. She had died the year before, at nineteen, a victim of tuberculosis. Reconstituted by a long tour of Europe, where he encountered ideas that gave him the makings of a new faith, Emerson embarked on a career as a writer and lecturer. Financially well situated because of his inheritance from Ellen, Emerson possessed the enviable freedom to follow his thoughts. He could marry again without worries about breadwinning, and in 1835, Lydia Jackson of Plymouth, Massachusetts, accepted his proposal. In September, when they married, she changed her first name as well as her last, becoming Lidian Emerson to indulge a husband who disliked the name Lydia.

Emerson took his bride to Concord, where they settled into the house on Lexington Road. He chose a room at the front of the house for his study and wrote at a round table with a rotating top. He piled it high with books and spun his way from Albert Brisbane's *Social Destiny of Man* and Richard Henry Dana's *Two Years before the Mast* to the philosophies, histories, and poems that launched his own explorations of nature, beauty, fate, Yankee capitalism, English society, slavery, self-reliance, prudence, Napoleon, Swedenborg, and whatever else he pleased. "Life is an ecstasy," he would come to believe, and he set about specializing in the whole of it.

The white-hot flame at the heart of his work, carried home from Europe, was transcendentalism. As he explained to curious Bostonians who gathered to hear him at the Masonic temple in 1842, transcendentalism took its name from an idea of the philosopher Immanuel Kant, who believed that his fellow philosopher John Locke had erred in saying that human beings know what they know entirely through information gathered by the senses. Kant insisted that humans also know by intuition, a form of knowledge transcending experience. Emerson described his transcendentalism as faith extrapolated to excess, granting intuition authority over experience. The transcendentalist, he said, "believes in miracle, in the perpetual openness of the human mind to new influx of light and power; he believes in inspiration, and in ecstasy."

He also believed in himself. "His thought,—that is the Universe," Emerson said. The world began and ended in his own mind: "I—this thought which is called I,—is the mould into which the world is poured like melted wax." The life of a proper transcendentalist overlapped little with the life of a proper Bostonian. True transcendentalists, Emerson said, "are not good citizens, not good members of society. . . . They do not even like to vote." Nor did they like most of the world's work, which struck them as "life without love, and an activity without an aim." Their disdain for the usual employments stoked a suspicion that transcendentalism was a fancy name for loafing, but Emerson felt otherwise. He and his fellow transcendentalists were "miserable with inaction" and longed for the universe to call them to some high purpose. But until the summons, he said, "[i]f I cannot work, at least I need not lie."

Disinclined to seek converts, the transcendentalists simply preached, sharing their beliefs in the unity of all creation, the innate goodness of their fellow humans, and God as a force within. Ultimately, nothing was sacred but "the integrity of your own mind," Emerson said. He sensed that his ideas would not appeal to everyone but hoped society would make room for a few transcendentalists even if they did no more than "eat clouds, and drink wind" because they stood for "thoughts and principles not marketable or perishable." Long after the mechanical and commercial wonders of their time had been superseded by even grander feats, Emerson predicted, the ideas of the transcendentalists "shall abide in beauty and strength."

Transcendentalism would evolve, but in its earliest phase, it asserted the supremacy of the self and sought to rescue the individual from society. As Emerson put it, society was "a joint-stock company, in which the members agree, for the better securing of his bread to each shareholder, to surrender the liberty and culture of the eater." In such a world, conformity was the highest virtue, individuality a menace. Transcendentalism would replace the joint-stock company with an infinity of sole proprietorships. The individual would answer not to community or convention but to conscience. It was a radical proposition, effectively shredding the social contract by detaching the individual from the world around him.

Emerson supposed that if every individual seriously undertook the business of improving the self, improvement of society would follow. He seemed not to recognize it, but it was much the same argument Adam Smith had made in economics: Allow a businessman to pursue his own interests in a free market, and he would become society's servant. To win out over his competitors, he would have to offer more than they did—lower prices, perhaps, or higher quality—and the public would be the gainer. Like Smith's laissez-faire economics, Emerson's laissez-faire spirituality flowed from the assumption that practitioners would be actuated by noble motives. It would be years before Emerson would consider what might happen when one noble conscience abraded another or when ignobility set up a stall in the marketplace.

Few answered his call to retreat to the cloisters of the glorious "I." Some of the resistance was undoubtedly pragmatic: who could survive on clouds and wind? A larger difficulty lay in the dissonance between this phase of transcendentalism and its times. Emerson might feel numbed by the blandness that flowed from mass production and mass marketing, but the new and thriving middle class of Americans delighted in it. Consumer goods of nearly every description were more accessible and less expensive than ever before.

Still, the *Dial,* the transcendentalist magazine founded in 1842, built its subscriber list up to a respectable three hundred. And if the circle of acolytes clustered around Emerson was small, it was choice, including (among others) Bronson Alcott, indefatigable social experimenter and father of Louisa May; Orestes Brownson, one of the few transcendentalists to engage himself seriously with the problems of New England's laboring classes; the poet W. E. Channing; Margaret Fuller, author and women's rights advocate; Elizabeth Peabody, who introduced kindergarten to the United States; Theodore Parker and W. H. Channing, preachers and social activists; George Ripley, founder of Brook Farm; and Henry Thoreau.

LIFE with the Emersons offered Thoreau an abundance of privileges, including opportunities to write for the *Dial,* but he sensed that as long as he stayed under Emerson's roof, his own life would be in abeyance. Only a few weeks after moving in, he asked the owner of Flint's Pond, on the outskirts of Concord, for permission to build a cabin there. He was turned down, a slight he would remember when he wrote *Walden.* Eighteen months into his stay at Emerson's, Thoreau wondered in his journal, "What am I at present? A diseased bundle of nerves standing between time and eternity like a withered leaf that still hangs shivering on its stem. A more miserable object one could not well imagine."

In April 1843, he left for New York City, which he sipped and promptly spat out. "It is a thousand times meaner than I could have imagined," he reported to Emerson. Thoreau had gone to the city as a tutor and hoped to establish himself as a journalist. After six months of homesickness and disappointment, he returned to his parents' house in Concord.

Still without a profession in the spring of 1845, he was in a receptive frame of mine when a friend pressed him to build a hut at Walden Pond "and there begin the grand process of devouring yourself alive. I see no alternative, no other hope for you." Thoreau went to see Emerson, who had recently purchased fourteen acres at Walden, and proposed to hack away the brush and plant a pine forest if Emerson would let him camp on the shore. Emerson assented at once, less for the trees than the fruit Thoreau himself might bear. The young man's poems and essays showed great promise, Emerson thought, and he hoped that Thoreau's talent would flourish in the woods.

Having borrowed some land, Thoreau next borrowed an ax. The borrowing was ticklish for a devotee of independence, and when he wrote about it in *Walden,* he wanted it understood that he had squared his account by sending the ax home sharp—"sharper than I received it." He started his labors in March, felling pines and (with more borrowed tools) hewing timbers, studs, rafters, and floorboards. Returning to his parents' house in the late afternoon, he followed the gleaming tracks of the new Fitchburg Railroad and marked the progress of spring by noting the arrival of one species of songbird after another. He knew these woods so intimately that when a friend inquired about a particular wild hibiscus, Thoreau named the day and place it would bloom.

In May he asked several acquaintances to help him put up the frame of his little house. He had not needed their assistance, he assured the readers of *Walden,* but sought it because house raisings struck him as fine occasions for neighborliness. On his own he covered the frame with boards pried from a shanty sold to him for $4.25 by an Irishman who had worked on the railroad. With nails, shingles, plaster, and whitewash, the bill for his new home totaled $28.

Basic as a birdhouse, Thoreau's cabin measured ten by fifteen feet.

There was a door at one end, a fireplace at the other, a window in each
of the long walls, and an attic above the eight-foot ceiling. He furnished his cabin with cot, desk, enameled lamp, three chairs, and the
barest assortment of kitchen utensils. When an acquaintance offered
him a doormat, he turned her down, saying that he had neither the
room for it nor the time to shake it. Best to "avoid the beginnings of
evil," he thought. Where there were doormats, gewgaws would follow.
His only concession to vanity was a tiny round mirror, most likely a
necessity for shaving. Outside he built a woodshed, dug a cellar, and
put up a privy. His bathtub was Walden Pond, a universe unto itself.
Afloat in still water, he said, "I too am a planet, and have my orbit, in
space, and am no longer a satellite of the earth."

SETTLED in at Walden, Thoreau went to work on his first book, *A
Week on the Concord and Merrimack Rivers,* an account of an 1839 outing with his late brother. Their peregrinations had taken them to
Lowell, where Henry was grieved to learn that canals and dams built
to harness waterpower for the mills had disrupted the annual migra-
tions of salmon and shad to spawning grounds upstream. "Poor shad!
where is thy redress?" he wondered. "When Nature gave thee instinct,
gave she thee the heart to bear thy fate?"

Of the hearts and fates in Lowell's factory workers, Thoreau had
nothing to say in this book, but he and Emerson regularly bewailed the
preeminence of money and its ministers. The merchant, the capitalist,
and the manufacturer ruled the nation as never before. "This class is the
controlling one in politics," Emerson and Thoreau's fellow transcendentalist Theodore Parker lamented in 1845. "It mainly enacts the laws
of this state and the nation; makes them serve its turn. It bought con-
gressmen and could "manufacture governors, senators, judges to suit its
purposes, as easily as it can manufacture cotton cloth."

As the literary critic Quentin Anderson has noted, the largest reality of American life in the age of Emerson and Thoreau was not the
republic, a realm that was both public and collective, but the market,
an arena for the individual pursuit of private gain. It was, Emerson

wrote, a time when "Things are in the saddle, and ride mankind." Emerson balked at the vast marketplace America had become because he felt it stifled the individual and the imagination. Business spoke with one dull voice, Mrs. Business seconded his platitudes, and government promoted "whatever will earn and preserve property." Even the so-called opposition newspapers were on the same side, attacking the rich but dreaming of a day when the poor too would be rich.

To Thoreau's exasperation, the man who rambled the forests because he loved them was dismissed as an idler, while the one who spent his day "shearing off those woods and making the earth bald before her time" won praise for his pluck. "As if a town had no interest in its forests but to cut them down!" In a marketplace, there was no value but market value.

"In America, we drag a pine-log to a mill, turn a crank, and it comes out the other end chairs and tables," Emerson remarked in his journal. The manufacturer drained New Hampshire lakes into Massachusetts rivers to increase his waterpower, and the merchant waxed opulent by the simple act of "bringing a thing from where it abounds, to where it is costly." It seemed to Emerson that Yankees and dollars had such "inextricable association that the words ought to rhyme." He wrote a rhyme of his own, "New England Capitalist," to describe this new breed taking over the world—a man of "conquering will" with dominion over the millions dependent upon his jobs and his custom, a tendency to devour both citizen and state, and an insatiable appetite for invention. Emerson exited with a challenge: "Now let him make a harp!"

A brave poem. Emerson put it in a drawer.

Thoreau inveighed against Mammon more sternly than any Puritan divine. While Emerson saw the California Gold Rush as no worse than other speculating, Thoreau considered it an abomination. He could not believe that God had intended man to grow rich by digging where he had not planted. Finding talk of business profane, Thoreau wished that it would be forbidden in front of children. He seethed at the sight of a raked-over cranberry bog left in a snarl by a greedy farmer racing his crop to Boston and New York, where, Thoreau mourned, the berries would be *"jammed,* to satisfy the tastes of lovers of Nature there." What torture for a man who gathered blackberries by starlight and felt more tenderness for the earth than for any of its human inhabitants.

In the 1840s, musing on the technological triumphs of the age, Emerson was an optimist, Thoreau a skeptic. Emerson hoped the railroads, the telegraph, and the factory would liberate humankind from drudgery and free up vast quantities of time for the imaginative life. Railroad iron was "a magician's rod," Emerson told a Boston audience in 1844. It "annihilated" distance, and the locomotives shuttling across the land wove "the thousand various threads of national descent and employment" into a single web, binding all Americans fast to America.

Alone in his study, Emerson could entertain doubts about the capitalist, but as he made the rounds of lyceums in the 1840s, he chose to share his dreams rather than his fears. He professed admiration for the merchant and spread Beacon Hill's shibboleth that trade fostered peace because war was bad for commerce. The complaint that trade substituted one aristocracy for another was unwarranted, he thought. The title of merchant was not hereditary, and upstarts with novel ideas regularly displaced merchants grown staid and complacent.

As railroad cars roared past Walden Pond at twenty miles an hour, Thoreau inhaled cargoes of coconuts, palm leaves, and timber and felt like "a citizen of the world," he said. But he grew to despise the shriek of the train whistle and the nightly panting of the locomotive. "It interrupts my dreams," he complained. "There is no sabbath." As far as Thoreau could judge, the railroad and the telegraph were no more than the "pretty toys" of a people bent on living fast but to no worthy purpose. What was the point of devising improved means to an unimproved end? he wanted to know. And why the haste to string telegraph lines from Maine to Texas, when Maine and Texas might have nothing of consequence to say to one another?

Both Emerson and Thoreau worried about the exploitation of those who built the capitalist's railroads, labored in his mills, and served in his household. It seemed unconscionable to Thoreau that so many had spent so much of their lives at the unsatisfying, ill-paid labor of digging in the dirt in order that the few might ride. A day's work on the railroad brought fifty or sixty cents, a train trip of thirty miles cost ninety cents. "We do not ride on the railroad; it rides upon us," he said. "The luxury of one class is counterbalanced by the indigence of another."

American factories soon would rival the English in savagery, Thoreau thought. Ever-narrower divisions of labor condemned humankind to ever-narrower lives. Where would the specialization stop? Thoreau understood that it increased profit and that profit was the capitalist's main goal but insisted that humankind needed loftier ambitions. "In the long run men hit only what they aim at," he warned. "Therefore, though they should fail immediately, they had better aim at something high." Thoreau protested the factory system by spurning textiles from the mills of Massachusetts and dressing in homespun.

The concentration of capital required for factories, railroads, and other large enterprises seemed to Emerson to turn capitalists into cannibals: "great merchants outwit and absorb the substance of small ones and every man feeds on his neighbor's labor if he can." As the strong grew stronger, commanding more power, more money, more jobs, the poor grew increasingly vulnerable to abuse. Fugitives from failing New England farms and a destitute Ireland poured into Massachusetts, creating a surplus of labor that depressed wages for decades. "What can be done for their relief as long as new applicants for the same labor are coming in every day?" Emerson wondered. Pained by the social as well as the economic gulf between rich and poor, Emerson sought to obliterate class distinctions in his own household by inviting his cook to begin dining with the family. He was rebuffed, his egalitarianism being no match for her sense of decorum.

The conscientious rich of Boston sought to palliate the injustices by institutionalizing their generosity, a task they performed with the zest they gave to founding banks and building factories. Between 1830 and

1850, the number of incorporated charitable and educational societies in the city rose from 26 to nearly 160. Ralph Waldo Emerson heartily disapproved. To his journal he confided that "strange and horrible" as it felt to say so, he was repelled by abolitionists, friends of the poor, prison reformers, soup societies—"the whole class of professed philanthropists." To him they were "an altogether odious set of people," boring and sanctimonious beyond bearing. In public he tempered his language but held to a tenet of his early transcendentalist faith: the true reformer reformed himself. Thoreau too resisted the charity boom. Organized philanthropy affronted his Yankee thrift by putting middlemen between donor and recipient, and he thought it wrongheaded to "go about mending the times—when we should be building eternity."

Emerson's bill of grievances against capitalism focused on its effects, Thoreau's on causes. *"Flint's Pond!"* he thundered in *Walden,* damning the man who had denied him permission to live on the shore. "Such is the poverty of our nomenclature. What right had the unclean and stupid farmer, whose farm abutted on this sky water, whose shores he has ruthlessly laid bare, to give his name to it?" By Thoreau's logic, the abolition of private property would prevent the accumulation of wealth, which in turn would eliminate poverty and crime, the evils tangled in wealth's train. Powerless to repeal the laws of property, mandates so ancient they had come to feel like laws of nature, Thoreau issued his own edict: "Simplify, simplify."

His contemporaries had reduced the world to "nothing but work, work, work," he lamented. Who could emancipate them if they would not? "Think, also, of the ladies of the land weaving toilet cushions against the last day, not to betray too green an interest in their fates! As if you could kill time without injuring eternity." The mass of men were leading lives of "quiet desperation," he thought, and blamed their low state on material desire run amok. Boston merchants scavenged the globe for Turkish carpets and Canton china and exotic foods, creating lusts that drove men to spend even more hours at work. Thoreau had a name for the individual who believed himself the owner of anything other than his life: fool.

The equation at the core of Thoreau's economics was straightforward: "the cost of a thing is the amount of what I will call life which is required to be exchanged for it." Forgoing tea, coffee, butter, milk, and fresh meat, he trimmed his grocery bill to a trifle and reckoned the savings in time, not dollars; where there was no bill, there was no need to waste a minute of life working to pay it. "I love a broad margin to my life," he said, and he had it. Pared to essentials (but supplemented by pies from home and frequent dinners with friends), life at Walden allowed him to survive on six weeks' paid work a year.

Thoreau's monkish renunciation of worldly pleasures drove Emerson to complain about the tedium of keeping company with "a man who does not know the difference between ice cream and cabbage and who has no experience of wine or ale." It struck Emerson as futile to try to "argue the wants down: the philosophers have laid the greatness of man in making his wants few; but will a man content himself with a hut and a handful of dried pease? He is born to be rich."

THOREAU ended his stay at Walden Pond on September 6, 1847, two years, two months, and two days after it began. He had lived deep and shaved close. He had also cut a broad literary swath, completing the final drafts of *A Week on the Concord and Merrimack Rivers* and the first draft of *Walden*. He went to the woods in hopes of learning what life had to teach and came away master of an unsurpassable lesson: "if one advances confidently in the direction of his dreams, and endeavors to live the life which he has imagined, he will meet with a success unexpected in common hours."

He left the woods because Emerson, soon to go to Europe for nine months, wanted him to stay with Lidian and the children. To refuse after accepting Emerson's manifold kindnesses would have been churlish. But a letter coinciding with Emerson's departure shows how disorienting Thoreau found the shift from Walden, which he loved, to another temporary perch and a future he could not envision. "I don't know whether mine is a profession, or a trade, or what not," he wrote the secretary of his Harvard class, who had asked for news of him. Thoreau itemized his full portfolio of occupations—schoolmaster, tutor, surveyor, gardener, farmer, housepainter, carpenter, mason, day laborer, pencil maker, glass-paper maker, writer, poet—and then dithered between describing himself as employed and boasting that he was not. "My present employment is to answer such orders as may be expected from so general an advertisement as the above—that is, if I see fit, which is not always the case, for I have found out a way to live without what is commonly called employment or industry attractive or otherwise." Dreading the thought that his classmates might consider him "an object of charity," he closed with a defensive flourish. Far from requiring help, he said, he was in a position to assist the needy, with "advice of more worth than money."

The query from Harvard poked a sore spot. The unimpassioned life was not worth living, in Thoreau's view, yet he was an oddjobsman by default, not passion. To live without money, as savages did, was to stand on "the unelastic plank of famine," to farm was to labor in perpetual danger of bankruptcy, to enter business or the professions was to chain oneself to an oar. Much as he admired Emerson's ability to make a living by his pen, Thoreau loathed the picture of his friend trotting from lyceum to lyceum, "repeating himself, shampooing himself." Thoreau stammered in defending his way of life to Harvard, but by the time he completed the seventh and last draft of *Walden* in 1854, he had figured out what he wanted to tell Harvard about theirs. His credo had come to him as he hurried away from a house where he had taken shelter during a summer storm.

[A]s I ran down the hill toward the reddening west, with the rainbow over my shoulder, and some faint tinkling sounds borne to my ear through the cleansed air, from I know not what quarter, my Good Genius seemed to say,—Go fish and hunt far and wide day by day,— farther and wider,—and rest thee by many brooks and hearth-sides without misgiving. Remember thy Creator in the days of thy youth. Rise free from care before the dawn, and seek adventures. Let the noon find thee by other lakes, and the night overtake thee every where at home. There are no larger fields than these, no worthier games than may here be played. Grow wild according to thy nature, like these sedges and brakes, which will never become English hay. Let the thunder rumble; what if it threaten ruin to farmers' crops? that is not its errand to thee. Take shelter under the cloud, while they flee to carts and sheds. Let not to get a living be thy trade, but thy sport. Enjoy the land, but own it not. Through want of enterprise and faith men are where they are, buying and selling, and spending their lives like serfs.

The very attractiveness of Thoreau's sojourn at Walden makes it easy to dismiss him as a romantic, yearning for a mode of life no longer feasible. It is equally easy to chide him for the fiction of his independence at Walden Pond, where he could not have lived without loans of land and tools and frequent invitations to dinner. But to dwell on the gap between the realities of Walden and Thoreau's aspirations for it is to miss his point. The world was speeding away from the direction of dreams, toward the marketplace, where nothing had value unless it could be bought or sold. He chose to stand aside and let the world pass, but not without reproaching the mass of men for throwing away life itself.

WALDEN and transcendentalism contended that the best of all possible lives was a journey deep into self, and both Emerson and Thoreau had begun by exhorting the individual to save himself by seceding from society. Secession was a natural reaction to the suffocations of their doggedly extrospective, grasping age, but it did not resolve the struggle between self and society. It merely substituted one self for another, and no matter how sacred one held the inner life, the individual devoted to the cultivation of his own imagination was no less selfish than the crass comer dedicated to the pursuit of wealth. Early transcendentalism was spiritual greed—devoid of the cannibalism Emerson deplored in the capitalist but ultimately sterile because a self acquires little meaning except in a social web. "Society is good when it does not violate me; but best when it is likest to solitude," Emerson had written in the 1840s. In such a vision, social bonds figured not as lifelines but as fetters. Social participation, seen by the Founding Fathers as vital to the well-being of a democracy, became an irrelevant if not unworthy application of one's energies.

Only when their lives were overtaken by the crisis of slavery did Thoreau and Emerson learn the moral limitations of the cult of self. In the summer of 1846, when he was still at Walden, Thoreau had walked into town one evening to pick up a shoe from the cobbler. Sam Staples, who served Concord as tax collector, constable, and jailer, stopped him in the street and mentioned his delinquency in paying the local poll tax, a levy imposed on males between the ages of twenty and seventy. Staples reminded Thoreau that he was several years behind and told him it was time to settle up. Thinking that Thoreau might not have the money, Staples volunteered to seek a reduction from the town selectman or to put up the money himself.

Thoreau replied that he had withheld payment and would continue to do so to protest the spread of slavery into newly annexed territory and the U.S. government's newly declared war on Mexico. When the constable noted that such a refusal put him in an awkward position, Thoreau encouraged him to resign. Staples warned Thoreau that if he did not pay, he soon would be locked up. "As well now as any time," said Thoreau. The constable marched him to jail.

Thoreau was elated. All Concord would know of his dissent, and perhaps some of his townsmen would follow his example. Whether they did or not, it seemed to him that in an unjust state, prison was the only suitable place for a just man.

In the morning, after allowing his prisoner to breakfast on brown bread and a mug of chocolate, Staples told him he was free to go. Someone, wisely requesting anonymity, had paid his tax. Thoreau was livid. Insisting that he had a right to stay because he himself had not paid, he refused to leave. Staples gave him an ultimatum: Walk out under his own power or be forcibly removed. Thoreau went peacefully and resumed life where he had left off, fetching his shoe from the cobbler. When an acquaintance invited him to lead an expedition just leaving for the local huckleberry barrens, he accepted. Within half an hour, Thoreau said, "the state was nowhere to be seen." He had gone to jail thrilled at the thought of being the talk of Concord, and going off to pick huckleberries was more theater, an ostentatiously silent soliloquy telling the world to go to hell.

Emerson found the performance "mean and skulking, and in bad taste," but the rest of his townsmen were simply curious about it. He explained himself to them on January 26, 1848, in "Civil Disobedience," a lecture setting forth the idea that the law of conscience was higher than civil law. When the two collided, the individual must defy the state and obey conscience. By paying their taxes, he told his fellow citizens, they were supporting the war and the spread of slavery whether they approved of such things or not. The only hope for change lay in resistance.

For the timid who agreed with him in principle but paid their tax because they feared for their families and property, Thoreau had little sympathy. "This is hard. This makes it impossible for a man to live honestly and at the same time comfortably." Their dilemma was one more argument in favor of the simple life. "You must hire or squat somewhere, and raise but a small crop, and eat that soon," he counseled.

Impressed, Thoreau's townsmen asked him to repeat his lecture, which he did a few weeks later. The word did not travel beyond Concord until much later, however, and Thoreau's philosophy of civil disobedience played no role in the campaign against slavery. But by writing about his willingness to go to jail rather than obey an unjust law, Thoreau gave Mahatma Gandhi and Martin Luther King Jr. their most powerful weapon.

EVENTUALLY Emerson came round to Thoreau's point of view. "The last year has forced us all into politics," Emerson admitted in a speech to his townsmen on May 3, 1851, a few weeks after Massachusetts authorities shipped a runaway slave back to Georgia. They were enforcing the new Fugitive Slave Law, drafted by Congress as part of the Compromise of 1850, a complex, Mephistophelean bargain intended to ease frictions between North and South. The requirement to return fugitive slaves was an old one but had been rarely enforced in the North. Under the new law, an affidavit of ownership from a slaveholder was all the commissioners needed to clap Negroes in chains and ship them south. Federal commissioners were empowered to issue warrants, form posses, and draft citizens to catch runaways. Citizens who refused faced fines or imprisonment. Runaways had no right to a jury trial, nor could they testify on their own behalf. Calling the law a "filthy enactment," Emerson vowed not to obey it. "An immoral law makes it a man's duty to break it, at every hazard," he declared.

Emerson exhorted the United States to follow the example of the British, who in 1834 had purchased the freedom of all the slaves in their West Indian colonies by paying the slaveholders £20 million. "I say buy,—never conceding the right of the planter to own, but that we may acknowledge the calamity of his position, and bear a countryman's share in relieving him," Emerson said. The cost of compensating American slaveholders was reckoned at somewhere between $2 billion and $3 billion, an unfathomable sum in an era when the federal government's annual spending ran to $6 million, but Emerson was willing to pay and believed his fellow citizens shared his sentiment. "The mechanics will give, the needle-women will give; the children will have cent-societies," he predicted. "Every man in the land will give a week's work to dig away this accursed mountain of sorrow once and forever."

In the spring of 1854, after a runaway named Anthony Burns was hunted down in Boston and arrested, abolitionists stormed the jail, President Franklin Pierce ordered up the militia, and Burns was carried back to Virginia aboard a federal ship. Indignation was rampant, but as Thoreau learned when he attended the next meeting of abolitionists in Concord, the anger evaporated with appalling speed. His townsmen had come together not to fight the demons on their doorstep but to flap their jaws about pro-slave villainies in far-off Nebraska.

Thoreau poured his fury into "Slavery in Massachusetts," an essay excoriating his friends and neighbors for their cowardice. News of his project spread, and he agreed to read his jeremiad at the Fourth of July celebration in the nearby town of Framingham. The trial of Anthony Burns was "really the trial of Massachusetts," he said. "Every moment that she hesitated to set this man free, every moment that she now hesitates to atone for her crime, she is convicted." Extending the argument he had made in "Civil Disobedience," Thoreau maintained that the law would never make men free: "it is men who have got to make the law free."

Since the capture of Anthony Burns, Thoreau said, "my old and worthiest pursuits have lost I cannot say how much of their attraction, and I feel that my investment in life here is worth many per cent less." The Fugitive Slave Law had even sullied his walks in the woods. "We walk to lakes to see our serenity reflected in them. . . . Who can be serene in a country where both the rulers and the ruled are without principle?"

Still, the fragrance of the summer's first water lily emboldened him to hope for a time when man would rise to the level of nature, which had played no part in the Compromise of 1850. The slavery of the South and the servility of the North would never yield flowers "to charm the senses of men, for they have no real life: they are merely a decaying and a death, offensive to all healthy nostrils. We do not complain that they *live,* but that they do not *get buried.* Let the living bury them; even they are good for manure."

Thoreau long had prized "brave speaking," calling it "the most entire and richest sacrifice to the gods." But he had learned that brave speaking was no match for brave doing. In 1846, after going to jail almost as a lark, he had realized that the individual courageous enough to resist authority possessed enormous power. Rather than secede from society, he decided, he would stand in its way.

Emerson reached the same conclusion by a different route. Facing the full implications of transcendentalism's belief in the unity of humankind, he saw that "the civility of no race can be perfect whilst another race is degraded." An injury to one injured all. He chose to believe that right would triumph over the self-interested forces of the marketplace, that "blessed necessity" would drive the country toward justice. To his ear, it seemed that the voice of right, "once very low and indistinct," was growing "ever more articulate, because it is the voice of the universe." And the voice demanded freedom.

6

LOOK AWAY, LOOK AWAY

THE NORTHERN VOICES raised against slavery went largely unheard in the South. Fearing bodily harm, abolitionists did not travel below the Mason-Dixon Line, nor did they press their cause in writing. Southern legislatures had banned antislavery literature in the belief that it would stir up more slave revolts like the 1831 Turner rebellion in Virginia, where a hundred blacks and sixty whites died before Nat Turner was captured and hanged. The state of Georgia promised that anyone caught disseminating material "inciting insurrection, revolt, conspiracy, or resistance, on the part of slaves, negroes or free persons of color" against Georgians would be "punished with DEATH."

After the Turner rebellion, legislators who represented the South in Washington adroitly stifled debate of the slavery question and managed to persuade one after another of their Northern colleagues that abolition, if left unchecked, would drive the South out of the Union. During the three decades between Nat Turner's rampage and the attack on Fort Sumter, Southerners censored the North and filled the silence in the national conversation by talking to themselves, fashioning ever more elaborate and prideful defenses of what they termed "the peculiar institution."

Consulting the Bible, they found God on their side. He had blessed Abraham with slaves and enjoined all in servitude to obey even harsh masters. Christ had spoken often of slavery, always without condemnation. A writer calling himself Amor Patriae proclaimed that "God never would have authorized slavery, had it not been intended as a blessing to mankind." Many Southerners agreed and shared Amor Patriae's view that whatever the faults of human bondage, they were the faults of errant masters, not of the institution itself. Looking to the American past, Southern political theorists observed that the Constitution permitted slavery, that eight presidents had owned slaves, and that a man's right to legally acquired property was inviolable. Contemplating the Negro, the South saw a being divinely ordained for slavery—able to withstand the heat of the cotton fields and the malarial dangers of the rice swamps and, to judge by reports of the suffering among free blacks in the North, unable to thrive on his own. Slavery rescued the Negro from barbarism, supported him from cradle to grave, and gave him the gift of Christianity. As one Baptist phrasemaker put it, "Instead of the gospel being sent to the heathen, God has in this case brought the heathen to the gospel."

Over two centuries, slaveholding had become many things to the South—economic necessity, social inevitability, inalienable right, sacred trust, source of power and prestige—all of which were on display in Savannah on March 2 and 3, 1859, at one of the largest slave auctions on record. The slaves belonged to Pierce Butler, an absentee planter and former husband of one of England's most celebrated actresses, Fanny Kemble. A prominent citizen of Philadelphia, Butler had run into hardships ascribed by some to the Panic of 1857 and by others to profligacy. Whatever the cause, the effect was that 436 slaves from two Butler family plantations were coming to the auction block. Pierce was said to be pained by the thought, and in deference to his feelings, the advertisements for the sale omitted his name.

The auction attracted wide notice because slave prices had been soaring. Cotton production doubled in the 1840s and again in the 1850s. The cotton boll's white fluff, which nature had designed as a protective cushion for the seeds of the cotton plant, proved wondrously serviceable. Picked, ginned, and dried, the fluff settled into flattish strands that were strong and easily twisted, characteristics ideal for spinning and weaving. Cotton fabric became one of the world's first mass-produced consumer goods.

By the time Pierce Butler's slaves were brought to auction, Southern planters furnished virtually all of the cotton used in New England's textile mills, three-quarters of England's, and a growing share of Europe's. Cotton was indeed king. Slave labor made farmers in the cotton belt four times richer than the farmers of the North, and it created almost twice as many large fortunes in the South as there were in the North. In 1860, 65 percent of the seven thousand Americans with estates worth $100,000 or more were Southerners.* The United States had a favorable balance of trade because of cotton, which accounted for more than half the value of America's exports. Without cotton, an 1853 report to the U.S. Senate concluded, "the balance-sheet would be a sorry exhibit of our condition as a commercial people, and of general prosperity."

The gentlemen of Beacon Hill shrank from discussing their debt to cotton and slaves, but David Christy, a journalist and defender of slavery, summed it up in his 1856 book, *Cotton Is King:* "To the superficial observer, all the agencies based upon the sale and manufacture of cotton seem to be legitimately engaged in promoting human happiness; and he, doubtless, feels like invoking Heaven's choicest blessings upon them. When he sees the stockholders in the cotton corporations receiving their dividends, the operatives their wages, the merchants their cottons, and civilized people everywhere clothed comfortably in cottons, he can not refrain from exclaiming, 'The lines have fallen unto them in pleasant places; yes, they have a goodly heritage.'"

As the wealth of Southern cotton planters grew, so did their sense of importance. In the mid-1850s, J. D. B. DeBow invited them to reflect that their cotton had done more than any other crop to lift humankind from barbarism. "You cannot civilize man until you first clothe his nakedness," he wrote in *DeBow's Review,* one of the South's most influential business publications. Before cotton there had been

---

*With the end of slavery, the wealth of the South collapsed. By 1870, five years after the Civil War, the Southern share of the nation's six-figure incomes had plunged to 20 percent.

"no cheap and abundant article raised by which the poor and helpless could be clothed on an extensive scale." Textile manufacturing "together with the vast production of cotton by slave labor in the South, have supplied the deficiency. . . . In this point of view, the culture of cotton becomes deeply interesting to the statesman and philanthropist."

In 1858, Senator James Henry Hammond of South Carolina prayed his Northern colleagues to remember their place: "You fetch and carry for us. One hundred and fifty million dollars of our money passes annually through your hands. Much of it sticks; all of it assists to keep your machinery together and in motion. Suppose we were to discharge you; suppose we were to take our business out of your hands;—we should consign you to anarchy and poverty."

OVER their grand imperium, planters saw only one cloud: a labor shortage. The importation of slaves had ceased in 1809, after Congress banned the practice, so the planter eager to expand in order to cash in on the boom could increase his workforce only by purchasing slaves from other planters, who generally needed hands as much as he did. As a result, the Milledgeville *Federal Union* reported in 1860, there was "a perfect fever raging in Georgia . . . on the subject of buying Negroes. The old rule of pricing a Negro by the price of cotton by the pound—that is to say, if cotton is worth twelve cents, a Negro man is worth $1,200.00, if at fifteen cents, then $1,500.00—does not seem to be regarded." While cotton prices had fallen by a third between 1857 and 1859, slave prices had risen by a quarter. "Men are demented upon the subject," the newspaper warned. "A reverse will surely come."

The planters who congregated in Savannah for the sale of the Butler slaves were less inclined to worry about reverses than rejoice in their present good fortune. Large auctions were rare, and this lot of slaves was choice. But the sale would have passed almost without notice had it not been for a young newspaper reporter from Horace Greeley's *New York Tribune*. A former actor who wrote humor and social satire under the *nom de plume* of Q. K. Philander Doesticks, P.B., twenty-seven-year-old Mortimer Neal Thomson slipped into Savannah at the end of February posing as a planter. He carried his auction catalog about town, mingled with planters inspecting slaves before the sale, and in general, he said, did his "little utmost to keep up all the appearance of a knowing buyer, pricing 'likely nigger fellers,' talking confidentially to the smartest ebon maids, chucking the round-eyed youngsters under the chin." As the planters penciled notes in their catalogues, Doesticks did likewise.

> For several days before the sale every hotel in Savannah was crowded with negro speculators from North and South Carolina, Virginia, Georgia, Alabama, and Louisiana, who had been attracted hither by the prospects of making good bargains. Nothing was heard for days, in the bar-rooms and public rooms, but talk of the great sale; criticisms of the business affairs of Mr. Butler, and speculations as to the probable prices the stock would bring.

The founders of Georgia would not have recognized the bustle that greeted Doesticks. Nearly deserted in the days of James Oglethorpe, Georgia had blossomed into the most populous state in the Deep South. The colony's ban on slavery had ended in 1750, and by 1860, 466,000 of the state's inhabitants (44 percent) were slaves. Savannahians still made their way through town by jogging right, left, and right around the squares Oglethorpe had plunked into the middle of the principal intersections, but the squares, once empty, were now fronted by elegant houses. Many had been built by slaves, and nearly all had been built by cotton, which is to say, by profits from the labor of slaves.

> The negroes were brought to Savannah in small lots, as many at a time as could be conveniently taken care of, the last of them reaching the city the Friday before the sale. . . . Immediately on their arrival they were taken to the [Ten Broeck] Race-course, and there quartered in the sheds erected for the accommodation of the horses and carriages of gentlemen attending the races. Into these sheds they were huddled pell-mell, without any more attention to their comfort than was necessary to prevent their becoming ill and unsaleable. Each "family" had one or

more boxes or bundles, in which were stowed such scanty articles of their clothing as were not brought into immediate requisition, and their tin dishes and gourds for their food and drink. . . .

In these sheds were the chattels huddled together on the floor, there being no sign of bench or table. They ate and slept on the bare boards, their food being rice and beans, with occasionally a bit of bacon and corn bread.

During her marriage to Pierce Butler, Fanny Kemble had spent a winter on the family's cotton plantation on Butler Island and its rice plantation on St. Simons Island, and she often commented in her journal on the poor diet of the slaves. Children begged her for meat, which was given only to slaves charged with ditch digging or other hard labor, "and to them only occasionally, and in very moderate rations." Field hands made do with two meals a day of corn or hominy. Although the Butler slaves were considered well treated, Fanny was struck by their fatigue and susceptibility to illness. She suspected that diet was to blame.

Southern planters often boasted that their slaves ate better than the factory hands of the North. Some did, especially when given permission to augment weekly food allotments with vegetables and chickens raised on their own and fish caught on Sundays, the one day a week they had to themselves. According to one Georgia slaveholder, "careful" slave households on his plantation regularly produced more food than they could eat and bartered the surplus for calico and tobacco at the local store. But reports of masters parsimonious with food are common, and slaves who did not get enough to eat often pilfered from the plantation storehouse. A fugitive slave from Georgia recalled that he and others often stole corn, which they took to poor whites to be ground into meal. In exchange for their services, the whites kept half. Infant mortality, chronic disease, and early death occurred more frequently among slaves than whites, patterns suggesting that however ample the slaves' food rations, their diet was nutritionally deficient.

As Doesticks worked his way through the shed, he was struck by the "expression of heavy grief" on every face.

[S]ome appeared to be resigned to the hard stroke of Fortune that had torn them from their homes, and were sadly trying to make the best of it; some sat brooding moodily over their sorrows, their chins resting on their hands, their eyes staring vacantly, and their bodies rocking to and fro, with a restless motion that was never stilled; few wept, the place was too public and the drivers too near, though some occasionally turned aside to give way to a few quiet tears. They were dressed in every possible variety of uncouth and fantastic garb, in every style and of every imaginable color; the texture of the garments was in all cases coarse, most of the men being clothed in the rough cloth that is made expressly for the slaves. The dresses assumed by the negro minstrels, when they give imitations of plantation character, are by no means exaggerated; they are, instead, weak and unable to come up to the original. There was every variety of hats, with every imaginable slouch; and there was every cut and style of coat and pantaloons, made with every conceivable ingenuity of misfit, and tossed on with a general appearance of perfect looseness that is perfectly indescribable, except to say that a Southern negro always looks as if he could shake his clothes off without taking his hands out of his pockets. The women, true to the feminine instinct, had made, in almost every case, some attempt at finery. All wore gorgeous turbans, generally manufactured in an instant out of a gay-colored handkerchief by a sudden and graceful twist of the fingers; though there was occasionally a more elaborate turban, a turban complex and mysterious, got up with care, and ornamented with a few beads or bright bits of ribbon. Their dresses were mostly coarse stuff, though there were some gaudy calicoes; a few had ear-rings, and one possessed the treasure of a string of yellow and blue beads.

Doesticks caught both the poverty and the splendor of the slave wardrobe. In Georgia and much of the rest of the South, shirts and dresses were stitched up from a yearly allowance of coarse white fabric called "Negro cloth"—seven yards for men, six for women. "Dat ole nigger-cloth was jus' like needles when it was new," an ex-slave remembered. "Never did have to scratch our back. Jus' wriggle yo' shoulders an' yo' back was scratched." Slaves were given shoes but often refused to wear them, behavior widely interpreted as proof of their incorrigible barbarism. The truth was that the shoes, New England's crudest and cheapest, hurt.

After six days in rough clothes (usually the same set) slaves dressed up for the Sabbath. Decorum led many to put on their shoes, however uncomfortable, for church. The women favored calico dresses, long white aprons, bright turbans, and hoop earrings; the men turned themselves out in an array of coats, hats, and an abundance of rings, sometimes several to a finger. By 1849, the Savannah *Republican* felt obliged to protest that in sartorial matters, slave women nearly outshone their mistresses and male slaves far surpassed their masters. This "ambition of dress is absolutely a disease," the *Republican* fretted.

As far as Doesticks could tell, the planters who came to inspect the slaves in the days before the auction did not notice the turbans or any other sign of the slaves' humanity.

> The negroes were examined with as little consideration as if they had been brutes indeed; the buyers pulling their mouths open to see their teeth, pinching their limbs to find how muscular they were, walking them up and down to detect any signs of lameness, making them stoop and bend in different ways that they might be certain there was no concealed rupture or wound; and in addition to all this treatment, asking them scores of questions relative to their qualifications and accomplishments. All these humiliations were submitted to without a murmur, and in some instances with good-natured cheerfulness—where the slave liked the appearance of the proposed buyer, and fancied that he might prove a kind 'Mas'r' . . .
>
> "Elisha," chattel No. 5 in the catalogue, had taken a fancy to a benevolent-looking middle-aged gentleman, who was inspecting the stock, and thus used his powers of persuasion to induce the benevolent man to purchase him, with his wife, boy and girl, Molly, Israel and Sevanda, chattels Nos. 6, 7 and 8. The earnestness with which the poor fellow pressed his suit, knowing as he did, that perhaps the happiness of his whole life depended on his success, was touching, and the arguments he used most pathetic. He made no appeal to the feelings of the buyer; he rested no hope on his charity and kindness, but only strove to show how well worth his dollars were the bone and blood he was entreating him to buy.
>
> "Look at me, Mas'r; am prime rice planter; sho' you won't find a better man den me; no better on de whole plantation; not a bit old yet; do

mo' work den ever; do carpenter work, too, little; better buy me, Mas'r; I'se be good sarvant, Mas'r. Molly, too, my wife, Sa, fus'rate rice hand; mos as good as me. Stan' out yer, Molly, and let the gen'lm'n see."

Molly advances, with her hands crossed on her bosom, and makes a quick short curtsy, and stands mute, looking appealingly in the benevolent man's face. But Elisha talks all the faster.

"Show mas'r yer arm, Molly—good arm dat, Mas'r—she do a heap of work mo' with dat arm yet. Let good Mas'r see yer teeth, Molly—see dat Mas'r, teeth all reg'lar, all good—she'm young gal yet. Come out yer, Israel, walk aroun' an' let the gen'lm'n see how spry you be"—

Then, pointing to the three-year-old girl who stood with her chubby hand to her mouth, holding on to her mother's dress, and uncertain what to make of the strange scene.

"Little Vardy's only a chile yet; make prime gal by-and-by. Better buy us, Mas'r, we'm fus' rate bargain"—and so on. But the benevolent gentleman found where he could drive a closer bargain, and so bought somebody else.

Elisha's forwardness might have surprised a Northerner, but it was behavior well-known to planters. Pierce Butler was importuned regularly by pregnant slaves and new mothers seeking lighter work. He responded with lectures on the duties of slaves to masters. Slaveholders did not always look away from the hardships of their slaves, and the slaves, like the powerless of all times and places, excelled at timing their requests for better treatment. When Fanny Kemble tried to coax a boy slave into confiding his dreams of freedom, he vaulted neatly over the briar patch and pressed for a favor more easily granted: "Oh no, missis, me no wish to be free, if massa only let we keep pig!"

Massa declined, insisting that his slaves had enough to eat and no means of supporting hogs. Fanny observed that masters who did grant favors to slaves regarded the benevolence as "undeniable proof of the general kindness with which their dependents are treated."

Like medieval French worshipers directing their prayers to the Virgin Mary in the hope of tempering the stern judgments of God, slaves often asked mistresses to intercede with masters. Fanny was easily enlisted after learning of the whippings and hard labor endured by female slaves, but Pierce cut her off. "Why do you believe such trash?"

he asked. "[D]on't you know the niggers are all d——d lairs?" He told
her that by sympathizing with their complaints, she was filling them
with attitudes sure to lead to whippings when she was no longer there
to stand between them and the lash.

Doesticks was equally disturbed by the handling of women slaves in
the sheds at the racecourse.

> The women never spoke to the white men unless spoken to, and then
> made the conference as short as possible. And not one of them all, dur-
> ing the whole time they were thus exposed to the rude questions of
> vulgar men, spoke the first unwomanly or indelicate word, or con-
> ducted herself in any regard otherwise than as a modest woman should
> do; their conversation and demeanor were quite as unexceptionable as
> they would have been had they been the highest ladies in the land, and
> through all the insults to which they were subjected they conducted
> themselves with the most perfect decorum and self-respect.
>
> The sentiment of the subjoined characteristic dialogue was heard
> more than once repeated:
>
> "Well, Colonel, I seen you looking sharp at Shoemaker Bill's Sally.
> Going to buy her?"
>
> "Well, Major, I think not. Sally's a good, big, strapping gal, and can
> do a heap o' work; but it's five years since she had any children. *She's
> done breeding, I reckon.*"

A healthy young woman who had demonstrated her capacity to bear
children—to "make little niggers for massa," in the plain words of one
of Pierce Butler's slaves—might command $800 or more. English
common law presumed that every human was born free, but after the
introduction of slavery, American colonial legislatures decreed that the
child of a slave was also a slave. The reasoning behind this departure
from old principles—reasoning that demonstrates the ability of determined minds to reason their way to practically anything—was that
since the Negroes had come to America as property, they and their offspring would continue to be property unless they purchased their freedom. The framers of the new doctrine enshrined it in a Latin phrase,
partus sequitur ventrem, meaning that the status of the infant followed
the status of the mother. Mothers, unlike fathers, could be identified

with certainty, and by fusing the status of mother and child, the philosophers of *partus sequitur ventrem* spared white males the twinges that might arise from pondering their responsibilities to their mulatto offspring.

Wills and other documents transferring female slaves from one owner to another routinely specified that their "future issue" would be the property of the new owner and his heirs. When Farish Carter, a plantation owner near Milledgeville, Georgia, purchased thirty slaves in 1821, the bill of sale gave him the right "to have and to hold the said slaves, and the future increase of the females of the same, to the only proper use and behoof of him the said Farish Carter, and his heirs and assigns forever."

IN the 1850s, with the demand for cotton growing faster than the slave population, some Southerners called for a reopening of the slave trade, and in the days leading up to the auction, Doesticks eavesdropped on several planters who cheered the proposition. Their dreams of the riches sure to follow from cheaper slaves inspired even grander ambitions of destroying abolitionism, diminishing the power of the North, and keeping the South forever free of the immigrant hordes washing ashore in Boston and New York. Those who favored more slave traffic liked to point out that it had never really ceased. Slaves were no longer transported from Africa, it was true, but they were often brought to the Deep South from Virginia and Maryland. In the early nineteenth century, they had even been carried down by Northerners canny enough to sell their human property before their states abolished slavery.

The absence of that sort of Yankee shrewdness among Southerners was obvious to Doesticks.

The Race-course at Savannah is situated about three miles from the city, in a pleasant spot, nearly surrounded by woods. As it rained violently during the two days of the sale, the place was only accessible by carriages, and the result was, that few attended but actual buyers, who had come from long distances, and could not afford to lose the opportunity. If the affair had come off in Yankee land, there would have been a dozen omnibuses running constantly between the city and the Race-course, and some speculator would have bagged a nice little sum of money by the operation. But nothing of the kind was thought of here, and the only gainers were the livery stables, the owners of which had sufficient Yankeeism to charge double and treble prices.

Making no effort to conceal his contempt, Doesticks also observed that when a slave was sold, his clothes were included in the bargain. "In the North, we do not necessarily sell the harness with the horse; why, in the South, should the clothes go with the negro?"

THE wealthiest planters, who thought of themselves as gentry, valued leisure more than the tedium and brow-furrowing discipline that went with the steady accumulation of capital. They delegated the management of their plantations to overseers and entrusted their financial destiny to cotton factors, who bought their cotton, extended the credit that saw them from one harvest to the next, and haggled with cotton brokers in New York and Liverpool.

Once a year, two hundred or so planters and businessmen roused themselves to attend regional conventions, where a vocal minority campaigned for diversifying the South's agriculture and building textile mills to keep more cotton profits at home. But inviting a planter to envision the beauties of factory life was like asking a poet to succumb to the enchantments of banking. Industry was alien, unsavory, best left to others.

Out of distaste for factories and finance came the fantastical notion that slavery was the only economic system in which capital and labor worked in perfect harmony. In two widely quoted books of the 1850s, *Sociology for the South, or the Failure of Free Society* and *Cannibals All! or Slaves without Masters,* George Fitzhugh, a Virginia lawyer, argued that class and exploitation were inevitable. Northern factory workers suffered more than Southern slaves, Fitzhugh said, because competition for jobs pitted laborer against laborer and enabled the capitalist to hold wages to subsistence levels.

While the ethic of free society was "Every man, woman and child for himself and herself," master and slave were bound to one another by the Golden Rule, Fitzhugh maintained. "Selfishness finds no place, because nature, common feelings and self-interest dictate to all that it is their true interest 'to love their neighbor as themselves,' and 'to do as they would be done by,'—at least, within the precincts of the family." Fitzhugh found it "passing strange" that abolitionism's brightest minds could not see that "their world of universal liberty was a world of universal selfishness, discord, competition, rivalry, and war of the wits." Millennia of human bondage had demonstrated that a world of masters and slaves was "the only natural society." By disrupting natural social relations, free society had forced man to become "bad and selfish."

Fitzhugh seemed almost to pity the capitalist with a conscience because his wealth so easily became "an instrument of oppression and wrong. . . . If you endow colleges, you rear up cunning, voracious exploitators to devour the poor. If you give it to tradesmen or landowners, 'tis still an additional instrument, always employed to oppress laborers. If you give it to the really needy, you too often encourage idleness, and increase the burdens of the working poor who support everybody. We cannot possibly see but one safe way to invest wealth, and that is to buy slaves with it, whose conduct you can control, and be sure that your charity is not misapplied."

THE census of 1860 showed slavery's hold on the South: of its 11,000,000 inhabitants, 4,000,000 were slaves. While slaves were owned by only 385,000 of the South's 1,516,000 free families, slaves and members of slaveholding households accounted for half the region's inhabitants. In the Deep South, the proportion was even higher: two-thirds in Georgia, Florida, Alabama, and Louisiana, and three-quarters in South Carolina and Mississippi. Most masters (88 percent) owned fewer than twenty slaves, but most slaves (75 percent) lived on plantations with more than twenty slaves. And although the 10,000 families who made up the so-called planter aristocracy were a tiny minority of slaveholders (2.6 percent), they owned 1,000,000 slaves.

The peculiar institution and the dependence on cotton put the Deep South on a peculiar economic footing. Like modern Third World nations that shortchange themselves by exporting natural resources as commodities rather than finished goods, the Deep South devoted the preponderance of its capital and labor to raising cotton, the riskiest and least consistently profitable phase of cotton production. When cotton prices rose, the one-crop economy fared well enough, but when they fell, no one was immune. Few would admit it, but the real King Cotton was the broker in New York or Liverpool. His was a rule of law, the law of supply and demand, and he never paid a penny more than he had to for a bale of fluff.

The consequences of the preoccupation with cotton rippled throughout Southern life. In the minds of the planters and all whose fortunes were tied to theirs, slavery became an economic essential on two counts: paying field hands would price American cotton out of world markets, and emancipation would wipe out the planters' capital.

Southern consumers felt the tyranny of King Cotton whenever they went to the store. As Fanny Kemble discovered, they routinely paid triple the going rate for comparable goods in the North. Prices were "fabulous," she gasped—"such as none but the laziest and most reckless people in the world would consent to afford." With little competition from Southern wares, Northerners priced as they pleased. Also, Congress had levied a series of tariffs on imports to protect infant U.S. manufacturing enterprises from lower-priced foreign goods— measures that benefited the industrial North more than the agrarian South. Needing more imports than the North, Southerners paid a disproportionate share of the tariff.

Cotton was also destroying the land. Agricultural periodicals preached the virtues of fertilizer, crop rotation, and drainage systems to prevent erosion, but few listened.

The Southern press made planters conversant with all of these issues, and the most progressive members of the Southern elite met annually to discuss them. Reports of their conventions brim with ambitious designs for improving agriculture, banking, and railroads and for keeping more cotton profits at home by building local textile factories, establishing local shipping lines, and cutting Northern middlemen out of the international cotton trade.

But the gulf between idea and action proved unbridgeable. The shimmering promise of Southern textile factories, for example, faded quickly amid disputes over the labor to run them. The idea of slaves as mill hands was inimical to many because of the plantation labor shortage and a fear that bringing large numbers of slaves into factories would enlarge their opportunities for conspiracy. By the 1850s, slaves were manning a handful of small Southern textile mills, which were generally prosperous, but the successes gave rise to new worries. Skeptics wondered about the market for Southern textiles given that 40 percent of the region's inhabitants were destitute slaves. The idea of selling to customers elsewhere—a strategy aggressively and profitably pursued by Lowell's manufacturers—did not figure in the discussions.

Nor did Southerners warm to the prospect of staffing the factories with white immigrants, as the Yankees had done. In the words of one Southerner who spoke for many, "There is no class in our country whose influence we have more reason to dread than that of the refuse population of Europe." Few saw that white immigrants would have supplied fledgling Southern textile enterprises with cheap labor and strengthened the region's political power. For purposes of congressional representation, three whites counted as much as five slaves. As immigrants swelled the North's population, the political scales tipped more and more heavily against the South.

"In contrast to the developments of a diverse Northern economy, planting was a specialty without professional spirit," historian Bertram Wyatt-Brown observed in *Southern Honor.* Since the days of John Winthrop, members of the Boston elite often had cooperated with one another to advance their individual interests as well as to maintain the power of their class. The elite of the South was an elite of autocrats, of men who eschewed association for independence no matter what the costs.

Early in the 1850s, *DeBow's Review* warned planters that cotton fac-

tors were manipulating the market by feeding newspapers false information about crop yields. Because cotton yields varied widely from
place to place, planters had no way to know whether they were headed
toward the low prices that went with bumper crops or the high ones
of lean years. Factors predicted big yields in hopes of scaring planters
into selling low. *DeBow's* thought the factors could be outflanked if
each county had a planters' society and exchanged information with
other counties throughout the South. Societies did exist here and there
but rarely took concerted action. Planters lived too far apart to hold
more than occasional meetings and hesitated to cooperate because they
suspected that individuals would break ranks whenever they spotted an
opportunity to do better on their own. Even the conventions were suspect. "[T]he sensible people of this section are nauseated with conventions," a Southern editor declared in 1851. "Nothing of importance has
ever been obtained by them, and they are generally relied on to do the
work which can only be done well by individuals." The refusal to associate or invest in diversifying the South's economy turned the planters'
cherished independence into a fantasy. They may have been lords of
their own plantations, but they were vassals of the cotton market.

BY the time the Savannah auction began, the slaves looked "more
uncomfortable than ever," Doesticks thought.

> [T]he close confinement in-doors for a number of days, and the driz-
> zly, unpleasant weather, began to tell on their condition. They moved
> about more listlessly, and were fast losing the activity and springiness
> they had at first shown. This morning they were all gathered into the
> long room of the building erected as the 'Grand Stand' of the Race-
> course, that they might be immediately under the eye of the buyers.
> The room was about a hundred feet long by twenty wide, and herein
> were crowded the poor creatures, with much of their baggage, awaiting
> their respective calls to step upon the block and be sold to the highest
> bidder. This morning Mr. Pierce Butler appeared among his people,
> speaking to each one, and being recognized with seeming pleasure by
> all. The men obsequiously pulled off their hats and made that inde-
> scribable sliding hitch with the foot which passes with a negro for a

bow; and the women each cropped the quick curtsy, which they seldom vouchsafe to any other than their legitimate master and mistress. Occasionally, to a very old or favorite servant, Mr. Butler would extend his gloved hand, which mark of condescension was instantly hailed with grins of delight from all the sable witnesses.

The room in which the sale actually took place immediately adjoined the room of the negroes, and communicated with it by two large doors. The sale room was open to the air on one side, commanding a view of the entire Course. A small platform was raised about two feet and a-half high, on which were placed the desks of the entry clerks, leaving room in front of them for the auctioneer and the goods.

At about 11 o'clock the business men took their places, and announced that the sale would begin. Mr. [Joseph] Bryan, the Negro Broker, is a dapper little man, wearing spectacles and a yachting hat, sharp and sudden in his movements, and perhaps the least bit in the world obtrusively officious—as earnest in his language as he could be without actual swearing, though acting much as if he would like to swear a little at the critical moment; Mr. Bryan did not sell the goods, he merely superintended the operation, and saw that the entry clerks did their duty properly. The auctioneer proper was a Mr. Walsh, who deserves a word of description. In personal appearance he is the very opposite of Mr. Bryan, being careless of his dress instead of scrupulous, a large man instead of a little one, a fat man instead of a lean one, and a good-natured man instead of a fierce one. He is a rollicking old boy, with an eye ever on the look-out, and that never lets a bidding nod escape him; a hearty word for every bidder who cares for it, and plenty of jokes to let off when the business gets a little slack. Mr. Walsh has a florid complexion, not more so, perhaps, than is becoming, and possibly not more so than is natural in a whiskey country. . . .

Mr. Walsh mounted the stand and announced the terms of the sale, "one-third cash, the remainder payable in two equal annual installments, bearing interest from the day of sale, to be secured by approved mortgage and personal security, or approved acceptances in Savannah, Ga., or Charleston, S.C. Purchasers to pay for papers." The buyers, who were present to the number of about two hundred, clustered around the platform; while the negroes, who were not likely to be immediately wanted, gathered into sad groups in the back-ground, to watch the progress of the selling in which they were so sorrowfully interested. The wind howled outside, and through the open side of the building the driving rain came pouring in; the bar downstairs ceased for a short time its brisk trade; the buyers lit fresh cigars, got ready their catalogues and pencils, and the first lot of human chattels was led upon the stand, not by a white man, but by a sleek mulatto, himself a slave, and who seems to regard the selling of his brethren, in which he so glibly assists, as a capital joke. It had been announced that the negroes would be sold in "families," that is to say, a man would not be parted from his wife, or a mother from a very young child. There is perhaps as much policy as humanity in this arrangement, for thereby many aged and unserviceable people are disposed of, who otherwise would not find a ready sale.

The first family brought out were announced on the catalogue as

NAME	AGE	REMARKS
1. George	27	Prime Cotton Planter
2. Sue	26	Prime Rice Planter
3. George	6	Boy Child
4. Harry	2	Boy Child

The manner of buying was announced to be bidding a certain price apiece for the whole lot. Thus, George and his family were started at $300, and were finally sold at $600 each, being $2,400 for the four. To get an idea of the relative value of each one, we must suppose George worth $1,200, Sue worth $900, Little George worth $200, and Harry worth $100. Owing, however, to some misapprehension on the part of the buyer, as to the manner of bidding, he did not take the family at this figure, and they were put up and sold again, on the second day, when they brought $620 each, or $2,480 for the whole—an advance of $80 over the first sale.

Robert, and Luna his wife, who were announced as having "goitre, otherwise very prime," brought the round sum of $1,005 each.

Eager to preserve his disguise, Doesticks occasionally put in a bid of his own—"a low bid," he said, "so low that somebody always instantly raised him twenty-five dollars," whereupon he would retreat. Planters who had noticed his bidding dropped by his table in the restaurant at Ten Broeck to deliver the sad news that while he had been eating lunch, his lot of slaves had been sold.

It seems as if every shade of character capable of being implicated in the sale of human flesh and blood was represented among the buyers. There was the Georgia fast young man, with his pantaloons tucked into his boots, his velvet cap jauntily dragged over to one side, his cheek full of tobacco, which he bites from a huge plug, that resembles more than anything else an old bit of a rusty wagon tire, and who is altogether an animal of quite a different breed from your New York fast man. His ready revolver, or his convenient knife, is ready for instant use in case of a heated argument. White-neck-clothed, gold-spectacled, and silver-haired old men were there. . . . These gentry, with quiet step and subdued voice, moved carefully about among the livestock, ignoring, as a general rule, the men, but tormenting the women with questions which, when accidentally overheard by the disinterested spectator, bred in that spectator's mind an almost irresistible desire to knock somebody down. And then, all imaginable varieties of rough, backwoods rowdies, who began the day in a spirited manner, but who, as its hours progressed, and their practice at the bar became more prolific in results, waxed louder and talkier and more violent, were present, and added a characteristic feature to the assemblage. . . .

A party of men were conversing on the fruitful subject of managing refractory "niggers;" some were for severe whipping, some recommending branding, one or two advocated other modes of torture, but one huge brute of a man, who had not taken an active part in the discussion, save to assent, with approving nod, to any unusually barbarous proposition, at last broke his silence by saying, in an oracular way, "You may say what you like about managing niggers; I'm a driver myself, and I've had some experience, and I ought to know. You can manage ordinary niggers by lickin' 'em, and givin' 'em a taste of the hot iron once in a while when they're extra ugly; but if a nigger really sets himself up against me, I can't never have any patience with him. I just get my pistol and shoot him right down; and that's the best way."

And this brute was talking to gentlemen, and his remarks were listened to with attention, and his assertions assented to by more than one in the knot of listeners.

The Southern planter survives in the American imagination as both gentleman and brute. The gentleman was an ardent partisan of agrarian life, built himself a fine house, committed poetry to memory during hours passed among his leather-bound classics, rode to hounds, helped his neighbors, and was kind to his slaves.

There were such gentlemen, men of intellect, attainment, and conscience, but they were as rare in the antebellum South as in any other time and place. The question of why the choice few have come to symbolize the many may never be answered. Even in the late twentieth century, six generations removed from slavery, the striking features of the standard tour of a Southern plantation are the guide's scant references to slaves and the tourists' assumptions, evident from their questions, of the gentility of the planter class. Like Germans dissociating themselves from the Third Reich, most white Americans, Northerners as well as Southerners, find it more congenial to identify with the gentleman planter than to consider the alternatives or imagine themselves enslaved.

Of the brute there is considerably more evidence, some from slaves but most of it supplied without embarrassment by the brute himself. The exchange that Doesticks reported on the proper management of truculent slaves was not a debate on the merits of brutality, it was a conversation flowing easily from a shared belief in the necessity of violence.

Except to outsiders like Doesticks and Fanny Kemble, the brutality was unremarkable. Slavery had normalized it, made it a fact of life. When Fanny tried to get Pierce to acknowledge that the flogging of female slaves was "abhorrent," he would concede only that it was "disagreeable." Her sense of the abhorrent appealed to a universal standard of human decency. His sense of the disagreeable answered only to his personal discomfort.

John Nevitt, a Mississippi cotton planter, kept a diary notable for the number of whippings it reports and chilling for the lack of emotion with which they are reported. "Maria who ran away on the 12th was brought home by Rubin," Nevitt wrote on August 21, 1827. "Gave her a light whipping and set her to making cotton bags." A few months later: "Maria was brought home by Jerry on the night of the 8th. Had her whipped severely and ironed with shackle on each leg connected with a chain. Weather clear and fine." Nevitt was not heartless. At Christmas he bought presents for his slaves and allowed them to hold a ball. When he slaughtered a steer, he shared it with them. "Gave the people permission to dig potatoes for the garden," he noted in 1832. "Increased their allowance to 4 lbs. meat. . . . Woodson brought home by Anthony. Gave him a good flogging and put him in the stocks." Brutality, like generosity, was all in a day's work.

Southern newspapers regularly carried advertisements offering rewards for the return of runaway slaves, and the distinguishing physical characteristics of the fugitives often included lash marks, broken noses, scars, and brands. The last aided in the return of missing property and helped fellow planters avoid the unwitting purchase of runaways.

Laws governing the treatment of slaves are impressive not for what they forbid but what they permit. In Savannah, slaves could be whipped no more than thirty-nine lashes a day, but they could be whipped for any conceivable offense, real or imagined. Some plantations, including Pierce Butler's, limited the number of lashes a driver or overseer could inflict, but where, Fanny Kemble wondered, was the limit on the master? "He may, if he likes, flog a slave to death, for the laws which pretend that he may not are a mere pretense, inasmuch as the testimony of a black is never taken against a white." In the absence of white witnesses, a planter or overseer who murdered a slave in Georgia faced no trial for the first offense. For additional murders, he (and it was always a he) could win acquittal merely by proclaiming his innocence under oath. Mutilation of a slave was a crime, punishable by a fine, but only if the act had been seen by a white man brave enough to testify against the offender.

The threat of the lash was said to be essential in controlling slaves, and there is no doubt that it was. What besides constant fear of brutal punishment would compel a slave to remain in bondage, working from sunup to sundown for no pay and only the meanest provisions of food, shelter, and Negro cloth? And how else could a master outnumbered by slaves ensure his own safety? New England villagers in danger might summon their neighbors, but in a world dominated by large plantations, master and overseer stood alone against the slaves. As Fanny realized during her stay on St. Simons, if the slaves chose to revolt, the island's handful of white residents would be dead before word of the mayhem reached the mainland.

Fear of such revolts led some planters to forbid their slaves to attend church or visit with slaves from other plantations, and Southern legislatures made it a crime to teach slaves to read. "The more I see of this frightful and perilous social system, the more I feel that those who live in the midst of it must make their whole existence one constant precaution against danger of some sort or other," Fanny wrote near the end of her stay in Georgia. She ignored the law and included a young slave in the reading lessons she gave her daughter.

One of the most moving testimonies of a slave's esteem for the written word was a manuscript left by a Savannah slave named London, who was literate in Arabic but untutored in English. While the pages he wrote would appear to be gibberish to most readers of Arabic, a scholar named William B. Hodgson discovered that when the manuscript was read aloud, it was the Gospels as heard in the dialect of Georgia slaves. London had written the sounds in Arabic characters, the only alphabet he knew. "Fas chapta ob jon," begins one passage transliterated back into the English alphabet by Hodgson. "Inde beginnen wasde wad; ande Wad waswid God, ande wad was God."

In a society where slaves outnumbered masters ten to one, an obsession with force was inevitable. But even obsession fails to account for what historian Daniel Jonah Goldhagen in *Hitler's Willing Executioners* called "surplus brutality"—force far in excess of the amount needed to secure the desired result. White Southerners regularly rebutted allegations of cruelty by asserting that a profit-minded master would no more harm his slaves than his livestock. But as Fanny Kemble discerned, the self-interest argument "answers nothing; the instances in which men, to gratify the immediate impulse of passion, sacrifice not only their eternal, but their evident, palpable, positive worldly interest, are infinite."

"I do not know what made Stevens so cruel-hearted to us poor slaves," said a fugitive from a cotton plantation owned by one Thomas Stevens. After fleeing to England, the slave changed his name to John

Brown and told his story to an abolitionist who turned it into a book, *Slave Life in Georgia,* published in 1855. Stevens "always wore a laughing expression, but this did not indicate his disposition, which was dreadfully savage," Brown reported. "Still, he always laughed, even when in a passion. In fact, at such times, and they were very frequent, he laughed more than at any other." Brown said that Stevens often whipped him, and once, while Brown was bent low to show Stevens a problem with a plowshare, Stevens "viciously raised his foot, which was heavily shod, and unexpectedly dealt me a kick with all his might." The kick broke the slave's nose and permanently damaged his right eye.

Brown ran away more than once before escaping for good. Like many other captured fugitive slaves, he was shackled with bells and horns, a fiendish iron contraption consisting of a pair of cuffs (one to be padlocked around the neck, the other around the crown of the head) attached to three-foot-long rods topped by bells. "The bells and horns do not weigh less than from twelve to fourteen pounds," Brown said. For the three months he was forced to wear them, his head and neck ached constantly, he said, and "I could not lie down to rest, because the horns prevented my stretching myself, or even curling myself up; so I was obliged to sleep crouching."

Stevens also volunteered Brown for medical experiments conducted by Thomas Hamilton, a local physician and planter. Hoping to make money with a nostrum to ward off sunstroke, Hamilton ordered a crew of slaves to dig a pit, build a fire in it, and remove the embers when the pit was hot. A plank and stool were lowered into the pit. Hamilton gave Brown a dose of his medicine and made him strip and descend to the stool. With wet blankets, Hamilton sealed off everything but Brown's head. Then he laid twigs on the blankets and set fire to them to keep the heat up. Brown lasted for half an hour before passing out. Hamilton felt the need for several more trials, but in order not to compromise Brown's productivity as a field hand, the doctor spaced his investigations three or four days apart. He also confined them to early evening, after Brown had finished his day's work for his master.

Stevens may have been uncommonly cruel, but surplus brutality was not rare. Even masters who chose not to inflict it themselves saw that it was done by delegating it to overseers or the local jails. Jailers whipped slaves for a fee ($1.25 in Milledgeville in 1832, $.50 in Savannah in 1853). Slaves sent to jail to be flogged often received the maximum number of lashes for several days running.

While the Christianity of the antebellum South stressed the mutual obligations of master and slave, the master's prerogatives had no bounds. As Fanny Kemble noted, "you are absolute on your own plantation." And the absolutism gave rise to both the gentleman and the brute. "The habit of command" endowed Southern planters with "a certain self-possession," Fanny thought, and from their love of leisure came "a certain ease." They were "impulsive and enthusiastic," their manners had "grace and spirit." But the peculiar institution had "infected them with . . . haughty, overbearing irritability, effeminate indolence, reckless extravagance, and a union of profligacy and cruelty, which is the immediate result of their irresponsible power over their dependents."

DOESTICKS was particularly incensed by the planters' ridicule of a female slave named Daphney, who was offered for sale with her husband, their three-year-old daughter, and an infant.

Daphney had a large shawl, which she kept carefully wrapped round her infant and herself. This unusual proceeding attracted much attention, and provoked many remarks, such as these:

"What do you keep your nigger covered up for? Pull off her blanket."

"What's the matter with the gal? Has she got the headache?"

"What's the fault of the gal? Ain't she sound? Pull off her rags and let us see her."

"Who's going to bid on that nigger, if you keep her covered up. Let's see her face."

And a loud chorus of similar remarks, emphasized with profanity, and mingled with sayings too indecent and obscene to be even hinted at here, went up from the crowd of chivalrous Southern gentlemen.

At last the auctioneer obtained a hearing long enough to explain that there was no attempt to practise any deception in the case—the parties were not to be wronged in any way; he had no desire to palm off on them an inferior article; but the truth of the matter was that Daphney had been confined only fifteen days ago, and he thought that on that account she was entitled to the slight indulgence of a blanket, to keep from herself and child the chill air and the driving rain. . . .

The day was the 2d day of March. Daphney's baby was born into the world on St. Valentine's happy day, the 14th of February. Since her confinement, Daphney had traveled from the plantation to Savannah, where she had been kept in a shed for six days. On the sixth or seventh day after her sickness, she had left her bed, taken a railroad journey across the country to the shambles, was there exposed for six days to the questionings and insults of the negro speculators, and then on the fifteenth day after her confinement was put up on the block, with her husband and her other child, and, with her new-born baby in her arms, sold to the highest bidder. . . . The family sold for $625 apiece, or $2,500 for the four. . . .

Many other babies, of all ages of baby-hood, were sold, but there was nothing particularly interesting about them. There were some thirty babies in the lot; they are esteemed worth to the master a hundred dollars the day they are born, and to increase in value at the rate of a hundred dollars a year till they are sixteen or seventeen years old, at which age they bring the best prices. . . .

And so the Great Sale went on for two long days, during which time there were sold 429 men, women and children. There were 436 announced to be sold, but a few were detained on the plantations by sickness.

At the close of the sale, on the last day, several baskets of champagne were produced, and all were invited to partake, the wine being at the expense of the broker, Mr. Bryan.

The highest sum paid for any one family was given for Sally Walker and her five children, who were mostly grown up. The price was $6,180.

The highest price paid for a single man was $1,750, which was given for William, a "fair carpenter and caulker."

The highest price paid for a woman was $1,250, which was given for Jane, "cotton hand and house servant."

The lowest price paid was for Anson and Violet, a gray-haired couple, each having numbered more than fifty years; they brought but $250 apiece.

Guy, chattel No. 419, "a prime young man," sold for $1,280, being without blemish; his age was twenty years, and he was altogether a fine article. His next-door neighbor, Andrew, chattel No. 420, was his very counterpart in all marketable points, in size, age, skill, and everything save that he had lost his right eye. Andrew sold for only $1,040, from which we argue that the market value of the right eye in the Southern country is $240.

The appraisers who had sized up the Butler family's slaves for the auction had concluded that they were worth, on average, $572 a head. The auctioneers had collected $708, a full 25 percent more. In two days, they had taken in more than $300,000.

As Doesticks departed, he saw a crowd of slaves collected around Pierce Butler.

[He] was solacing the wounded hearts of the people he had sold from their firesides and their homes, by doling out to them small change at the rate of a dollar a head. To every negro he had sold, who presented his claim for the paltry pittance, he gave the munificent stipend of one whole dollar, in specie; he being provided with two canvas bags of 25 cent pieces, fresh from the mint, to give an additional glitter to his generosity.

Doesticks caught a train north and spent the trip writing his report of the auction. The eight thousand words sprawling across the pages of the *Tribune* on March 9 were the talk of New York. The paper sold out and was reprinted March 11. Newspapers in Philadelphia, London, and elsewhere picked up the story, and the American Anti-Slavery Society turned it into a pamphlet. *A Great Slave Auction* failed to win the lasting fame of *Uncle Tom's Cabin,* but it gave an unsurpassed eyewitness account of the buying and selling of human beings.

For Doesticks, as for Fanny Kemble and most other strangers to the South, it was impossible to look away from the evils of slavery—brutality, uncountable deprivations and abasements, the sheer repugnance of the idea of one person owning another. For the stranger from a time long past the end of slavery, one disturbing question remains: How did six million white Southerners manage *not* to see the evil?

They were not blinded by greed. The planter aristocracy often acted against its own interests, refusing to spend even small sums on farm implements that would have increased productivity, refusing to diversify their crops, refusing to invest in textile manufacturing. Refusing became a point of pride, evidence of the South's superiority to the money-grubbing North.

The profits of slavery were real but notoriously unpredictable. Planters lived at the mercy of flood, drought, weevils, cotton prices, and a labor force that was highly inefficient. With no hope of improving their lives or the lives of their children, slaves had little reason but the lash to exert themselves. It should surprise no one that when they could lean on their hoes, they did. While the Yankee mill owner hired and fired at will to keep his overhead in line with the fortunes of his enterprise, the planter had to support his slaves in good years and bad.

It was inevitable that white Southerners would look away from Northern arguments against slavery. The abolitionist position was one of pure assault, offering the South almost nothing in the way of proposals or incentives for change. Ralph Waldo Emerson and a few others suggested that America free the slaves by compensating slaveholders for the loss of their property, but Americans never seriously explored the idea. Only in hindsight, after a civil war costing $3.3 billion and 640,000 lives, were the merits of the proposition clear.

A handful of Bostonians had claimed the moral high ground on the issue of slavery, but slaveholders considered the claim bogus. The Bible and the Constitution sanctioned slavery, and Southerners believed the North a hell of crime, vice, poverty, and war between capital and labor. Abolitionists were enemies of property and pawns of a Northern elite determined to tighten its grip on national affairs. Abolitionists were also hypocrites, eager to free the slaves but unwilling to live alongside them. Even Abraham Lincoln, the Great Emancipator, could not envision integrating blacks into American life. He wanted them to move to Africa.

To Southerners, the misery of slave life was Northern fiction. Proceeding from the assumption that the Negro was innately inferior (an assumption then shared by all but a handful of Northerners), the master saw himself not only as proprietor but as rescuer and protector of his slaves. The institution was peculiar, he admitted, but through it the Southern Negro had been given a life better than any he might know in Africa or the North. In the South he was housed, clothed, fed, civilized, and baptized. Some planters were so proud of the results of their two-hundred-year tutelage of the Negro that they opposed the reopening of the slave trade on the ground that the heathen newcomers would be unsuitable companions for their American brothers.

Brutality ceased to be seen as brutality and became a necessity— "disagreeable" to Pierce Butler (though not to everyone), legally permissible, increasingly unconstrained. Like modern urban beggars, whippings and other acts of violence were part of everyday antebellum Southern life, noticeable only to strangers. Just as there is comfort in seeing beggars as panhandlers, more cunning than needy, there was immense utility in thinking of slavery as merely peculiar. "Peculiar" wrapped jaggedness in the white fluff of preference, making slavery seem as harmless as any other difference between North and South. "Peculiar" disarmed critics by simultaneously admitting that slavery veered from the norm and demanding that it not be judged by the norm.

There is solace too in accepting the prevailing view that American slavery flourished because of avarice or some other moral pathology in the whites of the Old South—that they were in fact an identifiable "they," separate and different from "us" and guilty of wrongs we would not tolerate, much less commit. The facts suggest otherwise. Most Northerners were content to look away, feeling no more inclined to fight slavery than Southerners were to end it. Abolitionism did not become truly fashionable in the North until after the slaves were freed. Many New England merchants and cotton manufacturers disapproved of slavery but found it convenient to believe that because of the Constitution, slavery could not be abolished except by the Southern states themselves. Slavery persisted because it "seemed the dictate of trade to keep the Negro down," Emerson said. The commercial classes of New England had allowed the customer, North and South, to become "the jewel of our souls. Him we flatter, him we feast, compliment, vote for, and will not contradict."

The hard lesson of slavery is not about the evil of "them," it is about the unending complicity of "us." Mass indifference to mass injustice seems to be one of the sorrier constants of human history. In 1963, a century after the Emancipation Proclamation, Martin Luther King Jr. would write from his jail cell in Birmingham, Alabama, that the struggle for civil rights was as much against "the appalling silence of the good people" as against "the vitriolic words and actions of the bad people." Any day's headlines make plain that the unjust still thrive. "We" read, deplore "them," and look away.

Why Millionaires Should Not Be Shot

I N 1901, WHEN Andrew Carnegie agreed to sell his steel company to J. P. Morgan for $480 million, Morgan had himself chauffeured uptown from Wall Street to Carnegie's mansion on West Fifty-first Street to ratify the deal with a handshake. The visit was short—fifteen minutes—and Morgan left with a salute: "Mr. Carnegie, I want to congratulate you on being the richest man in the world."

It is hard to know whether Morgan was right, but if Carnegie's $300 million share of the transaction did not make him the world's richest man, he was certainly its most famous rich man, and famous less for the magnitude of his wealth than for his decision to give all of it away. His was a rags-to-riches tale with a surprise ending.

The tale was well known, even among children, thousands of whom heard it from Carnegie himself. In newspapers, magazines, and school auditoriums, Carnegie told of coming to America from the Scottish village of Dunfermline and going to work, at age twelve, as a bobbin boy in a Pennsylvania cotton factory. His parents had little money, which the adult Carnegie saw as a boon. "You know how people moan about poverty as being a great evil," he told the readers of the *Youth's Companion*. His youth had taught him otherwise. Poor children were close to their parents because no servants came between them, poor families were "loving and united" because everyone worked toward the common goal of survival, and poor homes were "sweet and happy and pure" because they were "free from perplexing care." To appreciate the nourishment of poverty, he said, one had only to look at history, which was full of great men who shared this "precious heritage."

After the cotton factory he moved on to a job as a boiler tender, which nearly doubled his pay but tormented him with nightmares of boiler explosions. He told no one, not wanting to violate his family's code of talking only about the "bright" things of life. From the menacing dark of the boiler room, young Andy ascended to a sunny telegraph office, was hired away by a superintendent of the Pennsylvania Railroad, and became a superintendent himself. After a couple of canny investments in his twenties, Carnegie went into business as a builder of iron railroad bridges. By his thirty-third birthday, in 1868, he had an income of $50,000 a year—a sum so large that it startled him into drawing up a rigorous set of orders for the rest of his life. "Beyond this never earn," he instructed himself.

> [M]ake no effort to increase fortune, but spend the surplus each year for benevolent purposes, Cast aside business forever except for others,—
>
> Settle in Oxford & get a thorough education making the acquaintance of literary men this will take three years active work—pay especial attention to speaking in public, Settle then in London & purchase a controlling interest in some newspaper or fine review & give the general management of it attention, taking a part in public matters especially those connected with education and improvement of the poorer classes—
>
> Man must have an idol. The amassing of wealth is one of the worst species of idolatry— No idol more debasing than the worship of money— Whatever I engage in I must push inordinately therefore I should be careful to choose that life which will be the most elevating in its character— To continue much longer overwhelmed by business cares and with most of my thoughts wholly upon the way to make more money in the shortest time, must degrade me beyond hope of permanent recovery. I will resign business at thirty five, but during the ensuing two years I wish to spend the afternoons in receiving instruction, and in reading systematically.

It took thirty-three more years and the Morgan deal for Carnegie to cast aside business forever, and as he inched toward his goal, he amassed a fortune capable of producing an annual income three hundred times greater than the $50,000 he considered alarming. He also helped to give the industrial corporation the shape it had for most of the twentieth century, eased the tensions he felt between money and morals by inventing modern philanthropy, and gave Americans one of their best-loved folk heroes, the millionaire.

As an industrialist, Carnegie had two gifts rarely found in the same person: he was an indefatigable innovator and a proficient imitator, full of original ideas but not too proud to borrow from others. At the Pennsylvania Railroad, he had shocked his elders by proposing that the best way to get freight moving again after a train wreck was to torch the cars blocking the track. The unthinkable soon became routine because it saved money and bolstered the railroad's reputation for do-or-die service. Carnegie was the first steelmaker to buy interests in iron ore mines and coalfields, a strategy that lowered his costs and tightened his control over raw materials. He was one of the first American businessmen to grasp the importance of making accountants independent of the operations they audited. Large businesses that failed to copy his practice would "go to ruin through dry-rot," predicted one early student of the corporate scene.

Heavily invested in iron making, Carnegie nevertheless kept watch on the long trial-and-error development of techniques for manufacturing steel. On vacation in Italy in 1879, he investigated at once when he read a newspaper account of a technical breakthrough. "It is too important not to invite our earnest attention," he wrote to one of his partners. A competitor was ahead of them, but Carnegie foresaw that he too could profit handsomely in steel.

It was unnervingly easy for the corporations of his day to raise money by issuing ever more shares of stock, hollowing themselves into husks that crumbled at the slightest pressure. Carnegie resisted. He also declined to play the dangerous game of baiting investors with large dividends. In Carnegie's view, earnings were not to be dispensed as largesse, they were meant to fund growth and seize the opportunities brought by financial panics. Happy the man with cash when the rest of the world clamors to sell.

Without the advice of management consultants, Carnegie understood that his company would prosper if it watched over each of the hundreds of steps involved in making iron and steel with the ultimate goal of offering customers the best quality and the best price. "[W]hat I fear most is that we will send out some imperfect boiler plate and fire box steel, and ruin the future," he wrote one of his managers in 1888. "We have our reputation yet to make, and no price is too great to pay for perfection. I hope you will take no risk. Far better not to sell."

There was no truer believer in the wares of the Carnegie Steel Company than Carnegie himself. From his office in New York, he made sure his steel found its way into the Brooklyn Bridge, the city's elevated railway, and the railroads, locomotives, ships, and skyscrapers being built by his fellow tycoons. With his full pockets, he could even help to finance their purchases.

Carnegie saw low costs as the key to low prices and low prices as the businessman's heroic contribution to society. After the Civil War, the spread of large-scale business organization and the quick march of technology enabled the entrepreneur to perform a sort of alchemy—lowering prices for customers while making a larger profit for himself. Commodore Cornelius Vanderbilt had pointed the way by splicing a dozen short railway lines into the New York Central, which cut freight costs by 80 percent, which in turn cut the prices of grain and goods transported from the Midwest. Vanderbilt, said Carnegie, "produced untold wealth for the community, and the profit he reaped for himself was but a drop in the bucket." Determined to do likewise for his customers, Carnegie pushed hard to restrain wages, replace muscle with machines, and fight the "extortions" of the railroads carrying his raw materials and finished goods. He also deployed an army of clerks to weigh the output of his blast furnaces so that the performance of one could be measured against the others. The result, he said proudly, was that "three pounds of finished steel are now bought in Pittsburgh for two cents, which is cheaper than anywhere else on earth."

To Carnegie, no detail was unworthy of consideration. More than once he gave instructions for taking minutes at a board meeting. He wanted to be informed of the tiniest change in costs. Bad news was to be relayed immediately to him, but disclosure of any news to the press was to be made with caution, the press being simply one more "department" in need of management.

His natural bonhomie led him to believe in the value of sounding "the note of sympathy, appreciation, friendship" in dealing with his subordinates. "You must capture and keep the heart of the original and supremely able man before his brain can do its best," he said in a speech called "The Human Side of Business."

To motivate his managers, Carnegie dangled the prospect of partnership and rarely hired outsiders, believing the practice unjust and unnecessary. "The heads of a great business who cannot discern the young geniuses around them will rarely select exceptional ability by going outside," he said. Prizing competition more than cooperation, he encouraged his partners to see themselves as horses in a race against one another. "It is never to be accepted by your partners that you can't compete with and whip others," he reminded a colleague. "This is what young partners are partners for." The young partners raced hard, prospered, and carried their senior partner far toward his fabulous riches. By 1892, the bridge-building firm Carnegie had started thirty years before was the largest, most diversified, most profitable steel company in the world.

With his compact frame and incandescently white beard, Andrew Carnegie looked like a powerhouse, and he was. He was curious about everything, had ideas about everything, had energy for everything. Affable and outgoing, he befriended statesmen and philosophers, delighted Tchaikovsky with a knowing imitation of his conducting style, helped President Ulysses S. Grant's widow with her finances, and furnished his friend Mark Twain with a memorable line: "Put all your eggs in one basket, and then watch that basket." Daniel Coit Gilman, the first president of Johns Hopkins University, told him, "All great men have their special feature. If I were asked what yours was, I should say, that which draws all men after him, pleasing everybody and offending nobody, doing the absolutely necessary ungentle things in a gentle way. . . . I like you."

Lots of people liked him. They felt they could seek his counsel on philanthropy (asking, for example, whether it was better to start at age forty with a relatively modest amount or work until sixty to accumulate a larger sum). Strangers sent him their treasures, including the tooth of a whale killed by the crew of the ship that had brought him to America. A lepidopterist named an African moth for him, hoping Carnegie would take pleasure in being forever identified with "one of the fairy forms which rise at dusk toward the light of the moon, and hover over the giant tree-tops flooded with the splendor of the equatorial night." There was a dinosaur, *Diplodocus carnegiei,* and a cactus, too, *Carnegiea gigantea,* said to be stout, upright, and strongly ribbed.

For more than a decade before his emancipation by J. P. Morgan, Carnegie gradually pared his involvement in managing the company in order to hurl his prodigious energy in other directions. He spent half of each year at his castle in Scotland, where he hosted an unending parade of guests. He wrote prolifically, dictating magazine pieces and several books. His unsolicited opinions on taxes, military spending, spelling reform, empires, and other matters turned up regularly in the mail pouches of presidents and prime ministers. But these were diversions. Most of his time was taken up with the monumental task of turning his fortune into a dynamo of social good.

No benefaction delighted him more than the one for which he is best remembered, the public library. Inspired by his father, one of five weavers who combined their meager collections of books to found the town library in Dunfermline, Andrew Carnegie ultimately gave $60 million to more than 2,500 public libraries. A lover of music who liked to think the sounds of the organ could transport souls "upward to the throne," he subsidized the purchase of more than 7,500 organs for churches in the United States and Britain. He was a veteran of many ocean crossings before he took swimming lessons and discovered the propulsive joys of the frog kick, but his ignorance of the art did not keep him from underwriting numerous public pools.

Carte blanche was not the Carnegie style. He agreed to give land for a cemetery on the condition that it be a "resting place for every human being, Pagan, Christian or Jew. . . . We poor mortals while living our short span are too sharply separated. Surely we should not refuse to lie down together at last upon the bosom of Mother Earth." When Carnegie donated a library, he paid for the building but expected the community to stock, staff, and maintain it. To receive a check for an organ, a church had to demonstrate that its finances were in good order. After looking at preliminary plans for the public baths he had promised Dunfermline, he challenged the size of the pool, trimmed the number of locker rooms and lavatories, and vetoed a proposed residence for the caretaker. "It is much more important to get the latest and best of things internally than to spend money uselessly in externals," he lectured the planners.

In 1889, having given away a few million dollars, Carnegie was eager to do in philanthropy what he had done in business: systematize and proselytize. His systems, laid out in a pair of essays that together became known as "The Gospel of Wealth," were straightforward. After pondering the useful purposes to which wealth could be put, Carnegie had decided which were best. There were seven. The founding of universities ranked first, churches last. Between came libraries, medical institutions, parks, public halls, and swimming pools.

Carnegie was equally definitive about modes of giving. The millionaire who left his fortune to his children ruined their characters. Charitable gifts at death were unwise because they were often ill spent and created the unseemly impression that the givers would not have left the money at all "had they been able to take it with them." The biggest danger was the softhearted millionaire who came to the aid of needy individuals. Such generosity was foolish at best, socially injurious at worst. It improved neither the individual nor the race, persons worthy of such assistance seldom needed it, it fostered dependency in people who needed to learn self-reliance, and the benefactor could not know enough about enough individuals to be sure that his wealth was put to good use. That left only one intelligent course: a millionaire must disburse his fortune during his lifetime and supervise the process.

Carnegie's proselytizing arose from a mélange of hopes, fears, and social convictions rooted in the ideas of Herbert Spencer, a nineteenth-century English philosopher who wrote pioneering works in psychology, sociology, and ethics. Master of a numbing prose style, Spencer nevertheless managed to pen one immortal phrase: "survival of the fittest." As Carnegie worked out the meaning of the term, it demonstrated that the rich had not succeeded through skulduggery or exploitation but through superior fitness. Among humans as among animals, the strong always triumphed over the weak. In flowing to the ablest members of a society, wealth obeyed the natural law of competition. Whether or not one approved of the law was immaterial, Carnegie said, "for good or ill, it is upon us, beyond our power to alter, and, therefore, to be accepted and made the best of. It is a waste of time to criticize the inevitable."

Spencer's theory also appealed to Carnegie's innate optimism because it seemed to promise that civilization would always advance. There was no need for communism, socialism, or any other radical social experiment, Carnegie wrote. "The blessed doctrine of evolution, the knowledge that humanity is endowed with an instinct for the good and the true and must turn to that as the sunflower to the sun, will keep us buoyant with hope as we ascend." Through the wondrous filter of survival of the fittest, each generation was destined to be stronger and finer than the last.

The roots of Carnegie's philosophy can be found in Spencer, but the branches shoot off in many directions. The definitive biography of Carnegie, by Joseph Frazier Wall, points out that Carnegie misunderstood Spencer on several key points and argues that American historians have overstated the influence of Spencer's "Social Darwinism" on the capitalists of the Gilded Age. The conventional interpretation holds that Carnegie, John D. Rockefeller, and others were mesmerized by the notion of survival of the fittest because it removed the taint of immorality from their ferociously competitive business tactics: How could they be evil if they were acting in accord with a law of nature? "A few of the great entrepreneurs . . . were moved to write, or to have ghostwritten, the story of their success, but one looks in vain through the pages of these success manuals for an expression of the Social Darwinist credo," Wall noted. He also observed that Carnegie and his fellow industrialists did not in fact let the law of competition take its natural course in a free market. They lobbied for legislation to further their interests and regularly entered into pooling agreements designed to ruin competitors and inflate prices.

Throughout his life, however, Carnegie was attracted to Spencer's ideas of survival of the fittest and the steady, upward progress of humankind. "All is well, since all grows better," Carnegie liked to say. Even before Spencer, the idea had gained currency through the writings of Frédéric Bastiat, a French economist, and Arthur Latham Perry, an American professor of political economy. Like Adam Smith before them, they believed that the best economy, for rich and poor, was a free one. In such a world, Bastiat wrote, "the good of each tends to the good of all, as the good of all tends to the good of each." Perry applied Bastiat to business, observing that the demand for labor grew with the accumulation of capital, "and capital therefore is the poor man's best friend." Capitalists needed productive enterprises for their capital, and productive enterprises needed workers. So capital and labor came together in "a relation of mutual dependence, which God had ordained and which, though man may temporarily disturb it, he can never overthrow." With the laws of God and nature on their side, the capitalists of the late nineteenth century were indeed blessed.

Carnegie had begun his gospel with the hope that if the wealth of the few could be administered for the good of the many, "the ties of brotherhood [would] still bind together the rich and poor in harmonious relationship." Underneath this hope lay an uneasy sense that the ties had begun to fray. The jobs and the vast array of cheap goods made possible by industrial capitalism were creating unprecedented heights of material well-being, but there were also rumblings from labor, the poor, and social critics. In *Looking Backward,* a best-selling novel published shortly before "The Gospel of Wealth," Edward Bellamy dipped his pen in lye to satirize the compassion of the rich for the poor:

[C]ommiseration was frequently expressed by those who rode for those who had to pull the coach, especially when the vehicle came to a bad piece in the road. . . . At such times the passengers would call down encouragingly to the toilers . . . exhorting them to patience and holding out hopes of possible compensation in another world for the hardness of their lot, while others contributed to buy salves and liniments for the crippled and injured.

A decade earlier, in *Progress and Poverty,* Henry George had looked at America and seen "an immense wedge . . . being forced, not underneath society, but through society. Those who are above the point of separation are elevated, but those who are below are crushed down." Society was like a boat, George said. Progress depended not on the total exertion of the crew but on the exertion directed at moving the boat forward. Society was an enterprise of man with man, not man against man, which meant that cooperation, not competition, was the fundamental law of nature.

Carnegie saw no need to answer George or Bellamy, although he gleefully reported that Herbert Spencer had read a few pages of *Progress and Poverty,* flung it down, and pronounced it "trash." "The Gospel of Wealth" did not address the discontented except to remind them that while the law of competition was "sometimes hard on the individual, it is best for the race, because it insures survival of the fittest in every department." He was preaching to his fellow millionaires, reminding them of Christ's warning about camels passing through the eyes of needles with more ease than rich men entering heaven. He closed by assuring them that salvation lay in shedding one's millions: "against such riches as these no bar will be found at the gates of Paradise."

It was a bravura performance. Industrialists applauded because Carnegie's equation of success with fitness assured them they were a superior class. By promising that the rich would do the proper thing and that they were the proper ones to do it, the gospel gave clergymen a balm for churchgoers who fretted about the wedge between haves and have-nots. William Lawrence, Episcopal bishop of Massachusetts and son of one of New England's wealthiest textile manufacturers, declared that godliness was "in league with riches" and that prosperity was making the national character "sweeter, more joyous, more unselfish, more Christlike." Lawrence admitted that there were abuses but believed they would disappear. Having learned how to win wealth, Americans would learn how to use it, he predicted.

Strivers welcomed the gospel because it validated their worship of success. Unlike impoverished Europeans, poor Americans did not dream of overthrowing the rich, they dreamed of joining them. The pull of dreams of wealth was so strong, wrote one critic of big business, that the United States had no home too poor to hope "that out of its fledglings one may grow the hooked claw that will make him a millionaire."

Americans took encouragement from Carnegie and from a Baptist minister named Russell H. Conwell, who exhorted them to glory in their material desires. Getting rich was a noble aspiration, Conwell asserted in "Acres of Diamonds," a sermon that made him a millionaire by drawing thousands of huge, paying crowds as "The Gospel of Wealth" spread across the land. Wealth, said Conwell, "is one great test of a person's usefulness to others. Money is power. Every good man and woman ought to strive for power, to do good with it when obtained." Here, from one of God's ordained, was a benediction for the ambitious, release at last from the manacles of ambivalence clamped on by the Puritans.

The Reverend Hugh Price Hughes, one of England's most influential Protestant clerics, begged to differ. Calling Carnegie and the rest of his class "an anti-Christian phenomenon, a social monstrosity, and a grave political peril," Hughes said that in a truly Christian country, millionaires would not exist because Jesus had forbidden the accumulation of wealth. Hughes took as his text Matthew 6:19, "Lay not up for yourselves treasures upon the earth." Carnegie's argument that great enterprises required great surpluses of wealth no longer held, Hughes maintained, because the individual capitalist had been supplanted by the corporation, with its legion of shareholders. Millionaires were not the natural result of competition, they were "the unnatural product of artificial social regulations. They flourish portentously in the unhealthy forcing-house of Protection, but everything else fades and dies beside them." Hughes assumed that Carnegie knew his claims of superior fitness were twaddle, but "if he thinks that he has made this great pile . . . off his own bat, let him set up business on a solitary island, and see how much he can net annually without the cooperation of 'his twenty-thousand men' and the ceaseless bounties of . . . Congress." From Moses to Edward Bellamy, Hughes added, no thoughtful person had ever imagined an ideal state without trying to provide against excess wealth.

Carnegie, who rarely paused to answer critics, took time for Hughes. In a reply defiantly entitled "The Advantages of Poverty," he insisted that poverty was a blessing and that laying up treasure was a public service.

> Consider the millionaire who continues to use his capital actively in enterprises which give employment and develop the resources of the world. He who manages the ships, the mines, the factories, cannot withdraw his capital, for this is the tool with which he works such beneficent wonders. . . . [I]t becomes the duty of the millionaire to increase his revenues. The struggle for more is completely freed from selfish or ambitious taint and becomes a noble pursuit. Then he labors not for self, but for others; not to hoard, but to spend. The more he makes, the more the public gets. His whole life is changed from the moment that he resolves to become a disciple of the gospel of wealth, and henceforth he labors to acquire that he may wisely administer for others' good. His daily labor is a daily virtue.

Hughes was not the only clergyman who found Carnegie's gospel long on questionable assumptions. Insisting that the concentration of wealth was the natural result of competition did not make it so, noted the Reverend William Jewett Tucker of Massachusetts. Nor was it necessarily so that wealth was best administered by the few. The issue was not "How shall private wealth be returned to the public?" but, "Why should it exist in such bewildering amounts?" Better to divide the pie fairly in the first place, through increased wages, than to expropriate it and then decide who did or did not deserve a slice.

Power and fairness were delicate issues in a nation that publicly professed the equality of all men but privately idealized the man whose wealth put him far above his equals. Carnegie tried to avoid these brambles as he avoided all brambles: he insisted they did not exist. Responsible rich men would do the right thing, as a "refuge from self-questioning" if nothing else. The responsible rich men, it went without saying, reserved the privilege of deciding what the right thing was and how it would be done. Mark Twain, who often teased Carnegie about his fortune, once wrote him asking for a dollar and a half for a hymnal. "Don't send the hymn-book, send the money," Twain said. "I want to make the selection myself." Believing that the rich would not have become so unless they were superior, Carnegie naturally believed that they should do the choosing. Like most of his class, he preferred philanthropy to higher wages because it gave him more control over the ultimate use of the money. He attributed his choice to prudence rather than a desire for control: higher wages were too often wasted "on more extravagant living." Carnegie's gospel also left much to chance. There was no way to compel millionaires to do as he did, no guarantee that the gifts would go where they were most needed.

ON occasion Carnegie complained that the way of the giver was hard, but no amount of criticism diminished his conviction or his determination to shame the greedy into embracing his faith. "I wish to see the 'Robber Baron' completely exterminated," he told a senator. "The Gospel of Wealth" was only one of Carnegie's attempts to set himself apart from the tycoons of his age. Even before delivering his sermon, he had unilaterally declared peace between capital and labor, confident that both camps were amenable to reason and that his reason would prevail because he had lived on both sides of the divide. Writing in the *Forum,* a leading journal of opinion, Carnegie had astonished his fellow capitalists (including his business partner Henry Clay Frick) by asserting that workingmen had the same "sacred" right to unions as manufacturers had to their alliances. He advised management to build loyalty by conferring regularly with committees of workmen, listening to their problems, and solving them whenever possible. He told of cutting the time between paychecks from four weeks to two after learning that when his workmen were short of cash, they had to pay merchants an extra 25 percent for the privilege of buying on credit. To avoid quarrels over wages, he urged business to adopt a sliding scale linking pay to prices so that employer and employed would prosper together in good times and share the burden in bad. Strikes and lockouts were pointless, he said, because the strong would always overpower the weak; capital and labor should settle their differences through arbitration. Free advice seldom being valued at more than the price, the appearance of Carnegie's article was followed by a rash of violent strikes and a bloody riot in Chicago's Haymarket Square.

Carnegie's denunciation of greed in "The Gospel of Wealth" and his sympathy with the aspirations of labor may have impressed some, but by 1892 it was plain that his own workers were not among them. As a three-year labor contract neared expiration at the company's plant in Homestead, Pennsylvania, management and representatives of the Amalgamated Association of Iron and Steel Workers found themselves squaring off for a conflict with no apparent resolution. The expiring contract tied wages to increases in productivity, and productivity had soared. Since most of the increase could be traced to $4 million worth of new machinery purchased by the company, management argued that the company deserved a larger share of the profits. Homestead's union, which represented a minority of the plant's 3,800 workers but bargained for all of them, strenuously disagreed. Because the new machines allowed one man to do the work of four, the union said, it hardly seemed fair to cut his pay. The company countered with talk of a recession. Demand had already slackened, and prices were falling, so the company's workforce and its lowest wage would have to be cut.

Once again Carnegie took out his pen, this time to write a book explaining the world of business to his workers. Saying that he was no longer involved in managing the company, he claimed to have no motive other than to give his audience "the truth about the questions of today." And the truth was that the world was awash in good things. Poverty was good because it sired greatness. Millionaires were good because they produced "the food of the race" in the form of employment and a rising standard of living. Corporations were good because they gave the small investor a chance to reap the same profits as the capitalist. Profits were good because the surplus from one enterprise furnished the capital for the next and gave the millionaire an incentive to risk his capital in new ventures. Even the "boiling" of the social engine, so feared by conservatives, was good because the steam turned the wheels of progress. Adding up all of these good things, Carnegie deduced that labor was better off than ever before and that its lot would continue to improve. But improvement would come gradually—through "evolution, not revolution."

The book went unpublished, perhaps because Carnegie sensed that it would inflame his workers. In addition to threatening cuts in staff and pay, the company announced that it would no longer recognize the union. Andrew Carnegie, friend of labor, drafted the announcement. "As the vast majority of our employees are Non-Union, the Firm has decided that the minority must give place to the majority," he wrote. "These works will therefore be necessarily Non-Union after the expiration of the present agreement." He pledged that pay at Homestead would be the same as at the company's other plants and held out the possibility that "desirable" employees laid off at Homestead might find work in another of the company's mills.

In the spring, Carnegie went off to Scotland as usual, leaving Frick, partner in charge of Homestead, with orders to shut the plant if the workers refused management's offer. Frick underscored the company's resolve by turning Homestead into a fortress complete with wooden palisade, searchlight, and electrified barbed wire.

At the end of June, the union declined Carnegie's terms, and all of Homestead's workers walked off their jobs. Expecting as much, Frick had hired three hundred armed Pinkerton guards to protect the mill. In hopes of reaching the factory unnoticed, they came by barge. The ruse failed, and on July 6, 1892, sharpshooters on the riverbank kept the barge under fire from dawn until four in the afternoon, when the Pinkertons waved a white flag. Promised sanctuary in the town jail, they came ashore only to be pummeled by a mob. By nightfall four

Pinkertons were dead, the rest injured. One of them told a newspaper reporter, "I am ready to go again, but I would rather have something else to do."

From Scotland Carnegie cabled his imperatives to Frick. "Never employ one of these rioters. Let grass grow over works. Must not fail now. You will easily win next trial." Within ten days Homestead was humming again, manned by workers who needed jobs more than they wanted a union. The company's victory was total—longer hours, lower pay, no union—but seven Pinkertons and nine strikers had been killed. Some American newspapers deplored the company's tactics, others deplored the violence of the strikers, but few delivered the sting of Carnegie's critics in Britain. The *Saturday Review* asked how this fervent democrat could "reduce his workmen's wages for the benefit of his own pocket, for all the world as if he were himself a Tory; and how, when the men exhibited the noble rage of freemen, he could hire barge-loads of bravos, who actually shot the sovereign people whom Mr. Carnegie loved so much." The *Sunday Times* of London accused him of exploiting workers "in order, presumably, that he may surround himself with still more luxuries, while flinging a library here and a swimming bath there to those among whom he deigns to dwell." Carnegie responded with his customary silence, but privately he wrote his friend William Gladstone, the British prime minister, "The pain I suffer increases daily. The Works are not worth one drop of human blood, I wish they had sunk."

However acute, Carnegie's pain did not lead to apologies or even to expressions of self-doubt. Just as he had sought to distance himself from the robber barons, he now backed away from Frick. Carnegie decided that his "young and rather too rash partner" could have prevented the mayhem by offering to wait until the workers agreed to accept the company's terms. Carnegie also claimed he had been helpless to intervene because he long since had removed himself from management. But his powerlessness had not kept him from barring Homestead's union or from telegraphing orders to Frick. Convenient as Carnegie found it to say that he no longer held the baton, he picked it up whenever he wanted, and his partners were more or less forced to stand by for the simple reason that he owned more than half the company's stock.

Early in 1893, Carnegie braved a trip to Homestead. No fact-finding mission, the trip was designed to help the citizenry forget what had happened. As he told the press, he had come to look to the future and bury the past, which he wanted "banished, as a horrid dream." Addressing the people of Homestead, he praised Henry Clay Frick and once more presented himself as a silent partner in the company's affairs. Eliding over his switch from friend to foe of unions, he declared that capital and labor were brothers and there could be no gain when they saw one another as enemies.

Carnegie left Homestead convinced that he alone understood the laborer. "No one knows the virtues, the noble traits of the true work-ing man who has not lived with them," he wrote to Whitelaw Reid, editor of the *New York Tribune*. During his visit he had talked with sev-eral workmen, all of whom had told him, "Ah, Mr. Carnegie, if you had only been here it never would have happened." Unfortunately, he had been "powerless," he told Reid. "I was all ready to return by the first steamer, but as my appearance on the scene would have implied Mr. Frick's virtual deposition and he had begged me not to do this, I remained abroad."

Soon after the journey to Homestead, Carnegie climbed back into the pulpit to preach the gospel of wealth, doubtless hoping his words would drown out those of his detractors. This time the public was more skeptical. Reporting that Carnegie had called philanthropy the "sweetest pleasure" of life, the Albany *Express* scoffed, "It is understood that in Homestead, Pa., there are opinions which do not exactly coin-cide with Mr. Carnegie's." In the judgment of *New York People,* the richest tycoon was the one who extracted the most from his workers, "and that's all there is to it. It is not a matter of brains, but of exploiting-power." The *Catholic Review* observed that if millionaires paid "the full amount of wages due by Christian justice, they would not have as much wealth as they now hold. They are carrying around as their own money that which ought to belong to their employees."

Pennsylvanians chose not to banish the horrid dream of Homestead. Carnegie offered to build libraries in forty-six of the state's towns, but twenty turned him down. In Pittsburgh, Carnegie's planned gifts of a museum, concert hall, and library met with such vehemence that he had to beg the indulgence of the citizenry. Fair play, he told them, required the people of Pittsburgh "to separate the donor and his many faults from libraries and music halls and art galleries, which have none." Having separated himself from the robber barons, Henry Clay Frick, and the tragedy of Homestead, Carnegie had no difficulty in asking that his munificence be detached from his methods.

Pittsburgh agreed to the gifts, and Carnegie went confidently on, sure that he was right, sure that he was misunderstood, sure that his gospel would prevail. When 1893 brought a stock market crash and a depression, he even softened his opposition to aiding the needy. Writing to a fellow businessman in Pittsburgh, he volunteered to put up as much as $5,000 a day to match funds raised by the local Citizens' Relief Committee.

> You know my views, and how often I have written and said that of every thousand dollars spent to-day in so-called charity, nine hundred and fifty dollars of it had better been thrown into the sea. But the business condition in this country, and especially in Pittsburgh, creates a temporary emergency in which money can be beneficially devoted, not to giving alms, but to giving work to worthy men who are idle through no fault of their own. . . . These are terrible times, but I trust that the people will not become discouraged. They will soon pass away, and the Republic will resume its prosperous career. Meanwhile they are fraught with precious opportunity for the rich to show that when real trouble comes, the rich and poor, employer and employed, are at heart brothers, allies essential to the prosperity of each other—not antagonists. If wealth does its duty in Pittsburgh in this crisis, the good feeling produced will be no small compensation, even for the suffering endured.

Was it possible to purchase good feeling? Carnegie hoped so, and despite Pennsylvania's hostility, he continued to believe that society gained more from the rich than vice versa. He made the point again and again, like a teacher who will not stop until the students demonstrate that they have learned the lesson. "While the commonweal obtains so much from the use of wealth, even in the hands of the few, what does the Millionaire receive?" he asked in one tutorial. Not happiness, he said. Great fortunes brought so many burdens that "much of the pleasure of life is forfeited." Not great luxury, except for an ostentatious and reprehensible few. The millionaire got "a living," and society got the rest. "It will be a great mistake for the community to shoot the millionaires, for they are the bees that make the most honey, and contribute most to the hive even after they have gorged themselves full."

Those who said millionaires at one end of the scale meant paupers at the other were wrong, Carnegie said. "Millionaires can only grow amid general prosperity, and this very prosperity is largely promoted by their exertions." The exertions were total. "The businessman pure and simple plunges into and tosses upon the waves of human affairs without a life-preserver in the shape of salary; he risks all." His fortune came from his profits, not his paycheck, and profits piled up in good times, when workmen's wages also rose. Capital and labor prospered together.

Carnegie liked to demonstrate the link between the fortunes of capital and labor by saying that the wages at Homestead were the highest in the world. But the claim was unfounded. As he was telling the press that wages averaged $2.90 a day in 1895, his own partner, Henry Clay Frick, was admitting to $2.20. And during the depression of 1893–94, when steel industry wages fell 14 percent, pay at Carnegie's company dropped by 60 percent.

Few of Carnegie's distinguished contemporaries dared to challenge him. E. L. Godkin of the *Nation* and the other leading pundits of the age were a timid bunch, and although they often lamented the predations of millionaires, they feared anarchists more than capitalists. As one historian of the period has observed, "more than any other group in America, businessmen represented property, and property represented order and stability." To pillory the capitalist merely gave aid and comfort to the bomb thrower.

The world as Carnegie saw it offered ample proof of the virtues of capitalism. Instead of railing against the "abnormal gains" of the few, the malcontent ought to join them, buying stock in their enterprises so that he too could share in the profits, Carnegie said: "the door is open, the path is free, and he can be shareholder and capitalist in any branch." Carnegie waved away the socialists by arguing that progressive industrialists were already working toward shorter hours, cooperative stores, pension funds, and other so-called socialist reforms. Communism was silly—a cult of "Rainbow Chasers."

So marvelous was the machine of capitalism that Carnegie, an inveterate social tinkerer, could think of only two improvements: profit sharing and taxes. Profit sharing, he decided in his seventies, would give workers an even larger stake in a company's fortunes than the sliding wage scale he had once advocated. In matters of tax policy, he was stoutly progressive—a proud traitor to his class. A steep federal tax on imported luxuries would hurt no one, he informed President Grover Cleveland in 1894. The masses did not indulge in such articles, and the wealthy would continue to buy what they pleased. After opposing an income tax, he eventually endorsed the idea and argued that it should be higher for the rich than the poor and higher on dividends and other unearned income than on wages. Carnegie also believed that a graduated inheritance tax would turn many a millionaire into a philanthropist. It apparently did not occur to him that such a tax might be avoided by spending the money.

WITH Carnegie's reverence for millionaires came a deep ambivalence about the have-nots. He esteemed poverty but loathed the poor, unaware of the paradox of viewing penury as the cradle of greatness while also believing that the ranks of the poor abounded in drunkards, vagabonds, and idlers. As relief rolls swelled and benevolent societies multiplied, so did tales of welfare cheats and bogus philanthropies. Carnegie swallowed them whole and insisted that every loafer sup-

ported by charity was "a source of moral infection to the neighborhood." He called for an end to the "mawkish sensibility" for the unfor-
tunates that softheaded social reformers called the "submerged tenth."
Those at the bottom had to be taught that "only through change of
habits can rewards of life be theirs." The only true charity was "that
which will help others to help themselves, and place within the reach
of the aspiring the means to climb."

Carnegie did not see the role that low wages played in keeping the
poor poor, nor did he sufficiently appreciate that many other penniless
families cherished the same high standards his own parents had had. In
Progress and Poverty, Henry George repeatedly used the word
"embrute" to describe poverty's effect on the human spirit, but in
Carnegie's mind, the poor were to blame for their brutishness while
poverty itself was a hallowed estate. He never thought to ask how, if
poverty were so honorable, the poor could be so devoid of honor.

Having written off the "submerged tenth," Carnegie focused his
philanthropy on what he called "the swimming tenth"—the hard-
working poor "who strive to keep their heads above water as self-
supporting and self-respecting members of the community." Of the
$350 million he gave away, more than 80 percent went to organizations
promoting education. Beyond the libraries were technical schools, colleges and universities, the Carnegie Institution for scientific research,
and the first pension fund for college faculty members.

In 1909, speaking at the dedication of the Brooklyn Public Library,
he remarked that Americans of the new century lived in an age of giving, with charitable organizations for every conceivable cause. He had
even heard of a Christian society for the conversion of the Jews, he
said, adding that he had also heard of an elderly Christian woman who
refused to contribute on the ground that "the Jews were quite rich
enough to convert themselves."

Andrew Carnegie was so rich that his greatest difficulty was getting
rid of his money. His coffers were like the Augean stables. He shoveled
and shoveled, but his wealth continued to pile up. By 1911, when he
was seventy-five years old and had given away $180 million, he still had

$170 million to go. Fearing he would die a hypocrite, he resorted to a gigantic shovel—a $125 million endowment, creating the world's largest philanthropic organization, the Carnegie Corporation of New York. Chartered to "promote the advancement and diffusion of knowledge among the people of the United States" through support of educational institutions, libraries, "useful publications," and other "appropriate" means, the Carnegie Corporation marked the end of an era. Just as the individual entrepreneur had been replaced by the corporation, the individual philanthropist was giving way to the foundation. The sums had grown too large, the tasks too complex, for administration by even the fittest member of the species.

Andrew Carnegie spent his life building bridges—spans across rivers, links between people and ideas. The millions he bestowed upon research and education gave passage from darkness to light, making the unknown knowable and carrying knowledge to the unknowing. His libraries, and the thousands of imitations they inspired, were bridges to learning, self-improvement, and pleasure. Free and open to all, they were a magnificent creation.

As a builder of bridges between social classes, Carnegie accomplished little. His relations with his own workers were paternalistic at best. When he laid a plank across the trench between capital and labor, neither side trusted that it would hold. He had leapt the canyon between poverty and wealth, but he seemed incapable of comprehending either condition except in terms of his own experience. He could not see the millionaire as anything but a hero, the creator of prosperity for the masses. By repeating this view in numberless speeches and magazine articles, Carnegie managed to give the millionaire's power, methods, and wealth more legitimacy, and a kinder face, than they had ever had. His view of millionaires would meet no serious challenge from Americans until the Great Depression.

Believing that an impoverished childhood was the surest springboard to achievement, Carnegie did not notice that the springboard failed 99 percent of the time. Nor did he pause to reflect that if poverty were indeed the ideal beginning of life, there could be nothing remarkable in the success of poor boys like himself. The contradictions are of more than historical interest, because they still complicate American attitudes toward poverty. Modern tales of poor boys who make good invariably present them as both the conquerors and the beneficiaries of poverty. The myth endures because it reinforces the American faith in the individual's power of self-transformation and assures the morally anxious that poverty does not embrute.

Carnegie read and traveled widely, thought about what he observed, diligently pursued facts, and then formulated his views. He had an open mind and felt no shame in changing it; what others derided as inconsistency, he regarded as intellectual evolution. But ultimately he was the soul of reasonableness, not of reason, unable to see the rickety assumptions under his grand conclusions. Assuming that the millionaire's success was proof of his superiority, he was blind to the contributions that governmental policies, business practices, and social conditions make to an individual's success or failure. While his unflagging optimism carried him over many hurdles, it also stunted his understanding of social unrest. Contemplating the violence at Homestead and the critics of his gospel, he found it easier to blame a handful of troublemakers than to face the breadth and depth of labor's discontent.

Still, when flaws are set against merits in the ledger of Andrew Carnegie, the net is an impressive gain. Others had recognized that capitalism is a more efficient tool for accumulating wealth than for distributing it, but Carnegie was virtually alone among his millionaire contemporaries in insisting that the imbalance needed redress. And while his mode of redress, philanthropy, could not spread wealth as broadly as higher wages or an income tax would have, his gospel burrowed into the American conscience. The example he set, and the vigor with which he set it, prodded many of the rich to large-scale generosity.

In the summer of 1919, the death of Andrew Carnegie made the front pages of newspapers on both sides of the Atlantic. First came the obituaries and then the inevitable inquiries: had he kept his promise to give away all his wealth? The gifts made during his life added up to $350,695,653. At his death, there was another $30 million. His will named beneficiaries for all of it: his largest foundation, a handful of favorite causes, longtime servants, the tenant farmers on his Scottish estate, and a private pension fund for old friends. The till was empty.

8

A SHARE OF THE PROFITS

I F THE WORLD had not exploded into war in 1914, the year
might have been best remembered by Americans for a piece
of news from a Midwestern boomtown called Detroit. On
January 5, the Ford Motor Company, a manufacturer of automobiles,
announced that it planned to double its workers' pay to the flabber-
gasting sum of five dollars a day.

Before the announcement, the company's founder and principal
shareholder, Henry Ford, had been largely unknown to the public, but
within days, citizens across the country knew precisely what they
thought of him. Fellow capitalists, who long had preached the virtues
of low wages, called him a turncoat and a fool. Labor organizers publicly conceded that the Five-Dollar Day was a "plum" for workers and
privately worried that Ford's generosity would render unions unnecessary. But most Americans cheered. Even Carnegie, who had done his
share to promote the idea that high wages would be squandered
because workingmen lacked the moral sturdiness to do otherwise,
offered his congratulations. Henry Ford was "a genius," Carnegie said,
"and this splendid gift to his employees foretells the coming of the day
when the distribution of wealth will be far more equal than it ever
has been."

Asked to explain his heresy, Ford told one journalist that he preferred making all his men prosperous to making "a few slave drivers in
our establishment multimillionaires." To another, he said, "Well, let me

put it this way: There's nothing left in life, when all is said and done, but good-fellowship, goodwill. Is there? Nothing else counts. And I like to see folks who work hard get their share. I would rather give our boys a part of the profits than do anything else." The philanthropy of Andrew Carnegie did not excite Henry Ford, and he had no interest in amassing more wealth for himself.

The profits Ford planned to share came from one of the world's most successful consumer products, the Model T. It had begun as a dream, and once the dream took hold, Ford gave himself to it with a fervor that bordered on the religious. "I will build a motor car for the great multitude," he pledged.

> It will be large enough for the family but small enough for the individual to run and care for. It will be constructed of the best materials, by the best men to be hired, after the simplest designs that modern engineering can devise. But it will be so low in price that no man making a good salary will be unable to own one—and enjoy with his family the blessing of hours of pleasure in God's great open spaces.

"This was constantly on his mind and there never was a day we got together that this thing wasn't in front of us," recalled Charles Sorenson, a Ford pattern maker who rose to production chief. Sensing the revolution portended by the dream, Sorenson pictured Henry Ford as Paul Revere and himself as Revere's horse.

Seven feet high and homely as a boiler, the Model T was essentially a pair of boxes on wheels—a large box for the passengers and a smaller one for the mechanical horses. Buyers of the first Model T's, made in 1908, had their choice of black, red, or dark green, but in 1909 Henry Ford decreed that a customer could have "a car painted any color that he wants so long as it is black." By making one model in one color, he meant to concentrate the company's energies on the Model T's technology. The resolutely drab cloak concealed a trove of marvels. The gears were easily shifted, the battery obliging—charms then rare in an automobile. Strong, lightweight steels eased the load on the engine. The suspension system quickly became the industry standard. Tough and dependable, the Model T triumphed over bad roads, no roads, snow, and mud.

From 10,000 cars in 1908, sales more than tripled to 34,000 in 1910, shot to 250,000 in 1913, and would top 1,000,000 in 1920. At $850, the Model T was a bargain of an automobile, and the price headed steadily downhill. By 1913, a new one could be had for $440. Between 1909 and 1913, the earnings of the Ford Motor Company swelled from $3 million to $27 million, and employment grew from 1,700 to 14,000. Henry Ford seemed to have found a way to make the industrial goose lay golden eggs.

THE man, like the machine, was singular. Born on a farm in Dearborn, Michigan, in 1863, Henry Ford was without doubt a genius. "He had a twenty-five-track mind and there were trains going out and arriving on all tracks at all times," a colleague said. "It didn't disturb him. He carried it all easily." Quickly bored and more intuitive than logical, his mind did "not know how to think consecutively, and I doubt if it would do so if it could," one of his executives observed. "It cannot endure the pace and burden of logic, and it cannot listen long to the man who is reaching conclusions through rational processes. . . . He does not reason to conclusions. He jumps at them." Ford read with difficulty and read little, which may explain why he exhibited scant curiosity—and much naiveté and suspicion—about the larger world. Bankers were "parasites," the Great War was part of a Zionist plot to take over the world, history was "bunk."

His eccentricities were many and pronounced, particularly in the realm of the human body. Admiring the shiny, thick hair of some young roustabouts in an oilfield, he too dabbed his hair with kerosene (Standard Oil No. 10, odorless only until it oxidized). For a time, he insisted that sandwiches of grass be served in the company dining room. He disapproved of sugar after his friend Thomas Edison told him the crystals lodged forever in the flesh. Distrustful of doctors, he once imported a Canadian specialist in horse limbs to examine a friend with a blood clot in his leg. Fearing that his dentist would overcharge him, he declined the customary courtesy of being billed after the fact. He took cash to his appointments and settled up on the spot.

Ford had one passion: machines. He collected them in quantities large enough to fill a museum, which he eventually built in Dearborn and named for himself. A colleague who had many occasions to observe Ford's fascination with engines, presses, and the like sensed that they were "living things to him, those machines. He was really a poet. Everything spoke to him. He had a queer feeling about machines just as some men have about horses. A real horseman can enter into the mental states of a horse. He could almost diagnose the arrangement of a machine by touching it. There was a peculiar sympathy between him and it."

A machine is an instrument of control, and control has had few swains as ardent as Henry Ford. While he boasted about the dearth of titles and hierarchy at the Ford Motor Company, the result was a structure that kept him firmly in command: he was the hub of the wheel, everyone else a spoke. Uncomfortable with experts, he insisted that the only way to get a job done right was to give it to a novice. The reason was plain to all who knew him: novices tended to be dependent and submissive, experts did not. As Ernest Liebold, Ford's longtime secretary, put it, "A man not having any particular experience or idea about a thing would keep in touch with Mr. Ford. Mr. Ford in that way was able to control what was being done." Mr. Ford had no skills, innate or acquired, in the arts of leadership and collegiality. He withheld praise because he believed that it puffed men up, and he had a low tolerance for opinions that clashed with his own. Subordinates who dared to dissent were silenced with sarcasm and insults. Liebold noted that once Ford had made up his mind, he was unswayable: "He would rather have the results prove him right or wrong [than] give in to any argument."

Slender and graceful, Ford loved to dance and often hosted parties with a dancing master in attendance. There were rebukes for guests who did not enjoy dancing or preferred their own footwork to Ford's. When he learned about regional variations in square dancing, he set out to eliminate them by hiring an orchestra to record the music in a version he hoped would become the standard.

Henry Ford's outsized impulse to control and systematize would turn factory workers into automatons and drive away many talented managers, but it also helped him to imagine and build a means of producing the first motor car affordable to the masses. Before the Model T, the building of an automobile had proceeded in much the same manner as the building of a boat. The chassis, like the keel, stayed put, and a few craftsmen gathered round to build and add parts till the car was finished. The method worked but was slow and expensive. Henry Ford's great invention was not the Model T but the machine that made it, a dazzlingly efficient behemoth where iron ore for steel came in one end and a shining new automobile rolled out the other.

The factory, first at Highland Park and later on a monumental scale at River Rouge, divided the labor of building an automobile into thousands of simple tasks. Each worker focused on one task, using nuts and bolts and bearings stocked in boxes over his workbench to eliminate wasted time and motion. His task done, he put the component on a slide, where gravity whisked it to the next man. Rather than use his best mechanics and engineers to build cars, Ford used them to design processes that would speed the work of the unskilled. Whatever could be automated was.

Machines were set close together and, where feasible, designed on the vertical to save floor space and lessen physical strain on the worker. To an outsider, the factory floor might look cramped, Ford said, but the machines were "scientifically arranged, not only in the sequence of operations, but to give every man and every machine every square inch that he requires and, if possible, not a square inch, and certainly not a square foot, more than he requires. Our factory buildings are not intended to be used as parks."

But neither were the mills to be dark and satanic. Concrete floors were sheathed in wood to alleviate fatigue and leg cramps. Believing cleanliness essential to morale, Ford deployed a janitorial army of hundreds, and, he wrote, "dark corners which invite expectoration have been painted white." A staunch foe of tobacco, Ford once ordered a manager to ban chewing in the plant. After five months of frustration, the manager gave up. Ford issued a new edict requiring chewers to buy little paper cuspidors from the company for a penny apiece. It was a source of managerial pride that the venture netted $2,000 in a month.

In 1912, when a manager told Ford about the conveyor belts he had just seen in a Chicago meat-packing plant, Ford quickly copied the idea. Ford's moving assembly line, fed by tributary belts carrying parts to the appropriate points along the line, appeared in 1913. Assembly time shrank by 88 percent.

SURVEYING their mechanical wonderland in 1913, Ford and his lieutenants saw only one flaw: employees hated their jobs. They worked nine hours a day, six days a week, for subsistence wages. Most had neither the money for a Model T nor the leisure to enjoy it. By the company's own admission, its foremen were "unintelligent and often abusive" in supervising their charges. Absenteeism was high (10 percent on a typical day), and most workers quit after a few months—easy to do in a time when the Sunday newspapers bulged with Help Wanted ads and paychecks were much the same everywhere. "Every Monday morning department foremen were at their wits' end, surveying the losses to other local establishments and trying to fit green employees into the gaps," Allan Nevins and Frank Ernest Hill wrote in their three-volume history of Henry Ford and his company.

The company's personnel chief, John R. Lee, was assigned to investigate. Well liked throughout Ford, Lee was described by one worker as "quiet, genteel, and what you would call a gentleman 100 percent." In talking with workers, Lee discovered that foremen were peremptory in firing employees, often demanded kickbacks for hirings and promotions, and occasionally resorted to physical brutality. The company also had allowed more than sixty wage scales to evolve over time and had given foremen broad latitude in setting pay—practices that sowed confusion and mistrust.

Problems abounded outside the factory as well. Between 1900 and

1910, as immigrants streamed into the United States, Detroit's population swelled from 287,000 to nearly 500,000 and would double in the next decade. Newcomers jammed into boardinghouses. The immigrant family lucky enough to find a house often squeezed into a corner of it and rented out the rest. Indoor plumbing being a novelty, the tenants frequently converted bathtubs to coal bins and bathrooms to storage space. "Water for washing had to be taken from the yard," a Ford representative reported after a visit to one such home. "Think, now, of a foundry man, when he comes home in the winter time, and needs a bath!" Children were sent to work, alcoholism and gambling flourished, merchants exploited the ignorance of the newcomers. Decades ahead of his time, John Lee understood that when employees come to work in the morning, they do not check their lives at the door.

Henry Ford was receptive to Lee's observations because they paralleled his own. In 1913, on a walk through the factory with his adolescent son, Edsel, they had seen two workers in a fistfight. Henry's embarrassment led him to wonder about the causes of such behavior, and he intuited that low wages were to blame. The Ford family and the handful of others who owned the company received huge dividends, Ford executives were rewarded with large bonuses, and Model T buyers reaped the benefits of falling prices, but the Ford worker remained mired in a poverty that worked against his better angels. Henry Ford concluded that sharing the wealth could change that. "Give them a decent income and they will live decently—will be glad to do so," he said.

What they need is the opportunity to do better, and some one to take a little personal interest in them—some one who will show that he had faith in them. . . . Blindfold me and lead me down there into the street and let me lay my hands by chance on the most shiftless and worthless fellow in the crowd and I'll bring him in here, give him a job with a wage that offers him some hope for the future, some prospect of living a decent, comfortable and self-respecting life, and I'll guarantee that I'll make a man out of him.

To Henry Ford, low wages were a scourge because they deprived the masses of purchasing power. "What good is industry if it be so unskillfully managed as not to return a living to everyone concerned?" he wanted to know. "No question is more important than that of wages—most of the people of the country live on wages. The scale of their living—the rate of their wages—determines the prosperity of the country."

Out of these convictions came the Ford Motor Company's announcement of the Five-Dollar Day, four thousand new jobs, and a reduction of the workday from nine hours to eight. Shortening the workday enabled the factory to run around the clock, on three shifts, a change intended to increase efficiency in order to keep Model T prices on the descent. And that in turn was intended to assure continued strong sales.

Ford was willing to share the wealth, but, like Andrew Carnegie, he worried that paying workers more than they needed to survive would lead them into self-indulgence. "We want to pay the men and pay them well so they can live well, but we don't want to make them reckless," he said. To save them from themselves, he decided that only about half of the celebrated five dollars would be paid as wages. The rest would be profit sharing, which a worker would not receive unless his personal life measured up to the standards of Henry Ford.

The profit-sharing plan was open to almost everyone with six months' service, the exceptions being men under twenty-two and the 1,500 women on the payroll. Both groups were excluded because of an assumption that they had no dependents, although a young man could become eligible by proving that relatives relied on him for support. Asked why women were treated differently, Ford officials offered various explanations: women were mercurial ("likely to throw up their positions at any time, without notice for any reason that may happen to influence them") and frivolous ("Women go to work to make a little more to put on their backs and swell around with when they are hunting for a man!"). Ford's women workers did not share in the profits until 1916, when President Woodrow Wilson, at the urging of

Helen Keller and other female suffragists, convinced Henry Ford to end the injustice.

The profit-sharing plan was one of the most ambitious experiments in human reformation ever undertaken by an American employer. To carry it out, Ford created a Sociological Department, headed by John Lee, and authorized him to organize a corps of one hundred investigators to look into workers' lives. Lee saw only good in the design. Detroit had become the Balkans in miniature, full of quarreling ethnic fiefdoms run by leaders determined to resist one another and fend off the forces working to turn all immigrants into some facsimile of the middle-class American. Lee hoped the Sociological Department would "break down the barrier" between the company and the various groups of newcomers and "get them on the plane we are" so that everyone would "understand what we are driving at."

By the end of January 1914, Ford investigators were crisscrossing Detroit in Model T's, knocking on employees' doors, and filing reports at headquarters. A company pamphlet explained that the investigator should spend his time "going from one place to another learning all he can about the men whom he is asked to investigate.

> He finds out how they live, what the conditions are in their homes, how they spend their evenings, what recreations they indulge in, how much money they have saved, how much they send abroad, how many persons are dependent upon them, and, in fact, everything possible that will aid in the smallest way to determine whether they are to receive a share of the Ford profits. . . . Please throw into the investigation of each case a deep, personal interest, and state as briefly and concisely as you can all of the facts and features necessary for well-rounded judgment. The honesty of a man in making frank statements, and the home conditions particularly, are of vital importance.

Calling on the family of James O'Brien, a foreman in the factory's paint shop, a Ford investigator found "a small house on the outskirts of town. All neat and clean. She looks prim. They look thrifty, live happily. The yard is in nice shape. Plants all covered. You can see they take an interest in what they have and care for it." The O'Briens were a model Ford family—tidy, prudent, content.

But for every James O'Brien there was a Joe Kostruba, a recent immigrant living in "squalid, cramped attic quarters" with a wife and five "grimy" children. Although Mrs. Kostruba worked, the family was in debt to the landlord, the butcher, and the grocer. They had no money in the bank, and cash on hand totaled six cents. The Ford Motor Company treated such discoveries as calls to action. The investigator ordered a basket of food, bought soap and clothing, settled the Kostrubas' bills, lent them fifty dollars, and arranged for Joe to be paid daily until the crisis passed. Ultimately the company resettled the Kostrubas in a five-room cottage and helped them furnish it.

Inevitably, the investigations bred resentment. Some workers felt spied upon, interfered with, and angry with Ford's claim to such a sweeping prerogative. To defuse these feelings and to persuade workers that the Sociological Department's mission was brotherly, Lee called the investigators together for a series of talks in the spring and summer of 1914. "Do not go into anybody's house in a way that you would not want them to come into yours," he counseled. He wanted them to proceed with "diplomacy, ingenuity and gentlemanly qualities." Questions were to be phrased carefully, compliments were as important as criticisms, and criticisms were to be accompanied by concrete suggestions for improvement. Arguments were to be avoided, as were questions "that anybody could twist or turn around against us and reasoned into news items to be spread broadcast through the country." All the company needed to know, Lee said, was that the employee was using his money wisely. But reaching such a conclusion put the investigator in the uncomfortable position of having to ask a man to show his bank book and divulge the details of his finances. "We are a little too greedy to know what Mr. Ford's plan has done," Lee admitted.

For outsiders who thought Mr. Ford a little too greedy to know what his employees were doing, Lee had a thoughtful answer. Rather than imitate other allegedly progressive employers, who were building gymnasiums and lunchrooms and beautifying their factories, Ford wanted to give the money directly to the workers, "but in a supervisory sort of way so that the employees would appreciate what it was for, and would use it for that purpose," Lee said. "Henry Ford believes, and so do I, that if we keep pounding away at the root and the heart of the family in the home, that we are going to make better men for future generations."

The company's preoccupation with family life stemmed from Henry Ford's disapproval of divorce and from an observation by one of his executives that family quarrels had "an almost immediate effect on the output of lathes and drill presses." The company sometimes moved unhappy couples to a new home in the belief that a change of quarters would help them "settle into proper relations." Investigators were told to overlook small domestic troubles but squarely face the large ones. When one party appeared to be more at fault than the other, the investigator was to convince the problem maker to admit the fault and the injured party to receive the admission "in the right spirit so that a satisfactory reconciliation may be effected." When the fault was joint, "each should be advised of the kindly feeling the other has in the matter. When this has been accomplished, and they have been called together, there is little doubt of a satisfactory result." It was to be understood that "the object of the Ford Motor Company is to *protect and build up happy homes* and in no way assist in tearing them down."

Divorce was not forbidden, but the divorcing worker who hoped to keep his profit sharing had to prove that his wife was to blame for the breakup. On this point, Henry Ford was motivated by more than a desire to preserve the family. He disliked the legal system and recoiled from the thought of Ford profits being frittered away on lawsuits and alimony.

Investigators were also instructed to verify that a worker who presented himself as married actually was and that the woman he introduced as his wife was indeed his spouse. If the couple could not produce a marriage certificate, the investigator was to ask for other evidence such as passports or children's baptismal certificates. "When accepting documents of this kind," Lee cautioned, "it is well to be certain that they are the property of the person offering them."

Mrs. Kostruba and other working wives were informed that they could no longer have jobs. Unless a wife promised to "stay at home and

assume the obligations she understood when [she] married," her husband would lose his profit sharing. The rules about a family's finances
were less stringent. "We do not consider any one thing preeminently
above all else," Lee explained to a branch manager seeking guidance in
a particular case. "Do not let the fact that he has or has not a bank
account weigh for or against him alone. Look at his habits, the kind of
life he leads, the way he takes care of his family. . . . Good manhood
and a manly standard is not a narrow thing and do not, therefore, let
your consideration of such be narrow."

Good manhood, in the view of Henry Ford and John Lee, was the
clean living embodied in the bourgeois code of virtue: sobriety,
fidelity, responsibility, thrift, industry, and a drive toward self-
improvement. When a worker violated the code—by drunkenness,
adultery, extravagance, or absenteeism—profit sharing was suspended.
The terms of reinstatement provided powerful incentives to reform. If
he returned to the path of righteousness within a month, he recouped
100 percent of the profits withheld. At two months, the share went
down to 75 percent. By the end of five months, he could recover only
25 percent, and if he had not redeemed himself in six months, he forfeited his job along with the profit sharing. The unskilled worker who
lived by the rules would take home almost $800 over six months, while
his unrepentant colleague received only $360, then lost his job. Profits
withheld from intractable workers were given to charity, a practice
meant to disarm cynics ready to accuse the company of keeping the
money for itself.

IN Lee's judgment, the stick attached to the Ford carrot was good for
workers and their families. The man who resented the investigations
tended to be the one who was "drinking up his income and beating
up his wife," Lee said. Everyone who joined the company was encouraged to think of himself as a partner, and the "man who enters into a
partnership with another agrees to conduct himself in a manner that
will not be detrimental to the business." Henry Ford asked no more
than he gave. Pointing out that suspensions were rare and dismissals

even rarer, Lee emphasized that the system had not been designed to punish. "The 'Help the Other Fellow' spirit runs through all we do."

The help included defenses against the flimflam artists drawn to the neighborhoods near the factory by the announcement of the Five-Dollar Day. Determined to keep their hands out of its workers' pockets, Ford instructed managers not to give workers' names to salesmen and forbade them to "form a partnership or have any interests whatever in any scheme to benefit [themselves], or any relative or friend out of the benefits derived by our employees through the profit-sharing plan."

During the profit-sharing plan's first two years, more than eight thousand Ford families decamped to better living quarters, their collective bank balances doubled, and the value of their other assets—mostly life insurance policies, homes, and building lots—swelled by 85 percent. When the U.S. Senate's Commission on Industrial Relations asked Henry Ford whether it was desirable for a corporation to assume so much control over employees, he replied:

> We do not undertake to say what corporations should do in general, but if employers . . . have a genuine, sincere and active interest in the improvement of the conditions of labor and the heartfelt personal interest in the welfare of their employees, no conditions that are irksome or distasteful will be laid upon the men.
>
> Theoretically, some persons may argue that we have no right to inquire how a man lives at home, so long as he does his work at the factory, but we are talking of conditions, not of theories. Our experience leads us to conclude, beyond doubt, that the interest taken in employees as to their individual welfare is most desirable from every standpoint, not only that of the employee and his family, but of the business itself.

The business itself had done well. Production had doubled to more than 530,000 Model T's a year, and in 1916, the company recorded net income of $57 million on sales of $207 million. Knowing that investigators would check up on them, workers went to work; the daily no-show rate dropped from one in ten to one in two hundred. Employee turnover was negligible, suspensions were rare, dismissals even rarer. Statistics from the production line showed impressive gains. A group of workers who had been making 750 radiators in nine hours began turning out 1,300 in eight. Fender makers boosted output by a third. The gas-tank fabricators managed to trim their ranks *and* increase production from 800 to 1,200 tanks per shift. The Five-Dollar Day turned out to be "one of the finest cost cutting moves we ever made," said Charles Sorenson, head of production. The link between higher pay and higher productivity was so strong that he wondered why no one before Ford had understood it. He suspected that similar schemes had not been tried elsewhere because the boards of directors of publicly owned corporations were answerable to stockholders, which was not the case at the privately owned Ford Motor Company.

In fact, nearly two hundred American employers had instituted profit sharing (minus Ford's investigative apparatus). Profit sharing tended to work as long as there were profits to be shared, but the cuts that came with hard times hurt labor more than capital. The tycoon could draw on his reserves of wealth and, if need be, exercise his borrowing power, while the factory hand seldom had more than his income. The imbalance in the burden sharing would lead labor unions of later generations to bargain for wage guarantees rather than take their chances on profits.

For Henry Ford, the sharing of profits was part economics, part theology. W. J. Cameron, a company spokesman and author of many of Henry Ford's essays, said that Ford "thought less of money than any man I ever knew," viewing it merely as one more factor of production, "like the coal pile."

"My gospel is work," Ford said, and he meant to live it by using his money to "make more work for more men." He saw that his employees had helped to create his wealth and believed that "after they have had their wages and a share of the profits, it is my duty to take what remains and put it back into industry in order to create work for more men at higher pay."

"There was something sacred to him about these jobs," Cameron said. "There was something beautiful to him in seeing men go to work in the morning and seeing them in their homes at night, in homes that they owned, and around their own gardens. He believed in that."

Because of the pleasure Henry Ford took in the early successes of the Sociological Department, one experiment in employee welfare easily led to another. Beyond helping a worker become an upstanding family man, for example, Ford aimed to make him thoroughly American. At the Ford English School, established in 1914, 160 employee volunteers taught the language to thousands of immigrant employees. Each class met for three hours a week for a course lasting six to eight months. The lessons, mainly recitations, were designed to teach the rudiments of English along with Ford's dictates on personal hygiene, household management, family relations, mathematics, geography, history, and civics. The course also featured a professor of table manners.

Foreign-born employees came to the school by invitation, but it was an invitation they could not refuse. As a company publication explained, "If a man declines to go to school, the advantages of the training are carefully explained to him. If he still hesitates, he is laid off and given a chance for uninterrupted meditation and reconsideration. He seldom fails to change his mind." Faced with losing their profit sharing, opportunities for promotion, or their jobs, most workers agreed to submit to the advantages of the training.

Ford counted more than fifty nationalities on its factory floor and mixed them willy-nilly in the classroom by way of convincing them that "they are, or should be, Americans, and that former racial, national and linguistic differences are to be forgotten." At a commencement ceremony held in a large auditorium, the stage was set with an immigrant ship on one side and a melting pot on the other. The graduates, clad in native costume and carrying suitcases, entered via the ship's gangplank, marched across the stage and into the melting pot, waited while their teachers stirred the pot with long ladles, and reappeared "dressed in their best American clothes and waving American flags."

In the last years of the twentieth century, as racial and ethnic groups throughout the world have struggled for recognition of their distinctive identities, Ford's Americanizing might be interpreted as one more attempt of the mighty to oppress the weak. Without question, the Ford English School helped to mold workers to the Ford manufacturing machine. Foremen no longer had to leap language barriers, which saved time, reduced errors, and improved safety. But the school also widened access to the opportunities of American society. Whether or not a graduate stayed at Ford, his knowledge of English gave him a mobility he otherwise would have lacked. Ultimately, the common language would help Ford laborers to unionize, something the workers in Andrew Carnegie's steel mills had found impossible for decades after the Homestead strike. As part of their anti-union vigilance, Carnegie and other industrialists routinely assigned Poles to work with Poles, Rumanians with Rumanians, and so on. Thus divided, they were more easily controlled.

With a mixture of motives, Ford opened its doors to Negroes, hiring them first as strikebreakers, then as regular employees in the most menial and dangerous jobs, and finally allowing them onto the assembly line and into departments of skilled workers. Between 1914 and 1941, more than half the Negroes employed by the automobile industry worked at Ford. Only at Ford could they take part in apprenticeship programs, work in racially integrated teams, and, in a few instances, hold supervisory positions.

They owed their opportunities to Henry Ford's personal interest and to a collaboration between the company and a leader of the city's Negro community. In 1919, Ford asked the Reverend Robert L. Bradby, pastor of the city's leading Negro church, to recommend his finest congregants for jobs at Ford. Bradby agreed and promised to exhort his flock to be "steady" in order to "prove the worthiness of colored industrial workers." Bradby also regularly visited Ford's factories, where he mediated racial disputes and encouraged the docility Ford wanted. As affirmative action goes, the 1919 Ford model was primitive, but it created opportunities matched by few other industrial employers at the time. Henry Ford's commitment to integration stopped at the factory gate, however. Fine as he thought it was for whites and blacks to work together, he believed that they should live, worship, and be educated among their own kind.

Ford hired ex-convicts and ordered that their pasts not be discussed. His willingness to give them a chance, Cameron said, arose from his belief that a criminal wasn't really a criminal but "a more adventurous type than the people he lived among; he had enough guts and initiative which if directed in the right channels would make him quite a man."

The disabled were present in large numbers. To place them, the company's chief surgeon, J. E. Mead, surveyed the 8,000 jobs being done in the factory and found that 670 of them could be done efficiently by legless men, 2,637 by one-legged men, none by armless men, 715 by one-armed men, and 10 by the blind. In 1918, 6,095 of the persons on the company's payroll had physical or mental debilities of one sort or another. Ford was even willing to take on tuberculosis patients, whose contagiousness made them pariahs elsewhere. Segregated from the rest of the employees, 900 of them worked in Ford's salvage department, where, it was proudly noted, their labors produced a monthly gain of $70,000.

Workers hospitalized with injuries often stayed on the payroll at their regular pay by doing minor assembly tasks for the factory. The company delivered nuts and bolts to their bedsides and furnished sheets of oilcloth to protect the hospital linens. In Mead's estimation, the work was therapeutic: "The men are much more contented, sleep better at night, eat better and I think recover more rapidly."

AT the end of 1915, as the Sociological Department and the profit-sharing plan neared their second anniversary, John Lee was transferred to Ford's office in Washington, and the social work portfolio passed to a newly hired executive, Samuel Marquis, dean of the Episcopal Cathedral in Detroit. As the dean's children told the story decades later in an interview with a company historian, Ford convinced their father to give up his prestigious ministry with the words "I want you, Mark, to put Jesus Christ into my factory."

Marquis embraced the mission. He changed the name of the Sociological Department to the Educational Department and rechristened investigators with the friendlier-sounding title of of advisers. Once a worker demonstrated that he and his family were living a proper Ford life, his name was added to an "honor roll," and the home visits ceased. The new arrangement allowed advisers to concentrate on hard cases. One Ford worker, for example, was fined fifteen dollars for drinking and made to accompany his adviser on an excursion to buy shoes and food and deliver them to a needy family. To Marquis's delight, the outing had exhilarated the miscreant. "Hell!" he told the adviser. "Why didn't you let me do more?"

In 1916, John Reed, the radical-left journalist about to become famous for his exploits in the Russian Revolution, came to Detroit to write about the profit-sharing revolution at Ford. Reed loathed Marquis on sight and told the readers of *Metropolitan* magazine that Marquis was "a man who for many years preached the gospel of Jesus Christ to the predatory rich so inoffensively that they built him the most sumptuous church in Detroit. He is a smooth-voiced, plausible gentleman with a practical mind."

Marquis proved unflappable. Asked how an employer could justify telling workers what to do with their money, he told Reed, "We try to help them, that's all. It is not a paternal system: it's fraternal. And we find that a man works better when the material conditions of his life are adequate, when he has saved his money, and when his home life is satisfactory." Asked if workers resented the company's intrusions, Marquis said that the kind of workers Ford wanted did not, and if anyone did, he was free to seek employment elsewhere. "I don't think you understand the spirit of our work," he told Reed. "You really can't do justice to it without first being around here for a couple of months."

The fraternal spirit fostered by Lee and Marquis was genuine. Lee had added lawyers and real estate advisers to help employees with mortgage applications, contracts, and the like. Through its own savings and loan association, Ford encouraged thrift and allowed employees to borrow small sums in emergencies. One production superintendent took special pleasure in helping immigrant workers bring family members to the United States.

The higher pay and tight constraints on dismissals gave Ford workers a security they had not known before 1914. Whatever their feelings about Ford's invasions of privacy, their protests were slight. Faced with a choice between good pay and perfect liberty, they inclined toward their wallets. And as objectionable as the company's social programs were in principle, in practice they proved surprisingly benign. One engineer acknowledged that some workers "would gripe to beat hell" about the company's prying but claimed that satisfaction was widespread: "They told me how they dressed the kids and how they got the wife a new dress and how they bought a new stove. . . . 'Come to the house and I'll show you the new curtains.' Boy, they were just tickled pink. They worked their heads off and worked overtime for free sometimes."

THE most serious weakness of the Five-Dollar Day was one the company could not forestall—inflation. Between 1914 and 1919, the cost of living in Detroit doubled, leaving workers no better off than they had been before the announcement of the Five-Dollar Day. To catch up, workers would have needed ten dollars a day, but in January 1919, the company decided that it could afford no more than six. It also turned up the speed of the assembly line, forcing (or enabling, depending on one's point of view) workers to produce more cars per shift.

To help workers stretch their dollars, the Ford Motor Company entered the discount retailing business. The venture started in 1920 with weekly sales of fresh fish, which the company bought wholesale by the boxcar, marked up slightly to cover handling costs, and sold at the side of the tracks near the factory. Soon ten Ford plants featured stores selling meat, fish, groceries, and household necessities such as soap and aspirin, dry goods, shoes, work clothes, underwear, and hosiery.

As plain and practical as the Model T, the stores offered a limited but choice selection of merchandise, all of it tested in the same laboratories where the company tested auto parts. Ford bought in bulk, sold in quantity, spent little on display, hired as few salesclerks as possible, and whisked customers through the store as if they were on an assembly line. Aisles were wide, goods were wrapped in advance wherever possible, and customers checked out at a row of grilled windows of the bank-teller variety. The shopper who wanted credit, delivery service, or fashion advice had to go elsewhere. As the Baltimore *Sun* explained to its readers, "You come there to buy cheap and get good stuff."

Word spread. Employees lent their identification badges to friends, and in 1926, Ford opened the stores to the public. Sightings of liveried chauffeurs and ladies in pearls and Packards were reported with glee. Proud of the success of its new sideline, the company announced that retail sales for the year topped $12 million and even turned a small profit.

Furious, Detroit's merchants called for a boycott of Ford automobiles. Boycott or no boycott, some newspapers warned, Ford's venture ultimately would backfire. Deprived of their livelihood, the retailers, their employees, and their suppliers would have no money to spend on cars. But other pundits credited Henry Ford with one more ingenious invention: how could low prices be anything but salutary for the general standard of living?

Now as then, the question has no universally satisfying answer. Shoppers who flock to the bargains at warehouse stores have reason to cheer, but this joy eludes small merchants who cannot stock enough goods to qualify for big-volume discounts, vendors under constant pressure to lower prices or lose their large customers, and the rank-and-file employees of these concerns, whose wages are relatively low. High wages may be inflationary, but low wages hurt the general prosperity, too, by leaving workers with little money to save or spend.

In the spring of 1927, the retailers of Detroit convened in a hotel ballroom, and after two splenetic hours yielded the floor to a young man who identified himself as the manager of the Ford stores. Although he seemed confident that expansion could easily push sales beyond $50 million a year, he announced that the stores would no

longer serve the public. The audience cheered, and the Ford Motor
Company rarely bragged about its stores again. Whatever their untoward consequences for other merchants, the stores saved the typical
Ford employee an estimated $500 to $600 a year—more than four
months' pay.

With the advent of the Six-Dollar Day in 1919, Ford dropped the
distinction between wages and profit sharing, eliminating the need for
the investigative work of the Educational Department. Marquis tried
to keep the social spirit alive with proposals for housing, pensions, life
insurance, and assistance for Ford families left destitute by the death of
a breadwinner. "I have on my desk at this moment the case of woman
whose husband was employed by this company," he wrote in 1920 to
Edsel Ford, who had succeeded his father as president. The widow, left
with young twins and a nursing infant, could not go to work, but work
could be brought to her. Marquis hoped the company would build an
apartment house, complete with nursery and workroom, for such
women. While the mothers worked, their children could be tended "at
a fraction of the expense which is entailed under present conditions,"
and mothers "would be near their families so as to relieve them of
worry." Marquis added that he had described his proposals to "men
familiar with what other companies are doing," and they had pronounced the ideas practical and "far ahead of any plan thus worked out
by any industry in this country."

But the concerns of Samuel Marquis no longer jibed with those of
Ford's management. While Marquis was pondering refinements in
human relations, Henry Ford was worrying about the survival of the
company. In 1919, wanting to consolidate his control of the company,
Ford had set aside his disdain for bankers and borrowed $75 million to
buy out several of his largest investors. He planned to repay the loans
in 1921 with profits from the Model T. In 1920, sales plunged.
Horrified by the prospect of losing the company to the dreaded "parasites," he slashed Model T prices by 25 percent. Sales rose, but the new
low price left little profit. To extricate himself from the crisis, he
turned a huge inventory of parts into one hundred thousand more cars

and forced his dealers to buy them. Those who refused lost their franchises.

The hard times led to a head-on collision between Marquis and Ford's production chief, Charles Sorenson. Assembly-line speed was turned up sharply as Sorenson pushed to cut costs and squeeze more work out of fewer men. Nearly twenty thousand workers were dropped from the rolls in 1921, and Marquis wanted a more humane approach to the layoffs. When they went to see Henry Ford to discuss their differences, Ford sided with Sorenson. Marquis resigned. Ford's great social experiment was over.

THE Model T had a few more good years, but in 1925, the unthinkable happened. General Motors caught up with Ford, finishing the year with the same market share (roughly 30 percent) and a much higher return on investment (35 percent versus 10 percent). The days when three out of five new cars on the road were Model T's could be glimpsed only in the rearview mirror.

To succeed, Henry Ford had reinvented work, remade the worker, and treated executives as replaceable parts. He had been willing to revise everything but the Model T, which he considered "the acme of motor car perfection." But by the mid-1920s, the shock absorbers, fuel gauges, and other innovations offered by competitors had broader appeal than the bargain price of the Model T. Consumers who did not share Henry Ford's antipathy to the lending class readily agreed to buy their cars on the installment plan, a practice popularized after World War I by the new General Motors Acceptance Corporation. By 1925, two-thirds of new cars were bought with borrowed money. G.M. also expanded the market for used cars, making it easy to trade an old automobile for a new one. In addition, G.M. offered its customers an abundance of choices—Buicks, Chevrolets, Oaklands, Oldsmobiles, and Cadillacs, some with six cylinders, some with eight, all available in an assortment of colors.

In 1925 Henry Ford capitulated on the color issue, offering the Model T in gunmetal blue, highland green, phoenix brown, and fawn gray, but otherwise he held fast. In 1926, after the acme of motor car perfection had been on the market for eighteen years, Ford declared it "a tried and proved product that requires no tinkering" and added that it would "continue to be made in the same way. We have no intention of offering a new car."

The folly ended in May 1927, when thousands of unwanted Model T's crowded the factory yards. One hundred thousand Ford employees lost their jobs—sixty thousand in Detroit, the rest in offices and dealerships across the country. The man who had preached the gospel of work and felt it his duty to create jobs had, by himself, destroyed more work than any other employer in a century of industrialism.

Henry Ford walked away from the wreck without a scratch. "I don't know that Mr. Ford ever admitted any mistakes," said his secretary, Ernest Liebold. The company used the moment to celebrate production of the fifteen millionth Model T. (That was a record, and it stood until 1972, when the beetle-bodied Volkswagen passed the Model T.) Ford spent a year and $100 million designing a new car, the Model A, and retooling the factories to make it. The car was an instant success. Available in seventeen variations and four colors, packed with the latest in technology and comfort, the Model A pushed Ford's market share back into the lead for a year or two.

Given an opportunity to return to Ford, the workers took it. Most had few alternatives, having been "deskilled" by the system of mass production perfected by Henry Ford. For good and ill, his interest in the quality of their lives was gone. "A great business," he declared in 1931, "is really too big to be human."

There was one legacy worth keeping. Between 1880 and 1900, as American workers staged 23,000 strikes against 117,000 businesses, employers had fought wage increases with arguments calculated to appeal both to self-interest and the common good. The first was an assertion that capitalists bore all the risks of their enterprises and thus deserved all the rewards, a notion that neglected the physical risks of industrial work as well as the value added by labor's increasing productivity. The second argument in favor of low wages held that labor was a cost like any other, to be purchased as cheaply as possible so that a greater good—low prices—might be enjoyed by all. In one bold move, the Five-Dollar Day, Henry Ford made it plain that the worker, along with the capitalist and the customer, deserved a share of the feast.

9

MORE GRACE, SWEETNESS, AND TIME

W ITH MUCH OF the rest of the American South, Nashville after World War I found itself suspended between past and present. Fading, to the regret of romantics and the relief of those who hungered for the modern, was the South where time slid slowly, day melting into day, season into season. Ahead, still vague but definitely on the approach, was a world that synchronized its life with railway timetables and factory whistles, kept an eye on the stock exchange ticker, and interrupted whatever it was doing to answer the telephone. ("What?" asked a disbelieving elderly gentleman on being told of the demands of Mr. Bell's invention. "It rings and you answer? Like a servant?")

The many blocks separating the stone and steel of Nashville's downtown from the tranquil, shaded campus of Vanderbilt University did little to muffle the clangor between past and present. Like their contemporaries elsewhere, the young poets who collected at the university's English department felt obliged to impugn their times, but at Vanderbilt the burden swelled to twice the usual size: one was required to scorn both the moonlight-and-magnolias version of the Old South and the mythologizers of progress, who joined the march and banged the drum without ever asking where progress was headed. But the past was not so easily dismissed. Years later, remembering his undergraduate encounters with other poets, Allen Tate noted that while World War I reconnected the South to the larger world, it also stirred memories of the Civil War: "With us, entering the world once more meant not the obliteration of the past but a heightened consciousness of it; so that we had, at any rate in Nashville, a double focus, a looking two ways."

For Tate, John Crowe Ransom, Donald Davidson, and a handful of other literary aspirants at Vanderbilt, the looking led first to a small movement to encourage Southern poetry and soon evolved into one of the most thoroughgoing literary examinations of American getting and spending since the 1840s, when Ralph Waldo Emerson and Henry Thoreau protested the nation's ironhanded new sovereign, the market.

In the beginning, 1921, the young poets met weekly in the home of James Frank, a Nashville businessman, aesthete, and amateur poet. After handing out carbon copies of their latest poems, the group set to work, analyzing the merits of every turn of phrase. Slender, handsome, and doctrinaire, Davidson planted his feet ("mule-like," Tate thought) and would not be budged from his ideals of beauty and rhythm. Tate, whose most arresting physical feature was a very high brow, said he longed to dislodge Davidson "with a blast of entrails and livers!" Ransom, erudite and reticent, retreated to a cloud of cigar smoke to hide his boredom with the squabbling.

A year later the poets christened themselves the Fugitives and started a magazine, the *Fugitive,* primarily to publish the work of Southern poets, themselves included. On a break-even budget of subscription revenues and contributions from Frank and a group of Nashville retailers, the *Fugitive* published some of the earliest work of Robert Penn Warren and numerous poems by Tate, Ransom, and Davidson. It also attracted the work of such well-known New York poets as Hart Crane and won the admiration of T. S. Eliot. The *Fugitive* seemed to draw acclaim from every quarter except the South. After months of trying to persuade local newspapers to write about the magazine, Davidson gave up. "All I want to do now is to let them go to hell," he grumbled to Tate. Even the publication of an anthology of the Fugitives' verse failed to stir Southern pride. One of the region's leading men of letters, W. T. Couch, complained that the writings of the Fugitives had been "consciously and very expertly modeled after Jeremy Bentham's definition of poetry, namely, a method of printing in which the lines do not reach the usual margins of the page."

When the *Fugitive* published its last issue in 1925, its editors laid the demise to understaffing. But when the *Fugitive* ceased to speak, the Fugitives did not. They continued writing poetry, took up literary criticism, and ventured into biography. Increasingly distressed by the spiritual vacuity and materialism of American life, they talked of founding a second magazine or a country newspaper to preach the virtues of the simple life as lived on the small farms of the South, to rebut Northern criticism of the South, and to challenge the wisdom of Southern openness to Northern industrialists, reformers, and tastemakers.

Particularly galling to Tate and his friends were the Eastern journalists who pontificated on Southern backwardness. Scores of them, including H. L. Mencken of the Baltimore *Evening Sun,* swarmed to Dayton, Tennessee, in the summer of 1925 to watch two of the nation's most celebrated lawyers, William Jennings Bryan and Clarence Darrow, settle the question of whether John Thomas Scopes or anyone else could teach Darwin's theory of evolution in the state's public schools. For Mencken, who had assigned himself the glee of deriding the class he named the "booboisie" and all other American lowbrows he could find, the Scopes trial had everything: bumpkins, barkers, Bible thumpers, and Bryan, the public figure he despised most.

For two weeks, Dayton was a carnival. Caged apes could be viewed for a fee, women and children clutching monkey dolls paraded around the courthouse, and a revival tent went up outside town. Mencken was impressed by the courtesy of the townspeople and the care the police took to keep perfervid fundamentalists from pestering the atheists who had come to town to cheer Scopes. A fair trial was out of the question, Mencken guessed, because it would be "no more possible in this Christian valley to get a jury unprejudiced against Scopes than it would be possible in Wall Street to get a jury unprejudiced against a Bolshevik." Mencken was right. Scopes was convicted. Although the state supreme court later overturned the conviction on technical grounds, the damage was done. Tennessee was a laughingstock. The day after the verdict, Bryan died of a stroke. Mencken wrote one of the meanest obituaries on record, linking Bryan to "the gaping primates" from the hills of Tennessee and remarking that he liked to rise "to the tune of cocks crowing on the dunghill."

Davidson and his fellow poets read the scorn of Northeastern opinion makers as one more act of Yankee aggression in a war that had never ended. As he dryly noted, Southerners did not make the Sacco-Vanzetti case or the Loeb-Leopold murder trial "the text of a moral lesson to be preached to the North," but Northerners regularly condemned the South and inserted themselves into Southern causes célèbres. What was needed, in his view, were not "occasional outbursts of indignation, but the steady flame of ethical purpose," a flame he did not see in the alienated intellectuals of the North.

To Davidson, the philanthropists and reformers who descended on the South for allegedly noble purposes were agents of Northern imperialism. While a cause such as compulsory public education might seem above reproach, Davidson pointed out that the real beneficiaries of the crusade were the Northerners who authored and published textbooks. In his opinion, when Tennessee's commissioner of education allowed "I see the traffic light" to replace "I see the horse" in rural school readers, he unwittingly surrendered to the conquerors. To Davidson, the Northerner's concern with Southern education paralleled "with remarkable precision the process by which the forward-looking Briton, speaking in the name of humanity, deplores Mahatma Gandhi's preference for loin-cloths and desires to fit him with a suit of tropical-worsted, British made."

THE collusion between North and South dated from the 1870s, when Henry Watterson, editor of the *Louisville Courier-Journal,* boasted to New Yorkers that the South intended to industrialize, commercialize, and generally "out-Yankee the Yankee." A few years later, the editor of the *Atlanta Constitution,* Henry W. Grady, ventured to New York to announce that the South had "found her jewel in the toad's head of defeat." Grady set forth his vision of a "New South"—reconciled with the North, determined to improve education, intent upon moving beyond an agricultural economy, and eager to turn itself into a profitable home for Northern capital.

In the minds of Davidson and Tate and their fellow poets, the New South was a sham, a Southern fantasy of a Northern fantasy of the South. It was also economically boonless. The Northern capitalists had come—to mine, log, and manufacture—and they had prospered, but Southern riches failed to materialize. Northern investment did little for the Southern laborer because most of the new factories specialized in rough processing rather than finished goods, and such operations employed unskilled workers at low wages. The gain to cities and states was negligible because they had been overgenerous to the Northerners, luring them with loans on highly favorable terms, light taxes, cheap power, and laws that kept wages low and factory hours long. Even the Southern businessman came up short, being more often invited to serve as functionary than as partner. Southern exports rose, but most were raw materials, which were bought cheap, turned into consumer goods in the North, and "sold back dear on a scale undreamed of twenty years ago," Davidson wrote. "The result of the process in the South has been a wholesale exportation of Southern cash and, more devastatingly, of physical resources—and all without adequate compensation." The profits went north.

A disappointment to many, the New South of the 1920s was a disaster for the farmer. Small-scale subsistence farming had given way to the large-scale planting of cash crops, especially cotton. Borrowing heavily to acquire more land and the tractors needed to work a big farm efficiently, the farmer was also in hock to merchants who extended credit between harvests at interest rates that often reached 75 percent. After a long slide, cotton prices soared during World War I. Believing that European textile factories destroyed in the war would not be rebuilt for years, Southern farmers began taking out loans to plant more cotton, speculate in land, or both. By 1920, Southern farmland fetched twice its prewar price and 150 times its cost at the turn of the century. The Europeans recovered more quickly than anticipated, the world cotton supply vastly exceeded demand, and the consequent dive in prices left farmers unable to pay bankers or merchants. Farm foreclosures and rural bank failures were commonplaces of Southern life for most of the 1920s.

Something had gone terribly wrong, and the poets wanted to stop it before it went further. In 1927, Tate told Davidson that they ought to meet every progressive's cry of *"Nous allons!"* with a firm *"Non! Nous retardons!"* Two years later he advocated that they start a movement of "Southern positive reactionaries" that would be "ambitious to the last degree," setting forth a conservative philosophy drawn from the Southern past and the aristocratic European tradition behind it and emphasizing the "possibilities it presents for perfection."

Their friend Andrew Lytle, who had turned his attention from poetry to theater, was in a similar mood. "I feel we ought to devote the next three or four years to a lucid and forceful restatement of our philosophy," he wrote Tate, "for when the industrial powers completely dictate, there will never again be the chance."

With no money to start a magazine or buy a country newspaper, they decided to launch their movement by publishing a book of a dozen essays about the South, all written by native Southerners. Sounding an unmistakably Confederate note, they called it *I'll Take My Stand*, a title they hoped would annoy Northerners and progressive Southerners alike. The book ranged over art, religion, education, and economics, made a case against the worship of progress, and dealt with the matter of race by urging Negroes to make themselves employable and to work toward making their communities "informed and productive." But none of these issues excited the authors so much as their idea that the South should be free to work out its own destiny.

Signing themselves "Twelve Southerners," the poets and their carefully chosen collaborators argued that because of the South's history and traditions, its destiny was agricultural rather than industrial. They were Agrarians, they said, and as they defined agrarianism, it was the theory that "the culture of the soil is the best and most sensitive of vocations, and that therefore it should have the economic preference and enlist the maximum number of workers." With Thomas Jefferson they believed that the best of all possible worlds would be peopled mostly by yeoman farmers. In such a world, nearly everyone owned property, a fact that minimized opportunities for the concentration of wealth and the exploitation that too often accompanied it.

According to the Agrarians, the North had sold itself long before to the devil of industrialism, but the South still had a choice. It could surrender to industrialism and become indistinguishable from the North, or it could take a stand and preserve its pastoral way of life. The choice had to be made soon, wrote Andrew Lytle. The small, self-sufficient farmer, the hero of agrarianism, was already being "turned into the runt pig in the sow's litter. Squeezed and tricked out of the best places at the side, he is forced to take the little hind tit for nourishment; and here, struggling between the sow's back legs, he has to work with every bit of his strength to keep it from being a dry hind one, and all because the suck of the others is so unreservedly gluttonous."

Like most of his coauthors, Lytle was a man of letters, but he intuitively grasped the human consequences of the Southern economy's tilt toward industrialism and cash-crop farming. While the highways being built throughout the South were presented as a blessing to the farmer, Lytle saw that they would be a decided hindrance unless the farmer could afford a truck. A man on foot was in danger on a highway, and the "hard, slick surface" of the new roads was "a shock to his mules' feet." It seemed to Lytle that those who gained most from highway construction were the road builders, makers and purveyors of automobiles and oil, and truck and bus lines.

The farmer succumbed to the blandishments of the tractor salesman in the hope that the tractor would make him rich but forgot that the purchase of one tractor would eventually necessitate the purchase of another because tractors could not reproduce. Lytle begged the farmer to remember that "a farm is not a place to grow wealthy; it is a place to grow corn" and urged him to hold firm against the imprecations of salesmen: "He should know that prophets do not come from cities, promising riches and store clothes. They have always come from the wilderness, stinking of goats and running with lice and telling of a different sort of treasure."

The treasure Lytle and his fellow essayists had in mind came from a life lived close to the land. Beholden to no one, small farmers were incorruptible, making them ideal citizens. Working the soil, they felt at one with nature and anchored in the universe. Operating on a small scale, they had little need of far-off markets, so ties to neighbors and community flourished. Above all, they were spared the soul-blunting dichotomy, endured by legions of clerks and factory hands, between living and making a living. On a farm, life was of a piece.

An agrarian society set more store by continuity and permanence than progress, and it was deliberately provincial—"decentralized, stable, local, and self-sufficient," in Davidson's words. Its attractions were "peace, stability, and leisure," which Davidson considered preconditions of "any intelligent pursuit of happiness."

Musing on "the most practical of all points—what is the end of living?" essayist and critic Stark Young guessed that the meaning of life might not be found in the "glittering narrowness" of an industrial society.

> It may be that the end of man's living is not mere raw Publicity, Success, Competition, Speed and Speedways, Progress, Donations, and Hot Water, all seen with a capital letter. There are also more fleeting and eternal things to be thought of; more grace, sweetness and time; more security in our instincts, and chance to follow our inmost nature . . . more of that last fine light to shine on what we do, and make the sum of it like some luminous landscape, all the parts of which are equable, distributed, and right.

The appeal of such a life was deeply felt even by Northern industrialists, said Tate, pointing to their pleasure in acquiring antebellum Southern mansions. "The middle-class capitalist has no confidence in the material basis of his life; his human nature demands a homogeneous pattern of behavior that his economic life will not give him. He

doubtless sees in the remains of the Old South a symbol of the homogeneous life." Tate conceded that man had "never achieved perfect
unity of his moral nature and his economics," but he thought the antebellum Southerner had come close: "He dominated the means of life;
he was not dominated by it."

Declaring industrialism "an evil dispensation," the authors of *I'll
Take My Stand* issued their call to action: "find the way to throw it off."

CONCEIVED and written in the roar of the twenties, *I'll Take My
Stand* was published toward the end of 1930, a year after the great stock
market crash. Most of those who reviewed the book agreed with
Henry Hazlitt of the *Nation,* who said that the problem with "these
typewriter agrarians" was not that their ideals were quixotic but that
they were "stupid." Industry must be humanized rather than exterminated, Hazlitt thought. The *Saturday Review* pointed out that Vanderbilt
University had been founded with a Northern industrial fortune and
that whatever success Southern agriculture enjoyed was inextricably
tied to industry and commerce: "Cotton became king only after the
invention of the cotton gin, and thereafter maintained his reign
through the healthy functioning of the industrial system with its factories, cities, ships, railways, banks."

Malcolm Cowley, literary editor of the *New Republic* and a friend of
Allen Tate, privately told him that he considered anti-industrialism
pointless: "we can no more defeat present tendencies than we can make
water run uphill." Cowley left the *New Republic*'s dismissal of the book
to another of Tate's friends, Edmund Wilson, who wrote an essay
damning the Agrarians without even mentioning *I'll Take My Stand.*
Wilson noted that some of the Agrarians had ventured out of the
South long enough to taste life in "dark basements in Greenwich
Village" and the cafés of Paris, but their disillusionment with the intellectuals they met in their travels had made them "think tenderly of the
South again." Building a Southern movement on "ancestor worship"
and protests of industrialism was absurd, Wilson said—like "trying to
lock the stable door after the colt has gotten away."

Furious, Tate told Wilson that he and other Northeasterners were blinded by their assumptions of superiority: "you are morally and spiritually bankrupt, and you won't have it that other people aren't." He called Wilson "a modern Orestes—driven by your curse of industrialism, hating it, but still cherishing it as if it were decreed in heaven. Whom the gods destroy they first make mad."

Cowley tried to console Tate with the thought that Wilson and the other naysayers were merely putting the Agrarians to a test they would have to pass anyway. To survive, their movement would "have to be strengthened by a lot of outside criticism and self-criticism before it hardens into a dogmatic creed. At this stage of the game, you oughtn't to be tender about it."

The Agrarians' plea for the preservation of Southern traditions and a distinctive regional identity struck Northeasterners as wrongheaded and hopelessly quaint. Even before the publication of *I'll Take My Stand,* Wilson had tried to dissuade Tate from idealizing the past: "Naturally we fortify our own souls by looking backward, but it is surely mistaken to talk as some people do, as if the future were to contain the realization of some ideal conditions of the past, or as if the future could never, under any circumstances, come up to the past." To Wilson, the overriding consideration was that "all humanity is in the same boat, and that all these problems ought to be thought out without too much regard for local habits and traditions."

Having taken their stand, the Agrarians refused to retreat. It was the critics who were wrong. Davidson was stung by their "scornful levity," particularly the charge that the authors were not men of the plow but men of the desk. While the critics assumed that a man who writes a book is "*ipso facto* incapable of steering a mule," Davidson wrote, the truth was that all of the authors came from rural backgrounds, and some of them still farmed to supplement "the meager stipend which the industrial order grudgingly permitted them to draw as poets and professors." He also resented the critics' insistence that the Agrarians meant to force their ideal on the nation. The authors, he said, "had never imagined that Southern principles, once defined, would apply just as benevolently in New York City as some wise men thought the Eastern metropolitan principles would apply in the South."

Still, the ferocity of the critics and the poor sales of *I'll Take My Stand* led Davidson to wonder what he and his fellow essayists might have done differently. Perhaps they should have kept their focus on the virtues of the South. Or attacked the East rather than industrialism, a strategy that might have won them allies in the West, where farmers were also hostages to the Eastern banks that held their mortgages. Perhaps the problem lay in their tentativeness. As he told Tate, "we have never quite made up our minds whether we are crusaders or not. We like to think of ourselves as crusaders. . . . But we don't actually do the crusading. We merely trifle with it a little." He proposed that the poets return to their desks and write another book, hoping that their words would spur others to action. "I believe we would be fools to give ground now, when the times are still malleable, and will be swayed, for better or worse within the next decade."

THE times were indeed malleable. The unemployment rate in 1933 topped 25 percent, personal income fell by half between 1929 and 1933, and farm income dropped by two-thirds. There was talk of revolution, but Davidson dismissed it. The fact that millions of jobless workers had endured their fate without showing more than "a caterwauling belligerency" led him to think that they were "the most spineless group of downtrodden that the world has ever seen, and not of the stuff of revolutionaries," he told Tate early in 1932. Davidson had little faith that the radicals of the left would do more than bark, and he predicted that Midwestern farmers, despite their strong political organization and their bitterness over bank foreclosures, were more likely to be *"used* in some cause than originate a cause."

Shortly before the election, Davidson met with William E. Dodd, a distinguished Southern historian soon to be named ambassador to Germany, and came away feeling that agrarianism's stock was about to rise. Dodd told Davidson he believed the unemployed masses in the cities would begin returning to the countryside to support themselves on small farms. In the short run, this might hurt farmers by shrinking the urban market for their produce, but Dodd seemed to suggest that if Washington took care of the farmer, many other economic problems would take care of themselves. Across the country, thoughtful citizens noticed that workers were idle and poverty was widespread, but land was abundant. Why couldn't government acquire farmland and move city dwellers back to the land for a fresh start? Among those caught by the idea was President Roosevelt, who enjoyed thinking of himself as a farmer from Hyde Park, New York.

Thrilled by the possibility of an urban exodus, Andrew Lytle and Lyle Lanier, an academic psychologist who had contributed to *I'll Take My Stand,* set themselves the challenge of devising a program that would shift five million Americans from town to country. Like Davidson, Lytle was convinced that the idea was right for the times. The whole industrial edifice was rotten and ready to be toppled by the slightest wind, Lytle told Tate. He hoped that the Agrarians could stir the wind before industrialists persuaded Roosevelt to prop up their edifice.

In several magazine articles in 1932 and 1933, John Crowe Ransom made the case for a rebirth of the subsistence farm, where the object was self-sufficiency rather than raising crops for cash—a place to grow corn, not a place to grow wealthy, as Lytle had put it. In Ransom's view, industrial capitalism had foundered because of overproduction, and capitalism applied to agriculture was yielding the same disastrous results. A pound of cotton cost seven cents to produce but brought only five cents in the market. In 1933, cotton farmers planted forty million acres despite the fact that warehouses were stuffed to the rafters with unsold cotton.

Ransom saw little risk in transplanting people to the countryside. Denmark had done it simply by lending the indigent money to buy land and get a farm going. Blessed with open spaces, the United States owned a magnificent opportunity for homesteading. Other Agrarians suggested grants of land and farm implements, loans to tenant farmers, taxes that fell more lightly on small farmers than on large-scale agricultural enterprises, lessons in farming, and cooperative villages to alleviate social isolation in thinly settled regions.

Over time, Franklin Roosevelt's New Deal helped farmers with programs that paid them to take land out of production, refinanced their mortgages, extended credit to agricultural cooperatives, resettled urbanites on farmland, moved farmers on depleted soil to better land, and made low-interest loans to help tenant farmers, sharecroppers, and farmworkers buy land, livestock, and implements.

The Agrarians wanted more. As they saw it, the New Deal's subsidies for plowing crops under had bailed out big farmers but thrown thousands of tenant farmers and sharecroppers out of work. "With one hand [the president] measures acreage to be ordered out of production, and with the other hand waves city men to the farm," Ransom wrote. "How is it possible for Mr. Roosevelt to increase the occupation of the land without damning commercial agriculture to a yet lower hell?" Loans, even at low interest rates, fell short of hopes for outright grants. The resettlement program, which included land-use planning and help with soil conservation, failed because the head of the federal Resettlement Administration saw no point in encouraging small farms, which were demonstrably less efficient than large ones. Cityfolk, even unemployed cityfolk, did not yearn for the farmer's life, nor did the farmer yearn for the model villages and other social improvements that fired the dreams of do-gooders on the Potomac.

The biggest changes the New Deal brought to the South came from the creation of the Tennessee Valley Authority (TVA) and the Rural Electrification Administration (REA), which started nonprofit cooperatives to construct rural power lines. Before the TVA and REA, much of the South paid exorbitant rates for electricity, and sparsely populated areas often had none at all because of the high cost of stringing wires across empty land. In the forty thousand square miles of the Tennessee Valley, which sprawled from Virginia to Mississippi, only 2 percent of farms had electricity. Widely seen as a godsend, the electricity brought by the TVA ended much of the drudgery of farmwork, increased productivity, and enabled farmers to do more of their own processing, which raised the market value of their crops. The TVA also cleared forests and rivers, built levees and dams to control floods, resettled many farmers on better soil, set up demonstration farms and soil management programs, and produced fertilizers and sold them cheaply to encourage their use. The possibilities unlocked by easy access to electricity even softened Allen Tate's opposition to industrialism. With small factories financed and owned by Southerners, he thought, the South could break the North's hold on manufacturing and Southern wealth would at last stay in the South.

Davidson was more skeptical. Three years of observation convinced him that the TVA, like countless ostensibly beneficent enterprises before it, was nothing more than a subsidy to "any migrating manufacturers who want to set up shop in the Tennessee Valley, and above all to the great monopolistic northern corporations which have a great many articles to sell to the Tennessee Valley people." To Davidson, the New Deal was the New South all over again, perpetrated this time by the federal government. And if President Hoover's America had been in pain, Davidson wrote, President Roosevelt's was "in a condition of anesthesia, from which sooner or later we must emerge into new pain, with every prospect that the operating surgeon may have sewed up several pairs of forceps inside the helpless carcass." Davidson saw Roosevelt trying to salvage the industrial economy and provide "a modicum of comfort to the human casualties of our false way of life" but "doing nothing to repair the false way of life."

With their antipathy to industrialism and their conviction that the small farmer enjoyed a life far superior to that of the factory worker, the Agrarians did not engage themselves with the problem of industrial unemployment except to suggest that the dispossessed should head for the farm. Ransom accused Northeastern liberals of being "a little maudlin in their glorification of the workingman. They are mystical. They have broken bread with laborers, and communed with them over their beers. They have liked the thrilling odors from the armpits of men who work with their hands, and they have admired the ox-like strength of laborers, and still more the ox-like herding together in

comradeship." But Ransom's prescriptions for labor sounded no different from those of the Northerners: job security, unemployment insurance, decent housing and health care, good education, and a work
tempo suited to humans rather than machines.

Tate's solution to the unemployment crisis was a modest proposal in
the vein of Jonathan Swift's. The good of humanity and the good of
the industrial economy were now one and the same, Tate said, and the
utmost industrial good demanded the utmost efficiency. Unproductive
property must be destroyed. He called on American capitalists to
shoulder this burden and dispose of the permanently unemployed.

"Society would suffer the least rupture, and be spared that violence
to its *sympathy*—a peculiarly modern refinement of feeling—if it quietly, and in the ordinary routine of industrial technology, *killed off about
eight million workers and their families,*" Tate wrote. "The employer would
draw up a schedule of extinction, beginning with the mother in order
to cut off first the reproducer. The older daughters would come next."
The method of destruction Tate left to the specialists, though he
favored lethal gas. He urged that every demise be accompanied by
some sort of "half-ceremony, to remind us that these people are half
human." In the interests of efficiency, the rite could be administered to
groups. Perhaps "a distinguished pastor of the church—whose
Protestant branches have marched in the vanguard of progress—could
be appointed to receive the herds at the pens." Writing in the spring of
1933, the season when Adolf Hitler came to power, Tate had no way
of knowing how soon the savagery he presented as satire would be
enacted in Europe.

To Davidson, the problem of industrial unemployment loomed
small against the problem of industrialism. He saw no gain in reviving
a system that pointlessly accelerated the pace of life, perpetrated "end-
less hostilities against nature," and offered no satisfaction other than a
paycheck. Labor being "one of the largest items in the human career,"
Davidson wrote, "it is a modest demand to ask that it may partake of
happiness." As he saw it, the city where the laborer worked was often
as impersonal as the factory, the insecurity of factory employment

made it difficult to put down roots, and feelings of community were rare and fragile.

Davidson also decried the rift that mass production put between the consumer and his conscience.

> Under industrialism, no man sees the end of his deed, no man faces the consequences of his act. And not knowing the end of his deed, he is precluded from becoming a moral agent. . . . If I buy coal for my fire, I do not ask how dark and deep the coal mines are. I must be warm. It is a commercial transaction. This man has a clock with a dial illuminated by a radium compound, a pretty device which he can read, for convenience, in the night. The girl who touched the dial with a radium-dipped brush is slowly dying. Her fingers and jawbones are rotting away. Nobody is responsible. It was a commercial transaction. The girl's family may of course recover damages from the manufacturing corporation—it is still a commercial transaction. Nobody know where anything comes from. Nobody knows where anything goes.

Ultimately, the remove would "sap and destroy the moral impulse and the social will," Davidson thought, and people would "become callous even to near consequences."

LIKE many intellectuals, Davidson and his fellow poets had a keen eye for problems but little zeal for solving them. Davidson wished the Agrarians had the mettle to empty their bank accounts and organize Southern farmers and merchants into a political party, but he suspected they never would. "That sort of thing simply doesn't happen among us," he declared, as if their condition were immutable.

In the winter of 1931–32, Tate had tried to rouse the group to action by proposing that they join Malcolm Cowley, Edmund Wilson, and a few others on a trip to Harlan County, Kentucky. The local coal miners had gone on strike for higher wages, and mine owners were refusing to allow food to be distributed to the strikers on the theory that when they got hungry enough, they would go back to work. Relief trucks were stopped at the county line, soup kitchens were dynamited or torched, and relief workers were arrested and charged with criminal syndicalism. Cowley and Wilson hoped to bully their way past local authorities and brandish their mightiest weapon, adverse publicity.

Davidson wanted nothing to do with "this vague trouble between operators and miners and communists and sundry asses of all descriptions," he told Tate. "I have a feeling that the Agrarians had better stay out of local quarrels."

Tate was livid. "If we can't protest in 'local matters,' where can we protest?" he asked Davidson. Writing to Ransom, Tate wondered where the Agrarians *would* take their stand if not in the South. "Are we then to be concerned with the quarrels of Boston or the Chinese?" Tate saw Harlan County as a chance for their group "to keep the ball rolling, and to keep on preparing the public attention for our later efforts."

Davidson assured Tate that he was not getting "weak-kneed," he was merely waiting for a big fight, and one they could win. He believed it would come because the severity of the Depression had so discredited industrialism that agrarianism was bound to thrive.

The Northerners' mission to Harlan County was a qualified success. Traveling in a convoy of three trucks filled with food, they arrived in Pineville, the seat of Harlan County, to be greeted by the mayor and the sight of machine-gun barrels poking through various windows. The mayor refused the visitors' request to talk with the miners, but the county attorney allowed them to distribute food on a road outside town. Before they went home, two of them were badly beaten, one for publicly reading that portion of the Kentucky State Constitution enshrining Jefferson's idea that citizens unhappy with their government had a right to revolt.

The Agrarians' decision not to go to Harlan County foretold much. There would be no activism, no linking up with kindred movements, and only the faintest attempts to take their ideas to the halls of government. They preferred to write and wait for their words to tip the world in their direction. But at least one of them, John Crowe Ransom, had begun to question pure agrarianism. After boning up on economics to write a book on land, Ransom concluded that the South needed some industry if only to spare Southern farmers the indignity of "feeding out of the hands of the Yankees."

Eventually the writings of the Agrarians attracted the notice of two men eager to wage their own crusades against capitalism as practiced by the big banks and corporations of the United States. The first to find them, in 1933, was a New York magazine publisher named Seward Collins, who was starting a political monthly to be called the *American Review*. Tate sized him up as "a fine and sincere fellow, to whom one half of the world is pure error, the other half pure truth, with no complications in between." Though Collins's magazine was "not precisely what we want," he told Davidson, "I doubt if we could do better at this time." Over the next four years, Tate, Davidson, Ransom, and several other Agrarians used the *American Review* to keep their ideas alive, contributing some seventy articles.

Fearful that the Depression would drive the United States to communism, Collins endorsed every conservative cause he encountered, including fascism. The Agrarians assumed that since they were not fascists, no one would confuse their politics with Collins's, but in 1936, they found themselves accused of fascism in print. Tate was troubled enough by the charge to respond in the *Marxist Quarterly* and the *New Republic*. Davidson worried less about being tarred with fascism than about imbroglios with intellectuals who asserted that if the United States did not turn to communism, it would embrace fascism, an argument he considered softheaded. The problem of the Agrarians' association with Collins solved itself in 1937, when the *American Review* folded.

The second outsider to seek an alliance with the Agrarians was a New Yorker named Herbert Agar, former London correspondent for the *Louisville Courier-Journal* and winner of a 1934 Pulitzer prize for *The People's Choice,* a history of the presidency. Agar was a fine example of a once common but now endangered species of American, the public-spirited citizen who considers it a duty to participate wholeheartedly in the political debates of his day. The economic crisis of the

1930s begged for sweeping reforms, and there was no shortage of Agars ready to share their remedies. Business leaders thought that Washington should help industry recover to stave off a proletarian revolution. Many on the left thought that communism was the only hope. Liberals proposed the middle course taken by the New Deal, with government checking the excesses of laissez-faire capitalism and installing an economic safety net under the citizenry.

Herbert Agar disagreed with all of the above. In England he had known and admired the distributists, a small group of intellectuals who rejected communism as well as capitalism. Believing that both systems turned the masses into dependents and that being a ward of the state was no improvement upon being a wage slave, the distributists advocated that every Englishman be given three acres and a cow. Hilaire Belloc, a novelist and critic who was the chief spokesman for distributism, also proposed that small businesses be taxed less than big ones in order to slow the accumulations of great wealth that seemed to be an inevitable consequence of capitalism.

Agar absorbed these ideas, considered them in light of the American experience, and worked up his own critique of prevailing opinion. In his view, a big business economy put too much property in too few hands, making it "vain to expect the watching millions to be filled with enterprise or endowed with responsibility or hope." Agar found "monopoly capitalism" the very negation of private property: it kept wages low and restricted property ownership to the fortunate few. By doing so, it strengthened the appeal of communism, which Agar considered a menace. He thought the liberals were wrong because their solutions snipped off the economy's dead branches without attacking the rot at the roots. They were temporizing, which set the stage for chaos and the rise of a fascist demagogue. What was needed, Agar said, was widespread ownership of property. Property conferred economic independence, and without economic independence, political choice was meaningless.

There was much in Agar's synthesis to appeal to the Agrarians. He disapproved of communism, fascism, and big business. He also thought of himself as a "Jeffersonian conservative," a label they might have chosen for themselves. Tate was the first of the Agrarians to get to know Agar and, after corresponding with him for a year or so, invited him to collaborate on an outline for the long-awaited sequel to *I'll Take My Stand*.

Davidson, who had thought that he would edit the sequel, was hurt, but Tate held firm. "We've vaguely consulted off and on for five years, and I am damned to hell if we have accomplished anything as a group," he replied. Agar was "a gift from the gods." He was also a leader, Tate said, "and not one of us is a leader that anybody will follow. We are an army made up of generals." In Tate's judgment, the Agrarians' critical moment had arrived; either they attracted a wider following or they died. "We can't go on writing our pleasant little laments for our own consumption, we've got to get into action or admit that we are licked," he told Davidson.

The action Tate and Agar hoped to get into was the presidential campaign of 1936. Roosevelt was sure to be reelected, and they saw their book as a source of fresh ideas for his second term. The book, *Who Owns America? A New Declaration of Independence,* appeared in the spring. Davidson had healed sufficiently to contribute an essay on the need for regionalism as a counterweight to nationalism and to the centralizing predilections of the New Deal. There were twenty more chapters, on economics, politics, farming, literature, religion, and other matters. Eight of the twelve Southerners who authored *I'll Take My Stand* were represented in the new book.

Industrialism, the villain of *I'll Take My Stand,* was reduced to a bit part in *Who Owns America?* The real villain, the authors argued, was monopoly capitalism. Among other crimes, monopoly capitalism created giant corporations that injured society by putting management in one set of hands and ownership in another. Managers, who made a corporation's business decisions, worked for shareholders, who cared for nothing but the price of their stock. In effect, shareholders were "geldings," Ransom declared. If a company got into trouble, shareholders displayed no proprietary concern, they merely instructed their brokers to sell the stock. The manager had been gelded, too, obliged as he was to "engage in cutthroat competition and drive down wages, all for the good of the company," which is to say for the good of the shareholders. Tate argued along similar lines and exhorted readers to look askance when big business pointed to staggering gains in the nation's aggregate wealth. Aggregate wealth could be immense without being widely distributed, leaving the bulk of the populace impoverished.

Overcast as the economic and political landscape appeared, Agar took hope from the cowardice displayed by business in 1933, when it feared that an American rendition of the Russian Revolution was imminent. The fight business mounted "would not have startled a meadow full of rabbits," Agar recalled in his bouncy prose.

> Instead it gave us the unusually pleasing sight of timid old men in New York, moving their gold to Switzerland or Great Britain, provisioning their yachts for a fast and long retreat, planning doubtless to buy some distant island where they would not have to face anything more outrageous than an occasional horseshoe crab. The great lords of banking, who are said to hold us in the palms of their hands, were as gentle as a hearth-side of altered cats. They asked the Government please to save them, please to protect them from the alleged anger of the public. They promised to be as good as gold, or even as good as silver if that was what the people wanted. They resorted to the last refuge of the poltroon: they laughed amiably at the most savage jokes against themselves.

Agar believed that the American people, born of revolution, would never consent to tyranny, and when they decided they wanted something, they would not be "headed off by anyone so readily frightened as our robber rabbits."

Who Owns America? prescribed less big government, less big business, less Northeastern dominance, a more equal balance between agriculture and industry, and true economic democracy in the form of broader ownership of property, including the means of production.

Reviewers found the authors naive and noted that much of their critique of capitalism had been borrowed from an influential study published a few years earlier, *The Modern Corporation and Private Property* by Adolf A. Berle Jr. and Gardiner C. Means. The answer to the question of who owned America seemed to be "I don't care." The book went largely unnoticed.

Undaunted, Agar proceeded with plans to launch a magazine and start an organization to build a constituency for his ideas. When he opened his pages to the Agrarians, they were cool. They disapproved of his decision to base the magazine in New York, home of monopoly capitalism, Northern imperialism, and everything else they deplored. They also feared that the Southern flavor of their ideas would disappear in the great stew Agar planned to make of distributists, decentralists, back-to-the-land advocates, consumer cooperatives, and other agrarian movements. Nor did the Agrarians share Agar's sunny conviction that the differences among the groups would ultimately matter less than the similarities. "If the magazine is launched as now planned," Tate told Agar, "it will become, in a year or two, an organ of eclectic liberal opinion, and if we are in the organization, Agrarianism will die a quiet death." Tate proposed that the Agrarians contribute to the magazine but not ally themselves with an organization they did not control.

Agar readily agreed to respect their separatism while welcoming their writing, and he published the first issue of his magazine, *Free America,* in the summer of 1937. The Agrarians had little to do with it. Tate, after serving briefly as literary editor, turned his energies to poetry, teaching, and literary criticism. Ransom had moved to Ohio to teach at Kenyon College and in 1937 was busy starting the *Kenyon Review.* Tired of politics and increasingly skeptical of Agrarianism, he returned to literature. Davidson abandoned his last hopes that the New Deal might prove a good deal for the South. The more he saw, the more he believed that Franklin Roosevelt's Southern policy consisted solely of a cold calculation of how much federal largesse was needed to win Southern votes. In 1939 Davidson was finally ready to admit that the wind was not blowing in the direction of agrarianism: "At the moment there is no getting around the fact that a large part of the human population not only is not disillusioned with industrialism itself, but actually likes or thinks it likes industrialism and wants to see it go on."

BY Pearl Harbor Day, Agar had returned to London to fight fascism, and the agrarianism of the Southern poets was dead, a casualty of self-inflicted wounds. They took their stand and held it—even when they might have gained the allies they needed to spread their ideas. Yet the Agrarians were surprised by the world's indifference to their vision. How could it be that so few wanted a life with more grace, sweetness, and time? A life independent of industrial leviathans inhuman when they functioned as planned and apocalyptically destructive when they did not. A life unfragmented, in which connections to nature, God, and community were felt, and lived, daily.

The vision was unimpeachable, but only as far as it went. If industry was a tyrant, so was nature. The Agrarian idyll of the yeoman farmer, secure and self-sufficient on his own slice of earth, omitted drought, flood, infestation, and soil depletion, not to mention the inability to compete with the efficiency of large farms. And as much as the Agrarians liked to imagine otherwise, farmers seemed as smitten as their city cousins with the material comforts made possible by technology and mass production.

The Agrarians spoke often of wanting to preserve the virtues of a "traditional" society, meaning the society of the Old South, in which they saw honor, courage, courtesy, and a strong sense of obligation to others. But one human's tradition can be the source of another's oppression, and the Agrarian poets had little enthusiasm for ideals of equality. Tate disagreed with egalitarianism on much the same ground that Andrew Carnegie had: "there has never been social equality anywhere, there never will be, nor ought there to be," Tate wrote. "Every class and race should get what it earns by contributing to civilized life." He believed that lynching would disappear when "the white race is satisfied that its supremacy will not be questioned in social crises." The tradition the Agrarians sought to preserve owed more to aristocracy than democracy. While some of the Agrarians later supported the struggle for civil rights, Davidson became an ardent segregationist. Given his eloquence and force of intellect, it is a mercy that he had no taste for oratory or activism.

Some have dismissed the Agrarians as escapists longing for a past that had not existed except for a privileged few. But once the Depression began, they engaged themselves with the practical implications of their ideas, particularly as they championed the movement back to the land. As poets, they had their limitations in economics, but they were no less thoughtful than many intellectuals of other bents.

In repudiating the collectivism they saw in big business and big government, the Agrarians were asserting the worth of two deeply ingrained American values: independence and individualism. They objected to collectivism, whether of the capitalist or socialist ilk, because it squashed the individual. What they did not see was that the choice no longer lay between independence and dependence but between old habits of laissez-faire and new needs for interdependence. The Agrarians were not the first or last to suffer from this form of blindness. The worldwide failure to recognize the primacy of interdependence may prove the ultimate threat to the preservation of life on earth. But a global economy rooted in interdependence, however necessary, will never be the American dream.

Like uncountable other purists, the Agrarians did more than any of their foes to relegate themselves to the footnotes of history. Between protest and power lies the swamp of politics. The Agrarians took their stand well short of the swamp, and their deepest question—What is the end of living?—survives only as an echo. But it is an echo worth straining to hear.

10

WE'LL DO IT!

THE FASCISM THAT Herbert Agar had gone abroad to fight
would prove cataclysmic, but many Americans, Allen Tate and
Donald Davidson included, balked at the thought of taking
part in a second world war. Few remembered the first one fondly, and
there had been little dimming of the isolationist fervor that buried
President Woodrow Wilson's hopes for U.S. membership in the League
of Nations. Protected by two gigantic moats, the Atlantic and the
Pacific, many Americans had difficulty believing that the dangers from
Europe and Asia were either clear or present. When Hitler invaded
Poland in September 1939, France and Britain declared war on
Germany, and the United States announced its neutrality.

The war news of the following year made Tate think that the
United States was "about to commit suicide," and shortly after
Christmas of 1940, Davidson predicted to Tate that President Franklin
D. Roosevelt, just reelected for an unprecedented third term, "would
make Hitler look like a piker, in totalitarian techniques; I expect to
wake up any morning and find that Augustus had been proclaimed a
god." Davidson was not alone in suspecting that Roosevelt, safe from
the voters for another four years, would use the war as a pretext for
dictatorship. Other skeptics considered it folly to encourage the free-
spending FDR to enlarge his purview from nation to world, and con-
gressmen accustomed to shipping home barrel after barrel of prime
New Deal pork feared that more spending abroad would mean less for
their constituents.

Ignoring his critics, the president proposed that the United States become "the arsenal of democracy." In a Fireside Chat a few days after Christmas, he told Americans gathered around their radios that Germany and its allies intended to conquer Europe, then press on until "all of us in all the Americas would be living at the point of a gun." The best way to stop them and to head off U.S. entry into the war, Roosevelt said, was to keep Britain's army and navy well supplied. Congress soon gave the president the Lend-Lease Act, which empowered him to send planes, ships, munitions, and other supplies to any country judged vital to the defense of the United States. By the war's end in 1945, Lend-Lease would provide matériel worth $50 billion to other nations.

In truth, the arsenal of democracy had opened for business well before the Fireside Chat, and the clientele included the U.S. military as well as friendly foreign governments. In 1939 France and Britain placed orders for 4,700 airplanes with American manufacturers, and the United States began the secret project to make an atomic bomb. In 1940 Washington presented Britain with fifty superannuated destroyers and authorized the building of fifty thousand planes for American armed forces.

Henry J. Kaiser of Oakland, California, had opened his branch of the arsenal in September 1940 at a meeting with representatives of the Technical British Merchant Shipbuilding Mission. They were looking for someone to build cargo ships, and officials of the U.S. Maritime Commission in Washington had suggested that Kaiser might be the man for the job.

It was Kaiser who had suggested that the Maritime Commission suggest him. Never having built a ship, he was a peculiar candidate, but in his fifty-eight years, inexperience had rarely been an impediment. A school dropout like his hero Andrew Carnegie, Kaiser had gone to work in 1895 at the age of thirteen, clerking in a dry-goods store in Utica, New York. At twenty-two he talked his way into partial ownership of a photography studio, soon acquired the whole enterprise, then transplanted himself to the West Coast and the construction business. Lacking Carnegie's mastery of free-market capitalism or Henry

Ford's mechanical gifts, Kaiser nevertheless possessed a form of entre-preneurial genius—a knack for anticipating and serving the needs of one very large client, the federal government. While most of his fellow citizens struggled through the Depression, Kaiser thrived as one of the principal recipients of the tax dollars appropriated for several of the nation's largest government-funded construction projects, including Hoover Dam in Nevada, Grand Coulee Dam in Washington, and the long cantilevered bridge linking San Francisco with Oakland. He thought big and was big—250 pounds. Bald and bespectacled, he draped his bulk in elegant suits and hinted at his boldness with garish neckties.

Well connected in Washington and preternaturally good at scenting opportunity, Kaiser had already maneuvered himself into position to be of service to a government at war. His first move was a small one, an alliance with a shipyard in Maine, formed early in 1940 in case ship-building proved a good line of work. He told the visiting Englishmen of the alliance and proposed to build thirty ships for them in Maine and thirty in California. When they asked to tour his California yard, he showed them a huge mudflat along the eastern shore of San Francisco Bay, near the small town of Richmond. Whatever astonish-ment the visitors may have felt they kept to themselves. Many years later, relishing his memories of the moment, Kaiser claimed that he had said, "There are our shipyards! It's true you see nothing but mud here. But it's space—space for thousands of workers to come together and mass materials. Just envisage the shipyard that can be built in a mat-ter of months to pour out ships."

Kaiser was out on a limb ("where I like to be," he liked to say), and despite the fact that this particular limb was attached to no discernible trunk, the British grabbed hold. They had little choice. During the first year of the war, they had lost more than one thousand cargo ships to German U-boats, and without ships they could not move sufficient supplies or troops to the Continent. Bombs dropped by the Luftwaffe had crippled British shipyards, the Nazis were commissioning new U-boats at the rate of one a day, and experienced U.S. shipbuilders were busy filling orders for several hundred American cargo vessels called for by Congress in the Merchant Marine Act of 1936. So the British agreed to fund construction of a shipyard for a man who had never built a ship and promised to pay him on a cost-plus-fee basis, guaranteeing a profit of $160,000 per vessel. The contract, nearly lost at sea as the Englishman carrying it home scrambled into a lifeboat after a U-boat attack, was signed in London just before FDR's Fireside Chat.

Overnight the mud began to sprout the world's largest shipyard. "I thought I would never stop hearing the sound of pile-driving," said Frank Vodich, who helped to build the yard and stayed on as a welder and supervisor. "POW! POW! POW! It went on every day for years." In time there would be four Kaiser yards at Richmond, with a total of twenty-seven shipways, plus thirty-one ways at three Kaiser yards along the Columbia River in Oregon and Washington. They turned out nearly 1,400 cargo vessels and more than 100 warships for the United States after filling the order from Britain. Most of the cargo carriers were 441-foot Liberty ships, big seaborne trucks with crews of eighty. The Liberty, a modified version of the British vessel, struck FDR as an "ugly duckling," but it was easy to build and sail, and it proved crucial to victory. The toting up done after V-J Day showed that the 2,700 Liberties built by Kaiser and others delivered supplies at the rate of 6,000 tons an hour throughout the war.

WHILE Kaiser the novice could not have foreseen that he would construct more Liberties and set more records than any other wartime shipbuilder, he proceeded as if shipbuilding were a contest he intended to win. "You knew from the beginning that working for Kaiser was going to be something out of the ordinary," said Charlotte Martin Adams, who joined the shipyard's purchasing department in 1941. The instant landscaping later standard in suburban housing developments was virtually unknown in the 1940s, but as soon as the Richmond yard's office buildings went up, in came thirty-foot trees, full-grown shrubs, blooming flowers, and a lawn. "It was like waving a wand and everything suddenly appeared complete—and perfect," Adams remembered.

Soon after Pearl Harbor, President Roosevelt had declared that speed was essential in mobilizing the economy for war: "Speed will save lives; speed will save this nation which is in peril; speed will save our freedom and civilization." Speed also paid, as Henry Kaiser had learned in his earliest days as a road builder. By finishing construction projects ahead of schedule, he reduced his costs and gained a reputation that helped him win more business. Speed also suited his temperament. Too impatient to wait for the mails, he ran up gargantuan telephone and telegraph bills. He made decisions quickly, assigned others to carry them out, and demanded daily progress reports.

He expected everyone in his employ to move at high speed, and a surprising number did. Ninety-eight percent of his shipyard workers were as ignorant of shipbuilding as he was, but they completed the first of the British ships, the *Ocean Vanguard,* in 244 days, an American record for a vessel of its class. (Even the ship seemed to have caught the Kaiser ethos, sliding down the way before the intended moment. It was christened at the last second by an admiral's wife who saw what was happening and let fly with the champagne bottle.) By the middle of the war, when most U.S. shipbuilders needed forty days to make Liberties, Kaiser finished the job in twenty-seven.

Kaiser surrounded himself with highly capable engineers and managers, just as Carnegie had, and when Kaiser's men turned to shipbuilding, they made the most of the tabula rasa of their big mudflat. Conventional ship construction began with the laying of a keel, after which hundreds of workers climbed inside to do their jobs. Working in close quarters tangled their ropes, hoses, and electrical lines, causing innumerable delays and hazards. At Richmond, ship sections would be made separately and stitched together later. The approach was not new—a New Jersey shipyard had tried it in 1912—but Kaiser raised modular construction to an art form. Spread out across the vast spaces of Richmond, workers were soon prefabricating bulkheads, decks, and eighty-ton sections of hull. Once finished, the modules were lifted into position by cranes and bolted into place. The 250-ton deckhouses, too heavy for the cranes, were cut into quarters with blowtorches, hoisted aboard, and then welded back together. Time lost in slicing and splicing was minuscule compared with time gained in building the deckhouses on the ground.

Kaiser also saved production time by substituting welds for 97 percent of the rivets used in shipbuilding and by "downhand" welding. Deckhouses and other modules were assembled on their sides or upside-down, allowing welders to point their rods downward rather than fight gravity by working overhead. By lessening muscle strain and fatigue, downhand welding sent productivity soaring. It also enabled women of average strength to perform the job for eight hours at a stretch.

Scores of Kaiser "expediters" were charged with speed and nothing but. "I was a gofer," said Lovie Amos, who expedited for a pipe-fitting crew. "I ordered the materials the crew needed from the warehouse, got them to the loading dock, and made sure everything got to the work site on time." As a messenger boy, Bob Kelly was often sent to railyards in search of boxcars headed for Richmond. When he found one, his job was to badger the railroad into hurrying it to the shipyards.

Kaiser considered expediting essential to prevent bottlenecks and to deal with myriad new complexities caused by wartime competition for steel and other raw materials. Steel manufacturers hesitated to expand to meet the surging demand because they believed it would vanish at the end of the war, leaving them no way to recoup their investment. Irked by delays in obtaining steel from major suppliers, Henry Kaiser loudly protested that they were favoring longtime customers. He sent bellicose letters to steel executives and forwarded carbon copies to President Roosevelt. "It is beyond the scope of human ability to construct steel boats without steel," he wrote in the summer of 1941 to Vice-Admiral Howard L. Vickery of the U.S. Maritime Commission, the source of nearly all of Kaiser's shipbuilding contracts. "We solicit your advice. Should we disperse the organization or sit and wait? Your counsel will be appreciated. We are on a penalty basis."

The penalties were part of a new type of federal contract intended to eliminate flagrant abuses of former cost-plus-fee arrangements. Congress had appropriated more than $500 million for the creation of eighty-one shipyards with the understanding that the yards would be built at cost. Fees would not be paid until ships were built, and the fees on Liberties and other merchant ships were set at 3 percent above estimated costs. There were bonuses for shipbuilders who delivered ahead of schedule and under budget, penalties for those who missed the targets.

Since the government would not begin paying for a ship until the keel had been laid, the steel delays disrupted Kaiser's cash flow, stunted his potential for bonuses, and limited the number of ships he might build. Fran Koser, a steel industry veteran, was put to work rounding up steel from smaller mills around the country. To get steel when he needed it, Kaiser sometimes paid suppliers more than the government allowed. In 1942, when the Office of Price Administration accused him of illegal tactics, Kaiser claimed that he had acted with one goal in mind: furthering the war effort.

Kaiser saw the steel shortage as one more opportunity for his brand of entrepreneurship, and while he publicly lambasted steelmakers, he privately engineered government loans of more than $100 million to build his own steel mill in Fontana, California, in 1942. The war had shifted government spending from public works to defense, and as went government, so went Henry Kaiser. By the war's end, his enterprises would receive government loans of $152.78 million and defense contracts totaling $5 billion—$4 billion for ships and the balance for cement, gravel, steel, and incendiary materials used in the firebombing of Japan.

TURNOVER, absenteeism, housing shortages, cultural clashes—all of the consternations that had beset the managers of Henry Ford's first big factory—descended upon Kaiser's shipyard executives. Anticipating that the draft would intensify the competition for employees, Kaiser dispatched hiring agents to Southern California, the Midwest, the East, and the South. All who signed on would be taught a trade, earn as they learned, and be well paid, Kaiser promised in a tantalizing booklet, *Serve Your Country and Yourself: Help Build War-Winning Ships at Richmond, California.* Wages started at $45.76 a week for unskilled workers, quickly progressed to $54.60, and rose to $87.40 for crew leaders. "How fast you climb is entirely up to you," the booklet said. Working conditions were described as spacious and airy. Richmond and the surrounding towns were said to be pleasant communities with "various types of attractive homes," and California offered redwoods, the ocean, and romance. The company promised to advance the recruits' train fare with the understanding that it would be repaid through a series of $10 deductions from their paychecks.

Some 38,000 recruits headed west to Kaiser shipyards, many of them in the company's "defense trains." "They spent three or four days on those old choo-choos, packed in like cattle," said Joyce L. Harvey, an interviewer in the company's massive hiring hall, a three-story building that filled a city block in the center of Richmond. "They came to us first. Most of them hadn't had any sleep. Often they were hungry because the train had run out of food. They hadn't had a chance to bathe, and there was no air-conditioning in the hiring hall. Sometimes there would be two thousand people standing in line, waiting for interviews. They were tired and cranky. Very often fights broke out."

The interviews often got "a little personal," Harvey recollected. "This was wartime, and defense employers worried about sabotage. We worked closely with the FBI. The forms we filled out contained quite a few details. For identification purposes, I asked one woman if she had any scars or other marks, and she said, 'Ma'am, I got a scar on my leg where a hog bit me.' Many of them could not read or write. We asked all the women if they could sew. If they said yes, we sent them to welding classes because someone at Kaiser had decided that if you could sew, you could weld."

After a few days in California, many of the newcomers felt hoodwinked. The wages and the jobs were everything Kaiser had promised, but Richmond was no El Dorado. As the population swelled from

23,000 in 1941 to 100,000 in 1945, new arrivals were blamed, often to their faces, for ills ranging from crowded schools to rising crime. "It didn't matter where you were from, they thought of you as Okies and Arkies," said Lovie Amos, who came out from Missouri with her husband. "We were not welcome. You could feel it in the tone of voice of people in the stores. Sometimes in the shipyard people would write things on the bulkheads, like 'Why don't the Okies take Japan? They took California without the loss of a man.' There were lots of jokes about people who had never encountered indoor plumbing before and didn't know how to use a gas or electric stove. I can understand why people in Richmond were upset, but it didn't make you feel so good at the time."

In 1942 Kaiser inadvertently exacerbated the tensions by taking part in a program devised by Los Angeles County judges, who had waived sentences for petty criminals willing to sign on at the shipyards. Seventy-four of the miscreants were ushered aboard buses and whisked to Richmond. Soon after they arrived, three were jailed for public drunkenness, infuriating the overworked police chief. As with England's decision to give debtors a fresh start in Georgia, the program benefited the exporters more than the importers. Kaiser quickly withdrew.

Housing in Richmond was scarce and expensive, forcing many of the newcomers to choose between "hot beds" and long commutes complicated by carpooling, the rationing of gasoline and tires, and the vehicular molasses on two-lane roads never intended for heavy traffic. "Many of the men I met slept in 'hot beds,'" Clifford Trotter, a Kaiser personnel manager, remembered. "The bed was yours for eight hours. Then you got up, took off your sheets, and the next man came in, made it up, and slept for eight hours. The beds were working around the clock." The housing shortage punctured many a dream of working hard, putting a little by, and bringing the family west. Homesickness was epidemic, particularly among Southerners, leading one shipyard official to theorize that "either the Southerners are more sentimental than the Northerners, or their wives treat them better."

The dissatisfaction emerged in the course of a company investigation of high turnover, and as soon as the dimensions of the difficulties were understood, expediters were assigned to resolve them. Kaiser pressed the Federal Housing Authority to speed approval of plans to build 21,000 apartments for families and 4,000 dormitory rooms in Richmond. To ease traffic congestion, Kaiser started a ferry service between San Francisco and Richmond and knocked together a commuter rail line from Richmond to Oakland, twelve miles south. New railroad cars being hard to get, the tracks were laid to fit some castoffs from New York City's Third Avenue line.

Kaiser also revised the handling of the "defense train" arrivals. Showers replaced the hiring hall as the first stop, buses began running around the clock to take recruits to their lodgings, directions to workplaces were given in detail, and the unhappy were referred to counselors whose job it was to address complaints. On the theory that "losing these men is the same as throwing needed material into the bay," supervisors were instructed to imbue workers with a sense of the importance of their contributions to the war effort.

Perhaps because of lessons learned in Richmond, the company was more successful in coping with the newcomers flooding into its yards at Swan Island and Vancouver, Washington, and Portland, Oregon. A few months of construction in 1941 transformed 647 acres of swampland into the town of Vanport, which instantly acquired a population of forty thousand. The second-largest city in Oregon, Vanport was also the nation's largest war housing project.

High turnover plagued Kaiser and the rest of the defense industry throughout the war. The draft accounted for much of it, but the physical demands of shipyard work, the difficulty of the commute, and the ease of changing jobs in a booming economy aggravated the problem at Richmond. Although employment at Kaiser's shipyards peaked at 197,000, by war's end, the company's personnel files bulged with records on 1,000,000 employees.

EARLY in the mobilization, actuaries at the Metropolitan Insurance Company predicted that on-the-job fatalities would rise because of long hours, constant deadline pressures, and lack of familiarity with the settings and processes of the work. Between Pearl Harbor and October 1943, industry claimed more than 7,000,000 casualties (injuries plus deaths), while the American armed forces would suffer 1,078,162 casualties during the entire war.

Industry increased its attention to safety, and by all accounts, Kaiser was vigilant and progressive. But shipyards were inescapably dangerous. Cranes moving raw materials and prefabricated modules sometimes dropped their loads. Falls—from ladders and scaffolds, into holds, off decks—were common. Hot rivets shot amok. Overhead work with tools that cut and burned steel sent shards of molten metal down collars. Welders wore hoods with tinted glass, but anyone else who looked the wrong way at the wrong moment risked an eye injury known as a flash. "That's when the welding rod flashes directly into your eyes," explained Lola Malone, a welder in Richmond. "Just a few seconds will give you one. It feels as if somebody poured sand into your eyes. It's fiery, and it grates." The symptoms persisted for twelve hours or more.

"Kaiser was really good about safety, but some people were just oblivious to what was going on around them," said Norman Merboth, leader of a welding crew. "I saw people leap from beam to beam just as though they were on flat ground. I saw guys wearing heavy tool belts fall into the drink and drown. The cranes sounded warning bells before they moved, but people occasionally got hit and killed because they weren't paying attention."

Steel-toed boots, hard hats, and safety goggles were part of the dress code, and women were instructed to tie up their hair to protect it from fire and whirring machinery. Jewelry, metal buttons, and anything else that might snag was forbidden. The U.S. Maritime Commission mandated that women's coveralls have drop seats and dress shields and that there be "no ornamentation such as puff type shoulders, extended or standing collars or neck pieces." Underwear selection, the commission decided, could be left to the women themselves "since climatic conditions will govern the choice."

Earplugs and masks against fumes were unheard of, as were the hazards of asbestos, which was used to sheathe miles of pipe. Former workers with lung ailments trace them to their shipyard days, and other wartime injuries live on as scars, limps, missing fingers, impaired joints, and hearing problems. The decibel level ranged from thunderous to excruciating. "One night I walked across a hold that had riveters and chipping guns working on it," said John B. Wilson, a welder. "My feet seemed to float across the deck, and I think they *were* from the vibrations of all those guns. I was actually surprised I was able to hear after I got clear."

The poor physical condition of the workforce added to the hazards as well to high absenteeism throughout the defense establishment. Many of Kaiser's imported workers, having grown up in isolated communities and without adequate nourishment or doctoring, were susceptible to flu, pneumonia, and a wide range of other ills. Men over sixty-five and boys under sixteen lied about their age to get shipyard jobs. "They needed people so bad, they didn't check," said Ray Baker, who went to work at age fifteen as a painter helper in the Vancouver yard.

Kaiser found that most of its attendance problems were attributable to illness and that illness was widespread because so many of the company's employees "were not physically capable of doing the job." Injuries, pregnancy, and nights on the town increased the toll. "For many months I had a standing order at the hiring hall for one hundred laborers a day," personnel manager Clifford Trotter recalled. "One of the reasons was that many of the people hired were drinking men. They worked till they got a paycheck, then went off and drank till they were broke, then came back to work."

Henry Kaiser took the health problems seriously and decided to transplant to the shipyards the system he had created for his construction crews on the Grand Coulee Dam project: a health care plan with its own hospitals and salaried doctors, funded with payroll deductions from employees who chose to participate. Weekly contributions of fifty cents covered doctors' visits and hospital charges. Kaiser established a foundation to run the program as a nonprofit endeavor and borrowed $700,000 to build or buy hospitals near the yards. Coverage was soon offered to workers' family members for an additional twenty-five cents a head. Kaiser's employee health care plan evolved into one of the country's largest health maintenance organizations.

By 1943, absenteeism at defense companies was serious enough to command the attention of the Senate's Special Committee Investigating the Defense Program, which monitored war production. At hearings held in March, the committee's chairman, Senator Harry Truman, noted that productivity was unsatisfactory and that deficiencies were likely to worsen as more troops went to war and needed ever-greater quantities of ships, planes, weapons, and supplies. Various members of Congress blamed labor unions, and one congressman had introduced legislation to punish absentees by drafting them.

Deeply offended, Philip Murray, president of the Congress of Industrial Organizations, called the idea "an insult to the American army." He blamed poor attendance on stresses that had not been fully addressed: overcrowding in defense towns like Richmond, long commutes, and poor health. None of those concerns, Murray noted tartly, would be solved by a punitive draft.

At a ship launching a few weeks later, Henry Kaiser said that all the talk of absenteeism had left Americans with the false impression that war workers were shirking their duties. In his judgment, the phenomenon worth noting was "presenteeism"—attendance averaging 93 percent at West Coast shipyards. But 7 percent of 197,000 workers added up to nearly 14,000 missing persons a day, and behind Henry Kaiser's public puffery, shipyard managers waged an unending campaign to improve attendance. A company honor society, Anchor Men and Women, awarded gold pins for eighteen months of perfect attendance. An employee handbook urged workers to limit their alcohol consumption: "You can't drink the town dry in one night, so why not leave some behind for your vacation when the war ends?" An essay contest invited suggestions for improving attendance. "I won first prize," said Harold Furst, who spent a year systematizing assembly processes. "A big part of the problem was that many people who worked in the shipyards were not used to coming to work every day. I said that if management would let people know what it was doing, they might come to work because they would understand why it was important."

"The shipyards were a melting pot," said Frances Herrington, who supervised a crew of keypunch machine operators in Richmond. There were Okies, Arkies, Texans, Hispanics, blacks, Chinese— Americans of nearly every extraction except Japanese. There were also goldbrickers, draft dodgers, and con artists, including one who volunteered to collect contributions for gifts for workers leaving for the military, then purchased trinkets and pocketed the change. Another was said to have punched the time clock for the day shift at eight o'clock in the morning, slipped back out with the throng going home from the graveyard shift, and passed his days at leisure. In the late afternoon, he slipped back in with the crowd arriving for the swing shift, retrieved his time card, and punched out with the day shift.

If the patriotism of defense workers was not as impassioned as the newsreels said, it was nevertheless a fact of many lives. "My father was a veteran of World War One and active in the American Legion," said Joyce Harvey of Kaiser's hiring hall. "My mother had never worked outside the home in her life, bless her heart. Both of them came up from New Mexico to work in the yards. They felt it was their patriotic duty."

Eva Yorton, who spent a high school summer vacation working in a warehouse and painting serial numbers on torpedo heads at Kaiser's Swan Island yard, recalled the excitement of watching ship after ship return from successful test runs. "It would come back with whistles blowing and a broom up on the mast to show that it was a clean sweep. Then they'd load that one up and ship it out. You felt really proud. Everybody was still in shock from Pearl Harbor. Most of the boys I knew were gone overnight. You felt like you were doing something to bring them back sooner."

EQUAL opportunity was an idea of the future, and the wartime willingness to hire women and minorities sprang from necessity rather than desire. With rare exceptions, supervisors were white and male,

leaving women and minorities clustered at the bottom of the hierarchy. There were few protests, in part because the social order of the
shipyard was the social order of the era. In addition, Kaiser workers
belonged to unions, which insisted upon equal pay for equal work, and
the pay was exceptionally good. While postal clerks earned about fifty
cents an hour and beginners at aircraft factories made sixty-eight cents,
Kaiser started workers at ninety-five cents. After the Depression, a
shipyard job seemed as good as a mining claim at Sutter's Mill. Frank
Lee, a Chinese-American from a family of ten children, dropped out
of high school at sixteen in 1942 to commute by ferry from San
Francisco to Richmond. With his wages, his family no longer needed
public assistance.

Madge Hart, a young mother recently separated from her husband,
supported her children by working as a tank cleaner, carrying rags and
buckets up and down ladders and climbing over and under pipes in the
bowels of ships. "We crawled on hands and knees and took extension
lights with us because it was dark down there," she remembered. "We
worked in pairs in case one of us got stuck. We cleaned up oil, put it
into five-gallon buckets. We were about the dirtiest crew that could
have been—just full of grease by the end of the day." Hart stayed until
the shipyards closed at the end of the war. "We lived in a government
housing project about a mile above the yards, and she walked to work,"
said her son, Leroy Hart. "She did great at supporting us. I was really
proud of her, as proud as a kid could be."

John Jones, a black man born and raised in Arkansas, was nineteen
when he heard about the Richmond shipyards from a friend already
on the payroll. "He told me to apply for a job as a tank scaler," Jones
said. "It was common labor, not even semiskilled. You went down into
the double bottoms of the ships and went along behind the welder,
scraping slag off the welded seams. Then a chipper would come along
and vee out the seams so that the welder could lay in another weld. It
was extremely dirty in there." Jones remembered cashing his check at
a local grocery store, where he saw his first silver dollars. He bought
himself a watch, went to the dentist, and sent money to his mother.

Jones and members of other minority groups who worked in

Kaiser's shipyards reported little overt prejudice and discrimination, at least in hiring. "In my case, being unskilled, I had nothing to protest against," Jones said. "I was assigned according to my abilities. The welders were men, women, white, black, and Mexican. Some whites probably moved up and got highly skilled. But during that time, after living through the Depression, the feeling was that you grabbed whatever you could to survive. You didn't have time to look around and see what the guy next door was doing." When he realized that he was unlikely to be promoted, however, he found a way to promote himself: "Chippers were paid ten cents an hour more than tank scalers, and I thought I could do the work. So I quit at yard two and got hired as a chipper in yard three."

Black employees at the company's shipyards in Portland, which were managed by Henry Kaiser's son Edgar, pressed harder for their fair share. When they pointed out the segregation in company cafeterias, Edgar ordered tables designated blacks only, whites only, and mixed groups. When they noted that residents of white dormitories were quartered in double rooms while black dormitories housed residents in rooms for twelve to twenty-four, Edgar asked the government for funds to convert the big dorm rooms to doubles to prevent discrimination and increase productivity.

The Boilermakers Union in Portland refused to admit blacks except as members of a separate auxiliary, forcing them to pay dues but not allowing them to vote. When a group of black workers refused to pay, union leaders pressured Edgar to fire them. The Fair Employment Practices Commission, which President Roosevelt had created in 1941, insisted otherwise.

Edgar steered a middle course through the turmoil. Afraid that whites might riot, he refused black demands for supervisory jobs. But he also tried to use his influence to talk the boilermakers into ending their discrimination and to persuade local merchants and restaurateurs to be more hospitable to blacks. While racial inequities never disappeared from the Portland yards, Kaiser provided jobs for 7,250 of the city's 7,500 black workers.

Because of the labor shortage, Kaiser, along with other defense contractors, welcomed women and put thousands of them to work. Eventually they held more than a quarter of the jobs in the Richmond yards. "I don't think the men resented us," said Mary Fabilli, an artist who worked as a steel checker and also designed graphics for company publications. "They knew it was necessary for us to be there."

There were incidents of sexual harassment (one of which was met with a roundhouse punch that sent the offender plunging down a hold), and workers gossiped about assignations deep in the hulls. "As far as I knew, that was mostly hope on the part of the men," said John Wilson. "I suppose there were available women, but I never worked with any."

Judging by the recollections of many former employees, there was more help than hazing for the women who went to work in the ship-yards. "If welding lines were too heavy for a woman to carry, I'd help her," said Joseph Horton, a cutter and burner. "And if a woman couldn't reach up in a corner to do some burning, I'd do it for her. That wasn't unusual." Within six months of their arrival in the yards, women welders were performing almost as well as their male counter-parts (ninety-four versus ninety-nine feet of flat welding per day, according to a company study). When management learned that much of the turnover among women was due to exhaustion from climbing ladders with heavy buckets and tools, the company's gynecologist was put to work designing a physical training program to teach women how to climb with loads.

Ann Cox Steppan and a friend, both recently out of high school, worked outdoors at night with an older colleague who had lost his toes to frostbite. "He kept after us to keep warm and be careful," Steppan recalled. One raw night he commandeered a canvas to tack to the open side of a shack that was their only shelter from the elements.

After discovering that Richmond employed thousands of mothers of young children, Kaiser built a day care center large enough for four hundred and opened smaller centers in apartment buildings and schools. Centers also went up near the yards in Washington and Oregon. Some operated around the clock. For about a dollar a day (a shade less than 10 percent of average pay), parents could leave children under the supervision of doctors, nurses, a psychologist, a nutritionist, certified teachers, and assorted assistants. Sick children were cared for in the center's infirmary so that mothers could go to work knowing their offspring were well tended.

"When I went to work in the shipyards, my husband and I had a ten-month-old and a three-year-old," said Lovie Amos. "I worked the day shift, and every morning as all the children arrived at the child care center, there was a registered nurse at the front desk in the lobby to examine them to make sure they weren't coming down with something. The children were divided into groups by age and overseen by teachers and teachers' aides. They offered the children activities appropriate for their ages and saw to it that they napped. A kitchen staff delivered breakfast and lunch and snacks to the classrooms. The older children were taken on field trips. The center operated under the jurisdiction of the Richmond school system, and when children turned five, they started school."

Immunizations were available for a nominal fee, haircuts at the going rate. At some Kaiser child care centers, parents could pay the staff additional fees to take care of the family mending and grocery shopping. A few centers offered dinner to go for sixty-five cents, a major convenience in a world without frozen foods or microwave ovens. Entrées were cooked in the center's kitchen and packaged with a vegetable, salad, and dessert.

Professionals on staff debated whether it was "fitting" to get involved in the minutiae of housekeeping but decided such services had merit because they gave working women "more time to be mothers." The dinner program was instituted to "lessen the load of the woman who is a worker, a wife, a mother, a shopper, a cook, a laundress."

First Lady Eleanor Roosevelt agreed. In 1943, after christening a Kaiser ship in Portland, she toured one of the company's day care centers and declared, "We must take care of the children. . . . Mothers can't work well on a war job if they have to worry about their youngsters."

Marvelous as Kaiser's child care centers were, the company had to stage a publicity campaign to persuade mothers to use them. Women, the staff discovered, felt guilty about turning child care over to others and about departing from "the usual cultural food pattern of preparing all of their family's food even through a strenuous period of war work."

With government paying the bills and putting a higher priority on productivity than penny-pinching, it was easy for Kaiser and other defense companies to establish fine day care programs. Kaiser's child care professionals, hoping their pioneering work would continue after the war, noted that work enabled many women "to discover that they have abilities which are income-producing and satisfaction-producing. It will be a tragic social loss if every woman who has done a good job of creating wealth (services or things needed) is forced out of her production role."

"I loved working in the shipyards," said Lovie Amos. "I think most women did. For a lot of women, this was the first taste of earning an income and testing their intelligence. To my way of thinking, that experience was truly the beginning of women's liberation. It was the first time I ever wore pants. My husband never did adjust to that. After the war, women were told, 'Go home.' I had no intention of going home. I went to work for a water district, stayed there, and worked my way to the top. I was the first woman to be a division manager."

Most women did go home. There was a boom in babies, and with the babies came a seemingly incurable case of amnesia. Americans simply forgot that they had done a first-class job of caring for small children at an affordable price, thanks to federal subsidies made available despite the crushing financial burden of war.   .

DESPITE absenteeism, turnover, debility, and the draft, Kaiser shipyard workers at Richmond, Portland, Vancouver, and Swan Island turned in an astonishing performance. Between April 1941 and August 1945, they built 1,094 cargo ships (821 Liberties, 219 Victory ships, and 54 others), 147 tankers, 55 troop transports, 87 combat transports, 50 small aircraft carriers, 45 landing ship tank vessels, and 12 frigates. They also repaired more than 100 war-damaged ships. The wartime expansion of the merchant marine created the largest armada in history, and Kaiser workers built more than a quarter of it. Their boss saw to it that their praises were sung, literally as well as metaphorically. Bandleader Fred Waring and a collaborator, Jack Dolph, memorialized Kaiser's speed in "We'll Do It," a song dedicated to Kaiser employees. While it never made the hit parade, the lyrics captured the Kaiser spirit: "Uncle Sam's in a jam and it's up to you and me! We'll do it! We'll do it! If it's got to be done, we'll do it! We'll go over, go under, go round or go through: If we start it, we finish whatever we do," and so on. In September 1942 Henry Kaiser persuaded President Roosevelt to travel to Portland for the launch of the SS *Joseph N. Teal,* a Liberty ship built in a record ten days—a full thirty days short of the average. Newspapers across the country applauded the deed.

"What has Oregon got that we haven't got?" Richmond's chief, Clay Bedford, asked on printed cards distributed to workers soon after the *Teal* was launched. They responded with more than 250 suggestions, management took the best of them, and work for the next ship was scheduled with unprecedented exactitude. The keel of the SS *Robert E. Peary* was laid at 12:01 A.M. on November 18, 1942. "The boat is now under construction and the men are so excited they're staying late and coming an hour or two early to watch the work," Bedford wired Henry Kaiser. So many were watching, in fact, that they had become a hazard. Company officials took to the public address system to ask them to go home. Four days, fifteen hours, and twenty-six minutes after construction had begun, the *Peary* was launched, complete with bath towels.

Nearly all of the 1,490 ships built by the Kaiser yards were merchant marine vessels, but in 1942, Edgar and Henry Kaiser ventured into warships with plans for the "baby flattop," an abbreviated aircraft carrier. By modifying an existing cargo ship design, Edgar and Henry thought they could churn out the little flattops as expeditiously as they made Liberties. They predicted the new carriers would pack several punches since they could engage in combat, protect convoys of troops and cargo ships from submarines, and provide air support for invading ground troops.

Sixteen admirals turned down the Kaisers' proposal. Undeterred,

Henry arranged to present his idea to the secretary of the navy and the president. Roosevelt approved, and the fifty baby flattops built at Vancouver figured in several Pacific naval campaigns. They also won praise from Prime Minister Churchill, who called them "the most effective instrument in destroying the submarine menace."

The ships were not flawless. The crews of the first baby flattops called them "Kaiser's coffins" because they were so bow-heavy that they nosed under the waves. Clay Bedford was summoned before the Truman Committee in 1944 to explain why cracks had developed along the welded seams of a worrisome number of Kaiser's Liberty ships. Bedford testified that fractures had declined as Kaiser gained experience and suggested that the problem may have owed more to bad steel than bad welds. To head off further problems, Kaiser had begun reinforcing crucial welds with rivets.

HENRY Kaiser spent much of the war fighting Washington and enjoying himself immensely as he bellowed for more workers, more steel, more of everything that would lengthen his lead over competitors. Washington bellowed back, complaining about excessive costs, broken rules, and missed deadlines. When deliveries fell behind schedule one summer, Admiral Vickery of the Maritime Commission wired Henry Kaiser, "I should very much like to know reasons for such failure, and hope they will be something outside of the usual line of alibis." Kaiser immediately replied that two navy fiefdoms were squabbling over the acceptability of minor modifications; one wanted to take a ship, the other did not. Meanwhile, "the perishables are aboard but no crew," Kaiser said. He seized the occasion to ask Vickery's help in speeding the flow of materials to other ships in progress.

With Andrew Carnegie, Henry Kaiser believed that a successful man was obliged to trumpet his accomplishments in order to spur fellow tycoons to even grander feats. By October 1942, only eighteen months after laying his first keel, Kaiser felt entitled to lecture a meeting of the National Association of Manufacturers on the meaning of industry's triumphs in mobilizing for war. Business ought not to congratulate itself, he told his audience. "This is no hour to rest upon achievements. We must move our objectives ahead as each new goal is attained. If an industry succeeds in doubling its output, that merely indicates the inefficiency that had grown up in the past." However well they were doing, Kaiser said, they should be exploiting the latest in engineering, technology, and management to do more.

While other manufacturers complained about labor, Henry Kaiser piously declared that labor relations were human relations. Addressing the Academy of Political Science a few weeks after his blunt words to manufacturers, Kaiser said that when a worker was "treated like a human being; when his ability, skill, and goodwill are properly recognized; when his ambitions and his anxieties are given due and just consideration, he is not only capable of superb loyalty but of performing veritable miracles in production."

With his keen nose for the coming thing, Kaiser promoted the idea that if the United States mobilized for peace with the intensity it had brought to war, it could reach "the highest ground which civilization has yet attained." The war had created electronics "almost literally out of the air, and a new world has opened up to us greater potentials than those which Columbus viewed when he sailed into the regions of the North American continent," he wrote in the pages of the *Progressive* in 1944. Refusing to accept the conventional wisdom that wars were followed by depressions, he predicted that American industry could be kept busy for twenty-five years supplying nations devastated by war.

Lena Horne, Dinah Shore, and other celebrities came to the yards to launch ships or perform for workers, partly to keep up morale and partly to keep up press coverage. The president's appearance at the launching of the *Teal* and Mrs. Roosevelt's christening of the first baby flattop led to news coverage that made Henry J. Kaiser famous.

Intrigued by the machinery of publicity and curious about his reputation, he hired the Opinion Research Corporation in 1943 to find out what the world thought of him. Eighty-eight percent of his fellow citizens recognized his name, making him more famous than Winston Churchill, who was known to 80 percent of those polled, but less

famous than Henry Ford, who scored 99.8 percent. The public saw
Kaiser as a man who got things done. Journalists cast him as a hero.
Only his fellow industrialists withheld praise, seeing "the whole Kaiser
performance [as] undignified and unworthy of the best tradition of
industry." Some business leaders derided him as a grandstander, while
others felt his boasts were bad for business because they made most
manufacturers look like underachievers. Still others feared that because
he owed his success to government, he would promote statism at the
expense of private enterprise.

The pollsters concluded that big business was wrong and Henry
Kaiser was right. In their judgment, he had proved the value of the
"industrial ceremonial," a staged event such as the four-day ship or a
public appearance in Washington. "Most industrialists rightly abhor
cheap publicity stunts," the pollsters said in their report. "They seek to
deliver honest achievement and to understate rather than overstate
their results. But we cannot overlook the fact that the enterprise system as we have known it in America depends not only on sound economic achievement, but on proper dramatization of that achievement
as well—on telling the story of the free enterprise system in terms the
public can understand."

In the essay written for the *Progressive,* Kaiser explained what enterprise meant to him. "Lay hold of this word 'enterprise,' which in its
origins means to undertake, and give it a new meaning; namely, to create, to build, to possess, to enjoy, and best of all, to *share. . . .* The use
to which wealth is put is vastly important, but the fact remains there
can be no social progress without it. Therefore, the production of
wealth—new wealth, serviceable wealth—is a lofty goal and worthy of
all our best powers." Although Kaiser must have understood the extent
to which his private fortune had been the product of public wealth,
the point was one he did not care to acknowledge.

ON August 12, 1945, Henry Kaiser joined the Harmonettes, a high
school girls' glee club, in singing "Oh, What a Beautiful Morning" and
watched the Richmond's last Liberty ship, the SS *Marine Snapper,* slip

into San Francisco Bay. Three days later, with Japan's surrender, the war was over. Three days after that, Kaiser was in Washington, telling the Senate's Special Committee Investigating the Defense Program to get on with the business of peace. "All I want is speed," he said. "There is no problem at all. The world is ours. We are going to have the greatest amount of business that ever was in existence and a productivity that will enthuse everyone, but not if the thing is dilly-dallied, dilly-dallied, dilly-dallied and nothing moved."

Some of the dilly-dallying involved the sale of a huge portfolio of industrial real estate owned by the government. During the war, Congress had appropriated $9.2 billion to build shipyards, factories, and other facilities that it believed business would not finance because the need for their goods would evanesce with the arrival of peace. At Geneva, Utah, for example, $200 million had been spent to build a steel mill to supply West Coast shipbuilders and other defense contractors. U.S. Steel had operated the plant throughout the war. Having no wish to enter the steel business, the government in 1946 accepted the only bid it received for the plant, $47.5 million from U.S. Steel.

Henry Kaiser entered the postwar sweepstakes for the government's industrial assets by negotiating inexpensive leases on a huge factory at Willow Run, Michigan, and two aluminum plants near Spokane, Washington. His dream of using Willow Run to enter the auto business would prove disastrous, but the aluminum venture became one of his biggest successes.

Wanting more, he tried to use the sale of the Geneva plant to renegotiate the terms of the $103 million in government loans that had built his mill at Fontana. In a contentious booklet entitled *Outrage in Steel*, Kaiser argued that since Washington had been willing to give U.S. Steel a bargain at Geneva, Kaiser Steel deserved equal treatment at Fontana. Government was unpersuaded.

In the fall of 1946, the House Committee on the Merchant Marine and Fisheries called Henry and Edgar Kaiser to appear at hearings resulting from an investigation showing that on an investment of $23 million, nineteen American shipbuilders had pocketed $356 million, a

fifteenfold gain in five years. The shipbuilders countered that the relationship between investment and return was irrelevant; what mattered
was the profit per ship, and that had been fixed by the government. As
the biggest and best known of the nineteen, Henry Kaiser was the
prime target of the investigation, and Marvin J. Coles, the committee's
general counsel, seemed intent on proving that Kaiser had exploited
the war to enrich himself at taxpayer expense.

Two things rankled the committee. One was the chasm between
Henry Kaiser's initial investment in shipbuilding ($100,000) and his net
profits from it ($41 million). The other was his insistence that he had
actually lost money during the war because of the high costs of starting his steel mill at Fontana.

Kaiser replied that since the government had imposed no minimum
capital requirements for shipbuilders, he had violated no rules. And
because of Kaiser's efficiency, its Liberty ships had cost the government
$840,000 apiece, compared with the $1.1 million averaged by the
twelve other yards where Liberties were built. Kaiser estimated that it
had pared $266 million from the government's wartime bill for ships.
Insisting that he loathed the idea of war profits, he said he would favor
any system Congress might devise to assure that there were none. "If
you want to put everyone in soup kitchens so no one makes a dime,
it's up to Congress to write the laws that way," he said. He pointed out
that at $152.78 million, his share of the government's wartime loans
came to one-half of 1 percent of the total. He also noted that his seed
capital for his shipbuilding ventures had included $13.75 million bor-
rowed from the bank and that he had borrowed millions more from
private sources to finance other war projects.

Coles observed that the government had agreed to pay half the
interest on the $13.75 million loan and wondered, at length, whether
Kaiser was personally liable for the loan. Kaiser said that only a lawyer
could answer the question with certainty but that he had taken the
obligation seriously. Coles hoped to create the impression that if Kaiser
himself had not been legally responsible for the debt, he could have
defaulted with impunity.

Frustrated by his inability to answer a number of detailed questions, Kaiser said, "In all fairness to me, I am operating twenty-eight industries, and my memory—I will not trust it to serve in answering questions before a committee when I am under oath." When he proposed that the concerns be presented in writing so that he could have an accountant investigate, the committee's chairman, Schuyler Otis Bland of Virginia, snapped, "The committee will decide what should be done. You try to answer the questions."

Kaiser's bald head "provided an excellent barometer of his temper" during the proceedings, a United Press reporter observed. "Pink meant that he was only medium sore; scarlet indicated that he was getting good and mad; purple proved that he had to restrain himself from chopping down the congressman and using him for a propeller shaft stuffing in a Liberty ship."

One member of the committee suggested that Kaiser's twenty-eight companies amounted to an enormous shell game, enabling him to hide profits by shifting money from enterprise to enterprise. Another expressed annoyance with the financial information at the committee's disposal, all of which had come from Kaiser. But the committee had few other sources because the auditing systems of the General Accounting Office and the Maritime Commission had broken down. Edgar Kaiser volunteered that whatever the current problems, those agencies had kept a close watch on the shipyards throughout the war and had found no irregularities.

The committee seemed aggrieved by the fact that the government had spent $109.6 million to build Kaiser's yards and the housing, transportation, and other support systems around them. But the property belonged to government, not to Kaiser, and if government had not been willing to make the investment, no one would have. By the time Henry and Edgar Kaiser testified at the hearings, the shipyards were ghost towns. Without a war, there was little demand for new ships.

In a newspaper column about the hearings, Eleanor Roosevelt wondered what the controversy was. "[W]e were grateful to these men of enterprise and daring when we needed them, and I do not think we should cavil now." The editorialists of *The New York Times* concurred: "We needed the ships desperately. We got them."

NEITHER Henry Kaiser nor his inquisitors nor Mrs. Roosevelt mentioned the extent to which World War II had transformed the economy. Throughout the war, the American economy was less a model of free enterprise than monopsony—a system organized around a single customer. By 1944, the federal government was spending 42 percent of the gross national product—more than $300 million a day—on the war, supporting millions of civilians who worked for defense contractors, millions more who worked for suppliers, and millions more in the retail and service establishments patronized by war workers. Wages, prices, and profit margins were prescribed by Washington, annoying industrialists, but it was Uncle Sam who kept their factories humming.

The monopsony worked well. The customer got the goods, business was virtually assured of not losing money, labor got full employment. Between 1941 and 1945, the gap between the poor and the rich shrank considerably: the incomes of the poorest 20 percent of Americans rose 111.5 percent, while the top 20 percent gained 76.7 percent. Kaiser's shipyard workers fared even better. The good fortune of Eduardo Carrasco, who went from earning less than $20 a week as a hotel busboy to more than $100 as a journeyman driller, was not atypical. Encouraged daily to buy war bonds (and unable to buy most durable goods, which were manufactured in small quantities to conserve resources), many employees amassed sizable savings. Workers at Richmond put an average of 10 percent of their pay into war bonds, and employees at Portland invested even more. "I bought war bonds and saved money like a good middle-class American," said Norman Merboth, who made nearly $25 a day in Richmond. "I was saving for a car and a house."

Desperation had become the mother of cooperation, and government had suspended the rules of business as usual in order to purchase the machinery of war: 296,000 warplanes, 5.8 million tons of aerial bombs, 87,000 warships, 5,000 cargo ships, 102,000 tanks, 2.4 million trucks, 370,000 artillery pieces, 20 million small arms, 44 billion rounds of ammunition, plus uniforms, boots, and mess kits by the millions. The war had made the United States an economic paradox—a welfare state that touched off "the greatest boom in the history of capitalism," as Eliot Janeway observed in his history of the mobilization. Average citizens, "far from being proletarianized, began to accumulate their own funds of capital. On the one hand, millions of working people joined the class of small investors while, on the other, capital went back to work."

11

THE MAN IN THE MIDDLE

FIRST SERGEANT WHITNEY Moore Young Jr. spent World War II fighting on two fronts, battling the Axis powers in Europe and racism in the U.S. Army. Born in Shelby County, Kentucky, in 1921, he had been raised on the campus of the Lincoln Institute, a Negro boarding school run by his father. Young volunteered for the army in the summer of 1941, a few weeks after graduating from Kentucky State Industrial College and a few weeks before his twentieth birthday. He had enlisted in the hope of going to medical school under a special training program but was assigned instead to the Massachusetts Institute of Technology for a crash course in engineering.

By 1944, when his unit landed in France, many of the one million Negro men and women wearing American military uniforms had had their fill of fighting for freedoms they were denied. The War Department had ordered the services to open their officer candidate schools to Negroes, but the directive was easily thwarted. Commanders simply refused to recommend black soldiers for the training. Negro newspapers, which often carried stories of racial discrimination in the military, were banned on many bases. Theaters and servicemen's clubs were segregated, and the amenities for blacks were decidedly inferior. So was much of the merchandise offered to them in post exchanges. In the American South, more hospitality was extended to the enemy than to blacks in uniform. German and Italian prisoners of war were allowed to eat in restaurants off-limits to blacks and were free to ride in the front of the bus.

Decades after the war, Young told a newspaper reporter that in his unit in France, "white officers would say, 'Fall in,' and the men would say, '_____ you.'" (Or so the newspaper's editors phrased the reply.) "Officers were being killed," Young said. "It got to the point where they were afraid to go out of their huts. They couldn't handle the men. The young blacks weren't reconciled to second-class status. They couldn't articulate anything like black pride, but they were able to criticize the hypocrisy of their having to fight for democracy."

A commanding six feet two, Young had a megawatt smile, a nimble wit, keen emotional antennae, and the self-possession of an aristocrat. Drafted as a go-between, Young astutely brokered a permanently conditional truce. "I would say to the brothers in the company, 'I agree you're getting a bad deal, but what's it going to take to get you to fall out tomorrow morning and do the job?' They'd tell me and then I'd go to the officers. 'The men ain't goin' *nowhere*,' I'd tell them, 'unless you do so-and-so. You can put them in the guardhouse but you're going to look bad. It's going to look like you don't have the skills of leadership.' So we'd extract the conditions." When fellow soldiers accused him of toadying to the white man, Young invited them to take his place. No one wanted it.

No one ever would. In his largest and longest-running role as a man in the middle, the ten years he spent as executive director of the National Urban League, Young would be pilloried by black militants for his courtship of powerful white business leaders, scolded by powerful white business leaders for his refusal to repudiate black militants, and mocked as an Uncle Tom in the pages of *The New York Times*. To his black critics, Young was a brother who had sold out. To whites, he sometimes seemed a man who would not stay bought, a renegade insufficiently mindful of those who paid the League's bills. To himself, he was a pragmatist. He said that on his commute to Manhattan from his home in the suburb of New Rochelle, he often debated whether he should get off the train at 125th Street in Harlem to please his black detractors (like Malcolm X, who said that Young did not "spend enough time among Negroes") or "go downtown and talk to an executive of General Motors about two thousand jobs for unemployed Negroes." Young passed much of his time in the company of such men as Henry Ford II and David Rockefeller, he said, for one reason: "They've got the jobs. *Somebody's* got to talk to the people who have something to give."

HEARTENED by his successes in negotiating better treatment for blacks in the army, Young decided to abandon his medical ambitions and devote his life to race relations. "I had seen how people could modify their attitudes when it became necessary to do so," he wrote later, "and I had seen how simple contact with Negroes had wrought deep changes in individuals who had never before questioned the myths about race they were brought up to believe." Young had married his college sweetheart, Margaret Buchner, before going overseas. Soon after the end of his service in the army, they settled in Minneapolis, where he began graduate study in social work at the University of Minnesota.

In September 1947, master's degree in hand, he joined the St. Paul office of the National Urban League as secretary. The St. Paul branch was one of about fifty local affiliates of the League, which had been founded in New York City in 1910 to combat discrimination against Negroes. While the National Association for the Advancement of Colored People (NAACP) staged public demonstrations, filed lawsuits, and tried to influence legislation, the League in its first years studied social problems with the idea of gathering evidence of discrimination and using the facts to persuade those in power that reform was necessary and just. Comparing the two Negro organizations, officials of the League liked to say that their group functioned as the State Department, the NAACP was the War Department, and the plight of their people demanded the best efforts of both.

The League grew rapidly during World War I, as more than three hundred thousand Southern Negroes moved north to fill jobs vacated by whites who had joined the armed forces or taken higher-paying work in munitions plants. Like the settlement houses and ethnic societies that helped immigrants adjust to their new surroundings, the League opened social clubs and recreational facilities, offered education and child care, and led campaigns to increase the supply and quality of housing. From the earliest days, employment was a paramount concern. "Not Alms But Opportunity," a League motto adopted in 1913, summed up the hopes, and the League tried to create opportunity by presenting its case to business, trade groups, and government. It was the first Negro group to back the struggling young American Federation of Labor.

The League—and Negro workers—fared best when employers were desperate. Railroads, shorthanded during the war, dispatched recruiters to the South and brought trainloads of blacks to jobs in the North. In 1915, the tobacco growers of the Connecticut River Valley turned to the League for help after losing their field hands to better-paying factory jobs. The collaboration opened two hundred permanent positions for blacks and, for the rest of the war, hundreds of summer jobs for black college students.

Whitney Young once told President Lyndon Johnson that black organizations always had operated with a double mission: "to make a case 'outside' (for Negro worth and Negro needs), while bucking up Negro morale 'inside.'" In the organization's early decades, local chapters of the League sometimes added a third: reminding blacks of what it took to succeed in a white world. Quoting from League materials, historian Nancy J. Weiss described the effort in Detroit:

A group of "earnest race men" affiliated with the Urban League and local churches established a "Dress Well Club" in Detroit "to create a better impression of the Negro by attention to dress, personal appearance and public behavior." In leaflets, the club urged blacks to hold to high standards in order to avoid intensifying "prejudice, race friction and discrimination." Proper deportment was especially critical under circumstances of interracial contact: "DON'T carry on loud conversations or use vulgar or obscene language in street cars, streets, or in public places," the Urban League admonished. "DON'T be rude and ugly to people on the streets. Be courteous and polite and thereby keep out of trouble." "DON'T make lots of unnecessary noise going to and from baseball games."

Concealed at the heart of such literature is the same sorry truth about power imbalances that infects popular advice to women in search of husbands: Success is unlikely unless subordinates conform to the demands of those whom custom has enshrined as superiors. Centuries of slavery followed by decades of servility had left Negroes nauseously well informed on the subject of how to comport themselves among whites. Pamphlets such as the ones distributed in Detroit may have helped a Southern Negro adapt to life in the urban North, but they may have done even more to persuade employers that job candidates presented by the League would be docile and well behaved.

After World War I, few doors opened. Some employers refused to meet with League representatives, citing policies against hiring Negroes as if policy were fixed by a divine power. Other employers agreed to listen but declined to help because of alleged difficulties elsewhere in their businesses. What would their white employees think? How would white customers react?

But after World War II, Whitney Young thought he sensed an easing of the burden. "I see a new day dawning in this whole field of race relations," he wrote his father in 1948. "Never before in history has public opinion been stronger for a more democratic society. All about the country we see evidences, small as they may be, of changing patterns. More and more, Negro youth are going to be called upon to identify themselves, not as Negroes, but as people whose success or failure in life depends on their own initiative and perseverance." He spoke from his experience at the St. Paul Urban League, which was gradually convincing more businesses to hire Negroes and to hire them for better jobs. Between 1948 and 1950, the number of local companies with Negroes on the payroll rose from 100 to 128. With the tutelage of Young and his colleagues, employers began to see that adding blacks to their staffs was not only decent but smart. The president of a St. Paul department store agreed to hire two Negro saleswomen when Young pointed out their value in serving the store's many Negro customers.

Successful, energetic, and immensely likable, Young soon had a fine reputation that stretched well beyond St. Paul. In 1950 he was named head of the League's affiliate in Omaha, and in 1954 he was appointed dean of Atlanta University's School of Social Work. He had his first taste of leadership in the South's budding civil rights movement in 1958, with a coup that desegregated Atlanta's public libraries. With the support of fellow members of several integrationist organizations, Young found a few black college students willing to present themselves at the desk of the main library downtown and ask for books not available at the three "Negro branches" they were supposed to use. The students were hustled to a downstairs room where they would not be seen by white patrons. Young notified the library's trustees and asked them to order an end to the humiliation. They refused. Young threatened to file a federal lawsuit, which was already prepared. The trustees buckled. It was a swift, satisfying victory, and one that probably would have delighted Andrew Carnegie, whose gifts to public libraries, including Atlanta's, had been inspired by the painful memory of his own exclusion from a private library when he was a boy.

The National Urban League declined to participate in such demonstrations, believing that it could accomplish more as an organization dedicated to racial harmony, a social agency working for equal employment and open housing and better social services, and a planning agency well connected to the white establishment (demurely described in a League brochure as "the most powerful economic, social and civic groups in America"). That was an estimable portfolio, but by the time the League celebrated its fiftieth anniversary, in 1960, paralysis had taken hold. Chronically short of funds, the League had stopped growing, and with the stultification came a timidity especially unfortunate at a moment when the cause of civil rights demanded uncommon bravery.

The Rockefeller Foundation, one of the League's oldest and largest benefactors, led the search for a new executive director for the League and found Whitney Young in Atlanta. When he was hired, the League's board of trustees, most of them prominent white businessmen, looked to him to cure the organization of its inertia. His friends hoped for the same. "Despite all the whoop-de-doo over FREEDOM RIDES and SIT-INS, both of which I applaud, I think the LEAGUE still has a place despite its lack of vigor these past few years," an acquaintance wrote from Baltimore; "to me it's obvious that any interracial outfit has to show boldness or shut up shop. With you in charge things should be different."

They were. Soon after he arrived at League headquarters, in August 1961, he astonished his colleagues by asking them to meet a tight dead-line. "We don't do things that fast," a seasoned staff member explained. Young explained back: "From now on we will." He also nudged the League toward the civil rights movement. He began by meeting regu-larly with the leaders of the NAACP and its Legal Defense and Educational Fund, the Brotherhood of Sleeping Car Porters, the Congress of Racial Equality (CORE), the Student Nonviolent Coordinating Committee, the Southern Christian Leadership Conference, and the National Council of Negro Women. United in their pursuit of equality, the groups disagreed fiercely and often about tactics. Young quickly earned their respect with his ability to mediate disputes and steer the combatants toward common ground. They hon-ored his finesse by dubbing him "chairman of the board" of the civil rights movement.

Young excelled at diplomacy because of his warmth and intelligence and because he was a preternaturally sensitive listener, able to disarm the aggrieved by making them feel understood and valued. Unlike most of his fellow humans, he welcomed confrontation. In his judg-ment, confrontation, which he defined as "any action which puts the people affected by a problem face to face with those responsible for and capable of dealing with it," was essential and inevitable. Young thought a leader ought to plunge into confrontations and try to make them "creative and constructive rather than destructive and self-defeating."

He regularly administered bracing doses of reality to white liberals who imagined themselves epitomes of tolerance and brotherhood. By the early 1960s, many whites found it easy to admit the injustice of racial discrimination, Young noted, but they insisted that reform would have to come from some quarter other than their own. Employers claimed that blacks needed better education before they could be hired and promoted, realtors insisted that blacks would be welcome in white neighborhoods when they had better jobs, and educators predicted that when housing segregation ended, school integration would follow. "Briefly," said Young, "it's always somebody else over there, never me."

In the summer of 1962, toward the end of his first year as head of the League, he boarded a city bus alone for a visit to Harlem. He started in midtown Manhattan, where he was one of two black passengers in a crowd of whites. As the bus moved uptown, the number of whites dwindled, and eventually all the faces on the bus and in the streets were black. Young was shocked. "One could not help but be aware, suddenly, that segregation had not been left behind in Atlanta," he wrote. He got out on 135th Street and walked one ramshackle block after another, past broken windows, debris, derelicts, and the "obviously unemployed." Talking to a few children, he was pained by "the enormity of the waste they symbolized," of the potential that would go unrealized "because they happen to be black." Even more disturbing was his sense that Harlem's devastation could not exist without the "cold apathy" of Northern whites. Their "'conditioned' disinclination to understand" seemed to him "as vicious as the more overt attitude of the South."

The devastation was still on his mind in September, when he addressed a meeting of the Southern Christian Leadership Conference, the civil rights organization headed by Dr. Martin Luther King Jr. A handful of exceptionally talented Negroes were succeeding in American society, Young said, but racism forced the vast majority to settle for the worst jobs, the worst housing, and the worst schools. "I am convinced that there are racists in this country who would prefer that this whole world be taken over by Communism rather than that a neighborhood be opened to a Negro family, or a job made available to a qualified Negro worker, or that a single Negro child be admitted to a classroom where his rights to an education will be assured. Khrushchev himself would have less trouble getting enrolled at the University of Mississippi than James Meredith, an American-born ex-serviceman."

In the white establishment, banks were particularly culpable, Young thought. After decades of seemingly willful ignorance of urban problems, bankers finally had begun expressing concern but seemed content to congratulate themselves on their newfound sympathy. As beneficiaries of economic progress and social stability, Young argued, bankers had an obligation to work "aggressively for social change in all areas of community life."

DURING 1962, Young's first full year on the job, the League's income more than doubled, rising from $340,000 to $722,000. He opened an office in Washington to improve communication with federal agencies in charge of issues of interest to the League. The organization had risen from its stretcher.

The recovery continued in 1963 with the creation of two innovative and highly successful employment programs. With funding from International Business Machines, Time, and other blue-chip corporations, the League started the Secretarial Training Project, an eleven-week course that cost students nothing and nearly always culminated in corporate job offers. The League also established its National Skills Bank, offering employers a central source of qualified black job candidates, all of them screened by League offices throughout the country. Over the next five years, the League trained more than three hundred secretaries and placed more than eighteen thousand blacks in better jobs in banking, medicine, and other fields.

Although the League was thriving under Young's leadership, by 1963 he had concluded that no matter how hard the League and other black organizations worked, and no matter how much they accomplished, they alone could not repair the damage of three centuries of racism. Blacks earned half as much as whites, held a disproportionate share of the lowest-paying jobs, and were twice as likely as whites to be unemployed. To redress the inequities, Young and the National Urban League called on the United States to launch a ten-year, $145 billion "domestic Marshall Plan," modeled on the U.S. aid program that had helped Europe to rebuild after World War II.

President John F. Kennedy had promised new laws to ban racial discrimination, but by itself, equality under the law would not close the economic gap between blacks and whites, Young said. To overcome the effects of past deprivations, blacks needed "a massive effort in employment, education, manpower training, youth motivation and family strengthening." Knowing that some would attack the domestic Marshall Plan as preferential treatment for Negroes, Young made the case that Negroes needed rights that were "more than equal," at least for a time. "Fair competition means starting from the same place in a relatively equal condition. It does not mean declaring, after one runner is halfway around the track and the other runner is just out of a sick bed, that the race shall now begin with equal access to the track."

For those who objected that the domestic Marshall Plan was a multibillion-dollar subsidy of blacks, Young had a compelling counter-argument: America was awash in subsidies. The federal government helped millions of veterans go to college, allowed tax deductions on mortgage interest and property taxes, built highways and commuter railroads that primarily benefited white suburbanites, allowed business to write off its investments, and paid farmers not to plant. "Only the poor get a very small slice of the subsidy pie," Young wrote; "everyone else gets a good helping."

Young characterized the domestic Marshall Plan as an investment rather than an expenditure and noted that money saved by stinting on social investments was sure to be spent elsewhere—on low-income housing, welfare, police, courts, and jails. By an estimate he made a few years later, the denial of equal employment opportunity to blacks cost taxpayers $20 billion a year, an expense he called the "bigotry budget."

AT an Urban League board meeting in the spring of 1963, Young told his trustees that A. Philip Randolph of the Brotherhood of Sleeping Car Porters had invited the League to join a summer march on Washington in support of civil rights. The minutes of the meeting show that the trustees loathed the idea. Some worried that participation in a political demonstration would be construed as lobbying, an activity forbidden to the League and all other tax-exempt organizations. One trustee argued that taking part in the march would somehow "dilute" the League's effectiveness by suggesting that "in all affairs having to do with the Negro the League was available." Others objected that "this kind of 'march' implies that the League can not get to Washington through the front door."

To the well-connected gentlemen of the board, mass demonstrations were unpalatable because they were the tactic of the powerless—of persons forced, as Martin Luther King put it, to "write their most persuasive essays with the blunt pen of marching ranks" because they had found no other way to get the attention of the powerful. Like the mid-nineteenth-century Boston Brahmins who opposed slavery but found the abolitionists a bit scruffy, the Urban League's trustees believed that racial injustice would be ended by their friends in high places, not by masses in the streets.

Young heard out the trustees, then pointed them in the direction he wanted to go. He had already told Randolph that he would consider joining the march but needed to know more. Young told his trustees that he thought he should attend the planning sessions for the event in order to make an informed decision about the League's involvement. He also cautioned them about the dangers of snubbing the march. Because of the League's long-standing commitment to equal opportunity, he said, a premature rejection of the march "might be misinterpreted among the masses of Negro citizens, to the damage of the League's effectiveness, leadership role and respect."

Ultimately Young prevailed by stepping into the middle, shuttling between his trustees and his fellow civil rights leaders. He convinced the organizers of the march to focus the day on the plight of blacks rather than on civil rights legislation promised by the Kennedy administration. And together the leaders decided to make the march interracial, share their speeches in advance in order to assure that they sent the nation a unified message about equality, and allow black militants to participate only if they promised to abide by the rules.

The next hurdle was the White House. In June, President Kennedy summoned Young, Randolph, King, and other civil rights leaders to Washington to remind them that the civil rights bill he had proposed would need every vote he could muster and that a mass protest by blacks could trigger a congressional backlash. "We want success in Congress, not just a big show at the Capitol," he said. "Some of these people are looking for an excuse to be against us. I don't want to give any of them a chance to say, 'Yes, I'm for the bill, but I'm damned if I will vote for it at the point of a gun.'"

Randolph said that he did not know whether the civil rights leaders *could* cancel the march. "The Negroes are already in the streets," he said. "It is very likely impossible to get them off." Young added that the only real choice at this point was between allowing the protest to go ahead spontaneously, with no guidance, and entrusting it to the leadership of "more responsible elements." (On this point, the leaders were bluffing. "I'm not sure that we were as sure as we pretended to be that we could keep this a nonviolent kind of experience," Young later confessed.)

James Farmer, head of CORE, the organization that had invented the sit-in, said that while he appreciated the delicacy of the president's situation, civil rights leaders also felt themselves on the line. If they called off the march and no legislation materialized, they would be "in a difficult if not untenable position," and the frustration among their followers might explode into violence.

King noted that every public demonstration he had led had seemed ill timed. He offered the hope that the march would "serve as a means through which people with legitimate discontents could channel their grievances under disciplined, non-violent leadership. It could also serve as a means of dramatizing the issue and mobilizing support in parts of the country which don't know the problems at first hand."

The subject of police brutality arose, and the president joked that they should not be too hard on Bull Connor, the Birmingham, Alabama, police commissioner who had ordered fire hoses and guard dogs turned against civil rights demonstrators. By horrifying the nation, said the president, Connor had done "more for civil rights than almost anybody else." Kennedy made one last plea. His stock with the public had fallen, he told them. The latest poll showed his approval rating at 47 percent, down from 60. "We're in this up to the neck. The worst trouble of all would be to lose the fight in the Congress. We'll have enough troubles if we win; but, if we win, we can deal with those."

After their meeting with the president, the leaders decided to hold their gathering at the Lincoln Memorial instead of the Capitol, shifting the spotlight from Congress to the president who had freed the slaves but not guaranteed their equality. With the approach of August 28, the day of the march, President Kennedy had a new worry: What if no one came? The organizers had promised one hundred thousand marchers, but a poor turnout might convince Congress that there was no pressing need for a civil rights bill.

His fear went unrealized. The demonstrators numbered more than two hundred thousand, the largest such crowd ever seen in the capital, and "No one could remember an invading army quite as gentle," wrote Russell Baker in *The New York Times.* By the handful and the busload they collected at the Washington Monument, where they snapped photographs of one another, signed a pledge that they would "not relax until victory is won," listened to songs from Odetta and Joan Baez, and drew strength from the proud, steadfast Jackie Robinson, who told the the world, "We cannot be turned back." The procession to the Lincoln Memorial, scheduled to begin at eleven-thirty, started spontaneously at eleven-twenty, when a drum and bugle corps struck up a tune.

Massed before the Lincoln Memorial, the crowd picnicked on the grass, talked, and waited for two o'clock, when the official ceremonies would begin. Mishaps were minor—a few ugly words from a few ugly neo-Nazis, a small boy lost and quickly found, an unexpected bath for a woman who tumbled into the reflecting pool between Washington's obelisk and Lincoln's temple. Order was the order of the day. The marchers were making history, and to judge by the "I Was There" buttons pinned to thousands of hats and shirts and dresses, they knew it.

The dais at the memorial was thick with celebrities—Harry Belafonte, Paul Newman, Burt Lancaster, Ossie Davis, Marlon Brando, Charlton Heston, Josephine Baker fresh from Paris, and comedian Dick Gregory, who told the throng, "The last time I saw this many of us, Bull Connor was doing all the talking."

Backstage, the mood was a mix of triumph and testiness. The Most Reverend Patrick J. O'Boyle, archbishop of Washington, announced that he would not give the invocation unless John Lewis, the impassioned young chairman of the Student Nonviolent Coordinating Committee, toned down his speech. Lewis obliged, but not for the sake of the archbishop. He did it for A. Philip Randolph, the revered seventy-three-year-old patriarch of the civil rights movement. When Randolph learned of the friction, he found Lewis and told him, "I've waited all my life for this opportunity. Please don't ruin it."

The spectacle of a white man threatening sabotage unless a black man did as told laid bare an anguishing dilemma: equal rights for the minority would never materialize without support from the white majority, but in exchange for their support, whites expected concessions. The civil rights movement, like Whitney Young himself, had to wage its struggle in the middle, in the no-man's-land between black and white. Victory lay not in destroying enemies but in the infinitely more complicated business of winning their cooperation.

Convinced that such a victory was impossible, Malcolm X, chief spokesman of the Black Muslims, spent the day of the march in a Washington hotel, where he told any reporter who would listen that the demonstrators were Uncle Toms who had come to town to beg favors from "the white man's government." Malcolm X soon would begin calling on blacks to reject the civil rights movement's dream of integration and its strategy of peaceful protest. Protest led nowhere, he contended. Demonstrators often ended up in jail, compounding their woes, and a protest was nothing more than "a reaction to what someone else has done. And as long as you're involved in it, you're in someone else's bag." To his mind, the only hope lay in building a separate society and making it economically self-sufficient. "Once you gain control of the economy of your own community, then you don't have to picket and boycott and beg some cracker downtown for a job in his business," he said.

As two o'clock neared, there was no sign of Marian Anderson, the great contralto, who had been invited to sing "The Star-Spangled Banner." Her performance was sure to remind the nation of how little had changed since 1939, when she had sung at the Lincoln Memorial after the Daughters of the American Revolution barred her from Constitution Hall. Caught in the traffic around the march, Anderson arrived after the national anthem had been sung by someone else.

"Let the nation and the world know the meaning of our numbers," Randolph said. "We are not a pressure group, we are not an organization or a group of organizations, we are not a mob. We are the advance guard of a massive moral revolution for jobs and freedom." Rabbi Joachim Prinz, head of the American Jewish Congress, spoke of his past in Hitler's Berlin, where "a great civilization had become a nation of silent onlookers," unwilling to speak out against hatred, brutality, even genocide. He exhorted all Americans to "speak up and act" not for the sake of the Negro but for the sake of "the idea and the aspiration of America itself."

Whitney Young used his turn at the podium to note that while different civil rights organizations used different strategies, "we are all united as never before on the goal of securing first-class citizenship for all Americans—*now.*" He urged blacks to keep on marching—to libraries, schools, and voter registration booths. Walter Reuther, president of the United Auto Workers, inveighed against the hollowness of a government that insisted on freedom in the newly walled city of Berlin but not in Birmingham.

John Lewis promised that blacks would march through the South "with the spirit of love" but warned that they would not be patient. "We do not want our freedom gradually, but we want to be free now." Excised was his pledge to march "through the heart of Dixie, the way Sherman did. We shall pursue our own 'scorched earth' policy and burn Jim Crow to the ground—nonviolently." Nor did Lewis deliver the part of his speech promising that if government failed to confer freedom now, "we will take matters into our own hands and create a source of power outside any national power structure."

Also missing from the day was CORE's James Farmer, who was in jail in Louisiana with 232 other demonstrators after clashing with police wielding tear gas and electric cattle prods.

To Martin Luther King fell the honor of delivering the day's last oration. He started slowly and with ferocity, talking of America's default on its promise that "all men, yes, black men as well as white men, would be guaranteed the unalienable rights of life, liberty, and the pursuit of happiness." The march was only the beginning, he warned: "those who hope that the Negro needed to blow off steam and will now be content, will have a rude awakening if the nation returns to business as usual." He was not advocating violence, he said, but he had grown impatient with those who were asking, "When will you be satisfied?" Not as long as Negroes were denied access to public accommodations, denied the vote, and confined to ghettos, he answered. He exhorted the marchers to "go back to Mississippi; go back to Alabama; go back to Georgia; go back to Louisiana; go back to the slums and ghettos of northern cities, knowing that somehow this situation can, and will, be changed. Let us not wallow in the valley of despair."

Then, as if sensing that he had to offer the multitude more nourishment than a "somehow" and an admonition not to give up, King began to extemporize. "So I say to you, my friends, that even though we must face the difficulties of today and tomorrow, I still have a dream. It is a dream deeply rooted in the American dream that one day this nation will rise up and live out the true meaning of its creed—we hold these truths to be self-evident, that all men are created equal." He spelled out the dream—of brotherhood, of freedom and justice, of the day when his four small children would "live in a nation where they will not be judged by the color of their skin but by the content of their character," of the day when all of God's children would be able to sing, with new meaning, of their sweet land of liberty. And then, said King, all Americans would speed toward the day when they would "be able to join hands and sing in the words of the old Negro spiritual, 'Free at last, free at last; thank God Almighty, we are free at last.'"

A black policeman on duty at the ceremonies said he had been "enthralled" by King's speech. "Oh, my God, it just seemed to move you almost off the platform, off the earth. A big ole ox like me, it made my eyes water a little bit." For him, King "brought to life the hope that someday we would walk together hand in hand, that despite all this, one day we could smooth out our differences."

The leaders of the march ended their day with a five o'clock meeting in the Cabinet Room at the White House, where they talked with the president for more than an hour, over canapés and sandwiches. Kennedy, who had watched some of the proceedings on television, complimented King on his speech and the organizers on the success of the event. He thought the march had made a powerful positive impression, which he reinforced later that evening with a written statement praising "the deep fervor and the quiet dignity" of the day. It had been, he said, a demonstration of "faith and confidence in our democratic form of government."

Whitney Young went home pleased with the march and the surge of vitality it gave to the National Urban League. Despite the apprehension of the trustees, the League's tax-exempt status went unchallenged. Young's stature, like that of the rest of the civil rights leadership, increased because the president of the United States had seen them as powers to be reckoned with. And by taking a leading part in an event that had moved the nation, Young said, the League had shown that it was "a truly sincere, concerned civil rights organization, and not just a social agency."

But Young's encounters with John Kennedy and his brother Robert, the attorney general, had left him unimpressed. In his view, they dealt with civil rights by reacting to events rather than by leading. Two months later, when the president's bill emerged from committee, Young thought it offered "only the bare minimum of what these crucial times demand." His judgment was excessively polite. The bill promised to ban racial discrimination at the polls in national elections but not in state or local ones. It also created an Equal Employment Opportunity Commission with investigative powers but no enforcement authority. And it proposed to desegregate restaurants and other public accommodations by allowing the Justice Department to assist those willing to sue for the right to frequent them. No *Profiles in Courage* here, Young thought.

IF Young ever strained against the two short leashes attached to a man in the middle, it did not show. No matter who tugged, he walked with grace. In 1964, when militant blacks wanted to stage a "stall-in" to tie up traffic around the New York World's Fair, Young, unlike Martin Luther King, had no hesitation in opposing the scheme. Like most others leaders in the civil rights mainstream, Young worried about the danger of auto accidents and thought that an act of harassment directed against the general public would do their cause no good. King eventually concurred, although he wondered why the Boston Tea Party and other public demonstrations were "sacred when they were engaged in by white Americans" but "always become wrong and ill-timed when they are engaged in by the Negro."

Young felt equally at ease in jousting with Richard Peters, the white editor of the *New York World Telegram & Sun,* who objected to Young's service as honorary chairman of a day honoring Adam Clayton Powell, Harlem's controversial congressman. "Whatever our personal feelings may be about him and many of his activities," Young wrote Peters, "the fact still remains that over 19 pieces of significant social legislation have come out of that Committee [Labor and Education] under his chairmanship—more than came out of the Committee in the last fifteen years from the other Chairmen." Young said his association with

Powell on this occasion was not a "love feast," as Peters had charged, it was "like endorsing rain when there is a drought."

That fall, as Young prepared for a National Urban League retreat, he sat down with a yellow legal pad and drew up a list of sixty-three issues he wanted to discuss. The list was notable not only for its length and breadth but for what it revealed about his courage in naming and confronting unpleasant realities on both sides of the racial divide. The Republicans were running archconservative Barry Goldwater for president against Lyndon Johnson, and Young was alarmed by a new brashness among white supremacist groups and by signs of a broad backlash among whites who were less overtly menacing but nonetheless resentful of black progress. Young also worried about exploitation of blacks by business, the effects of automation on black employment, covert discrimination, and the seeming ease with which progressive legislation could be obstructed. Within the black community, he was concerned about deficiencies of restraint and social controls, as well as fear, apathy, frustration, and despair. He also wanted to sound out his colleagues on a number of broader questions: Was the influence of the masses fact or fiction? What did they think of the business world's attempts to give blacks a stake in the system? How should they think about the desire of organized religion to become more involved in the civil rights movement? Who "owned" the League? And what could be done "to change the attitude of most whites (some considered 'more enlightened') from paternalistic to a more realistic point of view (working *with* the Negro rather than *for* him)"?

Shortly after Johnson gave Goldwater the biggest shellacking since Franklin Roosevelt's triumph over Alf Landon in 1936, Young sent a memo to the president noting that blacks had voted in record numbers. "We should like now to urge you to enlist this confidence—and the new political energy it has brought about," he wrote. Filled with hope by the size of Johnson's mandate and by his dream of turning America into the Great Society, blacks wanted to work with him on implementing the Civil Rights Act and waging the War on Poverty. "In other words, Negro citizens do not wish merely to benefit from the bounty that will flow from the Great Society; they wish also to contribute actively and constructively to its establishment."

Johnson's battle plans called for attacks on many of the targets Young had identified in the domestic Marshall Plan, but in place of the $145 billion Young thought necessary, the president asked for less than $1 billion. Much of it would be expropriated from the budgets of existing programs, and much of the rest would be approved but never funded by Congress. Young declined to protest, at least in public. Instead he used his cordial relationship with the Johnson White House to get what he could for the League, namely millions of dollars' worth of contracts from the U.S. Department of Labor to place thousands of unskilled workers in on-the-job training programs.

FROM his first days as head of the National Urban League, Young cultivated his relationships with business leaders as assiduously as he worked at strengthening ties to the civil rights movement. His success with his corporate constituency showed in the League's ledger, with business donations soaring from $70,000 in 1962 to $1 million in 1966, and in the jobs opened to blacks at corporations run by chief executives who got to know Whitney Young. In 1967, the year after he toured Eastern Europe for twelve days with the heads of Alcoa, Ford, IBM, Time, and twenty other large corporations, they added thousands of nonwhites to their payrolls.

The brightest and best business leaders enjoyed Young's company for the same reasons they enjoyed one another. Like them, he was accomplished, polished, smart, and articulate. He also was sufficiently self-assured to meet them as an equal, a man proud of what the National Urban League could contribute to their organizations. The moral arguments of Martin Luther King had touched the conscience of many a corporate chief executive, but it was Whitney Young who showed them how they could use their power as employers to fight racial injustice. Any company unsure of how to proceed could "take the easy way out and call the Urban League," Young told them. Across the country, League chapters stood ready to serve as consultants, drawing on decades of experience to help employers create training and apprenticeship programs. For positions higher up, the League's National Skills Bank could supply qualified candidates in virtually every trade and profession.

As part of what he called his "missionary work," Young converted chief executives to affirmative action by telling them about the successes of their peers at other corporations. United Airlines sent black pilots and flight attendants into the ghetto to talk about careers. In Dallas, Stanley Marcus informed the suppliers of his fancy department store, Neiman-Marcus, that he intended to favor vendors who were "taking positive steps toward employment and training people of minority groups."

Young also shared his own experience of integrating the National Urban League's headquarters staff, which had been 99 percent black when he arrived in 1961. After advertising itself as an equal opportunity employer, the League increased its white employment to 2 percent. Dissatisfied, Young ordered the personnel office to begin recruiting at white schools, an effort that raised white representation to 4 percent. Still not content, Young sent the staff a memo: "Until further notice, if two people, one Negro and one white, equally qualified, apply for a job, hire the white person." White employment rose to 7 percent. Determined to do better, Young ordered a study of the problems and found that most whites were rejected because they failed to meet several of the League's qualifications. Having never lived in slums or worked with the poor, they were ignorant of the ghetto. Young decided to relax the League's criteria, theorizing that if candidates had some of the qualifications, plus "decent instincts," they could learn the rest. The League began hiring whites and remedied their shortcomings with six months of exposure to the problems of the urban poor. After five years of trying, the headquarters staff, 30 percent white, satisfied Young's affirmative action ambitions.

Telling the story to a corporate audience, Young said that employers often complained that no blacks applied or that their businesses would suffer if they lowered their standards. Young maintained that if the National Urban League could make affirmative action work, so could they.

> There are Negroes who are ready and willing to serve in your organizations, and on your boards, if you'll but reach out and make an aggressive effort to find them. Just don't worry if their English might not be perfectly correct: It is better to say "I is rich" than "I am poor." . . . The Negro has said to America in a thousand ways, despite his suffering, "I believe in you." It seems that the time has come for the white community to say to the American Negro, "and I believe in you."

The sequel to Lyndon Johnson's success in convincing Congress to pass the Civil Rights Act of 1964 and the Voting Rights Act of 1965, which outlawed discrimination in employment and at the polls, was three summers of rioting in a hundred cities across the country. The official casualty list included 225 dead, 4,000 wounded, and $112 billion in property damage. Had there been a calculus for the emotional toll and for the disruptions to life and work caused by the destruction of homes and businesses, the final price tag might well have made the National Urban League's $145 billion domestic Marshall Plan seem a good buy.

After the worst of the rampages, in 1967, Whitney Young was much in demand in executive suites. Many business leaders were profoundly upset by the violence and alarmed by the rise of militant black groups such as the Black Panthers, who wore uniforms, openly carried firearms, and took pleasure in quoting Chairman Mao's provocative epigram, "Power flows from the barrel of a gun." Young used white fear to the League's advantage, telling business executives that they could either support "responsible Negro leadership or—by sheer apathy— accept and allow the irresponsible to take over." It was an effective sales pitch. The League's income, much of it from corporate donations, rose from $3 million to $4 million between 1967 and 1968.

Young shrewdly avoided the temptation to calm white fears or assuage white guilt. Sustained, the anxieties might produce substantive change, so Young used his speaking engagements to drill deep into white discomfort. At a meeting of the National Association of Home Builders, a white member of the audience rose and said the riots had made him lose sympathy with blacks. Young let the observation hang in the air for a moment, then took out paper and pencil and asked the man to tell him slowly, so it could be documented for posterity, what he had done for blacks before he lost sympathy. How many integrated housing developments had he built? How many Negroes had he employed, and in what kinds of jobs? And how many had he helped move into his neighborhood or join his church? The builder had nothing to say.

Young told the National Association of Mutual Savings Banks that they had hung a "white noose" around black ghettos. "You have distinguished yourselves by your thunderous silence and magnificent irrelevance," he said. They had discriminated in employment and lending and had done nothing to solve the problems of inner-city neighborhoods.

He rebuked the news media for turning whites against blacks by limiting news coverage of blacks to crime, poverty, and the most incendiary remarks of black extremists. "The white press creates monsters, and then blames Negroes for producing them," he told a meeting of Associated Press managing editors. Where were the stories of black weddings and births and funerals? Judging by American newspapers, where blacks appeared only as athletes, criminals, or welfare recipients, one would conclude that there was no such condition as "normal life" in the black community.

Young also went on the attack against Washington, making plain his fury with the House of Representatives for rushing repressive "riot control" measures through Congress but scoffing at a bill to exterminate rats in poor urban neighborhoods. "The rat control bill was treated as a great joke by men and women who never had to watch over their sleeping children at night lest they be bitten by rats," Young said. He saw this as a tragic failure of a "well-fed, well-housed leadership" ignorant of its own racism.

In the fall of 1967, testifying before a Senate subcommittee and the presidential commission investigating the riots, he voiced his anger with legislators who blamed the uprisings on extremists and demanded harsher law enforcement instead of more antipoverty programs. "Extremists didn't create the ghetto," Young said. "Extremists didn't create unemployment. They did not inflict upon Negroes inferior education. They didn't strip the ghetto of essential services, nor did they exploit the poor and rob them of their dignity." The explosion had been "a natural response to conditions which are intolerable." His case in point was Newark, where six days of mayhem, which had left 26 dead and 1,500 injured, were said to have been caused by a traffic ticket dispute between a policeman and a black cabdriver. Young reminded the panel that Newark had the highest percentage of substandard housing of any U.S. city, the highest crime rate, the heaviest per capita tax burden, the highest rates of venereal disease and maternal mortality, the second-highest infant mortality rate, and one of the nation's highest unemployment rates. "This was the scene of the rioting," Young said. "Can there be any doubt as to why?"

THE War on Poverty turned out to be a skirmish, $3 billion worth of saber flashing and only two notable victories: food stamps and the Head Start preschool program for poor children. Conservatives smirked that the war was over and poverty had won. But the warriors had put up a weakling's fight. The grand total expended on each poor American was $100. Funds for programs in cities, where needs were gravest, had been whittled from meager to infinitesimal. A 1968 Urban League study of 815 federally financed antipoverty programs in 79 cities found that most were well run but reached only about a tenth of the poor. And the army had retreated much too soon, heedless of the fact that it had taken eighty years for the nation's agricultural education and research programs to revolutionize farming and twenty for every working American to be covered by Social Security.

Early on, the War on Poverty was struck by a barrage of friendly fire from which it never fully recovered, a 1965 report on the Negro family by Daniel Patrick Moynihan, an assistant secretary of labor.

According to Moynihan, the deepest problem in the black community was the female-headed household.

"It's not about *the* Negro family at all," Whitney Young complained about Moynihan's report; "it's about *some* Negro families, and a small minority at that." Lost in Moynihan's prose was the fact that three-quarters of black families were headed by two parents. James Farmer, executive director of CORE, was incensed by Moynihan's deduction: "As if living in the sewer, learning in the streets and working in the pantry weren't enough of a burden for millions of American Negroes, I now learn that we've caught 'matriarchy' and 'the tangle of Negro pathology.'"

Moynihan professed his innocence, claiming that he had meant only to document a crisis in order to spur Washington to bolder action. "The point was to make people say, 'This unemployment is something we can't put up with, this slum housing is intolerable, we've got to do something about these terrible schools,'" Moynihan told *Newsweek*. "What else do you *do* about family structure?"

Given the multiplicity and interconnectedness of ghetto problems, family structure was a peculiar scapegoat, but the Moynihan report played to a widespread desire to believe that blacks had been done in by their own behavior rather than by white racism. And if the problems of blacks were the fault of blacks, where was the logic in spending large sums on social programs to help them?

To Young's consternation, Moynihan's thesis resurfaced in 1967 in a study undertaken to brief Congress for its next decisions on antipoverty programs. Young appeared before a Senate subcommittee and tried to broaden Washington's thinking. "Who concludes that a family run by a woman alone is inevitably disorganized?" he asked the senators. "Who but those women are storming the doors of the educational establishment to ensure a better education for their children?" Why was there no mention of the strengths of the black family, which had been a source of courage and solace through more than three centuries of oppression? Why attribute black "alienation" to a "lack of organization and social structure in the Negro slum" rather than to squalid housing, discrimination, poverty, and inadequate social services? "Is the root cause of alienation in the victims or in the assailants?" Young wondered. "Whose alienation should we be studying?"

The War on Poverty also fell victim to the greatest of the era's great tumults, the war in Vietnam. In the beginning, Young and many other black leaders shied away from opposing the conflict for fear of angering Lyndon Johnson, who had done more for their civil rights than any other president and who seemed their best hope for improving enforcement of the laws against discrimination. Martin Luther King was the first to break silence, in the spring of 1967. To him, the war was a phantasmagoria of immorality. It was white aggression against a nonwhite people, it drafted black men in disproportionate numbers and forced them to fight for rights they were denied, and it diverted funds from the War on Poverty. King also had come to feel that unless he acknowledged the wrong of the government's "massive" violence in Vietnam, he had no right to preach his creed of nonviolence to angry blacks in the ghetto.

At a party on Long Island in 1967, Whitney Young had warned King not to speak out, arguing that it was suicidal for the civil rights movement. "Whitney," said King, "what you're saying may get you a foundation grant, but it won't get you into the kingdom of truth." Young insisted that he was concerned not about pleasing the powerful but about helping the poor and, showing his hurt, added that the Reverend Dr. King was looking rather well fed.

The president tried to blunt King's influence by enlisting other black leaders for highly visible assignments. Young's turn came in 1967, when Johnson asked him to join a delegation going to South Vietnam to monitor the elections. Young tried to dodge this draft by citing his busy schedule. Johnson was ready for him. "Well, Whitney," he said, "I'm going to announce you as one of the team, and if you feel you can't serve your country, you explain it to the press."

Once more the man in the middle, Young sought to stay on the good side of his black constituency by setting his own agenda for the trip. Building on a visit he had made the year before to investigate the treatment of black servicemen, he held meetings throughout Vietnam in the hope of establishing a Veterans Affairs Department at the Urban League. He wanted to use his position as head of the League to spare them the experience of most Negro soldiers after World War II, when no one but family and friends, who could do little to help them, took an interest in their futures. The League soon began contacting service-men just before they were discharged to offer help in finding jobs, assessing skills, and making plans for further education.

Young did not speak out against the war until October 1969, months after Lyndon Johnson vacated the White House. By then Young had lost all faith in the sincerity of Washington's desire to conquer poverty. The 1969 federal budget for antipoverty programs was $1.9 billion, a sliver of the $25 billion allocated for Vietnam that year. But Young did not share the common assumption that the war in Vietnam had diverted funds from the War on Poverty. There was simply no evidence that money spent on guns would go for butter, he said. "More likely it would have been returned to private individuals and corporations in the form of tax cuts, as was done in 1964."

In 1968, foreseeing the abandonment of the War on Poverty, Young announced a "New Thrust" for the National Urban League. In addition to employment programs, nonviolent civil rights activism, and efforts to promote interracial cooperation, the League would open offices in poor neighborhoods "to sink roots deep into the ghetto and work to change the institutions that perpetuate inequities." Through these offices the League planned to organize tenants' groups to confront housing authorities and to improve relations with police departments, schools, and other public agencies.

With the New Thrust, Young hoped to stimulate the League's growth in yet another direction. There had been growing pains since his arrival in 1961—a lack of coordination in some areas, staff shortages, and a high rate of resignations because of low salaries—but overall, he deserved excellent marks. Because of his leadership, the League had grown in importance in the civil rights movement, won numerous federal contracts for minority employment programs, added local offices in thirty cities, increased its annual income fourteenfold, and persuaded scores of corporations to hire hundreds of thousands of blacks.

WHITNEY Young would never be radical enough to suit the younger leaders of the civil rights movement, who had tired of waiting for the end of public school segregation, the end of discrimination in employment, and the end of myriad other indignities. To the radicals, Young was a "moderate," a label that by the late 1960s had become a code word for "tool of the white power structure." Young maintained that he was as militant as they were, and that the differences between one civil rights group and another were differences of means, not ends. "Nobody who's working for black people is a moderate," he said. "We're *all* militants in different ways." He had chosen to do his part through the establishment, and he wanted to be judged by his results, not his milieu.

Malcolm X, assassinated in 1965, had envisioned a day when black capitalism would turn Harlem into a thriving community like Chinatown, where the Chinese controlled the neighborhood's economy, kept one another employed, and more or less ignored the rest of the world. To Whitney Young, separation was the problem, not the solution. The South had innumerable all-black towns, he noted, all of them impoverished. Malcolm X's idea of economic salvation through black capitalism was also a delusion, Young thought, because the urban crisis cut too broad and deep to be repaired by a handful of black entrepreneurs. In the late 1960s, when white conservatives began endorsing black capitalism, Young was convinced that they saw it as "a way to keep blacks from demanding the jobs and the managerial positions in the mainstream."

Radicals who came to Young's speeches to heckle were surprised to find themselves invited to share the microphone. He understood their frustration and treated them with respect because he wanted their respect in return, believed that the knottiness of civil rights issues defied any "monolithic solution," and understood the value of honest confrontation.

Nor did he shrink from using his respectability to disabuse liberal whites of their fantasies of brotherhood. After Martin Luther King's assassination in April 1968, a white journalist assured Young that most whites bore no ill will toward blacks. That was not the problem, Young replied. "The problem is that they have no will. They do nothing." His desk had been piled high with condolences from whites, he told the American Newspaper Publishers Association, but "Negroes don't want sympathy, they want action. We've had sympathy of well-meaning whites throughout history, and it hasn't done us much good."

When whites told him that the Black Panthers and other radicals were hurting the cause of civil rights, he asked why, if white America had been unable to prevent the rise of the Ku Klux Klan and the John Birch Society, it expected blacks to produce "nothing but nice little Lord Fauntleroys"? Whites did not have "a monopoly on crackpots," he said, "and I resent white people judging all black people by the Black Panthers."

However one felt about the Panthers, Young thought, citizens who claimed to cherish democracy ought to be alarmed by the numbers of Panthers being brutalized by police. Was the nation so weak that it could no longer tolerate dissent? he asked. "More and more it is becoming obvious that the real danger in America lies less in radical dissent than in official lawlessness and official disregard for democratic values and civil liberties." By ignoring the illegal harassment of blacks, white America was confirming the black community's "sense of shared danger and oppression."

Young boldly chose a bankers' convention as the place to deliver a defense of Black Power. The phrase was not a cry for domination, Young informed his audience. "It is an appeal for recognition, it is a cry of the dispossessed, of people who are today powerless and who are saying to American society: 'I am somebody, I have roots, I have pride, I have dignity, and I want to participate in those decisions that affect my family and those decisions that affect my children. I want a piece of the action.'"

Venturing into what he must have known was sensitive terrain for many fathers in the audience, he offered the opinion that their adolescent children were dropping out and turning on because of the hypocrisy of their elders. "That is what the kids—your kids—are uptight about," Young said. "They are uptight about our value system, and our order of priorities. They are wondering whether men like you at a meeting like this are going to deal only with fiscal matters and economic matters or whether you really want to deal with the human challenges of this society."

Little changed. At an industry conference a few months later, bankers roused themselves to write a resolution endorsing the idea of pooling $6 billion to address inner-city problems. ("Chicken feed," said Young; huge as $6 billion sounded, it represented a mere 2 percent of U.S. bank assets.) After the conference, no one acted on the resolution, and the chairman of the American Bankers Association leapt into the vacuum to reject the plan on behalf of the industry.

Hoping to thwart him, the National Urban League retained a black economic consultant to offer the conference participants assistance in raising the $6 billion. Bankers sent long, cool replies, often enclosing brochures describing their good works in the ghetto. As the consultant explained in a memo to Whitney Young, "the banks are attempting to make a case for what they have been doing, with the full knowledge that this has not been enough, but with the hope that we will think that it has been enough." Their idea of enough was making loans to ghetto residents if the loans were protected by government guarantees.

THE unfinished business on the civil rights agenda seemed to mean nothing to President Richard M. Nixon, Lyndon Johnson's successor. Nixon had not even flashed the customary early signal of goodwill toward blacks by inviting their leaders for a White House visit. To Whitney Young, it appeared that the nation had begun "moving backwards to an age of indifference and repression." The Nixon administration had relaxed guidelines that would have completed the integration of Southern schools in the fall of 1969—a full fifteen years after public school segregation had been declared illegal by the

Supreme Court's decision in the case of *Brown* v. *Board of Education*. " 'More time' is asked for," Young said in a bitter speech to the National Urban League's 1969 annual meeting. "How much more time do law-breaking districts need?"

The Justice Department had tried to weaken enforcement of the Voting Rights Act. After a much discussed reorganization, the antipoverty program had, said Young, "lapsed into an awful silence that indicates it is going to a quiet death." In the area of equal employment opportunity, no federal agency was given enough money or staff to enforce laws against discrimination in employment, most charges were set aside as soon as they were denied by the alleged offenders, no federal contractor had ever been dismissed for discrimination, and the government's dependence on voluntary compliance instead of penalties encouraged interminable negotiations instead of action. Young thought it unseemly of white politicians to "rant and rave about the need for law and order" while leaving civil rights laws to "rot away."

What Young saw as rot, Daniel Patrick Moynihan, now ensconced in the Nixon White House as counsellor to the president, saw as an opportunity. "The time may have come when the issue of race could benefit from a period of 'benign neglect,' " he wrote the president in a confidential memo dated January 16, 1970. (The phrase, he explained, came from an 1839 report by the earl of Durham, who believed that after "many years of benign neglect by Britain," Canada was ready to govern itself.) Except for those in female-headed households, which were desperately poor, blacks were making progress, Moynihan said, but the issue of race had been "too much talked about. The forum has been too much taken over to hysterics, paranoids and boodlers on all sides. We need a period in which Negro progress continues and racial rhetoric fades." Moynihan speculated that if less attention were paid to extremists, white and black, the focus could shift to consolidating the gains of the 1960s.

Once again Moynihan was transfixed by black "pathology"—by blacks who "injure one another," deliberately set fires, and use their "hatred" of whites as "an acceptable excuse" for acts of violence that he thought they might have committed anyway. In passing, Moynihan acknowledged "white racial attitudes" as the root of the problem, but he dwelled on the alleged virulence of antiwhite feelings of blacks in every class. "It would be difficult to overestimate the degree to which young, well-educated blacks detest white America," he wrote, apparently forgetting that young, well-educated whites felt much the same way because of the war in Vietnam, the repression of dissent, and the derailment of civil rights. Beyond his recommendation of benign neglect, Moynihan proposed that the Nixon administration conduct more research on crime and pay closer attention to the black "silent majority," working-class families who shared many of the concerns of their white counterparts, whom Nixon claimed to represent.

When Moynihan's memo was leaked a few weeks later to *The New York Times,* it was unclear whether he had been unmasked by conservatives who resented his past in the Kennedy and Johnson administrations or by liberals who saw him as a traitor. Whitney Young saw him as an opportunist and read the memo as further evidence of the nation's growing hostility toward blacks. Blacks still had to "fight for everything, fight for every advance," Young told John Slawson of the American Jewish Committee in a long conversation soon after the memo was made public. The fighting usually ended with some concession large enough "to prevent riots but not to remove the inequity," Young said. "There really is no serious effort to do more than to cool any potentially violent situation." When Malcolm X made the same argument in the early 1960s, Young thought it unduly cynical, but time had corroded his faith.

As for whites, Young felt they were suffering from "amnesia and duplicity." In 1963, he had welcomed the idea of including them in the March on Washington, but their subsequent inaction convinced him that the whites who easily protested egregious injustice vanished when the problems involved subtler forms of discrimination or called for "hard work to be done with less drama, less excitement when the cameras aren't around." Conservative working-class whites railed against affirmative action but were conveniently oblivious of privileges they

enjoyed. Many held high-paying union jobs that existed because workers of the 1930s and 1940s had been brave enough to picket and strike
and boycott. And many had benefited from the G.I. Bill of Rights,
mortgage-interest deductions, and other government subsidies of the
middle class. Young was especially disheartened by the silence of white
liberals, who were not speaking out against the race baiting of
Governor George Wallace of Alabama or against law-and-order conservatives calling for more police and harsher sentences rather than
attacks on poverty, discrimination, and other causes of crime. "You see,
black leaders cannot get to the silent majority," he explained. He was
not invited to address the John Birch Society, the Klan, "or even just
the conservative Republicans." If white liberals did not raise their
voices against white reactionaries, much bigotry went unchallenged.

YOUNG'S mounting frustration with the apathy of white America
was lost on *The New York Times Magazine,* which ran an unflattering
profile of him in the fall of 1970. The title asked, "Whitney Young:
Black Leader or 'Oreo Cookie'?" and the article answered, "Oreo
Cookie"—black outside but white inside. The article's author, Tom
Buckley, maintained that although whites respected Young, "he leads
few blacks." Of the Urban League's $35 million annual budget, only
$500,000 came from blacks, Buckley noted. Blacks considered Young's
outlook "incorrigibly middle-class," and he had been known to trade
his normally impeccable diction for the accents of his native Kentucky
when speaking to black audiences. Recruited by the Rockefellers for
his job at the Urban League, he consorted with corporate chieftains.
Unlike most other black leaders, he had refused to spurn the Nixon
administration, leading his black critics to theorize that he was plump-
ing for a presidential appointment. The League professed to be the
advocate of poor blacks in America's ghettos, but only after riots, assassinations, and drastic cuts in federal social spending had it opened
branches in the slums. Directors of some of the League's largest local
chapters found Young too conservative, and an unidentified "20-year
veteran of the [civil rights] struggle" told Buckley that the League

worked against black interests because it gave "white folks the illusion of progress while the rest of us are out there telling them that they'd better straighten up." This particular critic was especially incensed by the League's failure to file antidiscrimination lawsuits.

Buckley misread his man. The fact that blacks contributed so little of the League's budget did not signify their lack of support, it reflected the League's strategy of funding itself through corporate donations, foundation grants, and contracts with the U.S. Department of Labor and other governmental agencies. The change in Young's English, which to Buckley seemed the hypocrisy of a man who jived with the brothers and tap-danced for the man, also could be read as a sign of Young's skill as an intermediary. Union leaders, for example, routinely use one style of speech with management and another among the rank and file without changing the substance of the message. The suggestion of hypocrisy was also unfair in light of the rebukes Young had been delivering to white audiences since 1967, but Buckley either did not consult or chose to ignore Young's speeches.

How Young could be guilty of both elitism and an "incorrigibly middle-class outlook" seems not to have aroused the critical faculties of the editors of the *Times,* but both sins were adduced as evidence of his unconcern for the oppressed. Young, being human, did enjoy his access to the mighty. Had Buckley plumbed the question of who was using whom, he might have seen that Young's friendships with the elite benefited the Urban League and thousands of black job seekers exponentially more than they benefited Whitney Young. What Young saw in the middle class was not an outlook but a level of material well-being that he believed ought to be achievable by all who aspired to and worked for it. As he once put it, he wanted to live in a world where mediocre blacks had the same opportunities as mediocre whites.

While the Urban League might be faulted for the tardiness of its move into the ghetto, the lag did not prove Young's insensitivity. The very existence of ghettos affronted him. He fought housing segregation in the hope of enabling blacks to escape the slums and was tireless in crusading for massive public investment in poor neighborhoods.

Young had gone to Congress innumerable times to plead for more funding for cities, and he routinely urged business leaders to press for better public housing and better public education in order to trim the urban tax burden and the business expense of training workers in skills they should have mastered in school. He chose to conduct his campaign in boardrooms rather than the streets in hopes of persuading business leaders and policy makers to provide the multibillion-dollar transfusions necessary to resuscitate dying neighborhoods. His failures say little about his deficiencies and much about the nation's seemingly incurable case of a disease that novelist Kurt Vonnegut named Samaritrophia, which he defined as "hysterical indifference to the troubles of those less fortunate than oneself."

The Urban League's inactivity in the courts sprang not from a fear of upsetting white benefactors but from a long-standing division of labor among civil rights organizations. The League's main job was to fight discrimination in employment and housing. Lawsuits, freedom rides, sit-ins, and boycotts were the province of the NAACP, CORE, and others. And despite the suspicions of Buckley's anonymous sources, Young told friends that he was not pining for an appointment in the Nixon administration. But as long as it served his purposes to have the administration think of him as a desirable candidate, he did not give the White House a resolute "no." At the same time Buckley was researching his article, Young was using the administration's interest in him to angle for a huge increase in government contracts for the League.

To the Reverend M. Moran Weston, rector of St. Philip's Church in Harlem, the *Times* article was the work of the "errand boys of the racist power structure," who in his judgment had an "uncanny way of going for the jugular vein of every Black man who is serious about basic change and in position to do something about it." That was one of the most offensive implications of the piece. Northern liberals found it easier to admire a Martin Luther King, who spent much of his time confronting the South's most reprehensible bigots, than a Whitney Young, who wore a black-and-white equal sign on his lapel

and challenged powerful whites to use their power to fight discrimination.

In purporting to demonstrate that Young was incapable of being a
true black leader because he was a captive of the white establishment,
Buckley also suggested, inadvertently or otherwise, that Young was not
their peer. As A. Philip Randolph and five other prominent blacks
noted in a letter to the *Times,* "it is inconceivable that Mr. Buckley
would have written the same way about a white man. Thus Whitney
Young, a talented sociologist and an effective leader, is not even
granted credit for his own accomplishments."

Young was deeply hurt by the article but hoped that some good
might come of it. "Tom Buckley may very well have done us a favor,"
he wrote a friend, "for far from resulting in divisiveness, the article has
brought a storm of protest from persons in leadership roles in both the
black and white community."

A few days before Christmas of 1970, Whitney Young went to the
White House for a meeting with President Nixon and his cabinet.
Young outlined the economic crisis and deepening despair of
American blacks and proposed that the government retain the Urban
League and other experienced nonprofit organizations to manage a
wide range of federal social and economic programs. The president
asked questions, made suggestions, and instructed his staff to set up
partnerships of the sort Young recommended. Within weeks of the
meeting, the League was promised federal contracts for $28 million. It
was the largest deal Young had ever made for the League, and he had
prevailed with a White House renowned for its indifference to blacks.

Three months later, Young was dead. He had gone to a conference
in Lagos, Nigeria, and on March 11, 1971, during an afternoon at a
beach on the Atlantic, he drowned.

As head of the National Urban League for the last ten of his forty-
nine years, Young often had said that the League's goal was to work
itself out of a job. For one radiant moment in the middle of the 1960s,
the goal had seemed attainable. By the end of Young's life it had slipped

out of sight. A friend who spoke at Young's funeral recalled his appreciation of Tennyson's lines about the boundlessness of the universe: it was big enough for "boundless better" but also for "boundless worse." The world was boundless better for the work of Whitney Young, boundless worse for not helping him to finish the job.

A GREAT COMPULSION TO GO NORTH

AMID THE SOUND and fury of assassinations, riots, and anti-war protest of the late 1960s, the most serious challenge to the reigning cynicism about big business came not from social philosophers brooding on the banks of the Charles River or human potential utopians in Big Sur hot tubs, but from a foursquare Midwestern businessman, William C. Norris. Born in 1911 on a farm near Inavale, Nebraska, Norris was an electrical engineer who had spent World War II as a U.S. Naval Reserve officer on a cryptology team in Washington. He married a WAVE, Jane Malley, and at the end of the war cofounded an engineering research firm. Drawn by inexpensive space in a factory that had built glider planes during the war, the company soon decamped to St. Paul, Minnesota. In 1957 Norris and several associates pooled $600,000 to start a second business, which they christened with the aid of "a cardboard contraption resembling a three-columned slide rule," wrote James C. Worthy, Norris's biographer. "The first two columns listed terms common to digital computing, while the third contained generic words such as *company,* *corporation,* and so forth. Sliding these columns back and forth against one another yielded various three-word combinations. *Control Data Corporation* was the one Norris liked best."

Control Data delivered its first computer to the navy in 1960. Known as the 1604 (the sum of two street numbers dear to the designers), the machine was housed in a boxy gray aluminum cabinet.

Offsetting the Model T drabness was a curved, futuristic-looking oper-
ator's console sporting "enough switches and indicator lights to satisfy
the most devoted button-pushing buyer," wrote David Lundstrom in *A
Few Good Men from Univac,* a memoir of his engineering career at
Control Data. Designed for military uses and scientific research, the
$1.5 million 1604 was the fastest, most powerful, and most reliable
computer in the world.

In 1961, the company added a computer services division to serve
customers unable to afford $5 million computers but willing to rent
time on them. By 1963, sales of hardware and services had reached $63
million, employees numbered 3,500, and Control Data was ready to
sell its shares to the public. Lundstrom recalled that the value of the
company's stock ascended so steadily that one investor, an engineer at
a rival company, drew a graph with the stock price on one axis and
"Number of People I Have to Be Nice To" on the other. As the share
price rose, the crowd of persons to be kowtowed to shrank toward the
bliss of zero.

Preoccupied with the leaping and bounding of his company, Norris
gave scant thought to the links between business and society until early
in 1967, when he heard a talk by Whitney M. Young Jr. at a conference of corporate leaders in the Bahamas. The summer of rioting that
ended eighty-three lives in Newark, Detroit, and dozens of other cities
was still a few months away, but the causes were painfully familiar to
Young and every other black leader.

"Black America is an economic disaster area," Young would soon
write in *Beyond Racism.* While white families enjoyed a median
income of $8,300 a year in 1967, blacks straggled far behind, at $4,900.
Black unemployment was more than twice as high as white, and
although blacks represented only one-tenth of the population, they
made up a full third of the nation's poor. Young prescribed a simple
cure: jobs. And from years of collaborating with business, he knew that
progress came only when a corporation's chief executive made a long-
term, personal commitment to equal opportunity and required his
managers to do likewise.

In an interview nearly thirty years after his first encounter with Young, Norris remembered him as "personable, articulate, and persuasive." A studious reader of newspapers, Norris considered himself well informed on social issues, but as a young entrepreneur in St. Paul, he had been unaware of Whitney Young's work with the local branch of the Urban League. Running a new company had been "all-consuming," Norris said. "Going to that conference and having a few days free of the details of running a business allowed me to reflect a little bit." He began wondering—and soon allowed himself to wonder out loud in a speech to the St. Paul Jaycees—how corporations might "take a leading role, and a profitable one in the long term, to assist in solving social problems such as those of the underprivileged, pollution, and urban congestion."

Although Control Data had always had a policy opposing racial discrimination and a conviction that the workforce at each of its plants should mirror the community where it operated, the reality was a wan rendition of the ideal. The company's headquarters and all of its plants were in the suburbs—geographically, financially, and socially out of bounds for nonwhites living in the heart of the Twin Cities of Minneapolis and St. Paul. After meeting Whitney Young, Norris directed Control Data's personnel chief, Norbert Berg, to open an employment office in the predominantly black North Side section of Minneapolis and start a shuttle bus up to the company's plant in the suburb of Arden Hills.

On a Wednesday night in the middle of July 1967, after a parade in downtown Minneapolis, police broke up a fight between two young black women. Witnesses claimed that the women were pushed to the ground by the police, as was a young black man protesting their rough treatment. Within hours, North Side's main thoroughfare, Plymouth Avenue, was in flames. Stores were looted and burned, a lumberyard was destroyed, and fires were set at both ends of a tunnel connecting a church and school. On Friday, after a second night of Molotov cocktails, rock throwing, and window smashing, Plymouth Avenue was empty except for a handful of armed, helmeted National Guardsmen.

More than forty rioters had been arrested, and the fire chief, who confirmed twenty cases of arson, estimated the damage at $1 million.

Watching the violence, Norris had a revelation: Providing equal opportunity was not simply the right thing for a corporation to do, it was indispensable because "you can't do business in a society that's burning." Norris hurried to New York to see Whitney Young, who told him that until the rioters had jobs, "you're going to have trouble in Minneapolis and everywhere else."

Norris dispatched Berg and others to confer with North Side community groups, hear what was on their minds, and find out how Control Data might join their efforts to nurse the neighborhood to health. Black leaders told Berg that the people of North Side were tired of training programs that led nowhere, tired of empty promises by government. "We want jobs, and we want them where we live," they said.

Berg carried the message back to Norris and suggested that Control Data open a plant in North Side.

"Fine," said Norris. "Make it a new one."

Norris wanted a new plant because he believed it would "tell the people in the community that this isn't a trial, this is for real," Berg said. "Norris has a thing about pilot projects. He always said, 'We don't do pilot projects because that connotes that maybe they won't work.' So he left no room for failure."

NORRIS'S fear of failure is minuscule, his tenacity bottomless. He traces both qualities to the spring of 1934, when he had to cope with the death of his father, the Great Depression, and a drought that was, he said, "the worst in memory. People were losing their farms and had to sell their livestock. When my father died, I was a senior in engineering school at the University of Nebraska. I went home for the funeral, and I was standing at the graveside, and I heard somebody in the back say, 'Well, the kid'll never save the farm.' That stung me so hard. I remember that just as clearly today as the day it happened. I said to myself, 'I'll show that bastard.'"

Feed was scarce because of the drought, and Norris worried that the family's Herefords, a herd of 125 built by his father over twenty-five years, would not survive the winter. Selling the Herefords was not an option. Desperate farmers had flooded the market with cattle, pushing prices to one record low after another. Norris knew that if he chose to sell, the farm would be lost. "Things were really, really bad," he said. "I was scared and despairing, but at the same time I felt, Well, hell, there's nothing to do but work it out."

Walking through a parched cornfield on a summer afternoon, Norris noticed that the only thriving vegetation was a weed, Russian thistle. "I remembered as a small boy, helping my dad feed the cattle and noticing a cow pick an immature thistle out of the green alfalfa and eat it," Norris said. "So we decided to cut and stack the tender thistles before their prickly heads matured." Most of the neighbors declined to help for fear of being laughed at. He went ahead anyway. The cattle lived, spring rains ended the drought, and the farm was saved. "The experience gave me great determination," Norris said. "It taught me that even though things look impossible—hell, keep working."

Norris more or less ensured the survival of Control Data's new North Side plant by insisting that it make a product critical to the company's success. Management chose controllers—sophisticated, refrigerator-size devices that meshed a computer's slow-moving mechanical parts with its nanosecond-speed electronics. North Side was designated sole supplier of controllers for a line of computers the company sold around the world, an arrangement that meant the company would need the North Side plant as much as the community needed the jobs. "There was mutual dependence from day one," recalled Roger Wheeler, chief liaison between North Side and Control Data's headquarters in the Minneapolis suburb of Bloomington. "There was no way we could walk away from that."

Aware of the vastness of their ignorance of poverty and racism, Control Data executives tiptoed into North Side and proceeded by what one of them called "quiet conversation." They assumed nothing.

They presented ideas, and they probed for the true opinions of individuals reluctant to be candid with whites. Once Control Data was encouraged to open a North Side plant, the company organized more meetings in order to describe its standard operating procedures and ask how they were likely to be received. On the advice of community leaders, Control Data shortened its application from four pages to one. "The average applicant had no experience, no useful references, and for some there wasn't nearly enough space on the form to list all of the brushes with the law," Norris explained. With the new application, "in essence we were saying we are more interested in your future than in your past."

To allay suspicions of favoritism, Control Data agreed—though it was heresy in the personnel priesthood—to replace the usual weighing of merits with first-come, first-served hiring. The company also was willing to dispense with its standard preemployment physical examination, but community leaders pointed out that it would be a service to a population largely unable to afford health care. Control Data made the examinations optional and conducted them at the plant, sparing candidates the indignities they often endured on visits to other parts of town.

At the suggestion of community leaders, the announcement of the plant came from the local branch of the U.S. Office of Economic Opportunity (OEO), the agency charged with coordinating the antipoverty programs of President Johnson's Great Society. The thought was that the news of the plant would be more credible to North Side residents if it came from the black director of the local OEO operations than from the mayor's office, Control Data, or some other citadel of white power.

The mayor and the city's business leaders got their first word of Control Data's inner-city plans from an inner-city newspaper, the *Spokesman*. There were professions of annoyance in some quarters, but few could have been surprised. Norris seldom fraternized with the city's other corporate chieftains. Nor did he enroll Control Data in the Five Percent Club, a group of local corporations that proudly committed 5 percent of pretax earnings to charity at a time when most Fortune 500 companies donated 1.1 percent. Although Norris did not disapprove of the Five Percent Club, he regarded most nonprofit organizations as ineffectual because they palliated the symptoms of social ills rather than addressing the causes. "He believes that if all you have to give is money, that's fine," Berg added. "But if you could provide management, technology, and leadership, you should do that, too."

Pleasant but not outgoing, Norris seems immune to the charms of inner circles and the comforts of conformity. "Whenever I see everybody going south, I have a great compulsion to go north," he has said. There is nothing fancy about William Norris. A trim five feet eleven, he has the solidity, level gaze, and directness of a Frank Capra hero. Because he had spent his childhood on a farm and in a one-room schoolhouse, he told a journalist, "I knew who Bill Norris was." Implicit is the thought that he does not hunger for the approval of others. He is so unconcerned with public opinion that his executives once felt obliged to collar him and explain that if he did not get rid of his battered old Chevrolet, investors and employees might think Control Data was in trouble.

Apart from the complexities of raising a family that eventually included eight children, Norris has always lived simply. He starts his days with exercise, works long hours, takes evening walks, reads for work, fills notepads with ideas for work, and relaxes with crossword puzzles before bedtime. Comfortable without an entourage, he once negotiated a major acquisition in a phone booth up the road from a cabin in the woods.

To keep faith with the North Side community during the year the new $3.5 million factory would be under construction, Control Data opened for business in the fall of 1967 in a factory on Plymouth Avenue, scene of the summer's riots. The plant, across the street from a blackened husk of a building, had just been vacated by a pharmaceutical manufacturer fleeing to the suburbs.

The beginnings were inauspicious. The company found itself shopping for a second piece of real estate after learning that its proposed construction site was wanted for a playground. The temporary plant was also in jeopardy, scheduled for demolition to make room for a highway interchange. And despite the fact that the company had followed a black leader's suggestion to blanket the neighborhood with Help Wanted handbills, there was no rush to sign up with North Side's newest employer. "The people who lived there didn't believe we were serious," Berg said in an interview in 1997. "They had been misled so many times. When I told one woman what we wanted to do, she looked at me and said, 'That's too much sugar for a dime, honey.'" So when the North Side personnel office opened, everyone in the community waited for someone else to go first. "[I]t took a few brave people to walk in that door the first few days," Wheeler said.

Then the fates put away their hammers. Community leaders helped the company find a second construction site. The highway department moved Control Data to the bottom of its bulldozing schedule. And as the favorable impressions of the first job seekers spread through the North Side grapevine, the volume of applicants picked up. By the end of January 1968, more than two hundred candidates had filled out applications, and the first sixteen employees, fresh from two weeks of training, were on the factory floor.

Control Data had decided to focus its North Side hiring on the disadvantaged, a term with an official U.S. Department of Labor definition: "poor persons who do not have suitable employment and who are (1) school dropouts, (2) under twenty-two years of age, (3) forty-five years of age or older, (4) handicapped, or (5) subject to special obstacles to employment." Of the 412 employees on North Side's payroll in 1969, 70 percent were certifiably disadvantaged. Forty percent had worked three months or less during the two years before they were hired. "Establishing this employment objective required recognition and acceptance of the hard facts in that community and confidence in the ambitions of the people, together with conviction in our ability to help them learn," Norris said. "The key here is our decision that we would not lower our job performance standards to hire these people;

instead we would train them to be able to perform at the level of our job standards."

Inexperienced, poorly educated, understandably wary, the newcomers needed acculturation and an abundance of encouragement. Sensing the need for counselors who understood the pressures of inner-city life, Control Data hired black professionals with advanced degrees in sociology or psychology. New employees got to know the counselors during eight hours of discussing such topics as "To Work or Not to Work—That Is the Question," "The Problem with Gossip," "Working Together," "Handling Personal Problems," "Following the Chain of Command," and "How to Do Your Damnedest." In the parlance of the Great Society, these were "job-conditioning programs," designed to teach the mores of a world organized around teamwork, punctuality, regular attendance, high performance, work rules, supervision, and openness to constructive criticism. The goal was not to control workers' private lives, as Henry Ford's Sociological Department had tried to do, but to remove impediments to their success at work.

Whites at North Side also spent time in the classroom, learning about the emotional baggage of poverty and racism. To help blacks and whites get to know one another, the company sponsored picnics and organized bowling and softball teams. Black employees brought soul food to work and invited white colleagues to neighborhood restaurants. "All of this was very important in helping me and many of the other people who were white cross that race barrier," said Gary Lohn, a young Control Data executive assigned to do whatever it took to make the plant succeed.

Lohn's appreciation of the need for whites to travel toward blacks has been as rare in business as in other parts of American society. Ending discrimination was not enough, Whitney Young had explained a few years before in a speech to the clergy. "You have to reach out to the Negro and say, 'I want you.' You have to meet us 75 or 80 percent of the way." The failure to reach out helps to explain why, three decades after the enactment of civil rights and equal opportunity laws, minority members are still suing employers for racial bias. Even whites of goodwill seldom recognize the condescension implicit in the typical white approach to racial equality. "I will help you" is a way of saying, "You need help," a position decidedly less egalitarian than "I will move toward you" or "I need to change."

After a week in North Side's classroom, Control Data's newcomers headed for the assembly floor, where they were assigned to a dozen technical instructors and two trainers. The trainers, who had spent the week in class with the new recruits, worked the floor as "floaters," moving from one employee to another, offering advice and support to minimize the frustrations of mastering complex new tasks.

Entry-level jobs were divided into three categories so that workers who did not succeed at the first assignment could be transferred to a second, and if that proved unworkable, they could try yet again. Giving every employee three chances showed the community that Control Data was committed to the workers' success. The near total racial discrimination throughout corporate America until the 1970s made it impossible for Control Data to find experienced black candidates for the top job in the plant. To fill the void, the company created a new post, assistant manager, and offered it to a talented black engineer. He was treated the way corporate America had always treated its fair-haired boys, which is to say that he was given the responsibilities, opportunities, and training to move up.

The company also decided to think of its work rules at North Side as "funnel-shaped"—wider and more flexible in the first weeks of employment and narrowing gradually for six months until they matched the rules at other Control Data operations. When employees failed to show up for work, someone from the front office went looking for them, inquired about the problem, and tried to help solve it.

Turnover and absenteeism were high, and investigation of the problem at North Side revealed what Kaiser had discovered at its shipyards during World War II: women are often forced to quit or miss work to care for their children. Knowing that the problem was not unique to Control Data, Norris invited other local employers to collaborate on a day care center. Seven accepted, and with their subsidies plus federal funds, the center was able to provide child care for half the going rate and offer children a wide range of intellectually stimulating experiences. Absenteeism and turnover plunged.

As management deepened its understanding of the challenges of doing business in the inner city, Control Data's social work expanded. Counselors began helping employees with substance abuse problems and interceding with supervisors when personal stresses affected performance at work. Control Data's Commercial Credit Company subsidiary extended small loans to North Side employees, many of whom could not borrow from banks because of poor credit ratings or no credit history at all. At the company's request, the Minneapolis School District conducted evening classes at North Side to prepare high school dropouts for their General Equivalency Diploma exams. And Norris persuaded the company's law firm to send two attorneys to the plant for two afternoons each week to help employees resolve disputes with landlords, family members, and bill collectors. The lawyers also drove out a neighborhood predator who happily sold $200 vacuum cleaners for $500 (on the installment plan, at exorbitant interest rates) but was loath to service them.

Employees jailed over the weekend found Lohn waiting in court with bail bonds on Monday morning. One detainee, a woman wanted on drug-dealing charges in Chicago, was released after admitting that she had hung out with a bad crowd there but had moved to Minneapolis to start fresh. She and Lohn were excused from the courtroom, and Lohn waited while she went back to the jail to retrieve her belongings. She returned with two eighteen-year-old girls in tow. Newly arrived from South Dakota, they had been arrested during a joyride with some young hoods. The woman from North Side lectured the girls on the importance of straightening up and then convinced Lohn to hire them.

The thought and care Control Data put into North Side did not win every heart in the neighborhood. Some residents were convinced that the company was part of a white conspiracy to exploit the poor and keep black workers in the ghetto. Others, observing that most

North Side workers were women, concluded that the company was discriminating against men.

Though groundless, the complaints were taken seriously. Control Data provided evidence that North Side workers received the same wages and benefits as employees doing similar work elsewhere in the company. Rumors of the plot to ghettoize blacks had sprung from a misinterpretation of the ending of a program that had bused several workers to a suburban plant for technical and supervisory training; the bus service ended when the training did. Having no wish to discriminate against men, Control Data agreed to set a goal of hiring men and women in equal numbers.

For a time, North Side's managers were exhilarated by their new challenges, but as problems persisted, patience frayed. Supervisors accustomed to dealing directly with employees resented the intrusions of counselors asking wider latitude for troubled workers and insisting upon keeping the troubles confidential. Production managers, charged with meeting delivery schedules, had a low tolerance for excuses and poor performance. Years later Roger Wheeler admitted that executives responsible for the plant began to think, "My God, this is a dumb idea, we'll never be able to make this work." Some were ready to quit. "[North Side] was really just being kept going because everybody knew that they couldn't get Norris's permission to do anything else," Wheeler said. Six months into the new venture, Norris and Berg seemed to be the only ones who still believed that North Side ultimately could be as productive as Control Data's other factories.

Norris was not simply exhibiting his celebrated tenacity. He concurred with Whitney Young's judgment that substantive social change demanded commitment. He also valued every new source of labor because Control Data needed all the help it could find. Between 1959 and 1969, revenues had shot from $4.5 million to $1 billion and employment had grown from 380 to more than 14,000. (Nearly half the spurt resulted from the 1968 purchase of Commercial Credit Company, but even without the acquisition, Control Data's revenues were up more than a hundredfold.) And Norris sensed that the company's bright young engineers and managers wanted to apply their creativity to social problems. "Everybody at Control Data was thinking creatively," he said. "There was an environment of great innovation. I believe that people want to do good things. The idea of doing a job and helping other people at the same time was very stimulating to many of our employees."

Well before North Side proved itself, Norris authorized three more plants in impoverished areas. Its Capital Facility in the Northeast section of Washington, D.C., opened in 1968, creating one hundred jobs. When production managers in Washington complained that the human resources staff was too lenient with employees, and the human resources staff accused production managers of running a sweatshop, the conflict was resolved in favor of the human element. "The emphasis will be on successfully employing those individuals who have hitherto experienced a poor work record or none at all," a company memo stated. Productivity eventually would be judged by the same standards used at other plants, but "the production goals must be set such that the primary objective of employee development is attained. . . . The major point here is that production goals must be adjusted to people development goals."

The following year, after Norris expressed concern about the poverty of Appalachia, Control Data officials asked Kentucky's economic development office for help in finding a needy community for a new plant. The state showed them a pretty town with a small college. When the visitors reiterated their ambitions, they were taken to Campton, an isolated hamlet of five hundred in a county with a per capita income one-third the national average. The nearest jobs were so far from Campton that the unemployment figures included nearly every able-bodied adult in town. The Minnesotans convinced a local car dealer that if he would let Control Data move into the showroom and garage he had under construction, "he'd sell a heck of a lot more Chevrolets," said Norbert Berg. Control Data's infusion of 175 jobs enabled many in Campton to afford their first electricity and telephones.

In 1970, the company moved into one of St. Paul's poorest neigh-borhoods and converted a bowling alley to a bindery. The plant, which assembled and mailed computer manuals, reports, and other in-house publications, was the first to operate on "mother's hours"—a workday that coincided with the schoolday.

Control Data's plants in impoverished areas ultimately created more than 1,500 jobs and $6.5 million a year in wages. Workers were pro-moted regularly and had opportunities to move up further by transfer-ring to other plants. And the productivity skeptics were proved wrong. Within eighteen months, each of the plants performed as well as Control Data's suburban factories. Norris calculated that it had cost $2.5 million to bring North Side up to par. Federal funds for training the disadvantaged had defrayed $1 million of the expense, and he viewed the rest as "the equivalent of research and development for a product. Considering that we now have an efficient production oper-ation with an average tenure at more than five years, and considering what we have learned, the payoff is a handsome one."

BY 1977, ten years after the move into North Side, Norris's thoughts on the relationship between business and society had crystallized into a mission. He had concluded that solving social problems was not a sideline to the company's business, it *was* the business, and he wanted Control Data to concentrate on "addressing society's major unmet needs as profitable business opportunities." Embedded in his philoso-phy was a belief that philanthropy and government had failed in the social arena largely because they spent wealth rather than created it. By treating social needs as economic opportunities, Norris reasoned, busi-ness could do what Washington and charity could not: create markets, jobs, and prosperity.

How the company would turn social needs into profitable businesses was less clear. Norris is a visionary, but he is a visionary with a high tolerance for fog. Once, when Norbert Berg pressed him to explain a decision, Norris said, "Well, somewhere out in that direction there's an opportunity for us; when we get out there it will be evident." Berg was stunned to realize that he had been following a leader who did not always know where he was going. "Many times his strategic directions were just because his gut said this was the way it had to go," Berg said. "And then he would elicit from people the building blocks that made sense." On another occasion, after remarking that automation was bound to affect thousands of Control Data employees, Norris asked Berg what he intended to do about it. "He starts you with the end point and then makes you sweat to get there," Berg said. "It's an interesting form of genius."

With annual sales of $2.3 billion and more than fifty thousand employees, Control Data was thriving, but Norris worried that computer hardware was heading toward stiffer competition and shrinking profits. "One of the reasons that the idea of serving social needs was so appealing to me," he explained, "is that by moving toward service, toward the application of technology, we could get away from our dependency on hardware."

Knowing that Control Data could not meet every social need, Norris decided to weigh the possibilities in terms of the size of the need, its importance to society, the company's ability to address it, and the likelihood of developing a profitable business from it. The company would sell what it had learned. Extrapolating from its success in training the disadvantaged, for example, Control Data created Fair Break, a four-month course giving high school dropouts basic language and math skills, vocational education, self-confidence, and help in finding jobs. The social need was immense: unemployment among sixteen- to twenty-four-year-old minority youth seldom dropped below 30 percent, the high school dropout rate was on the rise, and many dropouts were soon caught in a nightmarish maze of poverty, public assistance, crime, and incarceration.

Fair Break delivered most of its instruction by computer, and despite the teaching establishment's initial disdain for education by machine, students found it friendly and personal. With computers, they could learn at their own pace and escape the all-too-familiar embarrassment of giving wrong answers in a classroom full of students. By 1982, ten thousand students had enrolled. Of the 83 percent who completed the course, nearly 80 percent found jobs.

Control Data also created a business called Human Resource Management Services to market its innovative personnel programs. The employee counseling begun in the early days of North Side, for example, had evolved into a company-wide program, Employee Advisory Resource, better known as EAR. EAR offered confidential assistance with personal and work problems, referrals for help with substance abuse and psychological difficulties, and a round-the-clock telephone hot line. After seeing that EAR saved Control Data an esti- mated $10 million a year by improving job performance, reducing absenteeism, and cutting the cost of benefits, the company began sell- ing its counseling expertise to hundreds of employers, helping them establish employee assistance programs.

The most ambitious of Norris's plans to prosper by filling social needs emanated from his faith in the power of computers to revolu- tionize education. Between 1972 and 1982, Control Data invested $900 million to develop and market its Plato system and twelve thou- sand hours of courseware—instructional software—for education and training of every description. Norris believed Plato would make edu- cation better, cheaper, and more accessible. The rural high school with- out enough students for calculus or third-year Latin, for example, could offer it by computer.

Plato spawned scores of imaginative partnerships with government, academia, business, and the nonprofit world but failed to enrapture public school teachers. Norris was unfazed. "History shows that more than two hundred years went by after the book was introduced before it was used by teachers," he said in 1982, at a celebration of Control Data's twenty-fifth anniversary. "Our plan provided for a few carefully chosen fields of entry where resistance to change would be the least and for a gradually increasing commitment of resources for whatever length of time required to be successful."

The visions of William Norris, like the visions of Henry J. Kaiser, presupposed a partnership between business and government, with government as the dispenser of contracts, tax incentives, and seed money for the development of promising new ideas. Since World War II, government had spent billions on research for defense, health, and the space program, and the only capitalists who complained about this sort of governmental tampering with the free market were those unable to find space at the trough.

Norris's notion of the cooperation necessary between private and public spheres reached far beyond Kaiser's. Believing that massive problems required massive resources, Norris hoped that business would tackle the challenges through coalitions with unions, schools, churches, government, and institutions in every other segment of society. Business could contribute leadership and management, but it could not succeed alone. In preaching the necessity of cooperation, Norris was delivering the sermon Americans like least. It challenges the national reverence for lone heroes—the pioneers, cowboys, and self-made men who scorn cooperation because they cannot bear the truth of sociologist James Stockinger's observation that "each of us lives in and through an immense movement of the hands of other people.

> The hands of other people lift us from the womb. The hands of other people grow the food we eat, weave the clothes we wear and build the shelters we inhabit. The hands of other people give pleasure to our bodies in moments of passion and aid and comfort in times of affliction and distress. It is in and through the hands of other people that the commonwealth of nature is appropriated and accommodated to the needs and pleasures of our separate, individual lives, and, at the end, it is the hands of other people that lower us into the earth.

But American fantasy glorifies the individual and insists that the economic side of life is a war best conducted under the rule of every man for himself. It is, as the French say it is, *le capitalisme sauvage.*

Control Data shareholders generally approved of Norris's philosophy and the company's strategy of seeking a balance between short term and long, sometimes forgoing immediate gains in pursuit of opportunities that management thought would yield substantially greater rewards later on. For five years, the strategy worked. Between 1977 and 1981, revenues set record upon record, rising from $2.3 billion to $4.2 billion, while earnings nearly tripled, reaching a record $171 million.

Wall Street was unimpressed. Record or not, profit of $171 million amounted to a paltry 4 percent of revenues. As one securities analyst wrote, "It is not for us to pass judgment on how appropriate it is for Control Data to spend large amounts of money to set up plants in the inner cities, subsidize urban redevelopment, and sponsor various projects in certain underdeveloped countries outside the United States. The fact remains that the cost of these projects is preventing operating profits from the business to flow through to the bottom line, and lowering return on investment." Another analyst praised the company's performance in the late 1970s but criticized Control Data for chasing "largely non-related long-range opportunities such as hydroponics, education and consulting, farming, and inner city renovation. The long-term outlook would be markedly better if the company were to narrow its focus and enhance internal operating margins."

Norbert Berg, like Norris, had no respect for the Street's demand for instant gratification. "There was a time when I would try to be rational and reasonable and halfway decent to these people," he said. "That didn't work. So I just started pointing out that they were too damn dumb to understand what we were doing."

But in 1982, with a crash in sales of computer peripheral equipment and steep losses on casualty insurance underwritten by Commercial Credit Company, the short term began to crowd out the long term. Competition from cheaper Japanese products accelerated the slide in peripherals, Commercial Credit was squeezed between falling profit margins and rising costs, and the rapid spread of the personal computer axed much of the demand for data services, especially for time-sharing on big mainframes.

The company's 1985 annual report began with the admission that "Control Data's financial performance in 1985 was the worst in its history." Frank as the sentence was, it proved something of an understatement. The company had lost $567 million, wiping out in one year all that it had earned in the preceding five. Diversification had gone too far, the complexity of the company's operations had splintered management's attention, and there was simply not enough money to do well everything that Control Data wanted to do.

In fact, the corporate wallet was empty. Control Data had tried to raise cash by selling Commercial Credit, but its operations sprawled in so many directions that no single buyer was willing to acquire the whole business. Control Data had also gone to Wall Street to raise $300 million in a securities offering but felt obliged to retreat when it found that it had underestimated the year's losses by $250 million. Frightened by the news, Control Data's bankers refused to advance any more money, pushing the company into default on $383 million of its debt. Ten thousand employees were furloughed in the debacle, among them chief executive Bill Norris.

Norris ascribed the catastrophe to the sudden emergence of global competition and to the foot-dragging of Control Data engineers and managers who preferred computer hardware to information services. A decade after his departure, he remained unapologetic for his stewardship. "Addressing social needs takes time," he said. "The return on investment can be just as great as on anything else, but not in the short term."

After limping along for several years, with revenues and payrolls steadily shrinking as one operation after another was closed or sold, the company in 1992 spun off its Control Data Systems subsidiary and rechristened itself Ceridian Corporation. (Ceridian, like Exxon, is an invented word; meaning nothing, it can signify anything.) Ceridian describes itself as a diversified information services company. Control Data Systems designs software and offers consulting services. So Norris was right: services survived, hardware vanished.

Fifty thousand jobs also vanished. If Control Data's severed employees fared as well as the millions of workers caught in the downsizing of the 1990s, 12 percent would never work again, 17 percent would be unemployed for at least two years, and only 26 percent would find work that paid as well as their old jobs.

Some critics blamed the crash of Control Data on the $900 million

Norris had invested in Plato, the computer that could teach everything. Other detractors cited Norris's outsized vision of corporate
social responsibility, a charge that is difficult to prove. His biographer,
James Worthy, pointed out that the company's social ventures never
amounted to more than a financial smidgen—less than 5 percent of
assets—and some were making money. In Berg's judgment, the only
cloudiness in Norris's vision was a tendency to miscalculate the time
needed to turn new technologies into workable business propositions.
"With technology, the business time frame is very, very difficult to pre-
dict," Berg said. "But that's the only place where I can see that Norris
went awry. Everything he saw in the future—the demise of super-
computers, the rise of computer-based education, private management
of schools and prisons, windfarms, and a return to agricultural methods using fewer chemicals and less energy—eventually came to pass."

The epic dimensions of Control Data's 1985 losses made it difficult
for many to see the real heroism in Norris's great compulsion to go
north. Like any true story with an unhappy ending, this one seems full
of wrong turns: if only the company had paid more attention to the
short term, if only Plato's $900 million had been invested elsewhere.
There were disappointments on the social front, too. In spite of
Control Data's success in North Side, no other large employers set up
shop in the neighborhood. Nor was there a corporate stampede toward
the business opportunities Norris thought he saw in social needs. With
pension fund managers and other institutional investors clamoring for
ever-greater returns to shareholders, Wall Street displayed less and less
tolerance for broad conceptions of corporate social responsibility.

By the 1990s, the divide between rich and poor was markedly wider
than it had been in the 1960s, when Norris offered his observation on
the impossibility of doing business in a world on fire. Between 1979
and 1993, while the incomes of the wealthiest quintile moved up 18
percent, incomes in the three bottom quintiles fell. By 1993, households in the top quintile earned 13.4 times more than those at the bottom, the widest gap on record. Measured by wealth rather than
income, the contrast was even starker: by 1995, the richest 1 percent of

Americans owned a full 40 percent of the nation's private wealth, double the share they enjoyed in 1976. The gulf between haves and have-nots reminded economist Lester Thurow of income patterns in "countries experiencing a revolution or a military defeat followed by occupation."

For all Norris had tried to do, society was still burning—underground this time, like the coal-seam fires that smolder for decades before hell breaks loose. What remained, though, was evidence of what a large corporation could do when it accepted its connectedness to the rest of society and understood its power to add to the common good. Plato fathered the educational software industry. Control Data's inner-city plants and its Fair Break course salvaged more than ten thousand of the allegedly unemployable. The employee assistance program pioneered at North Side spread to a thousand corporations with a million employees. Other successes—with mother's hours, day care subsidized by several employers, telecommuting for the handicapped—have been put to work elsewhere. Bill Norris had headed north under a high star, and it was still out there, waiting for other eyes to look up and see the light.

13

THE GOD BOX

FOR MUCH OF the 1980s, the light from Norris's star was eclipsed by the flare of a supernova over Wall Street. Between 1982 and 1987, as the Dow Jones Industrial Average tripled, the national conversation about money and morals was all about money. "Greed is healthy," investor Ivan Boesky assured the class of 1986 in a commencement address at the business school of the University of California at Berkeley. "You can be greedy and still feel good about yourself." The applause was immediate and warm.

Boesky's genius for buying and selling huge blocks of stock at opportune moments had not yet been revealed for what it was: a crime. He traded on the basis of confidential information, often purchased from investment bankers whose firms were negotiating mergers, acquisitions, and other deals likely to affect stock prices.

The 1980s teemed with deals, many of them made possible by the insight of the financier who came to personify the decade, Michael Milken. Born on the Fourth of July in 1946, Milken grew up in Southern California's San Fernando Valley, was a cheerleader in high school, and earned a Phi Beta Kappa key at Berkeley. To his graduate studies in business at the Wharton School in Philadelphia he carried a piece of information that may well have had broader and deeper ramifications than any find made in the city since Benjamin Franklin, out flying a kite in the rain, discovered electricity. It was common knowledge that low-rated corporate bonds paid higher interest to compensate for their higher risk, but sophisticates had discerned a hidden beauty in the arrangement. Chancy as the bonds appeared, the record showed that corporations rarely defaulted on them. Electricity had existed before Franklin noticed it, of course, and finance professors had perceived the rewards of betting on nags rather than Thoroughbreds before the phenomenon entranced Michael Milken. But unlike the finance professors, Milken seized the reins.

After Wharton, Milken joined the brokerage firm of Drexel Firestone, where he turned his newfound theory to prosperous use, buying and selling the bonds of "fallen angels," once-mighty corporations beset by tribulations of one sort or another. As the 1970s ended, he saw even grander applications for his specialty. New companies, trapped between high interest rates (the prime was on its way to 20 percent) and a comatose stock market, had no affordable source of the capital they needed for growth. Large, established companies were caught in another vise. Wall Street's downdraft had depressed their stock prices, but rampant inflation had boosted the dollar value of their real estate, machinery, and other assets. The discrepancy between market value and asset value meant that big corporations, like mansions in boomtowns gone bust, were easy marks for any stranger with a bankroll. Pondering these unhappy facts, Milken worked his way to an inspired conclusion: Drexel could make a killing by issuing low-grade bonds to finance entrepreneurs in need of capital and bargain hunters hoping to acquire a corporation or two. To compensate for the higher-than-average risk of such propositions, the bonds would carry higher-than-average interest rates.

The new bonds, which Drexel called "high-yield securities," were soon rechristened "junk bonds" by skeptics who predicted catastrophe as corporate raiders and fledgling entrepreneurs took on more debt than they could repay. Drexel disagreed, seeing no reason why high-yield securities would default more often than the bonds of fallen angels and noting that the new bonds would give pension funds and other institutional investors solid, predictable returns. Drexel even claimed a higher social purpose for the bonds, arguing that they spread wealth by putting it in the hands of visionary entrepreneurs and millions of plain folk counting on pensions and annuities. Such assertions might not be true, but since they had not been tested, they were at least not demonstrably false.

Once created, junk bonds had to be sold, and Milken the former cheerleader was a superb salesman. In 1987 his skill brought him $550 million—so much money, observed one Puck with a calculator, that Milken owed no Social Security taxes on anything he earned after 12:42 A.M. on January 1. To a point, the $200 billion worth of junk bonds brought to market by Milken and his imitators during the 1980s filled a genuine need by making capital available to new companies. But as the frenzy mounted, the junk got junkier, and bond analysts began joking about the difficulties of distinguishing the junk from the trash. By 1988, default rates on junk issued ten years earlier had reached 34 percent. Many junk-financed corporations escaped default by laying off thousands of employees or selling pieces of their companies at panic prices. Even high yield, the only sound reason to buy a junk bond, proved a mirage. After the junk market collapsed in 1989 and the returns for the decade were in, it was clear that the bonds had returned an average of 9.4 percent a year—the same as money market funds, which are virtually risk-free.

FERNAND Braudel, author of magisterial histories of the Mediterranean world and the origins of capitalism, once told a journalist that his study of thousands of years of Western civilization had taught him a comforting lesson: Worlds tended to fall apart at the top and be remade by people at the bottom. Braudel did not say so, but these triumphs of the powerless are not as surprising as they are made to seem. At work is an illusion of light and shadow, of eyes fixed on the radiance of the supernova and blind to the energies of life in the surrounding darkness.

Among the many things obscured by the intensity of the focus on Wall Street during the 1980s was the rise of a small organization at the other end of Manhattan, in an unprepossessing gray office building on the fringes of Harlem. Gold-leaf letters on the facade identify the beige hulk as the Interchurch Center, although many employees of the religious organizations quartered within seem to take a sheepish delight in the building's nickname, the God Box. Ecclesiastical administration is the main line of work in the God Box, but the building is also home to a small band of missionaries who have been proselytizing among the capitalists since 1971. Under the leadership of Timothy H. Smith, the Interfaith Center on Corporate Responsibility (ICCR) has pressed corporations to end employment discrimination and reduce environmental pollution, asked banks to forgive the debts of the world's poorest countries, argued that American manufacturers owe their Third World employees more than the prevailing local wage, fought human rights abuses in South Africa and Burma, and joined the crusade against smoking.

Moral suasion being a notoriously unreliable weapon, ICCR took aim at the Goliaths with a more promising slingshot, the corporate proxy statement. There was a time when shareholders were few and easily convened, but as they multiplied and dispersed, there was no practical way for them to exercise their suffrage except by proxy. Mailed to shareholders each year in advance of a company's annual meeting, the proxy typically solicits votes on such routine affairs as the election of directors and ratification of management's choice of auditors. Most proxy resolutions are put forward by management, but any investor who has owned at least $1,000 worth of a company's stock for a year has the right to sponsor a resolution for inclusion in the proxy and bring it to a vote at the annual stockholders' meeting. There are deadlines to be met, and the rules of engagement, set by the Securities and Exchange Commission, do not allow resolutions on "ordinary business"—areas deemed the exclusive domain of management. Beyond ordinary business lies a vast territory in which managements set company policy on social issues.

Corporate gadflies—individual shareholders with complaints against management—have been turning up at annual meetings since the 1930s, but the idea of mobilizing proxy votes to campaign for social

change dates from the protest movements of the 1960s. In 1967, after
the Eastman Kodak Company reneged on a signed agreement to hire
and train young, unemployed blacks in Rochester, New York, veteran
community organizer Saul Alinsky realized that Kodak would be a
poor target for a boycott, the classic economic protest tactic. Because
of Kodak's near monopoly on film, Alinsky felt that calling for a boycott "would be asking the American people to stop taking pictures,
which obviously would not work as long as babies were being born,
children were graduating, having birthday parties, getting married,
going on picnics and so forth." So he traveled the country and asked
churches with Kodak stock in their portfolios to assign their proxy
votes to FIGHT, a coalition of community organizations in Rochester's
poorest neighborhoods. Amid boos from shareholders, a FIGHT
spokesman presented the group's case on the floor of Kodak's annual
meeting and gave the company a deadline for announcing that it would
honor the agreement. Management refused, but the showdown was
widely reported, and a few months later, Kodak and FIGHT negotiated a new agreement.

Alinsky did not fully appreciate the power of the proxy until he saw
how it unnerved business leaders. "Corporate executives sought me
out," he wrote later in *Rules for Radicals.* "Their anxious questions convinced me that we had the razor to cut through the golden curtain that
protected the so-called private sector from facing its public responsibilities. . . . In all my wars with the establishment I had never seen it so
uptight. I knew there was dynamite in the proxy scare."

Three years after the Kodak skirmish, a small group of General
Motors shareholders calling themselves the Project on Corporate
Responsibility persuaded the Securities and Exchange Commission to
include two resolutions in the proxy for the company's 1970 annual
meeting. One called for the addition of three directors to represent
"the public interest," the other for the creation of a corporate responsibility committee to monitor performance in areas ranging from safety
to the environment. General Motors fought back with a $500,000
advertising campaign. Although the resolutions won only a sprinkling

of votes, churches, many of which had multimillion-dollar investment portfolios, were intrigued by the possibility of using their proxies as levers of social change. In 1971 the Episcopal Church went to General Motors with a resolution asking the company to withdraw from South Africa. General Motors opposed the idea and once again won the votes of all but a handful of shareholders. But before the year was out, the Episcopalians and five other Protestant groups founded ICCR to coordinate their proxy activities and submit resolutions urging Goodyear, Gulf Oil, International Business Machines, and Mobil to stop doing business in the white-ruled nations of Angola, Guinea, Mozambique, Rhodesia, and South Africa, all of which had execrable records in human rights. ICCR appointed Tim Smith, a twenty-eight-year-old social activist and graduate of Union Theological Seminary in New York City, as program director. He has been executive director of the organization since 1976.

Smith is six feet tall and as white and buttoned-down as the elite of corporate America, but his looks afforded him little cover. Corporate directors long accustomed to conducting business without interference from shareholders had little patience with "those damned ministers," as one Boston plutocrat called ICCR. In an interview in 1997, Smith recalled that Presbyterian executives at Gulf Oil were deeply offended by their church's efforts to persuade the company to leave Angola. "The corporate secretary told us that Gulf had always had loyal shareholders. What we were doing was seen as an act of disloyalty." Investors at odds with management were supposed to adhere to the Wall Street tradition of quietly selling their shares. "Before the birth of ICCR, many church portfolios were schizophrenic," Smith explained. "They had their investments in one pocket and their social values in another. They told us that they felt church-sponsored shareholder resolutions were inappropriate—a case of social justice leaders meddling in the investment side of the church."

Many of those who saw ICCR's mixture of money and morals as dangerously combustible took refuge in the free-market orthodoxy of Milton Friedman, Nobel laureate in economics and leading exponent of the idea that a corporate executive has no social responsibility beyond making as much money as possible for the company's shareholders. "Let me give you an example that has often impressed me," Friedman told an editor of *Business and Society Review* soon after ICCR's founding.

> During the 1930s, German businessmen used some corporate money to support Hitler and the Nazis. Was that a proper exercise of social responsibility? The people who preach this hogwash talk as if everyone is always in favor of the same things, and there is no problem about which causes the money should be spent to further. But, of course, that's not the case. How the employees might want to spend the money is one thing; how the stockholders might want to spend it is another; how the customers might want to spend it is still another. . . .
>
> Have you ever heard anybody suggest that the 'Mom and Pop' corner grocery store should sell food below cost to help the poor people who shop there? Well, that would obviously be absurd! Any corner grocery store that operated that way would be out of business very soon. The same is true on the larger scale.

In a 1970 *New York Times Magazine* article that became a sacred text among guardians of the corporate status quo, Friedman damned the call for socially responsible business practices as "pure and unadulterated socialism." Executives attracted to such ideas were "unwitting puppets of the intellectual forces that have been undermining the basis of a free society," he said. In his human cosmos, atoms were superior to molecules, society being merely "a collection of individuals and of the various groups they voluntarily form." Friedman invited readers to consider who would pay if a corporation voluntarily spent more than the law required because management decided to eliminate the company's pollution of a river near one of its plants. If the corporation raised prices, customers would foot the bill, provided they did not take their business elsewhere. If wages were lowered or raises deferred, workers bore the burden and might leave in search of higher pay. Culling the funds from profits took the money from shareholders. Spreading the cost among the relevant parties was no solution, either, according to Friedman, because it amounted to taxation without representation. He did acknowledge that the desires of business and society sometimes clashed, but he maintained that government, as the embodiment of the will of the people, would mediate the conflicts.

The frailties of Friedman's logic begin with his assumption that German businessmen who funded Hitler acted out of a sense of social responsibility. The German executive dedicated to enriching his shareholders—his highest duty, in Friedman's view—would have been feckless indeed had he not aligned his company with Nazi ambitions for a Thousand-Year Reich. Friedman's portrayal of society as a collection of individuals appeals to American convictions about personal freedom and self-made success, but it neglects society's role as the connection among individuals. "A person is a person by means of other people," says an African proverb. The American antipathy to such thinking does not detract from its merits. Friedman's pollution control equation omits the crucial fact that pollution itself has costs, which are borne entirely by citizens who have not consented to such an arrangement and (unlike shareholders, employees, and customers) reap no benefit from it.

Friedman's notion that corporations should not engage in philanthropy because management's choice of worthy causes inevitably differs from the choices of shareholders, employees, and other interested parties is not wholly unfounded, but public-spirited corporations have proved highly inventive at minimizing the friction. Some leave the decision to employees and match their contributions. Since the late 1960s, there has been growing support for the idea that corporations, like individuals, are members of society and ought to contribute to the social well-being, however defined. When shareholders have sued to prevent a corporation from giving away "their" profits, courts generally have sided with the corporation, reasoning that while shareholders might earn less in the short run, they ultimately benefit because a healthy society makes for a healthy economy. In effect, the courts have codified Bill Norris's idea that "you can't do business in a society that's burning."

The last three decades of the twentieth century have furnished little justification for Friedman's faith that when the interests of business and society are out of balance, government will even the scales. But because no other interest group is as well financed or as well represented in Congress and the executive branch, Washington has become the place where inequalities of power are added to inequalities of wealth.

ASSAILABLE as Friedman's case was, few progressive business leaders disputed him in public. Protests came from churches and from Whitney Young, who swiftly issued a rebuttal of Friedman's insistence that social reform is the task of government. "This might make sense if our society was divided into neat little cubbyholes with clearly defined responsibilities," Young wrote, or if business had "no influence upon elected officials or if it had no powers to influence the jobs, schools and housing in the country." But business decisions about plant locations, job training, and myriad other matters had "a social impact at least as important as those decisions made by mayors or government officials." In Young's judgment, past discrimination by business had contributed heavily to high unemployment among minorities. He agreed that corporations were not social agencies, but he thought it behooved business to use its money, skills, and power to "assist those of us who are trying to make the system work for all." Any corporate executive who ignored the social consequences of his business decisions was "fooling himself, hurting his country, imperiling the future of his business, and cheating his stockholders' right to future security."

Fortified by Friedman's contention that their job was to maximize profits, corporate managements with no interest in social change stood on the lid of the God Box, paying little attention to religious' investors shareholder resolutions or to the moral challenges hurled at annual meetings. ICCR's early resolutions asking American companies to exit South Africa left few scuffs on corporate armor.

South Africa had concerned human rights activists since the 1950s, when apartheid became government policy with laws that denied

them suffrage, classified all inhabitants by race, banned interracial marriage, forced nonwhites to live in designated areas, and curtailed their
freedom of movement. Foreign corporations, some willing to overlook
apartheid and some believing they could help to end it, were attracted
to the country's cheap labor, abundant natural resources, and the
prospect of one day marketing their South African–made products to
the rest of the continent.

In the summer of 1972, convinced that none of the racist white
governments of southern Africa intended to reform, the World
Council of Churches voted to purge its investment portfolio of stocks
in companies doing business in the region. The eighteen U.S. corporations on the list included some of the country's largest: General
Electric, General Motors, International Business Machines, Merck,
Polaroid, Texaco, and Control Data. The council had concluded that
corporate calls for reform were ignored by government and that any
good that foreign companies did by providing employment was more
than offset by the taxes they paid the oppressors.

The council hoped its 250 members would follow its example, but
some church leaders saw that opponents of apartheid might have more
power if they kept their stocks and used their standing as shareholders
to file resolutions asking the companies to leave. Given the resounding
defeats of previous church-sponsored resolutions, the Lutherans
seemed as preposterous as the rooster who told the horse, "Let us agree
not to step on one another's toes." But ICCR and its allies have never
cared as much about winning proxy battles as about convincing recal-
citrant corporations to accept their social responsibilities. And unlike
most contests between roosters and horses, this one is governed by
Securities and Exchange Commission rules that give an edge to the
roosters. If a resolution wins 3 percent of the vote the first time it
appears in the proxy, it can be submitted to another vote the following
year. Six percent suffices to keep it alive for a third round, and once it
captures 10 percent, it can remain indefinitely. A share of 5 to 10 percent is often enough to convince a management of the need for
change.

In the beginning of ICCR's corporate campaign against apartheid, Smith said, "some of us had a general belief that the people of southern Africa eventually would prevail in their struggle for liberation and that we might play a helpful role. I don't think we foresaw that we would be as effective as we were in persuading American banks and corporations to leave. In our initial discussions with banks that made loans to South Africa, we were talking at cross-purposes. We argued that they should pay attention to the social and human rights and political implications of their loans, and they argued that the lending process was strictly economic and shouldn't be politicized."

Why tacit support of apartheid was regarded as unpoliticized remains a puzzle. Self-interest? The human tendency to accord the facts of a situation more legitimacy than they deserve? Fears of reviving old resentments of ugly Americans? Whatever the reasons, many corporate boards decided that a multinational corporation ought to stay out of the politics of its host countries. At Control Data, the World Council of Churches' announcement sparked a series of thoughtful discussions of South Africa and reinforced the company's determination to foster equal opportunity wherever it did business. The company also concluded that it should "continue to do business without regard to whether or not a nation is controversial. In fact, no nation is without controversy; we must do business in that environment."

Pressure to leave South Africa intensified in 1976, as student uprisings spread throughout the country and led to the deaths of more than six hundred protesters. General Motors, still hoping for peaceful reform, announced that it would remain in South Africa but not increase its investment. Control Data chose to withhold further investment except in computer-based education for South African blacks.

To go or to stay? In 1978, as the lines hardened, *Forbes* magazine invited Bill Norris and Control Data senior vice president Norbert Berg to have it out with ICCR's Tim Smith and William P. Thompson, president of the National Council of Churches in Christ and a leader of the United Presbyterian Church. Smith and Norris shouted at each other, Thompson reminded the Control Data executives that as a shareholder, the Presbyterian Church had a right to be heard, and Berg reminded Thompson that Control Data had forty thousand shareholders.

> *Thompson:* I am asking you not to support the oppressors, which you are now doing despite your pronouncements to the contrary.
>
> *Norris* (very angry, with a trembling voice): I take very direct issue with that. Remember the five million Kulaks that Stalin murdered? There's just enough power in South Africa to solve that problem [the Stalin] way [if the whites] choose to. What you're talking about brings them closer to that alternative.
>
> *Thompson:* Friendly persuasion has not worked. [South African Blacks] are saying things to us such as "You are trying to polish our chains, and make them more comfortable, but instead we want them cast off." They also say, "We have been suffering for a long time and if the withdrawal of certain foreign concerns occurs we may continue to suffer but white South Africa will start feeling the pinch too."
>
> *Smith:* When are people finally going to recognize that the level of oppression in South Africa has come to such a stage that we are not going to talk about putting curtains on the windows of the concentration camp any longer?

ICCR members filed a resolution asking Control Data to halt sales to the South African government and to refuse to renew expiring contracts. Control Data, seeing the proposal as tantamount to leaving the country, urged shareholders to reject it, and the vast majority of those who cast their ballots sided with the company.

Although Control Data and many other U.S. companies struggled to promote racial equality, the terms of the struggle were dictated by the forces of apartheid. Earlier in the decade, when the South African government realized that the nation's labor shortage was hampering economic growth, it had given employers more latitude to improve conditions for nonwhite workers. In exchange, employers were expected "to make white employees feel they are still progressing ahead of the nonwhites," a senior Control Data official explained to the company's committee on corporate social responsibility. A segregated health care system excluded blacks from the best treatment, leaving

Control Data to try to "arrange for equal care." The company also had hoped to give each employee a $50,000 life insurance policy, but the only insurer willing to extend coverage to blacks charged exponentially more for their policies because of their shorter life expectancies. As a result, Control Data's white employees received coverage of $50,000, blacks only $12,500.

In retrospect, it is clear that apartheid was no more amenable to reform than slavery or any other evil. It needed destruction, not refinement. But for most of the 1970s, antiapartheid activists inside South Africa were as divided as Bill Norris and Tim Smith on the question of whether foreigners should go or stay. In 1977, persuaded by South Africans who thought the presence of progressive outsiders could hasten the fall of apartheid, Leon Sullivan, an American civil rights leader and member of the board of General Motors, drafted a code of conduct for U.S. companies doing business in South Africa. It asked them to integrate eating areas, rest rooms, shop floors, and offices; provide equal pay for comparable work; train and promote nonwhites; and fund improvements in housing, schools, and health care in nonwhite communities. Critics branded Sullivan an accommodationist, but many thoughtful U.S. business leaders, including Bill Norris, welcomed the code as a way to voice their commitment to reform. By 1985, more than half of the three hundred U.S. companies in South Africa had agreed to abide by the Sullivan Principles, as they became known. Fine as the principles were, however, they did not touch the fundamental injustices of apartheid. In 1987, Sullivan renounced his code and joined the forces calling for withdrawal.

More than 160 American corporations left between 1984 and 1988, responding to pressures from Congress, which in 1986 banned new U.S. investment in South Africa and restricted import-export traffic between the two countries; from consumer boycotts; from states and cities that refused to buy from corporations operating in South Africa; and from shareholders. ICCR not only led the shareholder campaign to get American companies out of South Africa, it advised and collaborated with many other groups in the U.S. antiapartheid movement.

"I don't think apartheid would have become a big issue in the United States without shareholder resolutions," said Paul Neuhauser, a professor of law at the University of Iowa, a longtime adviser to ICCR, and the author of the Episcopal Church's first resolution. "I did a study in the 1980s comparing private and public U.S. companies doing business in South Africa, and it showed that a much higher percentage of publicly held companies had left." Without shareholders to file resolutions and challenge chief executives at annual meetings, private companies were much freer to do as they pleased.

Norris and Berg never stopped believing that their company was a force for good in a place sorely in need of goodness. Passionately moral men who put their convictions to work throughout Control Data, they were understandably offended by what they felt were attacks on their honor. Years after his battle with the clergy over South Africa, Norris still described it as one of the most bitter experiences of his life.

Tim Smith expressed no regrets about ICCR's adamancy. "We took the companies' premise that by being there, they would bring about social change. But the massacres and the repression kept growing. By the mid-1970s, several major banks had come around to our point of view and decided that it *was* legitimate to integrate social and political factors into their lending. First they stopped lending to the government, and later they stopped lending to South African companies. The ending of bank loans and the first corporate withdrawals were turning points because then it was no longer just the churches saying that business should leave."

In the end, apartheid proved expensive as well as unconscionable. By 1975, the costs of running a police state and restricting the mobility of blacks, who made up most of the labor force, had brought the country's economic growth to a standstill. In a study for the Council on Foreign Relations, Stephen R. Lewis found that if South Africa had maintained its 1946–75 growth rate in the years after 1975, by 1987 the country's economy would have been nearly half again as large as it was.

———————

ICCR's zeal in the crusade against apartheid did not endear Smith to corporate America. Nor did his combativeness at annual meetings in the 1970s, when he sometimes accused managements of lying and used his turn at the microphone during question-and-answer sessions to make pronouncements rather than pose questions. His clashes with corporate leaders led one of them, the president of multinational agribusiness giant Castle & Cooke, to charge that ICCR was a front for Marxist groups plotting the destruction of capitalism. A 1980 *Fortune* magazine article, "The Corporation Haters" by Herman Nickel, spread the allegation further.

The idea that ICCR practiced shareholder advocacy as a subversive activity made no sense to Smith, who wondered how anyone could believe that churches with stocks and bonds worth billions would want to overthrow free enterprise. It was soon revealed that "The Corporation Haters" had been researched and written with money from several companies that had been the targets of ICCR shareholder resolutions.

Despite the opposition, ICCR grew steadily throughout the 1980s, and by its twenty-fifth anniversary, in 1996, it was a confederation of 275 Protestant, Catholic, and Jewish organizations with portfolios collectively worth more than $70 billion. Its shareholder resolutions regularly won the backing of several state and municipal pension funds, universities, and foundations. Labor unions had adopted ICCR's tactics to file scores of resolutions of their own.

ICCR's rise was paralleled by the growth of the social investing movement, which by 1995 had attracted hundreds of thousands of Americans and more than $600 billion to scores of mutual funds and other institutions that invest with corporate social performance in mind. Such portfolios often exclude weapons, tobacco, and alcohol stocks and assess a company's record in areas such as equal opportunity, human rights, and the environment. The drive to align money and morals has led to the creation of mutual funds focused upon the tenets of Islam (no profits from liquor, pornography, gambling, or charging interest), conservative Christian beliefs (no makers or purveyors of alcohol or tobacco, no sponsors of offensive television programs, no marketers of provocative lingerie), and the advancement of women (companies with women in top jobs, women on boards of directors, and advertising presenting positive images of women).

Once it became evident that overwhelming defeat of a resolution did not daunt ICCR, corporations showed more willingness to meet privately with Smith and his colleagues. "We learned how to talk to each other," Smith said. "ICCR got more sophisticated in negotiation, we tried whenever we could to create win-win solutions, and we started celebrating companies that show real leadership in social responsibility." Progressive managements began to understand that ICCR was worth a meeting or two because religious investors were often in the vanguard on issues likely to become the center of major public debates. ICCR, General Motors decided, was useful as a "social early warning system."

In 1986, "Darkie" toothpaste, marketed in Asia by affiliates of Colgate-Palmolive, was renamed and repackaged without its blackface logo after ICCR filed a shareholder resolution sure to have loosed a storm of embarrassing publicity. A long collaboration between ICCR and 3M led one of the company's subsidiaries to stop accepting cigarette advertising for its billboards. Having kicked the habit, the 3M division was one of the few outdoor advertising businesses whose financial health was unimpaired by the federal government's 1997 decision to ban tobacco ads from billboards.

"Our goal is not so much to file a resolution to raise the issue but to change corporate behavior," Smith said. "The resolution is just one tool for doing that." Doris Gormley, director of corporate social responsibility for one of ICCR's members, the Sisters of St. Francis of Philadelphia, views resolutions as "a tactic for starting a conversation. The conversation is the important thing because that's what will lead to change." Over time, more and more of ICCR's resolutions became measures of last resort, submitted only after negotiations broke down.

A look at the 185 resolutions filed in 1996 by ICCR and its members shows that the churches have become highly adept at appealing to corporate self-interest. "Initially, we argued the moral case," Smith said. "We still do that, but now we try to make an economic case as well because managements have to look after economic issues." Unocal, one of the world's largest energy companies, was asked by ICCR to pay more attention to pollution prevention because of research showing that prevention is five to eight times cheaper than mopping up. Citing the huge costs of dismantling nuclear reactors, ICCR members requested that two utilities, Detroit Edison and Union Electric, provide shareholders with reports comparing the costs of closing their reactors now rather than several decades hence, when their licenses expire. At issue, ICCR said, were a potentially large financial liability from growing stockpiles of radioactive waste; the expense of hiring the extra help needed to cope with the hazards of operating aging plants; and the possibility of a catastrophe of biblical proportions.

A resolution asking several corporations to sign an environmental code, the CERES Principles, asserted that sound environmental policy "increases long-term shareholder value by raising efficiency, decreasing clean-up costs, reducing litigation, and enhancing public image and product attractiveness." CERES (Coalition for Environmentally Responsible Economies) came into being after the supertanker *Exxon Valdez* bled eleven million gallons of oil into the chaste waters of Alaska's Prince William Sound in 1989. Among other things, CERES signatories promise to repair environmental damage, reduce waste, save energy, audit their environmental performance, and fully inform investors of environmental risks and liabilities.

Many who have declined to sign the CERES Principles have said that they live by high environmental standards of their own. W. Eric Aiken, a consistent foe of ICCR and the man he calls "the sainted Timothy," has offered still other reasons to refrain. President of the Proxy Monitor, a Manhattan-based adviser to pension funds and other institutional investors, Aiken characterized CERES as a toothless "expression of good intentions" with burdensome reporting requirements. Aiken also has opposed shareholder requests for full disclosure of potential environmental liabilities on the ground that corporations concerned about their reputation "are not apt to take foolish chances that could injure payrollers, the residents of host communities, or their own good names."

In the churches' antismoking campaign, jeremiads against "merchants of death" have given way to charts depicting the shrinking rewards of owning tobacco stocks. To improve the profitability of RJR Nabisco, ICCR and other investors asked the company to separate its tobacco operations from the rest of its businesses, a proposal that attracted an unusually high 37.6 percent of the votes. ICCR used the specter of major lawsuits by state attorneys general to persuade Kimberly-Clark to stop supplying packaging materials to tobacco companies and to argue that PepsiCo and Wendy's should make all their restaurants smoke-free.

Pointing to boycotts by consumers and by city and state governments, religious investors have called upon Unocal, ARCO, Texaco, and PepsiCo to withdraw from the totalitarian state of Myanmar (formerly Burma), where human rights abuses have included forced labor, military conscription of children, refusal to cede power to a democratically elected government, and frequent arrests and assassinations. Myanmar is small and far away, but between 1991 and 1996, protests by U.S. investors, college students, and social activists communicating through the Internet persuaded nineteen American corporations to leave. Early in 1997, PepsiCo agreed to end all its Burmese business relationships. "In many ways," Smith said, "Burma is easier than South Africa because there are fewer corporations involved. But when this effort started, I thought it was an issue without a natural American constituency, and I never guessed that the changes would come about as quickly as they have."

Experience explained part of the success, said Simon Billenness, a leader of the Burma campaign and senior analyst at Franklin Research and Development Corporation, a Boston-based money management firm and associate member of ICCR. "South Africa taught us which tactics worked, so we didn't have to reinvent the wheel for Burma. Also, there is a great deal of moral clarity about the problems.

Investment in Burma supports the military elite, so it is difficult for corporations to make the case that withdrawal will hurt the Burmese people. And our efforts have the endorsement of the country's rightful leader, Aung San Suu Kyi, a Nobel Peace Prize laureate who is respected around the world. She has asked us to use our liberty to help her people win theirs." The state of Massachusetts, New York City, and several other municipalities have pledged not to buy from companies doing business in Burma, a move that affects purchases from Japanese and European giants as well as from American corporations.

ICCR has been submitting shareholder resolutions on equal employment opportunity since 1974, when it asked nine companies for data on their women and minority employees and called for the election of more diverse boards of directors. Xerox replied that it opposed broadening the board because representatives of "special interest groups" would not serve "the best interests of shareholders as a whole." That was an astounding response, implying as it did that women or members of minority groups represent special interests, think alike, and have no more to contribute to a board than their gender or ethnicity. By 1996, smiling faces of women and minority executives had become a commonplace of the business press, but discrimination still pervaded high places. While 57 percent of American workers were women or members of minority groups or both, white males filled 95 percent of the senior management positions in the 1,500 largest U.S. corporations.

ICCR's recent equal opportunity resolutions have emphasized the potential costs of discrimination—from lawsuits, loss of government contracts, and consumer boycotts. The dangers are genuine, as Texaco discovered in 1996, when *The New York Times* published excerpts from taped conversations of senior Texaco officials making derogatory remarks about minority employees and discussing the possible destruction of documents related to a pending discrimination lawsuit. Picketers turned up at Texaco stations, Jesse Jackson called for a boycott, and offended customers cut up their Texaco credit cards and mailed them to the company's headquarters. The suit, brought on behalf of 1,400 nonwhite employees, cost Texaco $176 million.

Equal opportunity resolutions often cite a study showing that the stocks of companies committed to equality have been significantly better investments than stocks of corporations with poor records in equal opportunity (annual returns averaging 18.3 percent versus 7.9 percent over five years). One reason that inclusion turns out to be more lucrative than exclusion is that customers come in both genders and all colors.

The point is still not widely appreciated. In 1996, when Doris Gormley of the Sisters of St. Francis of Philadelphia mailed out a form letter to two hundred companies announcing that her order would withhold authority to vote its proxies for their candidates for director because their boards were all male and all white, T. J. Rodgers, chief executive of Cypress Semiconductor, sent back a tongue-lashing. "Bluntly stated, a 'woman's view' on how to run our semiconductor company does not help us, unless that woman has an advanced technical degree and experience as a CEO," he declared. In passing Rodgers noted that his five-man board did have one minority member, but he seemed more interested in hammering home the point that the boards of high-technology companies were dominated by white males in their fifties because they were the ones with advanced degrees in engineering and three decades of experience in the ferociously competitive global electronics business. "Unfortunately, there are currently few minorities and almost no women who chose to be engineering graduates thirty years ago," he said.

Rodgers told "the good sister" that he considered her demand for an integrated board "immoral," which he defined as "causing harm to people." Unless he put profits first, he said, he would jeopardize the security of Cypress shareholders, including the nuns in her order. If all American companies "were forced to operate according to some arbitrary social agenda, rather than for profit," all Americans would be worse off and charitable donations would plummet, he warned. He pointed out that the board she voted against had authorized generous pay and benefits for Cypress employees, was committed to protecting the environment, and made substantial contributions to local charities.

Rodgers was right about the dearth of women and minority group members with advanced technical degrees and decades of relevant success. But the shortage cannot be explained by his notion that they "chose" not to go to engineering school in the 1960s. All but a handful were excluded until 1972, when Title IX of the Equal Education Act forced professional schools to open their doors. It is difficult to conceive of a "woman's" view of semiconductors, equally difficult to imagine that the global efforts of any U.S. board would not be strengthened by a Madeleine Albright or a Carla Hills. While Gormley had not asked Rodgers to shave a penny from profitability, his response assumed that integrating the board would be all cost and no benefit. Strangest of all was the contradiction between his intransigence about the board and his pride in Cypress's good citizenship in other realms.

Gormley was stunned by the outburst. The form letter, which the Sisters of St. Francis had been sending to scores of corporations for a dozen years, typically brought "courteous, succinct, direct responses," she said. Rodgers had characterized it as a demand to fill quotas, but in fact it was a simple 140-word announcement of the order's vote and a request: "We urge you to enrich the Board by seeking qualified women and members of racial minorities as nominees."

Perhaps fearing the oblivion of Gormley's wastebasket, Rodgers forwarded his letter to Cypress shareholders and posted it on the company's Web site. After the episode was reported in *The Wall Street Journal,* Rodgers received more than six hundred letters, 91 percent in his favor. He took special pleasure in an approving note from Milton Friedman, who sent along a copy of his 1970 *New York Times* article. The fact that only 9 percent objected despite the bigotry of Rodgers's tantrum showed how little had changed since the time of Whitney Young.

Gormley got mail, too, mostly from Cypress shareholders who had read Rodgers's letter but not hers. Half took his side. "They were vitriolic," Gormley said, "although some of them defended our right as a shareholder to voice an opinion." Rodgers won the popularity contest but inadvertently handed Gormley a more substantive victory. The publicity made her a celebrity in corporate circles and drew invitations to speak and write in prestigious business forums.

The exclusion of minorities and women from a corporate board is easily ascertained, often requiring no more than a look at the customary board photo in the annual report. But the task of sizing up equality throughout a company depends heavily upon the availability of statistics. Since the mid-1970s, ICCR members have filed hundreds of resolutions asking corporations to share the data they submit each year to the Equal Employment Opportunity Commission. Even the Proxy Monitor, which rarely concurs with ICCR, favors the idea, reasoning that shareholders have a right to know whether violations of equal opportunity laws might subject a corporation to "potentially ruinous redress." ICCR has persuaded scores of corporations to provide the data, but scores more demur on the ground that shareholders, like other citizens, can get the information from the commission itself. That is a frustrating alternative. The commission takes months to fill the requests, and corporations have the right to refuse release of their numbers, a rule that leaves the fox firmly in control of the henhouse.

"BECAUSE it pays" will always carry more arguments than "Because it's right," but ICCR continues to file resolutions with no bottom-line benefits, including some that boldly promote moral causes at shareholder expense. Religion would not be religion if it did not prod humankind to look beyond what is to what might be. "Only the foolishness of faith knows how to assume the brotherhood of man and to create it by the help of the assumption," Reinhold Niebuhr wrote in 1927, when he was a young clergyman in Detroit, troubled by the deepening enmity between capital and labor. "A religious ideal is always a little absurd because it insists on the truth of what ought to be true but is only partly true; it is however the ultimate wisdom because reality slowly approaches the ideals which are implicit in its life. . . . The races and groups of mankind are obviously not living as a family; but they ought to. And as the necessity becomes more urgent the truth of the ideal becomes more real."

In the 1990s, as Third World countries struggle to service their $1.9 trillion debt to the West, they have virtually nothing left to spend on the rudiments of sanitation, safe water, health care, or education. In Mozambique, where annual earnings average $80, per capita debt runs to $311. Throughout sub-Saharan Africa, hunger, infectious disease, poverty, unemployment, and illiteracy are epidemic. ICCR has asked banks either to forgive the debts of the world's poorest countries or ease the payment terms. The Proxy Monitor has opposed such measures, saying that it cannot see how "feel-good commitments to lofty ideals in negotiating credit relief in Third World markets would serve any useful purpose for bank holding companies, let alone their investors."

Nor has ICCR made much headway with resolutions on wages paid by U.S. corporations doing business in the Third World. Corporations claim that their pay is "competitive" wherever they operate, and churches counter that in poor countries, the going rate rarely amounts to a living wage. In Mexico, where some seven hundred thousand workers assemble products for U.S. manufacturers, ICCR has found that many take home only half what they need to subsist. Because of Mexico's runaway inflation and unstable currency, dollars-and-cents discussions of the cost of living are quickly enveloped in a thick fuzz. ICCR has worked to reframe the issue with a purchasing power index showing how many minutes the average factory hand must work to buy a liter of milk, a kilogram of beans, and the other items in a market basket of necessities. The objective is to show the U.S. companies operating in Mexico that at current wage levels, there are not enough minutes in the week to earn a sustaining wage. Tim Smith believes that the Mexican government could "solve the whole problem by stepping in and setting wages at a sustainable level. But it is not a friend of the worker. Neither are the unions, which are very close to the government." But no government is likely to make such a move on its own for fear of losing jobs to countries with lower wages.

SO it is that the richest inhabitants of the richest nations amass even more wealth while pushing the poorest and weakest deeper into misery. By the United Nations Development Program's reckoning in 1996, the human race had reached a point where it took the combined earnings of the 2.3 billion poorest people on earth to equal the net worth of the world's 358 richest individuals. "All for ourselves, and nothing for anyone else seems, in every age, to have been the vile maxim of the masters of mankind," Adam Smith wrote in *The Wealth of Nations.* He hoped that free markets would end the vileness by abolishing monopolies, putting buyer and seller on an equal footing in every exchange. It was a fine dream, but two centuries of reality have shown that the greater the disparities of wealth between the parties, the more likely it is that the terms of the transaction will be set by the haves. Take it or leave it—the central freedom in Adam Smith's marketplace—is a specious liberty to a laborer free to choose only between pittance or no pittance.*

The dream of *The Wealth of Nations* is not an illusion, but any dream of freedom nurtures only a part of the human spirit. If independence is the prize flower in the garden, interdependence is the soil in which it grows. That has been the heart of ICCR's message as it has called attention, again and again, to the human consequences of corporate action. In the beginning, ICCR's agenda, like the peace and environmental movements of the early 1970s, had the feel of a radical manifesto. By century's end, it enjoyed broad support. Thoughtful Americans, including many in the business world, could disagree on means, but few doubted the value of such ends as protecting the environment, promoting equality, and ending corporate exploitation of the world's poor. "We don't see ourselves as the sole purveyors of moral

---

*Although Smith's present-day acolytes rarely mention it, he understood that employer and employee are rarely equals. In coming to terms, Smith wrote, "workmen desire to get as much, the masters to give as little as possible. . . . It is not, however, difficult to foresee which of the two parties must, upon all ordinary occasions, have the advantage in the dispute, and force the other into compliance with their terms. . . . In all such disputes the masters can hold out much longer. . . . Many workmen could not subsist a week, few could subsist a month, and scarce any a year without employment." *The Wealth of Nations, 1776* (rpt. Chicago, 1976), 74–75.

wisdom to business, and we don't see business as immoral," Tim Smith said, "but we consider it our mandate to act when we believe that business decisions are being made in a moral vacuum."

To free-market purists, the moralizing is still a form of interference bordering on sacrilege. Capitalism, say its champions, is the friend of democracy, rewarding individual enterprise over hereditary privilege and generating more wealth and more political stability than any other economic arrangement known to humankind. Still, shareholder advocacy as practiced by ICCR may prove useful to capitalism, saving it from self-destruction by restraining its inherent tendency to drive headlong toward the extremes of winner-take-all. If nothing else, the hell-raising of those damned ministers in the God Box has led investors and corporate managements into permanent contention with a permanently excellent moral question. As an ICCR flyer puts it, "Money talks. What do you want yours to say?"

"GREED is healthy" seemed a pitiable reply to that question even in a decade memorable for its worship of money. For all their cherishing of worldly goods, Americans always had sensed that wealth was not enough. John Winthrop believed that Massachusetts would thrive only if the inhabitants heeded Christ's call to love one another. James Oglethorpe and the Georgia Trustees, seriously underestimating the importance of self-interest, went too far in asking their charges to sacrifice private gain to public good. Benjamin Franklin blended money-making and public service so effortlessly that ideologues at both ends of the economic spectrum have claimed him as their own.

The power imbalance between the Lowell textile cartel and the factory girls enabled mill owners to jettison their ideals of employee welfare as soon as hard times threatened stockholder dividends. But the ideals—fair wages and humane working conditions—quickly became standards of justice for industrial society. After staking stupendously broad claims for the individual, Ralph Waldo Emerson and Henry David Thoreau came to see the inextricability of self and society and the duty of the privileged to use their power on behalf of the powerless. Looking away from slavery proved cataclysmic as well as immoral—four years of civil war, 640,000 lives, and the still-mounting cost of racism.

Boston's elite quietly founded and underwrote charities long before Andrew Carnegie began advertising his ambition to give away his fortune, but Carnegie's public celebration of giving touched a chord that continues to stir millions of Americans to act on their generous impulses. Nowhere else in the world do ordinary citizens give as much money and time to organized charity as in the United States. The robber barons who preceded Henry Ford argued that the capitalist, having risked his capital, deserved all the profits, owed labor as little as the market would bear, and benefited society most when he invested his profits in more job-creating enterprises. Ford's profit-sharing system, authoritarian as it was, demonstrated that paying workers more than they needed to survive contributes to the general well-being by enabling them to buy goods and services that keep other people employed.

The back-to-the-land idyll of the Tennessee Agrarians proved that they were better at poetry than economics. Still, their writings managed to capture the seriousness of the troubles a society can make for itself if it allows economic empires to operate with little regard for human consequences. The rules of capitalism as usual were suspended in the government-controlled economy of World War II, an event financed by the citizenry. Business did not go out of business, and the income gap between rich and poor was smaller than in any period since.

In hopes of persuading white America to make good on its promise of equality, Whitney Young detailed the high costs of inequality and convinced progressive business leaders that equal opportunity made good economic sense. Bill Norris of Control Data treated corporate social responsibility not as an adjunct to business but as business itself. Where others saw social problems—the unemployability of high school dropouts, for example, and productivity lost because of substance abuse or emotional difficulties—Norris saw opportunities for profit, through the creation of computer-based instruction and employee assistance programs. ICCR works on the social fabric from a skein of all these strands.

What would that fabric be like when the new century began? How strong? How closely woven? Wide enough to cover our dead-eyed sons and brothers in Lafayette Park?

The answers depended upon where one stood. From the enclaves of power and wealth, more powerful and wealthier than ever before, the holes and frayed edges were invisible. As Reinhold Niebuhr pointed out in the 1920s, another unabashedly materialistic time, "Good men do not easily realize how selfish they are if someone does not resist their selfishness; and they are not inclined to abridge their power if someone does not challenge their right to hold it."

Where the challenges would come from was no more predictable than it had ever been, but strange and interesting voices could be heard outside the walls. The voices of women economists, like Myra H. Strober of Stanford University, here to kick the pins out from under cherished economic assumptions. "The more those who are among the 'haves' are told that the world is characterized by scarcity and that the path to well-being is through selfishness and competition," she has written, "the less likely they are to behave in ways that foster altruism, cooperation, and a more equal sharing of economic goods and services." Problems routinely ascribed to scarcity are often problems of poor distribution, Strober noted, citing the mismatch between American hunger and American farm surpluses. Surely there is a better way to share the leftovers than to rely on guests in luxury hotels to give them to men on park benches.

There was the voice of Virginia Held, a philosopher, here to suggest that Americans do not need a new social contract so much as some other basis for social relationships. However necessary contracts might be between buyer and seller, they undermine the trust and cooperation needed to hold society together, she said. In place of the contract, she offered a model of social connection based on the bond between mother and child. Theirs is a world of permanent commitment, a world where the strong act on behalf of the weak and individuals understand that they cannot meet their social obligations by leaving one another alone. In short, Held was proposing a declaration of inter-dependence.

Voices of community development loan fund officers, here in search of depositors willing to accept smaller yields on some of their savings in order to finance low-interest loans to entrepreneurs and nonprofit organizations working to strengthen poor communities.

A young man, here to give his explanation for the squalor and vio-lence in the housing project where he lives. The people in charge, he said, did not do their jobs "tenderly and wholeheartedly."

And Eliot Rosewater, the creation of novelist Kurt Vonnegut, here to share the instruction he would give if called upon to usher babies into the world: "God damn it, you've got to be kind."

To turn out that way, the babies would need all the tenderness they could get, wholeheartedly given. And spare change, because without money, they would not be able to afford much in the way of morals. Goodness—this was going to be hard. But it was even harder to think why a people who had always had the most and aspired to the best would settle for less.

ACKNOWLEDGMENTS

As IS TRUE OF MANY books, this one is the product of untold hours of work in a room that to the casual observer seems blissfully empty and quiet but to the writer is a no-man's-land between those ancient, irreconcilable enemies, Self-Doubt and the Muse. Happily, a book touching on thirteen worlds, as this one does, offers an abundance of legitimate excuses for retreat to more peaceable ground. For giving me sanctuary as well as expert assistance, I thank the Baker Library at the Harvard Business School, the Bancroft Library on the Berkeley campus of the University of California, the Rare Book and Manuscript Library at Columbia University, Kevin Corbitt and Bruce Bruemmer of the Charles Babbage Institute for the History of Information Processing at the University of Minnesota, Blanche Parker and her colleagues on the reference desk at the Darien (Connecticut) Library, the Ford Motor Company Archives at the Henry Ford Museum in Dearborn, the Savannah branch of the Georgia Historical Society, the Special Collections staff of the Heard Library at Vanderbilt University, Chuck Kelly and Fred Bauman in the manuscript reading room at the Library of Congress, the library at the Lowell National Historic Site, the Center for Lowell History, Peter Drummey at the Massachusetts Historical Society, the Rare Books and Special Collections staff of the Princeton University Library, the Southern Historical Collection at the University of North Carolina, and, at Yale University, the Beinecke Library and the manuscripts and archives division of the Sterling Memorial Library.

For documents and answers to questions on a wide range of subjects, I am also grateful to the Detroit Public Library, the Ford Foundation Library in New York, the Lyndon Baines Johnson Library in Austin, the Minnesota Historical Society in Minneapolis, the National Urban League in New York, the Nixon Presidential Materials

Staff of the National Archives in College Park, Maryland, and the Franklin D. Roosevelt Library in Hyde Park, New York.

In the course of my research, I was the beneficiary of excellent work by four indefatigable assistants—Katina Lillios, Regina Blakely, Molly Shapiro, and Kendra Hurley. They deserve added thanks for their good cheer in the face of even the most tedious tasks. During research trips to Washington, Berkeley, Ann Arbor, and Nashville, David Anderson, Susan Edmiston, Gae Amorose, and Elly and Joel Glassman took excellent care of me, bestowing many generosities that I will always appreciate.

For their willingness to grant me interviews and the care they gave to these encounters, I especially thank Harold Sims and Margaret B. Young (on Whitney Young); Bill Norris and Norbert Berg of Control Data Corporation; Timothy H. Smith of the Interfaith Center on Corporate Responsibility; Doris Gormley of the Sisters of St. Francis of Philadelphia; and more than fifty men and women (named in the notes for chapter 10) who worked in Henry J. Kaiser's shipyards during World War II. I am particularly grateful to the *San Francisco Chronicle, Oakland Tribune,* and *Alameda Times-Herald* for printing letters inviting wartime Kaiser workers to contact me. I am indebted too to W. Eric Aiken of the Proxy Monitor, Simon Billenness of Franklin Research and Development Corporation, Nell Minow of LENS, and Professor Paul Neuhauser of the University of Iowa's law school for interviews on specific issues related to shareholder resolutions.

I thank the Bancroft Library at the University of California–Berkeley for permission to use the papers of Henry J. Kaiser and Edgar F. Kaiser; Margaret B. Young for permission to use the Whitney Young Papers; and the Ford Foundation for permission to cite a Ford-funded study of the National Urban League by Cresap, McCormick and Paget. (Full bibliographic information on these materials appears in the footnotes.)

To William W. Abbot, Ronald Bailey, John Morton Blum, Eleanor B. Sheldon, Clifton R. Wharton, Dolores D. Wharton, and Brenda Wineapple—who read various chapters and kindly shared their

knowledge, insights, and suggestions—I feel much obliged. I refrain from mentioning who read which chapters lest my attributions be misconstrued as their imprimaturs. Suffice it to say that these expert readers improved the book, and if it is still wanting, they should not be held accountable.

A number of the concerns voiced in this book I first explored in a monthly column for *Lear's* magazine, where for three years Anne Heller gave me a wonderful combination of elbow room and imaginative, tough-minded editing.

For imaginative, tough-minded agenting, I am grateful to Elaine Markson and her colleagues at the Elaine Markson Literary Agency.

At Clarkson Potter, this book began under the wing of senior editor Shirley Wohl and was completed in the care of editorial director Lauren Shakely. I thank both of them for their extraordinary faith and patience. Lauren edited the manuscript with elegance and generosity and assured its expeditious publication.

Six years in the cross fire of Self-Doubt and the Muse is seven more than I would wish on anyone, but as I come to the end of it on this July day in 1997, I am struck by how unweary I feel. Part of this state owes to the natural exuberance of finishing a book, but most of it flows from the immense gratitude and love for a group of close friends who continued to astonish me with their tenderness and attentions throughout this endeavor: Thelma Jean Goodrich, Mary Kay Blakely, Mary-Lou and Larry Weisman, Judith Daniels, K. C. Cole, Claire Gruppo, and Jerry Jellison. By their openheartedness, intelligence, company, and laughter, they have kept my spirits aloft.

The last decade of the twentieth century turned out to be an especially propitious moment to reflect on the history of the tension between money and morals in American life. Scholars in many disciplines are challenging old assumptions about the primacy and value of rationality, self-interest, and competition. Exciting alternatives are being put forward, elaborated, discussed, and debated around the world. What the ferment will produce is anyone's guess at this stage. Because most of this new work is theoretical and rooted in the social sciences while my approach is primarily narrative and historical, I have quoted little from these scholars. Nonetheless, in opening new worlds to me, they stimulated and broadened my thinking on several fronts. Particularly valuable were the work of Amartya Sen; the essays in Jane J. Mansbridge, ed., *Beyond Self-Interest* (Chicago, 1991) and Marianne Ferber and Julie Nelson, eds., *Beyond Economic Man: Feminist Theory and Economic Man* (Chicago, 1993); and Amitai Etzioni, *The Moral Dimension* (New York, 1988).

Sources

Chapter 1

More Than All the Wealth in the World

John Winthrop had no way of knowing whether the Puritan settlement of Massachusetts would succeed, but he did have a sense of the momentousness of his move from England to America. As a lawyer, he had acquired the habit of keeping records, and much of what is known about Massachusetts in the crucial decades from 1630, when his fleet arrived, until his death in 1649 comes from his accounts of events in letters, a journal, and other papers. The principal sources for this chapter are Winthrop's writings and the records of the Massachusetts Bay Company, of which he was governor. These documents are collected in the following volumes:

Nathaniel Shurtleff, ed., *Records of the Governor and Company of the Massachusetts Bay in New England.* 5 vols. (New York, 1968). Abbreviated in the notes that follow as *RGC,* with volume number followed by page number (e.g., 5:25).

John Winthrop, *History of New England from 1630 to 1649.* Winthrop's journal, with notes by James Savage. 2 vols. (Boston, 1825–26). Cited as *HNE.*

Robert C. Winthrop, *Life and Letters of John Winthrop.* 2 vols. (New York, 1971). Noted as *LLJW.*

Winthrop Papers. 5 vols. (Boston, 1929–1947). Referred to as *WP.*

Page   1 helped themselves. *WP,* 2:247–63; *LLJW,* 2:21–22; Edmund S. Morgan, *The Puritan Dilemma: The Story of John Winthrop* (Boston, 1958), 54.

1 (weights around the neck.) *WP,* 2:244.

2 "speak evil of the ways of God." John Winthrop, "A Model of Christian Charity," *WP,* 2:282–95.

3 without dread. Richard Dunn, *Puritans and Yankees: The Winthrop Dynasty of New England, 1630–1717* (Princeton, N.J., 1962), 4–5, 8.

3 emblem of the glory of God. David Leverenz, *The Language of Puritan Feeling: An Exploration in Literature, Psychology, and Social History* (New Brunswick, N.J., 1980), 41–42; Kai T. Erikson, *Wayward Puritans: A Study in the Sociology of Deviance* (New York, 1966), 47–48.

4 "grasshoppers." J. Franklin Jameson, ed., *Johnson's Wonder-Working Providence of Sions Saviour in New England,* 1656 (rpt. New York, 1910), 23.

4 unsurprised. Stephen Innes, ed., *Work and Labor in Early America* (Chapel Hill, N.C., 1988), 4–5.

4 "nakedness." *WP,* 1:295.

4 "Babylon." *WP,* 2:130.

4 "hiding place." *WP,* 2:91–92.

5 saw fit. Samuel Eliot Morison, *Builders of the Bay Colony* (Boston, 1958), 65–71.

6 "general destruction." *WP,* 2:112–34; Everett Emerson, ed., *Letters from New England: The Massachusetts Bay Colony, 1629–1638* (Amherst, Mass., 1976), 37–38; Alden T. Vaughan, *New England Frontier: Puritans and Indians, 1620–1675* (Boston, 1965), 21–22, 111–12. The nature of the "miraculous" plague is unknown, according to Vaughan. Most historians agree that it was not yellow fever, smallpox, jaundice, or typhoid. Possibilities include measles, bubonic plague, or a combination of diseases that descended simultaneously.

7 "His people." *WP,* 2:161; Dunn, op. cit., 8; Morison, op. cit, 66–68.

7 suet. Ibid., 2:147, 278.

7 "tears." Ibid., 2:201–2; Benjamin W. Labaree, *Colonial Massachusetts: A History* (Millwood, N.Y., 1979), 40.

7 terrors of the wilderness. Thomas Hutchinson, *The History of the Colony and Province of Massachusetts-Bay,* Lawrence Shaw Mayo, ed. (Cambridge, Mass., 1936), 19–23; Morgan, op. cit., 56–58.

7 stronghold of Puritanism. Morison, op. cit., 79–81.

8 "in all our troubles." *WP,* 2:265, 303–5; *LLJW,* 2:34–35.

8 first execution, *WP,* 2:268.

8 clear shot. Morison, op. cit., 81.

8 Many more were ill. Michael J. Canavan, "Mr. Blackstone's 'Excellent Spring.'" *Publications of the Colonial Society of Massachusetts* 11 (1906–7):296–97.

8 atonement. *LLJW,* 2:56–57.

8 (wooden chimneys). Emerson, op. cit., 82.

8 trade along the coast. Dunn, op. cit., 13.

9 "first brunts." Emerson, op. cit., 92.

9 fed on the job. *RGC,* 1:74, 76, 79.

9 fetch in England. Darrett P. Rutman, *Winthrop's Boston: Portrait of a Puritan Town, 1630–1649* (Chapel Hill, N.C., 1965), 166; *RGC,* 1:111.

9 town governments to monitor wages. *HNE,* 2:24–25.

10 make their own trades. Ibid., 1:161.

10 short weight. *RGC,* 2:169, 181.

10 discretion of the court. Ibid., 1:59–63.

10 fined and flogged. Ibid., 1:74–75, 82–83, 155, 180.

10 real evil. *HNE,* 2:136–37, 403.

12 "higher tribunal than man's can be." Ibid., 1:313–17, 2:4; *LLJW,* 2:280–83; Stephen Foster, *Their Solitary Way: The Puritan Social Ethic in the First Century of Settlement in New England* (New Haven, 1971), 109. Keayne's will appears in Bernard Bailyn, ed., *The Apologia of Robert Keayne* (New York, 1965).

13 "placed them." Quoted in Joseph Dorfman, *The Economic Mind in American Civilization* (New York, 1966), 1:117.

13 "this jurisdiction." *HNE,* 1:143; *RGC,* 1:274–75.

13 rum trade. *HNE,* 2:324; Gabriel Kolko, "Max Weber on America: Theory and Evidence," *History and Theory* 1 (1961):249.

13 "do good with it." Foster, op. cit., 111.

14 expense to the town. Foster, op. cit., 134–41; Charles R. Lee, "Public Poor Relief and the Massachusetts Community, 1620–1715," *New England Quarterly* 71 (1983):564–85.

15 Virginia and other colonies. *HNE,* 1:116.

15 surrounding towns. Stuart Bruchey, *The Roots of American Economic Growth, 1607–1861: An Essay in Social Causation* (New York, 1965), 19; Labaree, op. cit., 30.

15 economic incentives. *RGC,* 1:81, 114, 257–58, 327, 331; 2:61, 126–29.

15 woodlots. Ibid., 1:111; William B. Weeden, *Economic and Social History of New England, 1620–1789.* 2 vols. (Boston, 1892), 1:65.

15 not regularly employed in farming. Weeden, op. cit., 1:82.

15 Upward of fifteen thousand, Edward J. Perkins, *The Economy of Colonial America,* 2d ed. (New York, 1988), 1.

16 suppliers in England. *LLJW,* 2:296–97.

16 "indifferent men." Bernard Bailyn, *The New England Merchants in the Seventeenth Century* (New York, 1964), 46–48.

16 linen and wool. *RGC,* 1:294, 326; Marion H. Gottfried, "The

First Depression in Massachusetts," *New England Quarterly* 8 (1936):655–78.

16 "depart out of our jurisdiction." Morison, op. cit., 101; *WP,* 3:172–74; 4:173–75, 209; *RGC,* 1:283, 295.

17 "self-love too much." *WP,* 4:192–93, 413–14; Dunn, op. cit., 20.

17 "could make." *HNE,* 2:24; *LLJW,* 2:297.

18 "distempers." *WP,* 5:209.

18 bankruptcy of the ironworks. *RGC,* 2:126; Bailyn, *The New England Merchants in the Seventeenth Century,* 62–65; Gottfried, op. cit., 662–64; Morison, op. cit., 275–80.

19 conveyance. *RGC,* 2:193; Weeden, op. cit., 1:56.

19 feverish. Bernard Bailyn, *The Peopling of British North America* (New York, 1986), 65–69, 85.

19 "for such an end." Quoted in Everett H. Emerson, *John Cotton* (New York, 1965), 53.

19 "would starve all." Thomas Morton, *New English Canaan* (New York, 1967), 177.

19 monogamous marriage. Vaughan, op. cit., 235–38.

19 access to firearms. *RGC,* 2:16.

20 to a squaw, *HNE,* 1:60–61.

20 ravaged native cornfields, *WP,* 5:347.

20 "God allows to all men." *RGC,* 2:85.

20 threatened Puritan authority. Vaughan, op. cit., 122–45.

20 Rhode Island. Dunn, op. cit., 17–18.

21 exiled. Morison, op. cit., 119–26; *HNE,* 1:265–67, 292–98, 326–28.

22 inventory, *WP,* 5:333–37; *HNE,* 2:392.

CHAPTER 2
NOT FOR SELF, BUT FOR OTHERS

THE FOUNDING OF Georgia is one of the best- and worst-documented episodes in American colonial history. The Trustees' official papers, together with hundreds of letters from Georgia, have been preserved in the British government's Public Records Office. The colonists and their descendants were not so punctilious. Because James Oglethorpe often put other duties ahead of correspondence, the record of his ten years in Georgia is skimpy. Consequently Oglethorpe is "America's least known founding father," say Phinizy Spalding and Harvey Jackson, editors of *Oglethorpe in Perspective: Georgia's Founder after Two Hundred Years* (Tuscaloosa, Ala., 1989), 3. As guardians of the colonial documents that did exist, the Georgians were sometimes unlucky, sometimes careless. Many records were lost in a fire in 1776. Others, secreted for safekeeping in Maryland during the American Revolution, disappeared. More were lost when the state capital was moved from Milledgeville to Atlanta in 1868. The final unfortunate winnowing happened in the twentieth century, when a team of archivists decided to make room for new materials by discarding old ones.

But if Oglethorpe remains in shadow, there is no mystery about the course of the Georgia experiment. The Trustees wrote about the colony in letters and fund-raising pamphlets, the Georgians did not shrink from communicating their grievances to London, a few diaries and journals have survived, and the debate over slavery occasioned the writing of many pamphlets.

Principal primary sources used in writing this chapter include the following:

Allen Daniel Candler et al., eds., *The Colonial Records of the State of Georgia.* 27 vols. to date. (Atlanta and Athens, 1904–16, 1976–). Referred to in these notes as *CRSG,* with volume number followed by page number.

John Percival Egmont, *Manuscripts of the Earl of Egmont, Diary of*

Viscount Percival afterwards First Earl of Egmont. 3 vols. (London, 1920). Cited here as Egmont. Egmont's powerful political connections, his broad human sympathy, and his joie de vivre make his diary one of the most revealing and delightful in eighteenth-century English literature. Like the other Trustees, Egmont had many responsibilities and interests, but the diary amply demonstrates the depth of his concern for the colony.

E. Merton Coulter, ed., *The Journal of William Stephens, 1741–1745,* Wormsloe Foundation Publications (Athens, Ga., 1958, 1959). 2 vols. Referred to here as Stephens. William Stephens was appointed secretary of the colony in 1737 and later served as president. His journal, filled with hopes and disappointments, is the most vivid extant account of day-to-day life in colonial Georgia.

Page   24 "a million more." Peter Earle, *The World of Defoe* (New York, 1976), 115–17; Roy Porter, *English Society in the Eighteenth Century* (New York, 1982), 145–48; W. A. Speck, *Stability and Strife, England, 1714–1760* (Cambridge, Mass., 1977), 138.

   25 succumbing to infection. Porter, op. cit., 147; James Ross McCain, *Georgia as a Proprietary Province: The Execution of a Trust* (Boston, 1917), 18; Sidney Webb and Beatrice Webb, *English Prisons under Local Government* (London, 1922), 18–19. The Webbs observe (p. 29) that although Parliament passed the reforms, little changed because the government neither designated nor established an office to carry them out.

   25 "rest and sleep." Quoted in Porter, op. cit., 145–46.

   25 "more equally divided." Egmont, 1:264.

   25 release of ten thousand imprisoned debtors. Henry Bruce, *Life of General Oglethorpe* (New York, 1890), 44–47; Amos Aschbach Ettinger, *James Edward Oglethorpe, Imperial Idealist,* 1936 (rpt. New York, 1968), 88–89; Albert B. Saye, *New Viewpoints in Georgia History* (Athens, Ga., 1943), 12–13.

   25 "starving at large." Benjamin Martyn, *Reasons for Establishing the Colony of Georgia, with Regard to the Trade of Great Britain* (London, 1733), 18–19.

   26 "trade, navigation, and wealth." Quoted in Ettinger, op. cit., 118.

   26 "all there plentiful." Sir Robert Montgomery, "A Discourse Concerning the Design'd Establishment of a New Colony to the

South of Carolina, in the Most Delightful Country of the
Universe" (1717) in Peter Force, ed., *Tracts and Other Papers,
Relating Principally to the Origin, Settlement, and Progress of the
Colonies in North America, from the Discovery of the Country to the Year
1776* (Washington, 1835), 1:6–7.

27 "forget their sorrows." Martyn, op. cit., 5; Ettinger, op. cit., 122.

27 the new land. Egmont, 1:164; Harvey Jackson and Phinizy
Spalding, eds., *Forty Years of Diversity: Essays on Colonial Georgia*
(Athens, Ga., 1984), 10; *"Non sibi, sed aliis"* can still be seen on the
seal of the Georgia Historical Society; Paul S. Taylor, *Georgia Plan:
1732–1752.* Institute of Business and Economic Research,
Graduate School of Business Administration, University of
California (Berkeley, Calif., 1972), 18–20.

27 become self-sufficient. [James Oglethorpe], "Some Account of the
Designs of the Trustees for Establishing the Colony of Georgia in
America," in Albert Sidney Britt Jr. and Anthony Roane Dees,
eds., *Selected Eighteenth Century Manuscripts* (Savannah, 1980), 4–5.

28 "perfection of virtue." Martyn, op. cit., 38–39.

28 not wholly Christian. Egmont, 1:273, 299, 309, 389; 2:195.

28 for the indentured. David M. Potter Jr., "The Rise of the
Plantation System in Georgia," *Georgia Historical Quarterly* 16
(1932):114–35; Milton L. Ready, "Land Tenure in Trusteeship
Georgia," *Agricultural History* 48 (1974):353–68; Harold E. Davis,
*The Fledgling Province: Social and Cultural Life in Colonial Georgia,
1733–1776,* Institute of Early American History and Culture,
Williamsburg, Va. (Chapel Hill, N.C., 1976), 9, 11–12.

29 overly large holdings. Potter, op. cit., 120–21; Davis, op. cit.,
11–12; Ready, op. cit., 358–59, 368.

29 demanding gift of wilderness. H. B. Fant, "The Prohibition Policy
of the Trustees for Establishing the Colony of Georgia in
America," *Georgia Historical Quarterly* 17 (1933):286–92; Francis
Moore, "A Voyage to Georgia; begun the 15th of October, 1735,"
in *Our First Visit in America: Early Reports from the Colony of
Georgia, 1732–1740* (Savannah, 1974), 99; Bruce, op. cit., 99; Betty
Wood, "James Edward Oglethorpe, Race, and Slavery: A
Reassessment," in Spalding and Jackson, eds., *Oglethorpe in
Perspective,* 70–71.

30 "arse." Jackson and Spalding, eds., *Forty Years of Diversity,* 12;
Robert G. McPherson, ed., "The Voyage of the *Anne*—A Daily
Record," *Georgia Historical Quarterly* 44 (1960): 220–31.

30 "with food and care." *CRSG,* 20:5.

31 for the river. Historians have suggested three possible origins for the name "Savannah"—the Spanish *sabana,* meaning "flatlands"; a corruption of *Shawnee,* the name of a native tribe in the region; and *Shawano,* meaning "the southerners" in one of the indigenous languages.

30 comforts of Charleston. *CRSG,* 20:2–3.

31 his charges were alive. *CRSG,* 20:9–10, 16; E. Merton Coulter, ed., *The Journal of Peter Gordon, 1732–1735,* Wormsloe Foundation Publications, no. 6 (Athens, Ga., 1963), 35–36; Bruce, op. cit., 112–16; Jackson and Spalding, *Forty Years of Diversity,* 14.

32 promised by Sir Robert Montgomery. Ibid., 20:17; *Our First Visit in America,* 81.

32 lying-in. *CRSG,* 20:34–35.

32 mixing strong drink with Georgia heat. *CRSG,* 20:27–28; Egmont 2:211, 317, 476; *CRSG,* 20:27–28; Phinizy Spalding, *Oglethorpe in America* (Athens, Ga., 1984), 153.

32 doing business in Savannah. *CRSG,* 20:124, 137–38; 21:463; Stephens, 1:95–96; Bruce, op. cit., 114–15.

34 "eating trash." *CRSG,* 20:39–42; 21:114–19; 24:447; 25:115, 228–29; *Our First Visit in America,* 108.

34 more money for Georgia. Egmont, 2:41; *CRSG,* 20:13, 97–98; 22–1:158, 275–76, 283–85; 23:421, 356, 358–59, 482; Saye, op. cit., 96–97.

34 administrators of justice. McCain, op. cit., 69, 93–94; *CRSG,* 22–2:165; Saye, op. cit., 83.

35 "in the dark." Quoted in Spalding and Jackson, *Oglethorpe in Perspective,* 83.

35 pursuit other than agriculture. Potter, op. cit., 121; Ready, op. cit., 358–59, 368.

35 "guided by them." *CRSG,* 21:469.

35 "settle it with Negroes." Ready, op. cit., 360; *CRSG,* 22–2:111–12.

36 compound the confusion. *CRSG,* 22–2:172–73; Ready, op. cit., 354–60.

36 cleared up. Force, op. cit., 21; James Etheridge Callaway, *The Early Settlement of Georgia* (Athens, Ga., 1948), 48; Davis, op. cit., 11–12; Ready, op. cit., 357–58; *CRSG,* 20:97–98, 120–21, 334–36. Jones was also a military officer, a counselor to Oglethorpe and, for a time, the colony's treasurer. McCain (op. cit., 166) notes that there were many complaints about the inaccuracy of Jones's surveys.

36 marriage or bequests. Ready, op. cit., 368; Carole Watterson

Troxler, "William Stephens and the Georgia 'Malcontents': Conciliation, Conflict, and Capitulation," *Georgia Historical Quarterly* 67 (1983):12–13.

37 a larger good. *CRSG*, 1:414–15; 2:408, 421; Taylor, op. cit., 308–9; H. B. Fant, "The Labor Policy of the Trustees for Establishing the Colony of Georgia in America," *Georgia Historical Quarterly* 16 (1932), 6.

37 "useless also in Georgia." William A. Byrne, "The Burden and Heat of the Day: Slavery and Servitude in Savannah, 1733–1865." Ph.D. diss., Florida State University, 1979, 16–19, 27–28; Ready, op. cit., 361.

37 price gouging. *CRSG*, 20:120–21, 206–7; 22–1, 275–76.

37 available for hire. *CRSG*, 22–1:272–73; 23:159, 352–53; 25:9; Egmont, 1:309; Stephens, 2:5.

38 rarely convicted them. Taylor, op. cit., 72; *CRSG*, 21:56–59, 22–1:6, 20–21; Stephens, 2:28–29, 123, 243, 256–57; Davis, op. cit., 68.

38 honor their bills. Fant, "The Prohibition Policy of the Trustees for Establishing the Colony of Georgia in America," op. cit., 290; Milton Sidney Heath, *Constructive Liberalism: The Role of the State in Economic Development in Georgia to 1860* (Cambridge, Mass., 1954), 29; Melvin Herndon, "Timber Products of Colonial Georgia," *Georgia Historical Quarterly*, 57 (1973): 56–62; Milton L. Ready, *An Economic History of Colonial Georgia, 1732–1754.* Ph.D. diss., University of Georgia, 1970, 188.

38 do not share it. *CRSG*, 20:3–4.

39 crucial moment. Ibid., 20:152–54; 22–1:65; 23:199, 212; 24:186–87; Stephens, 1:23, 25; 2:156.

39 filled with mulberry trees. *CRSG*, 22-1:283–85.

39 "for her family." Stephens, 2:83–85, 90, 155–56, 167.

39 win her cooperation. *CRSG*, 23:468–69; 24:68–70.

40 "the least article." Ibid., 24:302; 25:5.

40 kind of labor. Ibid., 22–2:178; 24:227; 25:140, 414; 363–64; 26:23, 130–31; 26:287; Mary Thomas McKinstry, "Silk Culture in the Colony of Georgia," *Georgia Historical Quarterly* 14 (1930):230–31.

41 seven and one-half pounds of spun silk. *CRSG*, 22-2:336; 23:468–69, 153–55; 24:414–15.

41 "great pain." Ibid., 24:296, 414.

41 evanesced. Ibid., 26:92; W. Calvin Smith, "Utopia's Last Chance? The Georgia Silk Boomlet of 1751," *Georgia Historical Quarterly* 59 (1975):25–37; McKinstry, op. cit., 230; Reba C. Strickland, "The

Mercantile System as Applied to Georgia," *Georgia Historical Quarterly* 22 (1938):164.

41 stuff of Georgia's dreams. Egmont, 3:100; Britt and Dees, op. cit., 108.

42 "cheaper than ours." Spalding, op. cit., 64; Force, op. cit., 22–23; Potter, op. cit., 123; *CRSG,* 20:19–20, 364–67. In a quantitative study of the relative costs of slaves and indentured servants, Ralph Gray and Betty Wood concluded that slavery won out because it was exponentially cheaper. Georgia's founders, wrote Gray and Wood, "nursed a vain hope: a colony based on indentured white labor that was large enough to serve as a military deterrent to the Spanish could not be economically viable in its own right; a colony whose workforce was dominated by black slaves could not serve as an effective military buffer. In fact, the example set in the other American colonies suggests that subsistence-level, mixed farming is not the key to rapid settlement. Rather, the establishment of a fast-expanding export base . . . and rapid growth of linked industries stimulate population expansion in colonial outposts." Ralph Gray and Betty Wood, "The Transition from Indentured to Involuntary Servitude in Colonial Georgia," *Explorations in Economic History* 13 (1976):353–70.

43 revenge. *CRSG,* 22-1:73–76; Fant, "The Labor Policy of the Trustees for Establishing the Colony of Georgia in America," op. cit., 1.

43 leaving for other colonies. Troxler, op. cit., 6–8.

43 prosper only with slave labor. *CRSG,* 22-2:111–12; 23:172–73, 176, 195.

43 terror of their masters. Troxler, op. cit., 11; Force, op. cit., 52–53.

43 forty Negroes and twenty whites. *CRSG,* 22-2:232–36, 250.

44 "brim full of tears." Egmont, 3:105, 109, 175; Taylor, op. cit., 143–48, 169.

44 "ruin of the adventurers." Force, op. cit., 46.

45 "introduction of Negroes." Betty Wood, "Thomas Stephens and the Introduction of Black Slavery in Georgia," *Georgia Historical Quarterly* 58 (1974):34; Taylor, op. cit., 210–11; *CRSG,* 5:648–49.

45 "voluptuously." *CRSG,* 23:444–47.

45 from £510 to £16,320. Leslie F. Church, *Oglethorpe: A Study in Philanthropy in England and Georgia* (London, 1932), 295; *CRSG,* 25:295; Taylor, op. cit., 304.

46 "Christian religion." *CRSG,* 1:56–62; 25:290–94, 430–35.

46 charter in 1752. Taylor, op. cit., 285–86.

CHAPTER 3
VIRTUOSO

BENJAMIN FRANKLIN WAS born in 1706 and died in 1790. One of the most ingenious, versatile human beings known to history, he led a life filled with discovery, innovation, and accomplishment in science, literature and journalism, government, and philanthropy. He has been the subject of many fine biographies, including Carl Van Doren, *Benjamin Franklin* (New York, 1938), and Esmond Wright, *Franklin of Philadelphia* (Cambridge, Mass., 1986). Claude-Anne Lopez and Eugenia W. Herbert present a delightful personal portrait in *The Private Franklin* (New York: Norton, 1975). I. Bernard Cohen, pioneer of the history of science, explored Franklin's scientific life and times in *Benjamin Franklin's Science* (Cambridge, Mass., 1990) and *Science and the Founding Fathers: Science in the Political Thought of Jefferson, Franklin, Adams, and Madison* (New York, 1995).

Among the most intriguing interpretations of the American Revolution and the writing of the U.S. Constitution are Bernard Bailyn, *The Ideological Origins of the American Revolution* (Cambridge, Mass., 1967); Henry Steele Commager, *The Empire of Reason: How Europe Imagined and America Realized the Enlightenment* (Garden City, N.Y., 1977); Edmund S. Morgan, *Inventing the People: The Rise of Popular Sovereignty in England and America* (New York, 1988); Forrest McDonald, *Novus Ordo Seclorum: The Intellectual Origins of the Constitution* (Lawrence, Kans., 1985); Garry Wills, *Inventing America: Jefferson's Declaration of Independence* (Garden City, N.Y., 1978) and *Explaining America: The Federalist* (Garden City, N.Y., 1981); and Gordon S. Wood, *The Creation of the American Republic, 1776–1787* (Chapel Hill, N.C., 1969).

The primary source on Franklin is Leonard W. Labaree, ed., *Papers of Benjamin Franklin* (New Haven, Conn., 1959–). It is cited in these notes as *PBF,* with volume number followed by page number. Franklin's *Autobiography,* his 1733–58 prefaces to *Poor Richard's*

Almanack, and many other significant works can also be found in J. A. Leo Le May's excellent anthology, *Benjamin Franklin: Writings* (New York, 1987). Where possible, I have keyed the references to Le May's book, which is more widely available than the *Papers.* The anthology is cited here as *BFW.*

Page 49 "spun too fine." *BFW,* 1238.
      49 "to gain him," Ibid., 1192.
      49 "that help themselves." Ibid., 1201.
      49 "ends in shame." *PBF,* 1:353.
      49 "a great ship," *BFW,* 1235.
      49 "themselves with it!" *PBF,* 4:446.
      49 "rise up with fleas." Ibid., 1187.
      49 American coast. Robert G. McPherson, ed., "The Voyage of the *Anne*—A Daily Record," *Georgia Historical Quarterly* 44 (1960):227.
      50 waiting on the wharf. *BFW,* 1407, 1324–29.
      50 logic. Ibid., 1314, 1317, 1320–21.
      50 five-foot-nine-inch frame. Carl Van Doren, *Benjamin Franklin* (New York, 1938):90–91.
      51 "lovers of reading." *BFW,* 1380–81.
      51 from Cotton Mather. Ibid., 75.
      51 "desire of victory." *BFW,* 1361.
      51 ("a rational creature?"). *PBF,* 1:255–263.
      52 "make me ridiculous." Ibid., 1362, 1383–93.
      52 destroyed young Israel's pleasures. Herman Melville, *Israel Potter* (1855) in Harrison Hayford, ed., *Herman Melville* (New York, 1984), 467–87.
      52 "'thief of time.'" Mark Twain, "The Late Benjamin Franklin" (1870) in Louis J. Budd, ed., *Mark Twain: Collected Tales, Sketches, Speeches, & Essays, 1852–1890* (New York, 1992), 425–28.
      52 "Kiwanians." Charles W. White, *Benjamin Franklin: A Study in Self-Mythology* (New York, 1987), 1.
      52 "usually unconscious." J. A. Leo Le May and P. M. Zall, eds., *Benjamin Franklin's Autobiography: An Authoritative Text, Backgrounds, Criticisms* (New York, 1986), 289–99.
      53 into their home. Ibid., 1371; Van Doren, op. cit., 93–94.
      53 Rhode Island. Van Doren, op. cit., 107.
      54 trumpeted the almanac's success. *BFW,* 1203.

54 "scraps from the table of wisdom." Ibid., 1211.

54 "Opportunity is the great bawd" . . . "Haste makes waste." *BFW,* 1190–1283.

54 *"to stand upright."* Ibid., 1397.

55 "What good may I do in it?" Ibid., 1206.

55 "never saw each other." Ibid., 1193.

55 "leave contentedly." *BFW,* 1286.

55 "philosophical studies and amusements." Ibid., 1420.

55 "freely and generously." Ibid., 1417–18.

55 gave away the lightning rod, Ibid., 1278.

56 "may be thought of public advantage." Ibid., 295–97.

57 "one's country, friends and family." Ibid., 323–44.

57 "cure of his diseases." Ibid., 361–67.

58 his shrewdness. Ibid., 1422–24.

58 through the night. Ibid., 1425–26.

58 "Join, or die." Ibid., 375–77.

59 unified the colonies. Van Doren, op. cit., 211–13; *BFW,* 863, 1429.

59 perennial best-seller, Ormond Seavey, *Becoming Benjamin Franklin: The Autobiography and the Life* (University Park, Pa., 1988), 180.

60 "he that saddles him another." *BFW,* 1281.

60 reimbursements from Parliament. Esmond Wright, *Franklin of Philadelphia* (Cambridge, Mass., 1986), 165–66.

60 paper money. Lewis J. Carey, *Franklin's Economic Views* (Garden City, N.Y., 1928), 318.

61 "can make new ones." Van Doren, op. cit., 337–40, 351–52.

61 "prettiest fleeces on their backs imaginable." *BFW,* 568–69.

61 bordered on insult. Ibid., 613–15.

62 "the golden eggs?" Ibid., 633–34.

62 "cargoes of eunuchs." Ibid., 717–19.

63 "extravagance, vice and folly?" Quoted in John Patrick Diggins, *The Lost Soul of American Politics: Virtue, Self-Interest, and the Foundations of Liberalism* (New York, 1984), 55.

63 "part in their favor." [John Adams], *Discourses on Davila,* 1790 (rpt. Boston, 1805), 39, 69.

63 "imposter." Quoted in Diggins, op. cit., 85.

64 "characteristic of the species." Thomas Jefferson to Thomas Law (June 13, 1814) in Merrill D. Peterson, ed., *Thomas Jefferson: Writings* (New York, 1984), 1336–38.

65 "no government would be necessary." James Madison, "The Federalist No. 51," in Garry Wills, ed., *The Federalist Papers* (New York, 1982), 262.

65 "no other lawgiver." Michael Foot and Isaac Kramnick, eds., *The Thomas Paine Reader* (New York, 1987), 66–67.

65 "eternity a moment." L. H. Butterfield, ed., *Diary and Autobiography of John Adams* (Cambridge, Mass., 1961), 4 vols., 2:54.

65 "on the side of virtue." [John Adams], op. cit., 45.

65 low regard. Ibid., 25–28.

65 "blown down by the winds." Butterfield, op. cit., 3:244.

66 "heaven and earth to obtain it." *BFW,* 1131–32.

66 act on his suggestion. Max Farrand, *The Records of the Federal Convention of 1787,* 4 vols. (New Haven, Conn., 1911), 1:120.

66 "and share his practice." Ibid., 1:82–83.

66 send two members. Van Doren, op. cit., 749–50; *BFW,* 1134–38.

66 "not sure that it is not the best." *BFW,* 1139–41.

67 "and not a setting sun." Farrand, op. cit., 2:648.

67 "if you can keep it." Quoted in J. A. Smith, *Franklin and Bache: Envisioning the Enlightened Republic* (New York, 1990), 18.

CHAPTER 4
THE BEAUTIES OF FACTORY LIFE

THE LOWELL TEXTILE corporations were the nation's first large-scale industrial enterprises. Spectacularly successful and widely imitated, they had a profound impact on the course of American industry, which is to say on the lives of millions: workers, customers, shareholders, suppliers, and the slaves who kept them in cotton. Many of the corporate records of the Lowell companies have been preserved (primarily in the Baker Library at the Harvard Business School), and these documents illuminate numerous facets of finance and operations. More qualitative matters—the thoughts and attitudes that informed entrepreneurial and managerial decisions, for example, or the owners' reactions to labor unrest—are harder to trace. Most useful in this part of my quest were materials in the Center for Lowell History, the library at the Lowell National Historic Site, and Massachusetts Historical Society collections of papers by and about Francis Cabot Lowell, Nathan Appleton, Patrick Tracy Jackson, and Abbott Lawrence.

Lowell's early factory girls wrote prodigiously. Two of them published memoirs: Lucy Larcom (*A New England Girlhood,* 1890) and Harriet H. Robinson (*Loom and Spindle,* 1898). Scores of factory girls contributed to the *Lowell Offering* and the labor publications of their day. Much of the best of this writing is collected in Philip S. Foner, ed., *The Factory Girls* (Urbana, Ill., 1977) and Benita Eisler, *The Lowell Offering* (New York, 1977). Thomas Dublin's anthology, *Farm to Factory: Women's Letters, 1830–1860* (New York, 1993), enriches the group portrait with letters from factory girls to their families and friends.

Valuable secondary sources are Dublin's *Women at Work: The Transformation of Work and Community in Lowell, Massachusetts, 1826–1860* (New York, 1979); Robert F. Dalzell Jr., *Enterprising Elite:*

The Boston Associates and the World They Made (Cambridge, Mass., 1987); and David A. Zonderman, *Aspirations and Anxieties: New England Workers and the Mechanized Factory System, 1815–1860* (New York, 1992), 64–65. The newer studies have supplanted much earlier work, but older general accounts still useful include Norman Ware, *The Industrial Worker, 1840–1860: The Reaction of American Industrial Society to the Advance of the Industrial Revolution,* 1924 (rpt. Gloucester, Mass., 1959); Caroline F. Ware, *The Early New England Cotton Manufacture: A Study in Industrial Beginnings* (Boston, 1931); and Hannah Josephson, *The Golden Threads: New England's Mill Girls and Magnates* (New York, 1949).

Page 68 destruction by gin. Benjamin Franklin to Thomas Percival, October 15, 1773, in Leonard W. Labaree, ed., *Papers of Benjamin Franklin* (New Haven, Conn., 1959–), 20:443.

68 "any amount of value." Quoted in Lewis J. Carey, *Franklin's Economic Views* (Garden City, N.Y., 1928), 168–69.

69 "panders of vice," Thomas Jefferson to John Jay, August 23, 1785, in Merrill D. Peterson, ed., *Thomas Jefferson: Writings* (New York, 1984), 818.

69 "both public and private." Thomas Jefferson to George Washington, August 14, 1787, in Julian P. Boyd, Lyman H. Butterfield, et al., eds., *Papers: Thomas Jefferson,* 26 vols. (Princeton, N.J., 1950–90), 12:38.

69 a ban on the export of manufacturing technology. "Report on Manufactures," December 5, 1791, in Samuel McKee, ed., Alexander Hamilton, *Papers on Public Credit, Commerce and Finance* (New York, 1934), 178–274.

70 "arrive at independence." Quoted in Stuart Bruchey, *Enterprise* (Cambridge, Mass., 1990), 144.

70 his class in 1793. Ferris Greenslet, *The Lowells and Their Seven Worlds* (Boston, 1946); Robert Varnum Spalding, "The Boston Mercantile Community and the Promotion of the Textile Industry in New England, 1813–1860," Ph.D. diss., Yale University, 1963, 9–10.

70 "dilapidated fortunes." Robert Sobel, *The Entrepreneurs: Explorations within the American Business Tradition* (New York, 1974), 9; Spalding, op. cit., 12.

70 "any one bottom." Francis Cabot Lowell to Mr. Motley, October 1, 1812, in letterbook, vol. 4, Francis Cabot Lowell Papers, Massachusetts Historical Society.

71 "engage him for a year." Francis Cabot Lowell to John Peabody, April 8, 1803, loc. cit.

72 dividends averaging 20 percent. Nathan Appleton, "Introduction of the Power Loom, and Origin of Lowell" (Lowell, Mass., 1858), 15, Massachusetts Historical Society; Dublin, *Women at Work,* 17–18; Dalzell, op. cit., 30–31; Sobel, op. cit., 38.

72 "come into these mills." Appleton, op. cit., 15.

72 waiting list for job applicants. Dalzell, op. cit., 33.

72 cheaper imports, Peter Temin, "Product Quality and Vertical Integration in the Early Cotton Textile Industry," *Journal of Economic History* 48 (1988):897–98.

73 finished goods back down. John Coolidge, *Mill and Mansion: A Study of Architecture and Society in Lowell, Massachusetts, 1820–1865* (New York, 1942), 19; Dublin, op. cit., 18–19.

73 tumbling Merrimack. The Merrimack Manufacturing Company was owned largely by investors in the Waltham mill: Patrick Tracy Jackson, Nathan Appleton, Kirk Boott, John Boott, and Paul Moody, the mechanic who built the power loom based on the design Francis Cabot Lowell brought home from Britain (Spalding, op. cit., 34–35); *Handbook for the Visiter* [sic] *to Lowell* (Lowell, Mass., 1848), 11–12; Coolidge, op. cit., 20–21.

73 second-largest city in Massachusetts. "Statistics of Lowell Manufactures, January 1, 1835," Elisha Bartlett Papers. Manuscripts and Archives Division, Sterling Memorial Library, Yale University; Dublin, op. cit., 21.

74 "He is avoided." Nathan Appleton, "Memoir of the Hon. Abbott Lawrence," 5, presented to the Massachusetts Historical Society, March 13, 1856.

74 regardless of his character. In speculating on the effects of the values and interrelationships of the Boston elite, I relied primarily on writings of Nathan Appleton, Patrick Tracy Jackson, Abbott Lawrence, and Francis Cabot Lowell. Useful in broadening my understanding of the group were Betty G. Farrell, *Elite Families: Class and Power in Nineteenth-Century Boston* (Albany, N.Y., 1993), 39–59; Paul Goodman, "Ethics and Enterprise: The Values of a Boston Elite, 1800–1860," *American Quarterly* 18 (1966):437–51; and Frederic Cople Jaher, "The Boston Brahmins in the Age of Industrial Capitalism," in Jaher, ed., *The Age of Industrialism in*

America: Essays in Social Structure and Cultural Values (New York, 1968), 188–247. Dalzell, op. cit., 79–112, provides a comprehensive account and thoughtful analysis of the financial superstructure built by the group.

75 looms and other machines. Zonderman, op. cit., 64–65.

75 they took it. A thorough analysis of the group's technological achievements can be found in David J. Jeremy, "Innovation in American Textile Technology during the Early 19th Century," *Technology and Culture* 14 (1973):40–76.

75 addition of fences. On December 1, 1833, William Austin, agent of the Lawrence Manufacturing Company, wrote to Henry Hall, treasurer and chief executive, "I am anxious to have the millyard fenced in; too long have we been exposed to the assaults of thieves and incendiaries . . . it is somewhat remarkable that nothing of any consequence to the company has thus far been lost or injured, tho' so much exposed." Lawrence Manufacturing Company Records, Box MAB-1. Baker Library, Harvard Business School.

75 billiards, "XXIV. Kirk Boott and his experience in the British Army, read by James B. Francis, May 5, 1887," *Contributions of the Old Residents' Historical Association* 3 (1887), 326. Lowell National Historic Site library.

75 riding crop. Robinson, op. cit., 5. Other sketches of Boott can be found in "No. XI. Kirk Boott, by Theodore Edson, D.D., Read February 12, 1875," *Contributions of the Old Residents' Historical Association* 1 (1876), 87–97, Lowell National Historic Site library; "VIII. Kirk Boott. A Letter from Dr. John O. Green to Rev. Theodore Edson, D.D.," *Contributions of the Old Residents' Historical Association* 4 (1888), 110–12, Lowell National Historic Site library; Josephson, op. cit., 39–48.

75 monthly payroll deductions. Joseph W. Lipchitz, "The Golden Age," in Arthur L. Eno, ed., *Cotton Was King: A History of Lowell, Massachusetts* (New Hampshire Publishing Co., 1976), 98.

76 opened in 1823. Nancy Zaroulis, "Daughters of Freemen: The Female Operatives and the Beginning of the Labor Movement," ibid., 105.

76 earned anywhere else. Dalzell, op. cit., 32–36; Foner, op. cit., xviii–xix; Dublin, *Farm to Factory,* 10–11.

77 the girls themselves. Robinson, op. cit., 28; Foner, op. cit., xix–xx; 19; Norman Ware, op. cit., 88–89.

77 "college class." Quoted in Robinson, op. cit., 45.

77 "reflection on other matters." Foner, op. cit., 36–37.

77 "cotton mill is no worse." Ibid., 27.

77 "hurricane." Quoted in Zonderman, op. cit., 34–35.

78 Tremont, Lawrence, and Boott. *Handbook for the Visiter to Lowell,* 12–17; "Statistics of Lowell Manufactures, January 1, 1835," loc. cit.

78 11.4 percent, Caroline F. Ware, op. cit., 152–53.

78 industrial bank loans. Lance E. Davis, "The New England Textile Mills and the Capital Markets: A Study of Industrial Borrowing 1840–1860," *Journal of Economic History* 20 (1960):3.

78 "seeking to do so." Charles Dickens, *American Notes,* 1842 (rpt. New York, 1985), 60–62.

78 "great effort at excellence was being made." Anthony Trollope, *North America,* 1862 (rpt. New York, 1951), 247–51.

79 added $2 million to his fortunes. Spalding, op. cit., 61.

79 "useful article." Goodman, op. cit., 439.

79 "a rich man." Robert C. Winthrop, "Memoir of the Hon. Nathan Appleton, LL.D." (Boston, 1861), 60–61. Massachusetts Historical Society.

79 slide in dividends, Caroline F. Ware, op. cit., 333.

79 doubled since 1830, Lewis C. Gray, *History of Agriculture in the Southern United States to 1860* (Washington, 1933), 230.

79 1,500 . . . were men. "Statistics of Lowell Manufactures, January 1, 1835," loc. cit.

80 "immediate and irretrievable." Patrick Tracy Jackson, "Report on Manufactures of Cotton" in *General Convention of the Friends of Domestic Industry* [1832?], 110. Massachusetts Historical Society.

80 "good help in future." Dublin, *Women at Work,* 90, 96–98.

80 their later writings, Nathan Appleton, "Introduction of the Power Loom . . ." and "Labor, Its Relations in Europe and the United States Compared" (Boston, 1844). Massachusetts Historical Society.

81 nearly 2,000 . . . workers. Foner, op. cit., xxiii; Dublin, op. cit., 98–101.

81 "maintain profit margins." Dublin, op. cit., 161, 109.

81 three times as much as she was paid. Bernice Selden, *The Mill Girls* (New York, 1983), 125–26.

81 "entire services of such men," Nathan Appleton, "Introduction of the Power Loom . . . ," 29, loc. cit.

82 "a little more charity." Foner, op. cit., 75–76.

82 12.5 percent lower in 1845 than in 1844. Dividends in Caroline F. Ware, op. cit., 152; 1845 wage cut in Norman Ware, op. cit., 8.

82 *"black* southern slaves?" Foner, op. cit., 276.

83 "if they could help it?" Ibid., 160–61. Bagley's essay, "The Pleasures of Factory Life," is also reprinted here, 36–37.

83 "death-spreading monster." Ibid., 85.

84 "ease and idleness." Quoted in Zonderman, op. cit., 112.

84 their parlors. Foner, op. cit., 84.

84 "sovereignty in all places," Quoted in Norman Ware, op. cit., xv.

84 "confectioner." Henry A. Miles, *Lowell, as It Was, and as It Is,* 1846 (rpt. New York, 1972), 124–26.

85 "brightness of their ideas." Quoted in Zonderman, op. cit., 49.

85 rest of the company's employees. William Austin to Henry Hall, July 15, 1833; August 21, 1833; December 22, 1833, Lawrence Manufacturing Company Records, Box MAB-1. Baker Library, Harvard Business School.

85 fashionable. Eisler, op. cit., 28; Zonderman, op. cit., 76–78.

85 maladies of the 34 percent. Elisha Bartlett, M.D., *A Vindication of the Character and Condition of the Females Employed in the Lowell Mills, against the Charges Contained in the Boston Times, and the Boston Quarterly Review* (Lowell, Mass., 1841), 10–11, Bartlett Papers, loc. cit.

89 several more decades. Norman Ware, op. cit., 126–28, 138–39, 143; Foner, op. cit., 218–19, 235–46. The ten-hour movement and the role women played in it are chronicled in Teresa Anne Murphy, *Ten Hours' Labor: Religion, Reform, and Gender in Early New England* (Ithaca, N.Y., 1992).

89 "drivelling cotton lords," quoted in Selden, op. cit., 165.

90 "in this direction." Alexis de Tocqueville, *Democracy in America,* 2 vols., 1835 (rpt. New York, 1990), 2:160–61.

CHAPTER 5
IN THE DIRECTION OF DREAMS

I N AN ESSAY on wealth, Ralph Waldo Emerson (1803–1882) observed that political economy was "as good a book wherein to read the life of man, and the ascendancy of laws over all private and hostile influences, as any Bible which has come down to us." He understood that money is almost never mere: how it is got—and spent—reveals much about an individual's character. (He might have said the same of nations, which make their values real in their budgets and tax policies. If spending cuts are needed, does the nation look to welfare or to weapons? Does it tax capital gains, which are accrued largely by the rich, at the same rate as wages?)

Few tales in the American book of political economy are more compelling than the story of Emerson's time. Railroads, canals, and steamboats gave veins and capillaries to the body economic, furnishing manufacturers with cheaper, quicker access to distant raw materials and opening up vast new sales territories. Markets, heretofore mostly local and regional, grew increasingly national. Business did not quite become big business, but it mastered the requisite arts: raising unprecedented amounts of capital by selling stock to the public, organizing and reorganizing production on an ever-grander scale to increase efficiency, and marketing across vast territories.

Emerson and his good friend Henry David Thoreau (1817–1862), cultural sentries both, watched the advance of the economic juggernaut and sounded warnings against the dominance of the marketplace, the dehumanizing power of technology, the exploitation of labor, and the insipidity of a society in which business crowded out the rest of life. Thoreau and Emerson raised their objections and proposed their alternatives in writing, and their journals, essays, lectures, and books are the primary sources for this chapter.

Page 91 "huzzas." Quoted in Philip S. Foner, ed., *The Factory Girls* (Urbana, Ill., 1977), 60–61.

92 factories, not in phalanxes. Robert D. Richardson Jr., *Emerson: The Mind on Fire* (Berkeley, Calif., 1995), 337–38, 365–67; Anne C. Rose, *Transcendentalism as a Social Movement, 1830–1850* (New Haven, Conn., 1981), 140–43.

92 no true home. Henry D. Thoreau, *Journal,* 2 vols. (Princeton, N.J., 1989), 1:277–78.

93 "true account of it." Henry David Thoreau, *Walden,* 1854 (rpt. Princeton, N.J., 1989), 90–91.

93 "Judge," Walter Harding, *The Days of Henry Thoreau* (New York, 1965), 18.

93 "solitude." Thoreau, *Walden,* 135.

93 awkward in the parlor. Physical and personal traits described in Harding, op. cit., 124; George Hendrick, ed., *Remembrances of Concord and the Thoreaus: Letters of Horace Hosmer to Dr. S. A. Jones* (Urbana, Ill., 1977), 137; Henry David Thoreau, *A Week on the Concord and Merrimack Rivers; Walden, or, Life in the Woods; The Maine Woods; Cape Cod* (New York, 1985), 1041–42.

93 marched out. Joel Porte, ed., *Emerson in His Journals* (Cambridge, Mass., 1982), 467.

93 "H is military." Quoted in John McAleer, *Ralph Waldo Emerson: Days of Encounter* (Boston, 1984), 347–48.

93 around an elm, Porte, op. cit., 304, 391.

93 "delicious," Quoted in Robert D. Richardson Jr., *Henry Thoreau: A Life of the Mind* (Berkeley, Calif., 1986), 105.

93 "bearing of the soul." Thoreau, *Journal,* 1:146.

93 "brave the domestic government." Porte, op. cit., 161.

94 corporal punishment. Harding, op. cit., 81–88.

94 "doubledealing quacking" age. Porte, op. cit., 181.

94 "nervous, bustling, trivial" time. Thoreau, *Walden,* 329–30.

95 "complaisant." Emerson, "The American Scholar," *Essays and Lectures* (New York, 1983), 70.

95 cello of a voice. Richardson, *Emerson,* 6; Carlos Baker, *Emerson among the Eccentrics* (New York, 1996), 35–36.

95 the name Lydia. Gay Wilson Allen, *Waldo Emerson* (New York, 1981), 242.

96 "an ecstasy," Emerson, "Fate," *Essays and Lectures,* 963.

97 "in beauty and strength." Emerson, "The Transcendentalist," *Essays and Lectures,* 193–209.

97 menace. Emerson, "Self-Reliance," *Essays and Lectures,* 261.

98 "one could not well imagine." Thoreau, *Journal,* 2:447.

99 "meaner than I could have imagined." Walter Harding and Carl Bode, eds., *The Correspondence of Henry David Thoreau* (New York, 1958), 111.

99 camp on the shore. McAleer, op. cit., 344; Richardson, *Emerson,* 399.

99 songbird, Thoreau, *Walden,* 41.

99 bloom. Harding, op. cit., 329.

99 $28. Thoreau, *Walden,* 41–45, 60.

100 "avoid the beginnings of evil." Ibid., 67.

100 a privy. Harding, op. cit., 181–82.

100 "no longer a satellite of earth." Thoreau, *Journal,* 1:168.

100 "thy fate?" Thoreau, *A Week on the Concord . . . ,* 29–31.

100 "as easily as it can manufacture cotton cloth." Quoted in Richard A. McDermott, Ph.D. diss., "The Claim to Power: The Foundations of Authority in American Industry, Lowell, 1820–1850," Brandeis University, 1985, 74.

100 private gain. Quentin Anderson, "A Culture of One's Own," *American Scholar* 61:3 (Autumn 1992), 534.

101 "ride mankind." Emerson, "Ode, inscribed to W. H. Channing," in Harold Bloom and Paul Kane, eds., *Ralph Waldo Emerson: Collected Poems and Translations* (New York, 1994), 63.

101 when the poor too would be rich. Emerson, "The Young American," *Essays and Lectures,* 226.

101 "cut them down!" Thoreau, "Life without Principle," in Wendell Glick, ed., *Reform Papers* (Princeton, 1973), 136–37.

101 "chairs and tables." Porte, op. cit., 326.

101 waterpower, Porte, op. cit., 375.

101 "where it is costly." Emerson, "Wealth," *Essays and Lectures,* 990.

101 "ought to rhyme." Porte, op. cit., 236.

101 "a harp!" The poem was first published in Carl F. Strauch, "Emerson's 'New England Capitalist,'" *Harvard Library Bulletin* 10 (1956):245.

101 other speculating, Porte, op. cit., 454–55.

101 had not planted. Thoreau, "Life without Principle," Wendell Glick, ed., *Reform Papers* (Princeton, 1973), 141–42.

101 in front of children. Thoreau, *Journal,* 1:302.

102 "lovers of Nature there." Thoreau, *Walden,* 238.

102 starlight, Thoreau, *Journal,* 1:158.

102 fast to America. Emerson, "The Young American," *Essays and Lectures,* 213.

102 staid and complacent. Ibid., 220–21.

102 "no sabbath." Thoreau, "Life without Principle," Glick, op. cit.,
    136; *Walden,* 115–19.

102 say to one another? Thoreau, *Walden,* 52.

103 "it rides upon us." Thoreau, ibid., 92, 54.

103 "indigence of another." Ibid., 34–35.

103 "something high." Ibid., 26–27.

103 homespun. Ibid., 64.

103 "labor if he can." Porte, op. cit., 252.

103 "coming in every day?" Quoted in Richardson, *Henry Thoreau: A
    Life of the Mind,* 138.

103 sense of decorum. Rose, op. cit., 100.

104 from 26 to nearly 160. Paul Goodman, "Ethics and Enterprise:
    The Values of a Boston Elite, 1800–1860," *American Quarterly* 18:3
    (Fall 1966), 446.

104 "odious set of people," Porte, op. cit., 328.

104 reformed himself. Emerson, "New England Reformers," *Essays and
    Lectures,* 591–609.

104 donor and recipient, Thoreau, *Journal,* 2:148.

104 "building eternity." Ibid., 1:264.

104 "give his name to it?" Thoreau, *Walden,* 195.

104 "Simplify, simplify." Ibid., 91.

104 "work, work, work," Thoreau, "Life without Principle," Glick, op.
    cit., 136.

104 "quiet desperation." Thoreau, *Walden,* 4–8.

104 even more hours at work. Thoreau, "Life without Principle,"
    Glick, op. cit., 152–55.

104 fool. Thoreau, *Journal,* 2:178, 220; *Walden,* 91.

105 "exchanged for it." Thoreau, *Walden,* 31.

105 "broad margin to my life." Ibid., 111.

105 six weeks' paid work a year. Ibid., 69.

105 "wine or ale." Quoted in Richardson, *Emerson,* 463.

105 "born to be rich." Emerson, "Wealth," *Essays and Lectures,* 990–91.

105 "common hours." Thoreau, *Walden,* 323.

106 "worth more than money." Quoted in Harding, op. cit., 220.

106 bankruptcy, Thoreau, *Walden,* 33.

106 "shampooing himself." Quoted in McAleer, op. cit., 347.

106 "like serfs." Thoreau, *Walden,* 207–8.

106 "likest to solitude." Emerson, "The Transcendentalist," *Essays and
    Lectures,* 195.

109 "and eat that soon." Thoreau, "Resistance to Civil Government,"
    Glick, op. cit., 63–90; Harding, op. cit., 199–205.

109 "forced us all into politics." "The Fugitive Slave Law," Ralph Waldo Emerson, *Works,* edited by Joel Myerson, 12 vols. (New York, 1979) 11:179.

110 "filthy enactment." Quoted in Richardson, *Emerson,* 498.

110 "hazard." Emerson, "Fugitive Slave Law," op. cit., vol. 11, 186.

110 £20 million. Emerson, "Emancipation in the British West Indies," *Works,* 11:113.

110 "once and forever." Emerson, "The Fugitive Slave Law," op. cit., 208–9.

111 "good for manure." Thoreau, "Slavery in Massachusetts," *Anti-Slavery and Reform Papers* (Montreal, 1963), 26–41.

111 "sacrifice to the gods." Thoreau, *Journal,* 1:248.

112 "voice of the universe." Emerson, "Emancipation in the British West Indies," op. cit., 145–47.

CHAPTER 6
LOOK AWAY, LOOK AWAY

THE HISTORICAL PROFESSION'S discussions of American slavery have been almost as disputatious as the quarrels that culminated in the Civil War. One of the early twentieth century's leading scholars of slavery, Ulrich B. Phillips, argued in *American Negro Slavery* (New York, 1918) and *Life and Labor in the Old South* (Boston, 1929) that however objectionable slavery was in principle, in practice it had not been harsh and in fact had done much to advance the black race. The Phillips attitude perfumed *Gone With the Wind* and countless other movies and novels about the Old South, and it prevailed in the academy until the 1956 publication of *The Peculiar Institution* by Kenneth Stampp. Stampp unearthed plenty of evidence of the physical hardships of slaves.

Stanley M. Elkins made the case for the psychological damage inflicted by masters in *Slavery: A Problem in American Institutional and Intellectual Life* (Chicago, 1959). Elkins infuriated many with his argument that the sustained, systematic emotional abuse of slaves had left them psychologically incapacitated. In reaction to Elkins—and because of the gains of the civil rights movement in the 1960s and a growing sense of black pride in the 1970s—historians of slavery began to investigate the extent to which slaves had been agents rather than victims during the 240-year life of the peculiar institution. Out of these inquiries came a literature rich in appreciation of the strengths of slave culture, community, religion, and family life—works such as *The Slave Community* by John Blassingame (New York, 1972), *Roll, Jordan, Roll* by Eugene D. Genovese (New York, 1974), *The Black Family in Slavery and Freedom* by Herbert Gutman (New York, 1976), and *Black Culture and Black Consciousness* by Lawrence W. Levine (New York, 1977).

The computer entered the fray in the 1970s, most famously with the 1974 publication of *Time on the Cross: The Economics of American Negro*

Slavery by Robert William Fogel and Stanley L. Engerman. Quantitative analysis led them to challenge many earlier views of everything from the relative profitability of slavery to the conditions of slave life. From a material point of view, the authors said, slaves were better off than free whites working in the factories of the North. The authors also asserted that although slaves had been exploited, the "rate of expropriation" of their labor was lower than previously thought. *Time on the Cross* drew attacks on the authors' assumptions, their data, their methods, their conclusions, and their honor. The October 1975 number of the scholarly journal *Explorations in Economic History* devoted more than a hundred pages to critiques of *Time on the Cross.*

"The Mathematics of Slavery," a review by John Blassingame (*Atlantic Monthly,* August 1974), pointed out that only about 10 percent of the items listed in the bibliography are primary sources and objected to the book's reliance on "if, then" propositions: "For example, they argue that plantations produced large quantities of milk, grain, vegetables, and livestock, and that *if* most of this produce was not consumed by planters, that *if* most of the grain and vegetables was not fed to livestock, that *if* the surplus was not sold to cities, and *if,* instead, it was fed to slaves, then the slave's diet 'actually exceeded modern (1964) recommended daily levels of the chief nutrients.' From the historian's perspective, this approach has an Alice in Wonderland quality." Blassingame was also troubled by Fogel and Engerman's conclusion, based on 1860 data showing a mulatto population of only 10 percent, that sexual exploitation of slave women by white men was rare. As Blassingame noted, such a figure reveals nothing about how many times slave women were forced to have sex that did not result in pregnancy.

Fogel and Engerman asked that *Time on the Cross* be considered a preliminary report. *Without Consent or Contract* (New York, 1989) is Fogel's summary and analysis of more than two decades of wide-ranging slavery research by the Center for Population Economics at the University of Chicago. The book also surveys much other scholarship in the field and contains a long chapter on changing interpretations of slavery.

The literature of slavery—primary and secondary—is vast. I have confined my research primarily to materials about slavery on Georgia cotton plantations in the twenty-five years before the Civil War. Many of the primary sources I used are part of the collections of the Savannah branch of the Georgia Historical Society. A few came from further research in one of the nation's major repositories of plantation documents, the Southern Historical Collection at the University of North Carolina in Chapel Hill.

My principal source is "What Became of the Slaves on a Georgia Plantation?" An 1863 reprint of an article that first appeared in the *New York Tribune* on March 9, 1859, this eyewitness account of a slave auction is the work of Mortimer Neal Thomson (1831–1875), one of the paper's leading reporters. Because the source is evident from the text, I have not cited it in the notes that follow.

My second most important source is Frances Anne Kemble's *Journal of a Residence on a Georgian Plantation in 1838–1839* (referred to in this section as Kemble). I used the edition edited and introduced by John A. Scott (Athens, Ga., 1984). Fanny Kemble (1809–1893) was a well-known English actress and the former wife of Pierce Butler, owner of the slaves auctioned in Savannah. In 1863, when her *Journal* was published, the *New York Tribune* featured it prominently and used the occasion to reprint Thomson's article.

Page 113 "punished with DEATH." Quoted in Ruth Scarborough, "The Opposition to Slavery in Georgia Prior to 1860." Master's thesis, George Peabody College for Teachers 1933, 187–88.

113 stifled debate of the slavery question. See, for example, William Lee Miller, *Arguing about Slavery: The Great Battle in the United States Congress* (New York, 1996).

114 "heathen to the gospel." Quoted in Glen Jeansonne, "Southern Baptist Attitudes Toward Slavery, 1845–1861," *Georgia Historical Quarterly* 55 (1971):517. Biblical passages often cited in support of slavery are Genesis 17:1–14, Ephesians 6:5–8, Colossians 3:22–25, Titus 2:9–10, Matthew 18:23–35 and 24:14–30, and Luke 17:7 and 10. Other sources of contemporary pro-slavery arguments in the collections of the Georgia Historical Society in Savannah

include "Amor Patriae," "Slavery, Con. and Pro. or, a Sermon and Its Answer" (Washington, 1858), especially 13–14, 39–40; Samuel B. How, D.D., "Slaveholding Not Sinful: An Argument before the General Synod of the Reformed Protestant Dutch Church, October 1855" (New York, 1855); Christopher G. Memminger, "Lecture Delivered before the Young Men's Library Association of Augusta, April 10, 1851. Showing African Slavery to Be Consistent with the Moral and Physical Progress of a Nation" (Augusta, Ga., 1851); and David Brown, *The Planter: Or, Thirteen Years in the South. By a Northern Man* (Philadelphia, 1853), especially 39–41, 97, 139.

115 "of general prosperity." Quoted in Stuart Bruchey, ed., *Cotton and the Growth of the American Economy: 1790–1860* (New York, 1967), 73–74. Statistics from Lewis C. Gray, *History of Agriculture in the Southern United States to 1860* (Washington, 1933), 691–92, and Fogel, op. cit., 81–84.

115 "'goodly heritage.'" David Christy, *Cotton Is King,* 2d ed. (New York, 1856), 62–63.

116 "statesman and philanthropist." *Southern States: Embracing a Series of Papers Condensed from the Earlier Volumes of DeBow's Review, upon the Cultivation, Commerce and Manufacture of Cotton, together with Historical and Statistical Sketches of Several of the Southern and Southwestern States; Their Agriculture, Commerce, Etc.* (Washington, 1856), 174. James Dunwoody Brownson DeBow's review provided planters and businessmen with statistics, news, and agricultural advice, and DeBow also used it to defend slavery, promote Southern economic development, and champion secession. The only full-length biography is Ottis Clark Skipper, *J. D. B. DeBow: Magazinist of the Old South* (Athens, Ga., 1958).

116 "anarchy and poverty." Quoted in Eric L. McKitrick, ed., *Slavery Defended: The Views of the Old South* (New York, 1963), 124.

116 "A reverse will surely come." Quoted in Ralph Betts Flanders, *Plantation Slavery in Georgia* (Chapel Hill, N.C., 1933), 192–93.

116 Q. K. Philander Doesticks, P.B. Attempts to decipher Thomson's pseudonym compound the inanity. David E. E. Sloane, in the *Dictionary of Literary Biography* (11:492), writes that Q. K. stood for Queer Kritter, P.B. for Perfect Brick. Philander has a well-known meaning, Doesticks appears to have none. Thomson is listed in the *Dictionary of American Biography* and was the subject of a fond but not exhaustive master's thesis by Fletcher D. Slater ("The Life and Letters of Mortimer Thomson," Northwestern University, 1931). Mortimer Neal Thomson published several best-selling books

about life in the seedier purlieus of New York in the 1850s. He was also the author of *Plu-ri-bus-tah* (1856)—set to the meter of Longfellow's *Hiawatha*—a book-length indictment of the moral climate of the era.

117 most populous state in the Deep South. *Historical Statistics of the United States, Colonial Times to 1970, Part I* (Washington, 1975).

118 nutritionally deficient. Kemble, 99, 162, 169; Robert Quarterman Mallard, *Plantation Life before Emancipation* (Richmond, 1892), 31–32; F. N. Boney, ed., *Slave Life in Georgia: A Narrative of the Life, Sufferings, and Escape of John Brown, a Fugitive Slave* (Savannah, Ga., 1991), 47–48. Robert William Fogel, *Without Consent or Contract* (New York, 1989), surveys historians' studies of slave diet (132–48) and mentions (159) a quantitative study of ex-slave narratives by Stephen C. Crawford showing that stealing was reported more than eight times as often on plantations where slaves were underfed than on those where they had enough to eat.

119 hurt. Eugene D. Genovese, *Roll, Jordan, Roll* (New York, 1976), 551–52.

120 the *Republican* fretted. Quoted in William A. Byrne, "The Burden and Heat of the Day: Slavery and Servitude in Savannah, 1733–1865," Ph.D. diss., Florida State University, 1979, 126.

121 supporting hogs. Kemble, 84–85.

121 "dependents are treated." Ibid., 102.

122 between them and the lash. Ibid., 210–211.

122 $800 or more. Ibid., 127.

122 *partus sequitur ventrem,* Kenneth Stampp, *The Peculiar Institution,* 193–94; Farish Carter Papers, bill of sale, September 24, 1821 (Southern Historical Collection, folder 65). Other examples in Arnold and Screven Family Papers: On November 4, 1786, Jonathan Bryan, a Georgia planter, signed a legal document leaving "my Negro girl named Hagar" as well as "her future issue" in trust to two men for his granddaughter, Helen Wylly; on January 7, 1829, Martha Richardson "in consideration of the natural love and affection which I bear to my grand niece Elizabeth M. Screven," made a gift of thirteen slaves "and the future issue and increase of the said females slaves to have and to hold . . . forever" (Southern Historical Collection, Box 7, folders 140 and 148).

123 before their states abolished slavery. Curtis P. Nettels, *The Emergence of a National Economy, 1775–1815* (New York, 1962), 190.

124 New York and Liverpool. The role of the cotton factor is well described in Lynn Willoughby Ware, "The Cotton Trade of the

Apalachicola Chattahoochee River Valley, 1840–1860," Ph.D. diss., Florida State University, 1989, 19–24, 139ff., and in Nelson Miles Hoffman Jr., "Godfrey Barnsley, 1805–1873, British Cotton Factor in the South," Ph.D. diss., University of Kansas, 1964.

125 "charity is not misapplied." George Fitzhugh, *Cannibals All! or Slaves without Masters,* 1857 (rpt. Cambridge, Mass., 1960), 217–19. Fitzhugh's thinking is summarized and critiqued in Eugene D. Genovese, *The World the Slaveholders Made* (New York, 1969), 158–63.

125 they owned 1,000,000 slaves. Statistics from Bruchey, op. cit., 165–66; Gray, op. cit., 482.

126 "consent to afford." Kemble, 118.

126 few listened. George B. Crawford, "Cotton, Land, and Sustenance: Toward the Limits of Abundance in Late Antebellum Georgia," *Georgia Historical Quarterly* 72 (1988) 215–47; Eugene D. Genovese, *The Political Economy of Slavery* (New York, 1967), 85–89.

127 did not figure in the discussions. Norris W. Preyer, Why Did Industrialization Lag in the Old South?" *Georgia Historical Quarterly* 55 (1971):378–96; Stampp, op. cit., 397–98. Other sources on Georgia's industrial beginnings are Richard W. Griffin, "The Origins of the Industrial Revolution in Georgia: Cotton Textiles, 1810–1865," *Georgia Historical Quarterly* 42 (1958):355–75, and J. G. Johnson, "Notes on Manufacturing in Ante-Bellum Georgia," *Georgia Historical Quarterly* 16 (1932):214–31.

127 "refuse population of Europe." "A Baptist Minister," "Slavery: A Treatise Showing That Slavery is Neither a Moral, Political, Nor Social Evil" (Penfield, Ga., 1844), 31.

127 more heavily against the South. Ronald T. Takaki, *A Pro-Slavery Crusade: The Agitation to Reopen the African Slave Trade* (New York, 1971), 25.

127 "without professional spirit," Bertram Wyatt-Brown, *Southern Honor* (New York, 1982), 177.

128 better on their own. *Southern States: Embracing a Series of Papers . . . ,* 137–38.

128 "by individuals." Quoted in Weymouth T. Jordan, "Cotton Planters' Conventions in the Old South," *Journal of Southern History* 19 (1953):332. Between 1839 and 1861, region-wide planters' conventions met twenty times at various cities in the South. A parallel series of commercial conventions met between 1845 and 1871. The commercial-convention movement is broadly covered

in Vicki Vaughn Johnson, *The Men and the Vision of the Southern Commercial Conventions, 1845–1871* (Columbia, Mo., 1992), and treated more particularly in Herbert Wender, "The Southern Commercial Convention at Savannah, 1856," *Georgia Historical Quarterly* 15 (1931):173–91.

132 his personal discomfort. Kemble, 161.

133 all in a day's work. John Nevitt, diary, 1826–32 (Southern Historical Collection).

133 unwitting purchase of runaways. Franklin, op. cit., 207; Boney, op. cit., 28n; Flanders, op. cit., 263.

133 real or imagined. Byrne, op. cit., 280.

133 "never taken against a white." Kemble, 79.

133 against the offender. Byrne, op. cit., 75–76.

134 reached the mainland. Kemble, 284.

134 gave her daughter. Ibid., 302.

134 "ande wad was God." Byrne, op. cit., 164–65.

134 the desired result. Daniel Jonah Goldhagen, *Hitler's Willing Executioners* (New York, 1996), 400.

134 "are infinite." Kemble, 80.

135 his day's work for his master. Boney, op. cit., 22, 28, 41–43, 76. A variation on the bells and horns described by Brown can be seen in Edward D. C. Campbell Jr. with Kym S. Rice, eds., *Before Freedom Came: African-American Life in the Antebellum South* (Richmond and Charlottesville, Va., 1991), 3.

136 several days running. Farish Carter Papers, May 31, 1832 (Southern Historical Collection); Byrne, op. cit., 280.

136 "absolute on your own plantation." Kemble, 272.

136 "irresponsible power over their dependents." Ibid., 353.

138 $572 a head. Malcolm Bell Jr., *Major Butler's Legacy: Five Generations of a Slaveholding Family* (Athens, Ga., 1987), 327.

138 buying and selling of human beings. Publication details from Sloane, op. cit., 495; *Atlantic Monthly* (September 1859), 386–87.

140 Southern states themselves. Thomas H. O'Connor, *Lords of the Loom: The Cotton Whigs and the Coming of the Civil War* (New York, 1968), 50.

141 "will not contradict." Ralph Waldo Emerson, "Emancipation in the British West Indies," *Works* (New York, 1979), 11:123–24.

141 "the bad people." James M. Washington, ed., *A Testament of Hope: The Essential Writings and Speeches of Martin Luther King, Jr.* (San Francisco, 1986), 296.

CHAPTER 7
WHY MILLIONAIRES SHOULD NOT BE SHOT

THE 274-VOLUME Carnegie Papers in the Library of Congress contain correspondence, business records, manuscripts, newspaper clippings, and other materials. In the notes for this section, citations from the papers are indicated by CP followed by the volume number and the page number, when available.

Carnegie was not introspective (or if he was, he took unusual care to conceal it), so his autobiography offers little insight into the man or the times. It is also unreliable on the Homestead strike. But it does convey his charm and vitality.

Many of Carnegie's most significant writings, including several excerpts from his autobiography, are collected in Joseph Frazier Wall, ed., *The Andrew Carnegie Reader* (Pittsburgh, 1992). The definitive life—a model of biography and of business history—is Wall's *Andrew Carnegie, 1970* (rpt. Pittsburgh, 1989). The *Reader* is referred to here as *ACR*, the biography as Wall.

Page 142 "richest man in the world." Quoted in Wall, 789.
    143 "precious heritage." Andrew Carnegie, "How I Served My Business Apprenticeship," *ACR*, 33–34.
    143 nearly doubled his pay, Carnegie, *The Autobiography of Andrew Carnegie* (Boston, 1920), 33.
    143 iron railroad bridges. Carnegie, "How I Served My Business Apprenticeship," *ACR*, 31–39.
    143 "reading systematically." Carnegie, December 1868 (CP 3:561).
    144 corporate scene. Wall, 151, 587; R. W. Raymond to Carnegie, February 8, 1900 (CP 73:14006–7).
    144 profit handsomely in steel. Carnegie to W. P. Shinn, March 23, 1879 (CP 4:602).
    144 financial panics. Wall, 322.
    145 "better not to sell." Carnegie to W. L. Abbott, December 29, 1888 (CP 10:1686).

145 finance their purchases. Wall, 291; Louis M. Hacker, *The World of Andrew Carnegie, 1865–1901* (Philadelphia, 1968), 357.

145 "drop in the bucket." Carnegie, "Your Business and Wealth," ms., n.d. (CP 247:8); Edward C. Kirkland, *Dream and Thought in the Business Community, 1860–1900* (Ithaca, N.Y., 1956), 155.

145 "extortions," Carnegie to Henry Clay Frick, February 7, 1896 (CP 36:7117–21).

145 against the others. Carnegie, *Autobiography,* 130.

145 "on earth." Carnegie, "How I Served My Business Apprenticeship," *ACR,* 39.

146 in need of management. Carnegie to J. A. Leishman, September 2 and 10, 1895 (CP 32:6334–36, 6354).

146 "do its best," Carnegie, "The Human Side of Business," in Burton J. Hendrick, ed., *Miscellaneous Writings of Andrew Carnegie* (New York, 1933), II, 9–10.

146 "going outside," Carnegie to Charles Scribner's Sons, December 30, 1896 (CP 40:7822).

146 "are partners for," Carnegie to W. L. Abbott, September 1889 (CP 10:1739).

146 most profitable . . . in the world. Wall, 583–84.

146 conducting style, Excerpt from Tchaikowsky's diary, May 6, 1891, in (CP 12:2116).

146 Ulysses S. Grant's widow, Julia D. Grant to Carnegie, December 14, 1900 (CP 80:15386–87).

146 "watch that basket." Carnegie, "How to Win Fortune," *New York Tribune,* April 13, 1890.

146 "I like you." Daniel Coit Gilman to Carnegie, December 10, 1893 (CP 101:18954).

147 (a larger sum.) J. G. Schmidlapp to Carnegie, December 10, 1890 (CP 12:2014).

147 whale, Carnegie to Captain Newbury, September 17, 1903 (CP 98:18519).

147 "equatorial night." W. J. Holland to Carnegie, May 2, 1896 (CP 37:7290–91).

147 dinosaur. Hacker, op. cit., 372.

147 strongly ribbed. The Desert Laboratory of the Carnegie Institution, November 2, 1908 (CP 253).

147 several books. In addition to the autobiography, his books include *Round the World* and *Our Coaching Trip,* privately published accounts of his travels; *Triumphant Democracy,* a hymn to his adopted homeland and a best-seller on both sides of the Atlantic; and *Empire of Business,* a collection of essays.

147 library in Dunfermline, *Autobiography,* 46.

147 $60 million. In a summary of his philanthropic contributions (CP 256).

147 more than 7,500 organs, Carnegie, prepared statement, January 7, 1915 (CP 247); Wall, 830.

147 public pools. Carnegie to W. M. Frew, February 16, 1896 (CP 36:7136); Carnegie, "The Gospel of Wealth," *ACR,* 151.

148 "Mother Earth." Carnegie to Benjamin Gemmill, October 13, 1896 (CP 39:7645).

148 stock, staff, and maintain it. Carnegie, speech at the Brooklyn Library, 1909 (CP 254).

148 lectured the planners. Carnegie to John Ross, December 12, 1899 (CP 70:13583–84 and 78:15006–7).

148 supervise the process. Carnegie, "The Gospel of Wealth," *ACR,* 129–54. The two essays, "The Problem of the Administration of Wealth" and "The Best Fields for Philanthropy," appeared in the *North American Review* in June and December 1889. A British periodical, the *Pall Mall Gazette,* reprinted both under one title, "The Gospel of Wealth," and the name stuck.

149 "criticize the inevitable." *ACR,* 131.

149 "as we ascend." Carnegie, "Socialist Articles" (CP 246).

150 inflate prices. Wall, 376–79, 390.

150 "all grows better," *Autobiography,* 339.

150 "never overthrow." Hacker, op. cit., 71–72.

150 material well-being, Carnegie, "The Gospel of Wealth," *ACR,* 131.

151 "crippled and injured." Edward Bellamy, *Looking Backward* 1888 (rpt. New York, 1982), 38–39.

151 fundamental law of nature. Henry George, *Progress and Poverty,* 1879 (rpt. New York, 1955), 9, 508.

151 "trash." Carnegie, "The Advantages of Poverty," in Edward C. Kirkland, ed., *The Gospel of Wealth and Other Timely Essays* (Cambridge, Mass., 1962), 52. Henry George was both wildly popular and widely scorned. *Progress and Poverty* outsold all previously published American works of economics. He argued that poverty was caused by the ownership of property, land speculation, and the charging of rent. As a remedy, he urged adoption of his Single Tax to confiscate all unearned income from rent and land speculation. But poverty also existed in countries where land speculation was virtually unknown. George's theory also failed to account for unearned income from stocks and bonds or for poverty caused by the effects of boom-and-bust business

cycles. *Progress and Poverty* is more successful as a work of social criticism, a passionate objection to the increasingly visible rift between the haves and have-nots.

151 "gates of Paradise." Carnegie, "The Gospel of Wealth," *ACR,* 132, 154.

152 "make him a millionaire." Henry Demarest Lloyd, *Wealth Against Commonwealth* (New York, 1894), 524.

152 "when obtained." Russell H. Conwell, "Acres of Diamonds," quoted in Richard M. Huber, *The American Idea of Success* (Wainscott, N.Y., 1971), 55–61.

153 provide against excess wealth. Hugh Price Hughes, "Irresponsible Wealth, III," in Hendrick, op. cit., 183–86.

153 "a daily virtue." Carnegie, "The Advantages of Poverty," op. cit., 72–75.

153 "bewildering amounts?" William Jewett Tucker, "The Gospel of Wealth," *Andover Review* 15 (1891), 637, 645.

154 "self-questioning," Carnegie, "The Advantages of Poverty," op. cit., 66–67.

154 "make the selection myself." Quoted in Wall, 825.

154 "more extravagant living." Hendrick, op. cit., II, 208–9.

154 giver was hard, Carnegie, speech in Montgomery, Alabama, 1909 (CP 254).

154 "exterminated," Carnegie to A. P. Gorman, January 2, 1894, (CP 24:4528–29).

155 arbitration. Carnegie, "An Employer's View of the Labor Question," *ACR,* 95–99.

155 $4 million, Carnegie to Charles Scribner, October 21, 1895 (CP 33:6454–55).

155 have to be cut. Wall, 541–42, 550–51.

156 "evolution, not revolution." Carnegie, untitled ms. (CP 249).

156 another of the company's mills. Wall, 541–42.

156 barbed wire. *New York Sun,* July 6, 1892.

157 "something else to do." *New York Sun,* July 8, 1892.

157 "next trial." Quoted in Wall, 565.

157 "loved so much." Quoted in *New York Sun,* July 8, 1892.

157 "deigns to dwell." *Sunday Times,* July 31, 1892.

157 "I wish they had sunk." Carnegie to William Gladstone, September 24, 1892 (CP 17:3198–3200).

158 more than half of the company's stock. Henry Phipps Jr. to Carnegie, September 1, 1897 (CP 44:8648–52). Phipps noted that Carnegie owned 58.5 percent of the firm.

158 enemies. Carnegie, prepared statement for reporters, January 1893.

158 "I remained abroad." Carnegie to Whitelaw Reid, March 20, 1893 (CP 19:3572–73).

159 "belong to their employees." Newspaper clippings (CP 263).

159 turned him down. Paul Krause, *The Battle for Homestead, 1880–1892* (Pittsburgh, 1992), 238.

159 "which have none." Ibid., 229.

159 "the suffering endured." Carnegie to Robert Pitcairn, December 26, 1893 (CP 24:1–3).

160 reprehensible few. Carnegie, "Socialist Articles" (CP 246).

160 "a living," Carnegie, ms., n.d. (CP 247:105).

160 "gorged themselves full." Quoted in *New York Times,* April 11, 1902.

160 prospered together. Carnegie, "The Advantages of Poverty," op. cit., 55; *Empire of Business* (New York, 1902), 189–90.

160 dropped by 60 percent. Wall, 624; Henry Clay Frick, statement in *New York Tribune,* 1895; *Express & Star* (Britain), September 2, 1892 (CP 30). Wage figures vary from one account to another, but the higher amounts claimed by Carnegie were not typical.

161 bomb thrower. John G. Sproat, *"The Best Men": Liberal Reformers in the Gilded Age* (Chicago, 1982), 152.

161 "in any branch." Carnegie, ms. chapter entitled "Distribution of Wealth," n.d. (CP 247).

161 socialist reforms. Carnegie, "Socialism: 'Individualism versus Socialism,'" *ACR,* 262–71.

161 "Rainbow Chasers." Carnegie, "Socialist Articles," February 3, 1908 (CP 246).

161 Profit sharing, Carnegie, "Socialist Articles," January 17, 1908 (CP 246).

161 what they pleased. Carnegie to Grover Cleveland, December 14, 1894 (CP 29:5556–61).

161 than on wages. Carnegie, "Socialist Articles," January 17, 1908 (CP 246); "Socialism: 'Individualism versus Socialism,'" *ACR,* 263.

161 into a philanthropist. Carnegie, "The Gospel of Wealth," *ACR,* 136.

162 "rewards of life be theirs," Carnegie, ms., n.d. (CP 247:16).

162 "means to climb." Carnegie, "The Advantages of Poverty," *ACR,* 67–69.

162 "the swimming tenth," Carnegie, speech at the Brooklyn Library, op. cit.

162 faculty members. Wall, 871–79.

162 "convert themselves." Carnegie, speech at the Brooklyn Library, op. cit.

165 Will details from Wall, 882–83.

CHAPTER 8
A SHARE OF THE PROFITS

ALTHOUGH HENRY FORD is one of the most famous figures in American history, he is also one of the least knowable. His three volumes of autobiography, the many articles that appeared under his name, and his correspondence offer limited insights because they were written almost entirely by others. Their high-flown phrases sound nothing like the simple speech recorded by journalists who interviewed Ford and described by men who worked closely with him.

Longtime associates of Ford left many recollections and observations of him, and their facts and opinions coincide sufficiently to provide an impression of the man's character. But it remains an impression rather than a full rendering, since the Ford they "knew" struck them as elusive and disconnected. After Ford's death, one of these executives told a Ford Motor Company historian, "You know, he never was in the present very much. . . . What did he belong to? . . . He was a member of society but he wasn't in society. What was he in? He had a tremendous impact on society but he lived in his own idea. He lived on the fringes of the community all the time, physically and intellectually" (Ford Archives, W. J. Cameron, *Reminiscences,* 135–36).

Fortunately, the difficulties of discovering who Ford was are offset by the ease of learning what he did. The collection of documents in the Ford Motor Company Archives at the Henry Ford Museum in Dearborn, Michigan, is one of the most comprehensive industrial archives in the world. In addition to holding a vast range of corporate documents, the archives contain numerous lengthy oral histories of Ford executives, engineers, and others who have played significant roles in the company. These *Reminiscences,* as they are called, proved a valuable complement to the financial records, correspondence, memoranda, legal documents, pamphlets, press clippings, and other materials on the Five-Dollar Day and the employee-welfare experiment that followed. Documents in the Ford Archives are catalogued by accession number and box number and in the following notes appear with the accession number first and the box second (e.g., 293:1).

page 166 "plum," *The Masses,* n.d. (940:16). *The Wall Street Journal* accused Ford of committing "economic blunders, if not crimes," and *The New York Times* predicted "serious disturbances" because Ford's plan was "dead against all experience." Newspapers quoted in David L. Lewis, *The Public Image of Henry Ford: An American Folk Hero and His Company* (Detroit, 1976), 71.

166 "than it has ever been." Andrew Carnegie in a United Press interview, n.d., in a notebook of newspaper clippings, Ford Motor Company memos, and letters on the Five-Dollar Day (683:1).

167 "anything else." Loc. cit.

167 no interest in . . . wealth for himself. Ford frequently expressed his lack of interest in personal wealth or philanthropy. The following statement is typical: "My wealth is not my own. It belongs jointly to me and the men who helped me to create it. I regard myself but as the administrator of this wealth for others. It is not mine to give away to so-called charities. There is something bigger and better than charity—that is, justice. Justice demands that I take this wealth which labor has created and reinvest it in such a manner that labor will have still more and greater opportunities." S. S. Marquis, "The Ford Profit-Sharing Plan" (293:1).

167 "open spaces." Henry Ford with Samuel Crowther, *My Life and Work* (Garden City, N.Y., 1912), 73.

167 Revere's horse. C. E. Sorenson, *Reminiscences,* 73, 615.

168 no roads, snow, and mud. Allan Nevins and Frank Ernest Hill, *Ford: The Times, the Man, the Company* (New York, 1954), 387–395; E. G. Liebold, *Reminiscences,* 814–18; Ford, op. cit., 72; Anne Jardim, *The First Henry Ford: A Study in Personality and Business Leadership* (Cambridge, Mass., 1970), 63.

168 1,700 to 14,000. Nevins and Hill, op. cit., 645–48.

168 larger world. W. J. Cameron, *Reminiscences,* 22–24, 95–96, 135–36, 190B; Liebold, op. cit., 983–90, 1332, 1388; Samuel S. Marquis, *Henry Ford: An Interpretation* (Boston, 1923), 50–51.

169 on the spot. Liebold, op. cit., 1036–38, 1305–6; Cameron, op. cit., 179–87.

169 "between him and it." Cameron, op. cit., 80–81.

169 "any argument." Liebold, op. cit., 1334, 1339, 1369, 1487.

170 the standard. Liebold, op. cit., 1363–65; Cameron, op. cit., 207.

170 Whatever could be automated was. O. J. Abell, "The Making of Men, Motor Cars and Profits," *Iron Age,* January 7, 1915, 33–41ff.; William Pioch, *Reminiscences,* 13, 45, 47; W. C. Klann, *Reminiscences,* 28; Ford, op. cit., 78–79, 111–13. By the mid-1920s, the Rouge was the largest industrial complex in the world, with 93 structures on more than 1,000 acres, 160 acres of floor space, 93 miles of railroad tracks, and 27 miles of conveyor belts. (Lewis, op. cit., 160–61.)

171 $2,000 in a month. Ford, op. cit., 113–14; George Brown, *Reminiscences,* 89; W. C. Klann, *Reminiscences,* 234–53.

171 88 percent. Klann, op. cit., 21–23; David Gartman, *Auto Slavery: The Labor Process in the American Automobile Industry, 1897–1950* (New Brunswick, N.J., 1986), 280–82.

171 "into the gaps," Nevins and Hill, op. cit., 517; excerpts from statement of Henry Ford, U.S. Congress, Senate, Commission on Industrial Relations, 1915 (940:16); untitled document, S. S. Marquis Papers (940:17).

171 confusion and mistrust. Nevins and Hill, op. cit., 529; Brown, op. cit., 90; Frank Hadas, *Reminiscences,* 90–91.

172 at the door. A. E. Gruenberg, "Human Interest Story, Number Twelve," S. S. Marquis Papers (940:17); Nevins and Hill, op. cit., 526.

172 wealth could change that. Cameron, op. cit., 58–63; Nevins and Hill, op. cit., 533.

172 "a man out of him." Quoted in Jardim, op. cit., 119.

173 "prosperity of the country." Ford, op. cit., 116.

173 "reckless." Ford quoted in Brown, op. cit., 91.

174 end the injustice. Excerpts from "Profit Sharing Plan" pamphlet (940:17); Stephen Meyer III, *The Five Dollar Day: Labor Management and Social Control in the Ford Motor Company, 1908–1921* (Albany, N.Y., 1981), 140; John Reed, "Industry's Miracle Worker," *Metropolitan,* October 1916; "Ford Puts Women on Equality Wage," *New York World,* October 25, 1916; Ford Motor Company, "Minimum Wage & Profit Sharing," General Letter 206, October 17, 1916 (683:1); Nevins and Hill, op. cit., 547.

174 "driving at." Ford Motor Company, "Ford Sociological Department, 1914–1921," n.d. (940:17).

174 "vital importance." S. S. Marquis, "The Ford Profit-Sharing Plan," 46, 49–50 (940:17).

174 "care for it." Investigation record, January 28, 1914 (940:17).

175 furnish it. F. W. Andrews, "Human Interest Story, Number Nine,"
    n.d. A 1916 summary by the Sociological Department states that
    in 1914, only 47 percent of Ford families passed muster with the
    investigators. By 1916, 87 percent of employees were leading
    Ford-approved lives (940:17).

175 Lee admitted. "Mr. Lee's Talk to First Group of Investigators, April
    15th, 1914"; "Mr. Lee's Talk to Second Group of Investigators,
    April 16th, 1914"; Summary of State of Workers, Results of
    Investigations of Sociological Department, 6, S. S. Marquis Papers
    (940:17).

176 "drill presses." Quoted in Meyer, op. cit., 124.

178 "all we do." Marquis, "The Ford Profit-Sharing Plan," Accession
    293, Box 1; "Henry Ford's Idea of Brotherhood," *Manufacturers'
    News,* May 14, 1916; Lee to C. F. Reynolds, April 29, 1914
    (509:1); Lee, "The So-Called Profit Sharing System in the Ford
    Plant" (940:17); Meyer, op. cit., 112–13, 141.

178 "through the profit-sharing plan." Ford Motor Company secretary
    to branch managers, February 4, 1914 (509:1).

178 the business itself. Ford, excerpt from statement to U.S. Congress,
    Senate, Commission on Industrial Relations.

179 the privately owned Ford Motor Company. Lee, "The So-Called
    Profit Sharing Plan . . ."; Nevins and Hill, op. cit., 530; Marquis,
    "The Ford Profit-Sharing Plan," 4; Sorenson, op. cit., 602–3.

179 nearly two hundred American employers, Stuart D. Brandes,
    American Welfare Capitalism, 1880–1940 (Chicago, 1970), 83–90.

179 "coal pile." Cameron, op. cit., 51.

179 "higher pay." Quoted in Marquis, *Henry Ford: An Interpretation,*
    38–39.

180 "He believed in that." Cameron, op. cit., 20.

181 otherwise would have lacked. Marquis, "The Ford Profit-Sharing
    Plan," 8–9; Nevins and Hill, op. cit., 557–58.

182 their own kind. David L. Lewis, "History of Negro Employment
    in Detroit Area Plans of Ford Motor Company 1914–1941," 2–4,
    10, 16–17 (940:17); August Meier and Elliott Rudwick, *Black
    Detroit and the Rise of the UAW* (New York, 1979), 6–17.

182 "quite a man." Marquis, "The Ford Profit-Sharing Plan," 12;
    Cameron, op. cit., 82.

182 "recover more rapidly." J. E. Mead, "Rehabilitating Cripples at
    Ford Plant," *Iron Age,* September 26, 1918, 739–42; Mead, "Salvage
    of Men," Detroit: Ford Motor Company, 1919 (940:17); Nevins
    and Hill, op. cit., 561–62.

182 "Christ into my factory." Barbara Carritte, Roger Marquis, Mrs.

Johnson, *Reminiscences,* 11; Allan Nevins and Frank Ernest Hill, *Ford: Expansion and Challenge, 1915–1933* (New York, 1957), 64.

183 "do more?" Marquis, "The Ford Profit-Sharing Plan," 7–8, 14–15; Nevins and Hill, *Ford: Expansion . . . ,* 334; Ford Motor Company Executive Committee, General Letter 249, November 20, 1917 (683:1); Marquis, "Henry Ford's Idea of Brotherhood," op. cit.

183 "couple of months." Reed, op. cit.

184 bring family members to the United States. Marquis, "The Ford Profit-Sharing Plan," 7–8; Summary of Sociological Department Work for 1924 (940:17); Meyer, op. cit., 107–8; Klann, op. cit., 110.

184 "for free sometimes." Hadas, op. cit., 97.

184 more cars per shift. Keith Sward, *The Legend of Henry Ford* (New York, 1948), 61, 75; Klann, op. cit., 154.

186 more than four months' pay. "The Row about Henry Ford's Stores," *Literary Digest,* April 16, 1927, 12–13; Mills Wellsford, "Henry Ford: Retailer," *Dry Goods Reporter,* April 23, 1927; Wellsford to F. H. Diehl, April 27, 1927 (390:1); newspaper clippings (940:16); Nevins and Hill, *Ford: Expansion . . . ,* 346–47; Liebold, op. cit., 229.

186 "any industry in this country." S. S. Marquis to Edsel B. Ford, June 28, 1920, S. S. Marquis Papers (940:17).

187 lost their franchises. Sward, op. cit., 74–77.

187 Marquis resigned. After Marquis left, J. E. Mead, the company's chief surgeon, added employee welfare to his responsibilities for health and education, and the Educational Department once again became known as the Sociological Department. See J. E. Mead, April 1, 1921 (940:17).

187 experiment was over. In "Detroit Motors," Edmund Wilson allows a former factory hand to talk at length about his experience at Ford when Sorenson was in charge: "It's not human—I could just bust when I talk about it—break the spirit of an elephant, it 'ud. . . . The bosses are thick as treacle and they're always on your neck, because the man above is on their neck and Sorenson's on the neck of the whole lot—he's the man that pours the boiling oil down that old Henry makes. There's a man born a hundred years too late, a regular slave driver—the men tremble when they see Sorenson comin'. He used to be very brutal—he'd come through and slug the men. . . . I cahn't understand a man committin' suicide and not takin' Sorenson with 'im!" (In *The American Jitters: A Year of the Slump* [New York, 1932], 50–52.) See also Nevins and Hill,

Ford: The Times, the Man, the Company, 648; Nevins and Hill, *Ford: Expansion . . . ,* 329–30, 352–54, 519; Sorenson, op. cit., 240–41.

187 rearview mirror. Arthur J. Kuhn, *GM Passes Ford, 1918–1938: Designing the General Motors Performance-Control System* (University Park, Pa., 1986), 312–315.

187 assortment of colors. Jardim, op. cit., 250; Sward, op. cit., 194–205; Alfred P. Sloan Jr., *My Years with General Motors* (Garden City, N.Y., 1964), 151–52.

188 fawn gray, Lewis, op. cit., 189.

188 "no intention of offering a new car." Quoted in Jardim, op. cit., 251.

188 dealerships across the country. Kuhn, op. cit., 282–83; Sward, op. cit., 201.

188 "too big to be human." Liebold, op. cit., 1382; Lewis, op. cit., 193–95; Sward, op. cit., 200, 205; Kuhn, op. cit., 312; Nevins and Hill, *Ford: Expansion . . . ,* 525.

188 117,000 businesses, Brandes, op. cit., 1.

CHAPTER 9
MORE GRACE, SWEETNESS, AND TIME

T HE AGRARIAN WAY of life has been idealized by philosophers and historians since the fifth century B.C., when Xenophon declared that the tilling of the earth made men virtuous because the greater their devotion to the soil, the richer their rewards. Aristotle thought agriculture particularly conducive to democracy. Its demands gave citizens little time for the disputatiousness of politics, and since farming supplied "the necessaries of life," there would be scant cause to envy the wealth of others. In American history, the agrarian ideal is most commonly associated with Thomas Jefferson, who reasoned that farmers were politically incorruptible because they were economically independent. (For a fuller discussion of these and other sources of agrarianism, see Richard M. Weaver, "The Southern Phoenix," *Georgia Review* 17 [963]:6–17.) I use the lowercase agrarian in writing about agrarianism in general and reserve the uppercase Agrarian for Donald Davidson, Allen Tate, John Crowe Ransom, and their colleagues. They were variously known as Agrarians, Nashville Agrarians, Southern Agrarians, Tennessee Agrarians, and Vanderbilt Agrarians. The terms are interchangeable.

Principal manuscript collections consulted were the papers of Allen Tate (ATP in these notes) and John Peale Bishop in the Department of Rare Books and Special Collections at Princeton University and, in the Department of Special Collections of the Heard Library at Vanderbilt University, the papers of Donald Davidson (cited here as DDP), Andrew Lytle, Frank Owsley, and John Crowe Ransom.

Page 191 themselves included. Alan Tate, "The Fugitive, 1922–1925," *Princeton University Chronicle* 3 (1941):75–84; Tate to Davidson, December 7, 1922 (DDP); Paul K. Conkin, *The Southern Agrarians* (Knoxville, Tenn., 1988), 16–17.

191 "go to hell," Davidson to Tate, October 8, 1922, and December 17, 1922 (ATP).

192 "margins of the page." W. T. Couch, "The Agrarian Romance," *South Atlantic Quarterly* 36 (1937), 419.

192 into biography. Davidson edited the *Nashville Tennessean's* book page from 1923 to 1930, published several volumes of poetry, and wrote social criticism, much of which appears in his books, *The Attack on Leviathan* (1938) and *Still Rebels, Still Yankees* (1957). He is also the author of a two-volume history of the Tennessee River, *The Tennessee* (1946, 1948). In addition to writing poetry, Ransom founded and edited the *Kenyon Review* and wrote several works of literary criticism: *God Without Thunder* (1930), *The World's Body* (1938), *The New Criticism* (1941), and *Beating the Bushes* (1972). Tate's poetry appeared in several volumes. He also wrote two biographies, *Stonewall Jackson* (1928) and *Jefferson Davis* (1929), and three volumes of literary criticism: *Collected Essays* (1959), *Essays of Four Decades* (1969), and *Memoirs and Opinions* (1975).

192 country newspaper, Davidson to Tate, May 9, 1927, and Ransom to Tate, spring 1930 (ATP).

193 "dunghill." William Manchester, *Disturber of the Peace: The Life of H. L. Mencken,* 1950 (rpt. Amherst, Mass., 1986), 162–85.

193 "preached to the North," Davidson, "Trials by Jury and Otherwise," *The Tennessee* II (New York, 1948), 204; "Expedients vs. Principles— Cross-Purposes in the South," *Southern Review* 2 (1937):650.

193 intellectuals of the North. Davidson, "The Dilemma of Southern Liberals, No. 1," ms., n.d., 18A (DDP).

193 "British made." Davidson, "Expedients . . . ," op. cit., 651–52.

194 Northern capital. Virginia Rock, "The Making and Meaning of *I'll Take My Stand:* A Study in Utopian-Conservatism, 1925–1939," Ph.D. diss., University of Minnesota, 1961, 190, 194.

194 as partner. C. Vann Woodward, *Origins of the New South, 1877–1913* (Baton Rouge, La., 1951), 291–92, 309–11. Woodward develops the idea that in economic matters, the South of this era served largely as a colony of the North.

194 "compensation." Davidson, "Expedients . . . ," op. cit., 652–53.

194 reached 75 percent. Woodward, op. cit., 197.

195 most of the 1920s. H. Thomas Johnson, "Postwar Optimism and the Rural Financial Crisis of the 1920's," *Explorations in Economic History* 11 (1973–74):178–80, and Thomas Lawrence Connelly, "The Vanderbilt Agrarians: Time and Place in Southern Tradition," *Tennessee Historical Quarterly* 22 (1963):29–30.

195 "presents for perfection." Tate to Davidson, March 1, 1927, and August 10, 1929 (DDP).

195 "the chance." Lytle to Tate, January 31, 1929 (ATP).

195 "informed and productive." Robert Penn Warren, "The Briar Patch," Twelve Southerners, *I'll Take My Stand* (New York, 1930), 246–64.

196 "maximum number of workers." Ibid., pp. xlvi–xlvii.

197 "a different sort of treasure." Andrew Lytle, "The Hind Tit," Twelve Southerners, op. cit., 201–45. Noting the sequence of Lytle's essay and the one that preceded it, the critic Malcolm Cowley inquired, "Was it a brave jester who put 'the hind tit' as an answer to 'Whither Southern economy'?" Cowley to Tate, December 15, 1930 (ATP).

197 "stable, local, and self-sufficient," Davidson to Tate, December 29, 1929 (ATP).

197 "pursuit of happiness." Quoted in Rock, op. cit., 464.

197 "equable, distributed, and right." Stark Young, "Not In Memoriam, But In Defense," Twelve Southerners, op. cit., 358.

198 "not dominated by it." Tate, "What Is a Traditional Society?" *American Review* 7 (1936):376–87.

198 "throw it off." Twelve Southerners, op. cit., xlviii.

198 exterminated, Henry Hazlitt, "So Did King Canute," *Nation* 1323 (1931):48–49.

198 "ships, railways, banks." *Saturday Review* (1930), 467–68.

198 "water run uphill." Malcolm Cowley to Tate, August 15, 1930 (ATP).

198 "gotten away." Edmund Wilson, "Tennessee Agrarians," *The American Jitters* (New York, 1931), 169–75.

199 "they first make mad." Tate to Wilson, August 8, 1931 (Andrew Lytle Papers).

199 "tender about it." Cowley to Tate, August 21, 1931 (ATP).

199 "come up to the past." Edmund Wilson, *Letters on Literature and Politics, 1912 to 1972* (New York, 1977), 164–65.

199 "local habits and traditions." Ibid., 163–64.

199 "poets and professors." Davidson, "The Southern Agrarians," ms., n.d., 2 (DDP).

200 "apply in the South." Davidson, " 'I'll Take My Stand': A History," *American Review* 5 (1935):306.

200 "within the next decade." Davidson to Tate, January 23 and October 29, 1932 (ATP).

200 dropped by two-thirds. Arthur M. Schlesinger Jr., *The Coming of the New Deal* (Boston, 1959), 3, 27, 263.

200 "originate a cause." Davidson to Tate, January 23 and October 29, 1932 (ATP).

201 their edifice. Lytle to Tate, February 23, 1933 (ATP).

201 five cents, Lytle, "They Took Their Stand: The Agrarian View after Fifty Years," *Modern Age* 24 (1980):114–20.

201 get a farm going. Ransom, "The State and the Land," *New Republic* 70 (February 17, 1932):8–10.

201 grants of land and farm implements, Frank Owsley, "The Pillars of Agrarianism," *American Review* 4 (1935):529–47.

202 thinly settled regions. Other participants in the back-to-the-land movement of the Depression era are discussed in Edward S. Shapiro, "Catholic Agrarian Thought and the New Deal," *Catholic Historical Review* 65 (1979):583–99; Edward S. Shapiro, "Decentralist Intellectuals and the New Deal," *Journal of American History* 58 (March 1972):938–57; William H. Issel, "Ralph Borsodi and the Agrarian Response to Modern America," *Agricultural History* 41 (1967):155–66; and Jess Gilbert and Steve Brown, "Alternative Land Reform Proposals in the 1930s: The Nashville Agrarians and the Southern Tenant Farmers' Union," *Agricultural History* 55 (1981):351–69.

202 sharecroppers out of work. Gilbert and Brown, op. cit., 357, 363.

202 "lower hell?" Ransom, "Happy Farmers," *American Review* 1 (1933):526.

202 Potomac. Schlesinger, *The Coming of the New Deal,* 371–72, 380.

202 only 2 percent, ibid., 320–21.

203 market value of their crops. Edward S. Shapiro, "The Southern Agrarians and the Tennessee Valley Authority," *American Quarterly* 22 (1970):801.

203 stay in the South. "Noted Author Visions South as Industrial," *Chattanooga Times,* November 4, 1936, 12 (ATP).

203 "Tennessee Valley people." Quoted in Shapiro, "The Southern Agrarians and the Tennessee Valley Authority," op. cit., 803–4.

203 "carcass." Davidson, ms. frag., n.d. (DDP).

203 "false way of life." Davidson, "'I'll Take My Stand': A History," op. cit., 320.

204 humans rather than machines. Ransom, "What Does the South Want?" in Herbert Agar and Allen Tate, eds., *Who Owns America? A New Declaration of Independence,* 1936 (rpt. Washington University Press of America, n.d.), 191–93.

204 "at the pens." Tate, "The Problem of the Unemployed: A Modest Proposal," *American Review* 1 (1933):129–48.

204 "hostilities against nature," quoted in Rock, op. cit., 464.

205 "near consequences." Davidson, ms. frag., n.d., 4–5, 12 (DDP).

205 "doesn't happen among us," Davidson to Tate, October 29, 1932 (ATP).

206 right to revolt. Tate to Davidson, December 17, 1931 (ATP); Davidson to Tate, December 15 and 19, 1931 (ATP); Cowley to Tate, February 3, 16, and 26, 1932 (ATP); Page Smith, *Redeeming the Time: A People's History of the 1920s and the New Deal* (New York, 1987), 517–20.

207 "hands of the Yankees." Ransom to Tate, October 25, 1932 (ATP).

207 "do better at this time." Tate to Davidson, April 8, 1933 (DDP).

207 seventy articles. Paul K. Conkin, *The Southern Agrarians* (Knoxville, Tenn., 1988), 108.

207 *New Republic.* Edward S. Shapiro, "American Conservative Intellectuals, the 1930s, and the Crisis of Ideology," *Modern Age* 23 (1979):370–80.

207 softheaded. Davidson to Tate, May 26, 1936 (ATP).

208 inevitable consequence of capitalism. Conkin, op. cit., 111–12, and A. N. Wilson, *Hilaire Belloc: A Biography* (New York, 1984), 184–87. Belloc laid out his philosophy of Distributism in *The Servile State* (1911).

208 political choice was meaningless. Shapiro, "American Conservative Intellectuals . . . ," op. cit., 375–76.

209 "made up of generals." Tate to Davidson, September 28, 1935 (DDP).

209 "we are licked." Tate to Davidson, quoted in William E. Leverette Jr. and David E. Shi, "Herbert Agar and *Free America*: A Jeffersonian Alternative to the New Deal," *Journal of American Studies* 16 (1982):194.

209 second term. Conkin, op. cit., 123.

210 good of the shareholders. Agar and Tate, op. cit., 183–84.

210 the bulk of the populace impoverished. Agar and Tate, op. cit., 91.

210 "robber rabbits." Agar and Tate, op. cit., 96–97.

211 win Southern votes. Davidson to Tate, March 27, 1937 (ATP).

212 "see it go on." Andrew W. Foshee, "The Political Economy of the Southern Agrarian Tradition," *Modern Age* 27 (1983):165. See also Davidson, "An Agrarian Looks at the New Deal," *Free America* 2 (June 1938):3–5.

212 indifference to their vision. Lytle, "They Took Their Stand . . . ," op. cit., 120.

212 "social crises." Tate, "A View of the Whole South," *American Review* 2 (February 1934), 424–25.

CHAPTER 10
WE'LL DO IT!

THE PRIMARY ARCHIVAL sources are the Henry J. Kaiser Papers and Edgar F. Kaiser Papers at the Bancroft Library, University of California, Berkeley. Both collections are more impressive for their mass than their comprehensiveness. The Kaisers' preference for doing business by phone and in person may explain the absence of letters and other papers on many points. Both Kaisers regularly assigned personnel managers and others to study and report on employee matters, productivity, and other aspects of their shipyard operations. A number of these reports survive, and their candor reveals much about the day-to-day challenges facing wartime industry and about the Kaisers' admirable drive to identify and solve problems. In the citations that follow, materials from the Kaisers' papers are indicated by HJK or EFK, followed by box and folder numbers.

After doing research in these papers and reading about the U.S. economy during World War II, I realized that while I had learned a great deal about the management of the shipyards and Henry Kaiser's relations with Washington, I knew almost nothing about the one million men and women who built the ships. In 1996, through notices that the *San Francisco Chronicle, Oakland Tribune,* and *Alameda Times-Herald* kindly ran as letters to the editor, I was able to conduct telephone interviews and exchange letters with many former Kaiser shipyard workers: Charlotte Martin Adams, Teddy Allen, Lovie Amos, Jack C. Andrews, Ray Baker, Bert Bruzzone, Evelyn Canby, Eduardo Carrasco, Stanley Robert Chan, Frank Cheney, Robert Cook, Hank Cunningham, Mattie Dawson, Maxine Deetz, Ruth Dyer, Mary Fabilli, Adele Fash, Thomas Fee, Harold Furst, Frances Harrington, Joyce L. Harvey, Dale Hester, Joseph Horton, Charles Jackson, John Jones, Bob Kelly, Sylvia Warren Kittelson, Fran Koser, Eilean E. Lear, Del Ledesma, Frank Lee, Lola Malone, Ralph Martinez, Leon Mason, Norman Merboth, Madge Hart Perry, Gerald Ponsi, Robert J. Rice,

Glenn Ruggiero (son of the late Frank O. Ruggiero, who helped to construct ships' boilers at Richmond), Marshall Sanders, Marie Scott, Ann Cox Steppan, Victor Steppan, John B. Stolp, Charles A. Stone, Thomas William Streib, Clifford Trotter, William F. Van Gelder, Frank Vodich, Paul Watt, Don Welch, Dallas Wilcox, John B. Wilson, Harry Yetter, and Eva Yorton. Their accounts immeasurably deepened my understanding of life and work in the shipyards, giving me feelings, perspectives, color, and texture absent from the papers of the men at the top of the Kaiser shipbuilding enterprises. I am especially indebted to Tom Leonetti (son of the late Frank Leonetti, a welder leaderman at Richmond) for sending me a video of a company-produced film that enabled me to see many of the processes and places described by wartime employees. The information they supplied is cited here only when the source is not evident from the text.

Readers seeking a full picture of the United States during World War II will be well rewarded by John Morton Blum, *V Was for Victory: Politics and American Culture During World War II* (New York, 1976). One of the liveliest and best oral histories of women's work experiences in this period is Nancy Baker Wise and Christy Wise, *A Mouthful of Rivets: Women at Work in World War II* (San Francisco, 1994). More than five hundred thousand persons moved to Northern California during the war, and many other areas of the West also boomed. The changes are well chronicled and analyzed in Gerald D. Nash, *The American West Transformed: The Impact of the Second World War* (Bloomington, Ind., 1985).

Page 214 "proclaimed a god." Donald Davidson to Allen Tate, January 19, 1941 (Allen Tate Papers).

214 for their constituents. Eliot Janeway, *The Struggle for Survival,* 1951 (rpt., New York, 1968), 18–19.

215 $50 billion to other nations. Doris Kearns Goodwin, *No Ordinary Time* (New York, 1994), 194–95; Harold G. Vatter, *The U.S. Economy in World War II* (New York, 1985), 30.

215 for American armed forces. Vatter, op. cit., 4–5.

216 garish neckties. Lester Velie, "The Truth about Henry Kaiser," *Collier's,* July 27, 1946 (HJK 259:12); details of Kaiser's early life

and the beginnings of his shipbuilding career are from "Henry J. Kaiser: A Biography," prepared by the Kaiser companies shortly after his death in 1967, and from "The Prefabricated Captain," a history of Kaiser's shipbuilding, which appeared in a company publication. Neither source is dated or paginated.

216 "to pour out ships." "Kaiser Shipbuilding During World War II," n.d., 1 (EFK 62:1).

216 "where I like to be," "Henry J. Kaiser: A Biography."

217 just before FDR's Fireside Chat. Mark S. Foster, *Henry J. Kaiser: Builder in the Modern American West* (Austin, Texas, 1989), 70; Emory S. Land, *Winning the War with Ships* (New York, 1958), 21; Walter W. Jaffee, *The Last Liberty: The Biography of the SS Jeremiah O'Brien* (Palo Alto, Calif., 1993), 23–24.

218 "our freedom and civilization." Quoted in Samuel M. Levin, "The Impact of War on Technology," *Essays on American Industrialism: Selected Papers of Samuel M. Levin* (Detroit, 1973), 106.

218 finished the job in twenty-seven. *Fore 'n' Aft,* April 14, 1944 (HJK 288:3); "Kaiser Ship Production During War: Summary Report" (HJK 285:11); *Fore 'n' Aft,* February 1, 1946 (HJK, 298:21); "Kaiser Shipbuilding During World War II," 4, 6–7; Donald M. Nelson, *Arsenal of Democracy: The Story of American War Production* (New York, 1946), op. cit., 245; Land, op. cit., 24, 168–69; "The Prefabricated Captain."

218 daily progress reports. Generalizations about HJK's management style are based upon my reading of his papers and interviews with former Kaiser workers, with a few details from Foster, op. cit., 234–39.

219 building the deckhouses on the ground. The 1912 precedent for Kaiser's prefabricating technique was pointed out by Admiral Howarld L. Vickery, who took pleasure in needling Henry Kaiser, in a December 24, 1942, letter to him (HJK 15:36). The construction methods are described in "Kaiser Shipbuilding During World War II" and "The Prefabricated Captain."

219 eight hours at a stretch. Frank J. Taylor, "Freighters from the Assembly Line," *Nautical Gazette,* March 1942, 17–19 (HJK 287:7); "Kaiser Shipbuilding During World War II," 3.

219 speed and nothing but. HJK, speech to Academy of Political Science, November 10, 1942, 3–4 (HJK 262:17).

219 no way to recoup their investment. James Houlihan, *Western Shipbuilders in World War II* (Oakland, Calif., 1945), 7 (HJK 289:19); Vatter, op. cit., 27.

219 "a penalty basis." HJK to Howard Vickery, August 13, 1941 (HJK 26:15); Kaiser complaints to steel executives (HJK 316:35).

220 missed the targets. Houlihan, op. cit., 7; Nelson, op. cit., 246;
    Henry Kaiser, report to U.S. Senate Special Committee
    Investigation, n.d. (HJK 15:21); Grant's Pass, *Oregon Courier*
    editorial, August 28, 1942 (HJK 13:69).
220 firebombing of Japan. Foster, op. cit., 90–96, discusses Fontana's
    beginnings; "Kaiser Financing" (HJK 156:17).
221 deductions from their paychecks. Jean Johnson, Report of the
    Industrial Relations Department, Contract Recruits Section,
    February 1943 (HJK 20:32); *Serve Your Country* . . . (HJK 288:3);
    "The Prefabricated Captain."
222 rising crime. Katharine Hamill, ms. for *Fortune* magazine,
    December 18, 1944, 1 (HJK 24:13).
222 Kaiser quickly withdrew. Marilynn S. Johnson, *The Second Gold
    Rush: Oakland and the East Bay in World War II* (Berkeley, Calif.,
    1993), 37.
223 contributions to the war effort. Jean Johnson, op. cit.; Clay
    Bedford to Carl W. Smith of the Federal Housing Administration,
    March 25, 1942 (HJK 15:14); "The Transportation and Housing
    Problem as It Affects Labor Turnover in the Richmond Shipyards,"
    company report, February 1943 (HJK 288:6); see also HJK 287:20
    and Alyce Mano Kramer, *The Story of the Richmond Shipyards,* 1945
    (HJK: 288:5).
223 largest war housing project. D. Lester Lynch, "Vanport, Oregon's
    Second City," *Western Construction News,* August 1943, 351–54;
    "Vanport City, U.S.A.," *The Bo's'n's Whistle,* May 20, 1943, 8–9
    (EFK 64:4).
223 1,000,000 employees. "The Prefabricated Captain."
224 entire war. Actuaries' report cited in Levin, op. cit., p. 111; defense
    workers' casualty figures from Sidney R. Garfield, M.D., first
    annual report of the Permanente Foundation Hospitals, November
    14, 1943 (HJK 287:20).
224 "climatic conditions will govern the choice." U.S. Maritime
    Commission directive, February 15, 1943 (HJK 287:16), and
    author interview of Charlotte Martin Adams.
225 "after I got clear." Other workers who told me of shipyard injuries
    include Lovie Amos, Mary Fabilli, Bert Bruzzone, Joseph Horton,
    Thomas William Streib, and Don Welch.
225 wide range of other ills. Garfield, op. cit. (HJK 287:20); Sally
    Bolotin to Clay Bedford, November 6, 1942 (HJK 287:17); Jean
    Johnson, op. cit.
225 "not physically capable of doing the job." Kaiser Company, Inc.,

Vancouver Yard, "Report on Labor Utilization," February 28, 1944, n.p. (EFK 64:9).

226 one of the country's largest health maintenance organizations. Kaiser, "The First Fifty Years," 23 (HJK 259:26); Foster, op. cit., 214–15.

226 a punitive draft. Donald H. Riddle, *The Truman Committee: A Study in Congressional Responsibility* (New Brunswick, N.J., 1964), gives an admiring account of the committee's work and its chairman. U.S. Congress, Senate, Special Committee Investigating the National Defense Program, *Hearings,* March 24, 1943, 901–25 (HJK 286:4).

226 "presenteeism," HJK, speech, April 1943 (HJK 262:31).

226 perfect attendance. Kramer, op. cit., 64.

226 "when the war ends?" Employee handbook, Richmond Yards 3 and 3-A, 6 (HJK 288:26).

227 pocketed the change. Author interview with Maxine Deetz.

227 punched out with the day shift. Author interview with Glenn Ruggiero.

229 7,500 black workers. Nash, op. cit., pp. 102–4; Foster, op. cit., 80–81.

230 more than a quarter of the jobs in the Richmond yard. Kramer, op. cit., 61.

230 climb with loads. "Women in Shipbuilding: A Graphic Portrayal of the First Six Months' Experience of Women Employed in the Kaiser Shipyards, July to December 1942," January 1, 1943 (HJK 289:20); Kramer, op. cit., 70.

231 "laundress." *Washington (D.C.) Star,* November 23, 1942 (HJK 285:10); Kramer, op. cit., 61–62; several undated publications of the Child Service Department of Kaiser's Portland Yard: "Meeting Needs: The War Nursery Approach," Kaiser Child Service Centers Pamphlets for Teachers, no. 4; "Extra Service to Parents & Children"; "Home Service Food"; "The Medical and Nursing Program"; "Publicising the Centers to Workers" (EFK 62:2 and 62:3).

231 "their youngsters." Stub Nelson, "Mrs. F.D.R. Kept on Go," *Oregonian,* April 6, 1943 (EFK 64:10).

232 war-damaged ships. Associated Press dispatch of April 21, 1943 (HJK 285:11); *Fore 'n' Aft,* February 1, 1946 (HJK 289:21); "Kaiser Shipbuilding During World War II," 5–6.

233 applauded the deed. "We'll Do It!" (HJK 289:7); photo of President Roosevelt, Henry Kaiser, and Edgar Kaiser at the *Teal*

launch, September 23, 1942 (EFK 62:11); "Kaiser Shipbuilding During World War II," 2.

233 complete with bath towels. Clay Bedford to HJK, November 9, 1942 (HJK 14:30); Clay Bedford to HJK, November 10, 1942 (HJK 15:55); "Kaiser Shipbuilding During World War II," 4; "The Prefabricated Captain."

234 "the submarine menace." "Kaiser Shipbuilding," ms., n.d., 2 (EFK 62:1); "Kaiser Shipbuilding During World War II," 5–6. The first baby flattop, the SS *Casablanca,* was christened by Eleanor Roosevelt on April 4, 1943 (HJK 285:10).

234 "Kaiser's coffins," *Time,* September 4, 1944, 62 (HJK 285:10).

234 reinforcing crucial welds with rivets. Clay Bedford testimony, 10200–9 in U.S. Congress, Senate, Special Committee Investigating the National Defense Program, *Hearings* (Part 23), 1944 (286:1). According to "The Prefabricated Captain," bad welds caused only 8 of the 4,694 vessels ordered by the U.S. Maritime Commission to be lost at sea during the war.

234 other ships in progress. Howard Vickery to HJK, September 1, 1944; HJK to Howard Vickery, September 2, 1944 (HJK 27:15).

235 to do more. HJK to National Association of Manufacturers, October 29, 1942, 6 (HJK 262:16).

235 "miracles in production." HJK to Academy of Political Science, November 10, 1942, 5 (HJK 262:17).

235 devastated by war. HJK, "America Can Win the Peace!" *Progressive,* May 29, 1944, 1–2 (HJK 153:29).

235 Lena Horne, Dinah Shore, Kramer, op. cit., 76, 81.

236 "in terms the public can understand." Claude Robinson, "Henry Kaiser: A Study in the Psychology of Business Heroics," Opinion Research Corporation, February 3, 1943.

237 "and nothing moved." *Oakland Tribune,* August 13, 1945 (HJK 285:11); HJK testimony, 4062, U.S. Congress, Senate, Special Committee Investigating the National Defense Program, August 18, 1945 (HJK 286:6).

237 aluminum . . . one of his biggest successes. Foster, op. cit., 93, 100–1, 196.

237 equal treatment at Fontana. *Outrage in Steel* (HJK 151:1).

240 "We got them." U.S. Congress, House. Committee on the Merchant Marine and Fisheries, *Hearings,* September 23–26, 1946, pp. 41, 43, 50, 53, 56, 61, 63–64, 96, 104, 110, 147, 150, 154 (HJK 287:3); "The Prefabricated Captain"; "Kaiser Financing," a statement prepared by the company for the hearings (HJK

156:17); on the extent of private financing of Kaiser's war work, HJK to Jesse Jones, April 19, 1946 (HJK 154:20); and newspaper clippings including the United Press story, September 25, 1946; Eleanor Roosevelt, "My Day," *Washington Daily News,* September 26, 1946; *New York Times,* September 26, 1946 (HJK 156:15). If Henry or Edgar Kaiser contacted Eleanor Roosevelt about the hearings in the hope of generating the kind words in her column, it was apparently not by mail: Mrs. Roosevelt's 1945–52 correspondence in the Franklin D. Roosevelt Library at Hyde Park, New York, contains no letters to or from the Kaisers.

240 top 20 percent gained 76.7 percent. James McGregor Burns, *Roosevelt: Soldier of Freedom* (New York, 1970), 460; Vatter, op. cit., 19, 143.

240 invested even more. The 10 percent figure was noted in December 1942 (HJK 287:20). Portland's war bond purchases won praise in 1943, but HJK was asked to use his "personal intervention" to improve performance at Richmond (HJK 21:41). "forced out of her production role." "Who Will Need a Postwar Nursery School?" Kaiser Child Service Centers Pamphlets for Teachers, no. 3, n.d., 2–3 (EFK 62:3).

241 mess kits by the millions. William Manchester, *The Glory and the Dream* (Boston, 1974), 296.

241 "capital went back to work." Janeway, op. cit., 130.

CHAPTER 11
THE MAN IN THE MIDDLE

THE NIGHTMARES OF the 1960s included assassinations, a pointless war that would end fifty-eight thousand American and two hundred thousand Vietnamese lives, riots in a hundred cities, and untold acts of violence against nonviolent civil rights demonstrators by "lawful" authorities wielding firearms, clubs, guard dogs, fire hoses, and cattle prods. There seem to be as many versions of this anguishing period as there are chroniclers of it, but in the decade's civil rights struggle—a labyrinthine tale in itself—at least one thing can be said with certainty: No one did more to advance the cause of equal employment opportunity than Whitney M. Young Jr., executive director of the National Urban League from 1961 until his death in 1971. He did his share of marching, but most of his "missionary work," as he called it, was among the powerful white men who ran America's largest corporations. The Reverend Jesse Jackson said that Young had the most difficult job in the movement, selling civil rights to the white establishment. By influencing the influential and by using the National Urban League to help them recruit and promote members of minority groups, Young helped hundreds of thousands of blacks through the gates of corporate America.

My chief sources for the chapter were the correspondence, memos, speeches, and other documents in the Whitney Young Papers of the Columbia University Rare Book and Manuscript Library (materials from which are cited here as WYP, followed by the box number). Young's camaraderie with the inhabitants of the upper echelon of American business excited the suspicions of younger, more militant blacks, who sometimes derided him as "Whitey" Young or "Uncle Whitney." His speeches to white business leaders and his testimony at congressional hearings make clear that the pejoratives were undeserved. He spoke bluntly to white audiences about their racism, making his case with facts, figures, and pointed examples. The intolerant could ignore Whitney Young, but it was seldom possible to refute him.

Many of Young's ideas for fighting racism and poverty appeared in his newspaper column, "To Be Equal," which was syndicated in one hundred papers, and his two books, *To Be Equal* (New York, 1964), and *Beyond Racism: Building an Open Society* (New York, 1969). Three decades after their publication, the columns and books make painful reading. The quality of life among the urban poor (most of whom are not white) has continued to deteriorate, the gap between rich and poor continues to widen, segregation still abounds, and the attendant suffering still fails to move the vast majority of white Americans.

Among secondary sources, two works by Nancy J. Weiss were particularly valuable: *Whitney M. Young, Jr. and the Struggle for Civil Rights* (Princeton, N.J., 1989), and *The National Urban League, 1910–1940* (New York, 1974). John Morton Blum gives an excellent overview of the period in *Years of Discord: American Politics and Society, 1961–1974* (New York, 1991), and Robert Weisbrot's *Freedom Bound: A History of America's Civil Rights Movement* (New York, 1990) is a valuable introduction to its subject. Nicholas Lemann, "The Unfinished War," *Atlantic Monthly* (December 1988 and January 1989), examines the politics of the War on Poverty.

My account of the March on Washington relies primarily on *The New York Times* of August 29, 1963, which provided superb eyewitness reports by James Reston, Gay Talese, Russell Baker, and Nan Robertson, among others. I have rounded out the story with anecdotes from a few other sources, noted separately in this section.

Except where otherwise indicated, information on National Urban League programs and finances comes from the organization's annual reports.

Page 243 front of the bus. John Hope Franklin, *From Slavery to Freedom: A History of Negro Americans,* 3rd ed., New York, 1967, 580–91. The story of black soldiers in uniform being forced to ride in the back of Washington, D.C., buses while Italian prisoners of war rode in the front was told in my presence in March 1995 by Bruce Llewellyn, a successful black entrepreneur who served in World War II.

243 "fight for democracy." Quoted in Tom Buckley, "Whitney Young:

Black Leader or 'Oreo Cookie'?" *New York Times Magazine,*
September 20, 1970, 32ff.

243 six feet two, application for special vehicle identification,
September 25, 1970 (WYP:31).

243 No one wanted it. Buckley, op. cit., and Weiss (1989), 34.

244 "the people who have something to give." David Gallen, ed.,
Malcolm X as They Knew Him (New York, 1992), 184; Weiss
(1989), 173, 355.

244 "brought up to believe." Weiss (1989), 34.

244 joined the St. Paul office, ibid., 40–43.

244 best efforts of both. Nancy J. Weiss (1974), 29, 67–68.

245 American Federation of Labor. Memo from Guichard Parris and
Lester Brooks to WMY, April 10, 1969 (WYP:21).

245 jobs in the North, Weiss (1974), 93, 98–102.

245 "bucking up Negro morale 'inside.'" "Outline of Memorandum to
President Johnson, Future Civil Rights Strategies" (WYP:Box 29a).

246 "baseball games." Weiss (1974), 118–19.

246 How would white customers react? Ibid., 176–77.

246 "initiative and perseverance." Whitney M. Young Jr. to Whitney
M. Young Sr., April 30, 1948 (WYP:1a).

247 the store's many Negro customers. Weiss (1989), 41–43.

247 The trustees buckled. Ibid., 60–62.

247 ("the most powerful economic, social and civic groups in
America.") "The Urban League," n.d. (WYP:29a).

248 "things should be different." Sidney Hollander to WMY, January 5,
1962 (WYP:2).

248 "From now on we will." Weiss (1989), 87.

248 "chairman of the board," Weiss (1989), 338–39; Weisbrot, op. cit., 80.

249 "self-defeating." WMY, "Building Ghetto Power," June 1969 draft
for *Social Services Outlook* (WYP:29a).

249 "never me." WMY, speech to Urban League of Westchester
County, April 30, 1961 (WYP:161).

249 "as vicious as the more overt attitude of the South." WMY, notes
in a folder dated 1962 (WYP:122).

250 "all areas of community life." WMY, speech to the Southern
Christian Leadership Conference, September 27, 1962 (WYP:124).

251 "everyone else gets a good helping." WMY, "To Be Equal," March
20, 1968 (WYP:215). The Domestic Marshall Plan is outlined in
National Urban League, "A 'Marshall Plan' for the American
Negro," in Alan F. Westin, ed., *Freedom Now!* (New York, 1964),
48–51. Young's comment about "equal access to the track" appears
in "Ford Foundation Presentation Draft Version," n.d. (WYP).

251 "bigotry budget." WMY, "America's Bigotry Budget," U.S. Congress, Senate, Labor and Public Welfare Committee on Employment, Manpower and Poverty, 1967 (WYP:199).

252 "through the front door." Minutes of executive committee meeting, April 11, 1963 (WYP:12).

252 "the blunt pen of marching ranks," Martin Luther King Jr., *A Testament of Hope: The Essential Writings and Speeches of Martin Luther King, Jr.,* in James Melvin Washington, ed. (San Francisco, 1986), 304.

253 abide by the rules. WMY, interview with Dr. Albert Gollin, July 26, 1967 (WYP:9).

253 (bluffing.) Ibid.

254 need for a civil rights bill. Arthur M. Schlesinger Jr., *A Thousand Days: John F. Kennedy in the White House* (Boston, 1965), 968–72.

255 "Please don't ruin it." Courtland Cox, John Lewis, and James Forman, quoted in Henry Hampton and Steve Fayer, *Voices of Freedom: An Oral History of the Civil Rights Movement from the 1950s through the 1980s* (New York, 1990), 164–66.

256 "in his business." George Breitman, ed., *Malcolm X Speaks* (New York, 1966), 38–39.

256 voter registration booths. WMY, August 28, 1963 (WYP:126).

257 not in Birmingham. Taylor Branch, *Parting the Waters: America in the King Years, 1954–63* (New York, 1988), 883.

258 " 'free at last.' " King, op. cit., 217–20.

258 "smooth out our differences." William H. Johnson Jr., quoted in Hampton and Fayer, op. cit., 168.

258 "not just a social agency." WMY, Gollin interview, loc. cit.

259 sue for the right to frequent them. Blum, op. cit., 121–22.

259 No *Profiles in Courage* here. Weiss (1989), 145.

259 "engaged in by the Negro." Martin Luther King to Dorothy Height, April 21, 1964 (WYP:38).

260 "a drought." WMY to Richard Peters, September 14, 1964 (WYP:1).

260 ("rather than *for* him")? Notes, n.d. (WYP:14).

261 "contribute to . . . its establishment." Leadership Council on Civil Rights to Lyndon Johnson, November 11, 1964 (WYP:38).

261 their payrolls. Weiss (1989), 344–48, and National Urban League annual reports.

262 "training people of minority groups." WMY, "To Be Equal," January 17, 1968 (WYP:215).

263 "and I believe in you." WMY, speech to Chrysler Management Club, May 17, 1967 (WYP:146).

263 "barrel of a gun." Weisbrot, op. cit., 236.

263 "take over." WMY, speech to Chrysler Management Club, loc. cit.

264 nothing to say. WMY, speech to Businessmen's Employment Luncheon, Newark, N.J., February 7, 1968 (WYP:260).

264 "white noose," WMY, speech to National Association of Mutual Savings Banks, May 26, 1969 (WYP:179).

264 "normal life," WMY, statement on race relations coverage, Associated Press Managing Editors Association, January 16, 1968 (WYP:260).

264 ignorant of its own racism. WMY, speech to Akron Bar Association, November 10, 1967 (WYP:146).

265 black cabdriver. WMY, speech to Radio Program Conference, December 9, 1967 (WYP:150).

265 "any doubt as to why?" WMY, testimony, U.S. Congress, Senate, Subcommittee on Government Operations on the Full Opportunity and Social Accounting Act of 1967, July 27, 1967 (WYP:200).

265 meager to infinitesimal. WMY, speech to Akron Bar Association, loc. cit.

265 a tenth of the poor. WMY, *Beyond Racism,* 92.

265 Social Security. Peter F. Drucker, "The New Meaning of Corporate Social Responsibility," *California Management Review* 26:2 (Winter 1984), 56.

266 headed by two parents. WMY, *Beyond Racism,* 58–60.

266 bolder action. Weisbrot, op. cit., 245–46.

266 "family structure?" "The Negro Family: Visceral Reaction," *Newsweek,* December 6, 1965.

267 "Whose alienation should we be studying?" WMY testimony, U.S. Congress, Senate, Special Subcommittee on Evaluation and Planning of Social Programs of the Labor and Public Welfare Committee, July 8, 1969 (WYP:201).

267 angry blacks in the ghettos. King, op. cit., 232–39.

267 rather well fed. Weisbrot, op. cit., 250.

267 "you explain it to the press." Weiss (1989), 350.

268 an interest in their futures. Whitney M. Young, "Home from Vietnam," *Sphinx,* February 1967. *Sphinx* is the magazine of Young's college fraternity, Alpha Phi Alpha.

268 "as was done in 1964." Young, *Beyond Racism,* 88–89.

268 New Thrust, National Urban League annual reports and materials (WYP:19).

268 growing pains, Cresap, McCormick and Paget, "National Urban League Study of Organization and Management Practices" (March 1969), II-2, 3. Ford Foundation Library.

269 "militants in different ways." Buckley, op. cit.

269 not his milieu. Weiss (1989), 175, 232; Nancy J. Weiss, "Whitney M. Young Jr.: Committing the Power Structure to the Cause of Civil Rights," in John Hope Franklin and August Meier, eds., *Black Leaders of the Twentieth Century* (Urbana, Ill., 1982), 343.

269 "mainstream." WMY, "We ARE Separated—That's the Cause of All Our Woes," *Ebony,* August 1970, 90ff.; Peter Goldman, *The Death and Life of Malcolm X* (New York, 1973), 78.

270 "monolithic solution," WMY, speech to Congress on Racial Equality, July 6, 1968 (WYP:162); Weiss (1989), 121, 185.

270 "They do nothing." WMY, "To Be Equal," April 5, 1968 (WYP:215).

270 "hasn't done us much good." WMY, speech to American Newspaper Publishers Association, April 23, 1968 (WYP:160).

270 "sense of shared danger and oppression." WMY, "To Be Equal," December 31, 1969 (WYP:217).

271 "human challenges of this society." WMY, speech to National Association of Mutual Savings Banks, loc. cit.

271 government guarantees. Ghettonomics Inc. to WMY, September 5, 1969 (WYP:16).

272 "rot away." WMY, "To Be Equal," October 28, 1970 (WYP:219).

273 claimed to represent. "Text of the Moynihan Memorandum on the Status of Negroes," *New York Times,* March 1, 1970.

273 "when the cameras aren't around." WMY, Gollin, op. cit.

274 bigotry went unchallenged. WMY, in interview by John Slawson, March 16, 1970 (WYP:29a).

275 antidiscrimination lawsuits. Buckley, op. cit.

275 mediocre whites. WMY, commencement address, Bryn Mawr College, May 26, 1968 (WYP:161).

276 mastered in school. WMY, "To Be Equal," November 18, 1970 (WYP:219).

276 "less fortunate than oneself." Kurt Vonnegut, *God Bless You, Mr. Rosewater* (New York, 1965), 54.

276 "do something about it." M. Moran Weston to WMY, September 22, 1970 (WYP:11).

277 "his own accomplishments." Randolph et al., *New York Times Magazine* (October 18, 1970).

277 "storm of protest," WMY to Shirley Gould, October 14, 1970 (WYP:11).

277 indifference to blacks. WMY, White House press conference, December 22, 1970, transcript reprinted in *Sphinx,* May–June 1971, 23ff.

278 "boundless worse." Lyndon A. Wade, (WYP:11).

CHAPTER 12
A GREAT COMPULSION TO GO NORTH

A MERICAN CORPORATE SOCIAL responsibility had many beginnings. Andrew Carnegie invented the socially responsible tycoon—ruthless in business but willing to direct his private wealth to the public good (as defined by him). The socially responsible employer is sometimes said to have been invented in 1875, when H. J. Heinz put Aggie Dunn in charge of the well-being of the young women in his pickle factory. Henry Ford carried Heinz's notion to extremes with his Sociological Department, a brigade of snoops who visited employees at home to determine whether they were living in accord with Ford's principles.

Since World War II, progressive corporations have invoked the concept of enlightened self-interest to explain their charitable contributions, participation in community affairs, and initiative in areas ranging from education to the environment. William C. Norris, cofounder and chief executive officer of Control Data Corporation, appreciated the interdependence of business and society more than most postwar business leaders, and he devoted a large part of his considerable energy to putting his understanding into action. My account of his endeavors is based largely on research done at the Charles Babbage Institute for the History of Information Processing at the University of Minnesota. I relied primarily on materials from the Control Data Corporation collection (CDC in the notes that follow) and the papers of James C. Worthy, a former member of the company's board of directors and author of *William C. Norris: Portrait of a Maverick,* the only full-length biography of Norris to date.

Of special interest in the Control Data collection were Norris's speeches as well as memos, minutes, and reports on the company's activities in the social arena. Unless otherwise noted, information on the company's financial performance and the size of its workforce came from Control Data's annual reports to shareholders. For my purposes, the most valuable part of James Worthy's papers were the Worthy Transcripts (WT here), which are transcripts of interviews of Norris and several other Control Data executives: Norbert Berg, Thomas Kamp, John Lacey, Gary Lohn, Robert Price, and Roger Wheeler. Some of the interviews were conducted by Worthy, others by authors and journalists who wrote about Norris and Control Data, still others by Control Data executives gathering information for a history of the company.

To add to my understanding of individuals, events, and ideas central to my account, I interviewed Norris and Berg. Details on the Minneapolis riots of 1967 came from the newspapers in the archives of the Minnesota Historical Society.

Page 279 glider planes during the war, James C. Worthy, *William C. Norris: Portrait of a Maverick* (Cambridge, Mass., 1987), 14, 24.

279 "the one Norris liked best." Ibid., 33.

280 most reliable computer in the world. Ibid., 40–41; David Lundstrom, *A Few Good Men from Univac* (Cambridge, Mass., 1987), 67; William C. Norris (author interview, September 18, 1996).

280 rent time on them. Control Data Corporation, *Report from the "Social Needs and Business Opportunities" Conference,* September 22–23, 1982, 32 (CDC).

280 bliss of zero. Lundstrom, op. cit., 53, 67.

280 every other black leader. *Report of the National Advisory Commission on Civil Disorders* (New York, 1968), 115–16. This panel, most often referred to as the Kerner Commission (after its chairman, Otto Kerner, governor of Illinois), was convened by President Johnson after the riots. Assigning an accurate dollar value to the damages proved difficult, the commission found. Early estimates of property damage proved to be exaggerated, but most calculations omitted costs incurred by city fire and police departments as well as state and federal governments, costs borne by inner-city residents and shopkeepers displaced by the destruction of homes and businesses, and the intangible yet real costs of "fear, distrust, and alienation."

280 to do likewise. Whitney M. Young Jr., *Beyond Racism* (New York, 1969), 3–4, 23–24, 27, 111–12, 114.

281 "and urban congestion." Norris, speech (CDC, Box 3BIA, Folder A), and interview with author.

282 damage at $1 million. *Minneapolis Star,* July 22, 24, and 25, 1967.

282 "and everywhere else." Worthy, op. cit., 107–8.

291 "stimulating to many of our employees." Norris, interview with author; Norris, interview with Ralph Nader and Bill Taylor, October 2, 1984, 46 (WT); Norris, interview with Jeannye Thornton, May 14, 1984 (WT); Norris, "Back to the Countryside via Technology," *Technology Series No. 5,* January 1978, 2 (CDC); Norris, "Technology and the Inner City—Experience and Promise," *Technology Series No. 8,* September 1978, 4 (CDC); Norris, speech to Houston Minority Group Symposium, February 18, 1969 (CDC); "Control Data Corporation: Minneapolis, Minnesota, and Washington, D.C., Synopsis" (N. Berg Subject Files, CDC); Worthy, op. cit., epigraph, 108, 131; Worthy interviews of Norbert Berg, Thomas Kamp, John W. Lacey, Gary Lohn, and Robert Price (all in WT); Gary Lohn, interview with Robert Price, February 28, 1982, 13–15, Executive History Narratives (CDC); Conference Board, *Business and the Development of Ghetto Enterprise,* n.d., 29, 31, 79, 95; Council on Foundations, *Corporate Giving: The Views of Chief Executive Officers of Major American Corporations,* May 1982, 9.

291 "people development goals." R. D. Conner to R. G. Wheeler, May 11, 1970; B. L. Hanson to R. G. Wheeler, June 2, 1970 (CDC, Box CD3BIA).

291 electricity and telephones. Speech to Second Annual Industrial Placement Conference, July 30, 1969 (CDC, N. Berg Subject Files).

292 schoolday. Control Data, "Our Corporation's Contributions to Solving Social Needs—A Report from Control Data Corporation," n.d., 6–8.

292 "a handsome one." Control Data Corporation, "Social Responsibility Report 1978," 5; Norris, "Technology for the Inner City—Experience and Promise," op. cit., 4.

292 markets, jobs, and prosperity. Worthy, op. cit., 126–34.

293 "form of genius." Worthy interview of Norbert Berg (WT).

293 "dependency on hardware." Norris, interview with author.

293 developing a profitable business from it. Norris, "Technology for the Inner City—Experience and Promise," op. cit., 2.

294 nearly 80 percent found jobs. Memo from G. H. Lohn to Corporate Social Responsibility and Concerns Committee,

February 23, 1977 (CDC, Box 3CIG); Worthy, op. cit., 144; Control Data Corporation, "Report from the 'Social Needs and Business Opportunities' Conference," 1982, 3; Control Data Corporation, "Social Responsibility 1978," 2.

294 employee assistance programs. Control Data Corporation, 1981 annual report, 6, and "Social Responsibility 1978," 10.

294 "required to be successful." Control Data Corporation, "Report from the 'Social Needs and Business Opportunities' Conference," 1982, 3, 6.

295 could not succeed alone. Norris, "Harnessing Technology for Better Urban Living," *Technology Series No. 6,* April 1978, 11.

295 "into the earth." Quoted in Robert N. Bellah, et al., *The Good Society* (New York, 1991), 104.

296 "lowering return on investment." Ulric Weil, report dated September 2, 1980.

296 "enhance internal operating margins." Stephen T. McClennan, report dated March 4, 1981.

296 "what we were doing." Worthy interview of Norbert Berg, loc. cit.

296 big mainframes. Ford S. Worthy, "Does Control Data Have a Future?" *Fortune,* December 23, 1985, 24–26.

297 the preceding five. Worthy, op. cit., 12–13.

297 $383 million of its debt. Ibid. and Control Data Corporation, 1985 annual report, 1–3.

297 "not in the short term." Norris, interview with author.

297 their old jobs. Lester Thurow, "Almost Everywhere: Surging Inequality and Falling Real Wages," in Kaysen, op. cit., 388.

298 some were making money. James C. Worthy, op. cit., 13, 203–4.

298 "came to pass." Berg, author interview, December 2, 1996.

299 "followed by occupation." Thurow, op. cit., 383–84; "Here We Go Again," *Nation,* August 26–September 2, 1996, 18–19.

CHAPTER 13
THE GOD BOX

THE FIRST TWENTY-FIVE years of the Interfaith Center on Corporate Responsibility, 1971–1996, coincided with immense changes in society, politics, and the economy. American women went to work in unprecedented numbers, but even with two incomes, most American families were not as well off in 1996 as they were before 1973. Affirmative action, a far-reaching social experiment in equal opportunity, was tried and abandoned. The federal government's welfare state, in place since the New Deal, was dismantled. The global marketplace, dreamed of for centuries, became a reality.

ICCR's shareholder activism has addressed many of these issues and others as well. Although I have focused on ICCR's shareholder resolutions, it should not be left unsaid that the organization and its members are also active in social investing and the campaign to attract more money to so-called alternative investments, which often produce low returns but provide affordable (and much needed) capital for businesses and nonprofit endeavors in distressed urban neighborhoods and poor rural communities.

For this chapter my principal sources were interviews with Timothy H. Smith, executive director of ICCR; ICCR's newsletter, *Corporate Examiner;* and the January 1996 edition of ICCR's *Proxy Resolutions Book,* which is, unless otherwise noted, the source for all summaries and quotes on the group's 1996 resolutions. "Inspired by Faith, Committed to Action," the 25th anniversary edition of *Corporate Examiner* 25:5 (November 1, 1996), is the source for several thumbnail descriptions of earlier resolutions. I also interviewed W. Eric Aiken, president of the Proxy Monitor, and have quoted from his organization's recommendations on several proxy resolutions; Simon Billenness, a senior analyst with Franklin Research and Development Corporation, in Boston; Doris Gormley, O.S.F., director of corporate responsibility of the Sisters of St. Francis of Philadelphia; and Paul

Neuhauser, professor of law at the University of Iowa and an attorney for ICCR.

The greed and exhibitionism of the 1980s, treated in passing at the beginning of this chapter, have been well chronicled in Connie Bruck, *The Predators' Ball* (New York, 1988); Michael Lewis, *Liar's Poker* (New York, 1989); Bryan Burroughs and John Hellyar, *Barbarians at the Gate* (New York, 1990); and James B. Stewart, *Den of Thieves* (New York, 1991). In its March 16, 1992, issue (pp. 78–100), *Forbes* magazine allowed Michael Milken to tell his version of the story.

Page 300 immediate and warm. James B. Stewart, *Den of Thieves* (New York, 1991), 223.

302 January 1. Robert B. Reich, *The Work of Nations* (New York, 1991), 199.

302 34 percent. Benjamin Stein, *A License to Steal* (New York, 1992), 164.

302 risk-free. Patricia O'Toole, "Flipping Risk in the '80s," *Lear's* (December 1989), 27–28; "How I Became a Junk-Bond Airhead," *Lear's* (June 1990), 35–37; "Poor Michael Milken," *Lear's* (February 1991), 21–22; "Winkling the Bumpkins and Other Tales of Greed," *Lear's* (March 1992), 30–32.

302 at the bottom. L. Minard, "A Chat with Fernand Braudel," *Forbes* (June 21, 1982), 132–34ff.

302 since the 1930s, Jonathan Z. Larsen, "Sharecroppers," *Manhattan, inc.* (February 1986), 71–82. Larsen's account is a delightful history of corporate gadflies.

304 "proxy scare." Saul Alinsky, *Rules for Radicals* (New York, 1972), 171, 175; P. David Finks, *The Radical Vision of Saul Alinsky* (Ramsey, N.J., 1984), 201–28; Sanford D. Horwitt, *Let Them Call Me Rebel: Saul Alinsky, His Life and Legacy* (New York, 1989), 493–94.

305 levers of social change. Andrew J. Hoffman, "A Strategic Response to Investor Activism," *Sloan Management Review* 37 (Winter 1996), 51–52; David Vogel, "Trends in Shareholder Activism: 1970–1982," *California Management Review* 25:3 (Spring 1983), 68–69.

306 "larger scale." "Milton Friedman Responds," *Business and Society Review* 1:1 (Spring 1972), 6.

307 mediate the conflicts. Milton Friedman, "The Social Responsibility of Business Is to Increase Its Profits," *New York Times Magazine* (September 13, 1970), 32–33ff.

307 "by means of other people." Keith Ovenden and Tony Cole, *Apartheid and International Finance* (New York, 1989), epigraph.

307 healthy economy. Margaret Blair, *Ownership and Control: Rethinking Corporate Governance for the Twenty-first Century* (Washington, 1995), 215.

308 "future security." Whitney M. Young Jr., "To Be Equal" (November 18, 1970). Whitney Young Papers, Box 219, Columbia University.

309 resolutions asking the companies to leave. "World Church Unit to Liquidate Stocks to Protest Racism," *New York Times* (August 23, 1972), 1.

310 "in that environment." Committee on Corporate Social Responsibility, minutes of September 14, 1972, meeting (Control Data Corporation Archives, Box 3CIG).

310 computer-based education for South African blacks. Control Data statement, October 24, 1977 (Control Data Corporation Archives, Worthy subject files, Box 4/5, folder 28).

311 "any longer?" Excerpts from Robert J. Flaherty, "Revolution, Sayeth the Churchman; One Soul at a Time, Says a Businessman," *Forbes* (February 6, 1978), 31–33.

311 urged shareholders to reject it, Committee on Corporate Social Responsibility, minutes of April 21, 1978, meeting (Control Data Corporation Archives, Box 3CIG).

312 $12,500. Committee on Corporate Social Responsibility, minutes of April 25, 1973, meeting (Control Data Corporation Archives, Box 3CIG); R. G. Wheeler, speech to Lutheran Church meeting, May 9, 1979 (Control Data Corporation Archives, Box 3BIA, Folder V).

312 joined the forces calling for withdrawal. Richard Rothstein, "The Starbucks Solution," *The American Prospect* 27 (July–August 1996), 26–32.

313 nearly half again as large as it was. Stephen R. Lewis, *The Economics of Apartheid* (New York, 1990), 166–67.

314 targets of ICCR shareholder resolutions. S. Prakash Sethi, *Up against the Corporate Wall,* 4th ed. (Englewood Cliffs, N.J., 1982), 460, 468–69; Herman Nickel, "The Corporation Haters," *Fortune* (June 16, 1980), 126–36; Morton Mintz, "Infant-Formula Maker Battles Boycotter," *Washington Post* (January 14, 1981), A2.

314 Labor unions . . . resolutions of their own. Paul Sweeney, "Clash by Proxy," *Across the Board* (May 1996), 23. Nearly 20 percent of the shareholder resolutions appearing in 1995 proxies were proposed by labor.

315 (images of women). Social Investment Forum, *South Africa: Major Responsible Investment Trends in the U.S.,* September 1995; Manuel Schiffres, "Ethical Investing the Right Way," *Kiplinger's* (April 1996), 53–55.

315 public debates. Hoffman, op. cit., 51–52.

315 billboards. ICCR/3M news release (May 2, 1996).

317 restaurants smoke-free. Social Investment Forum, *Tobacco's Changing Context: A Challenge and Opportunity for Institutional Investors* (1996), 1; "Kimberly-Clark to Leave Tobacco Business," *Corporate Examiner* 23:10 (1994), 1; "1996 Proxy Season Report," *Corporate Examiner* 25:1 (July 19, 1996).

317 "as quickly as they have." The Internet has proved useful in mobilizing world opinion against the government of Myanmar. In 1996, a Web site established by Zar Ni, a Burmese exile and graduate student at the University of Wisconsin, (http://www.freeburma.org) billed itself as the world's largest human rights campaign in cyberspace.

318 as well as from American corporations. "Local Burma Laws under Fire," *Investing for a Better World* (April 15, 1997); Nancy Dunne, "Massachusetts' Burma Law Row Flares," *Financial Times* (June 14–15, 1997).

318 1,500 largest U.S. corporations. Federal Glass Ceiling Commission, *A Solid Investment: Making Full Use of the Nation's Human Capital* (Washington, 1995), 6, 10.

319 $176 million. "Texaco: Lessons from a Crisis-in-Progress," *Business Week* (December 2, 1996); "Protestors Pressure Texaco at the Pump," *Salt Lake Tribune* (November 17, 1996).

319 (7.9 percent over five years). Federal Glass Ceiling Commission, op. cit., 3.

321 prestigious business forums. T. J. Rodgers, "Profits vs. PC," *Reason* (October 1996), 36–42; Doris Gormley, author interview (June 19, 1997). Gormley also supplied a copy of her form letter.

321 henhouse. Ann Taylor, "Public Accountability and EEO Disclosure: Breaking Down Barriers to Equality," *Corporate Examiner* 24:6 (January 26, 1996), 3A–D.

322 "ideal becomes more real." Reinhold Niebuhr, *Does Civilization Need Religion?* (New York, 1927), 44–45.

322 Mozambique, Christian Aid, "Not Waiving but Drowning," n.d.

322 subsist. The Reverend David Schilling, "Maquiladora Workers Deserve a Sustainable Living Wage," *Corporate Examiner* 23:10 (1994), 3A–D.

323 358 richest individuals. United Nations Development Program, Human Development Report, 1996.

323 "masters of mankind," quoted in Stein, op. cit., 178.

326 "their right to hold it." Reinhold Niebuhr, op. cit., 60–61.

326 farm surpluses. Myra H. Strober, "Can Feminist Thought Improve Economics?" *American Economic Review,* 84:2 (May 1994), 145–46.

327 declaration of interdependence. Virginia Held, "Mothering versus Contract," in Jane Mansbridge, ed., *Beyond Self-Interest* (Chicago, 1990), 287–304.

327 "be kind." Kurt Vonnegut, *God Bless You, Mr. Rosewater* (New York, 1965), 110.

INDEX

ABOUT THE AUTHOR

P ATRICIA O'TOOLE'S LAST book, *The Five of Hearts: An Intimate Portrait of Henry Adams and His Friends* (1990), was a finalist for the Pulitzer Prize and the National Book Critics Circle Award. For her writing on business and society, she has received a Front Page Award as well as an Emma from Radcliffe College and the National Women's Political Caucus. Her articles, essays, and reviews have appeared in a wide range of publications, and she teaches in the Writing Division of the School of the Arts at Columbia University. She lives in Manhattan.